Praise for *The State*

"Theorists of politics will welcome this book, in which Philip Pettit uses genealogical methods to explore the implications of his republican ideas for an understanding of polity and state. It is a topic that demands our attention as we watch how states frustrate as well as advance the purposes for which they were constituted. Pettit's exploration yields an extraordinarily sophisticated set of insights into the relation between state and legitimacy."
—Jeremy Waldron, *New York University*

"Philip Pettit continues to inspire. This groundbreaking book offers original answers to questions any political philosopher needs to ask: What kind of entity is the state? Why are we justified in holding such an entity responsible? What possibilities are feasible in terms of its structure and functioning?"
—Victoria Costa, *College of William & Mary*

"An extremely impressive and philosophically rich book, in the grand tradition of Hobbes and Locke, and, more recently, Rawls and Raz. There is every reason to believe that this book will become essential reading for anyone working in political philosophy, political theory, legal theory, and related areas today."
—Daniel Viehoff, *New York University*

THE STATE

The State

PHILIP PETTIT

PRINCETON UNIVERSITY PRESS

PRINCETON & OXFORD

Published by Princeton University Press
41 William Street, Princeton, New Jersey 08540
99 Banbury Road, Oxford OX2 6JX

press.princeton.edu

All Rights Reserved

Library of Congress Cataloging-in-Publication Data

Names: Pettit, Philip, 1945– author.
Title: The state / Philip Pettit.
Description: Princeton : Princeton University Press, 2023. | Includes bibliographical
    references and index.
Identifiers: LCCN 2022019122 (print) | LCCN 2022019123 (ebook) |
    ISBN 9780691182209 (hardback) | ISBN 9780691244396 (ebook)
Subjects: LCSH: State, The—Philosophy. | Justice—Philosophy. | BISAC: POLITICAL
    SCIENCE / History & Theory | PHILOSOPHY / Ethics & Moral Philosophy
Classification: LCC JC11 .P44 2023 (print) | LCC JC11 (ebook) |
    DDC 320.1—dc23/eng/20220812
LC record available at https://lccn.loc.gov/2022019122
LC ebook record available at https://lccn.loc.gov/2022019123

British Library Cataloging-in-Publication Data is available

Editorial: Rob Tempio & Chloe Coy
Production Editorial: Ali Parrington
Jacket Design: Chris Ferrante
Production: Erin Suydam
Publicity: Kate Hensley & Charlotte Coyne
Copyeditor: Joseph Dahm

This book has been composed in Arno

Printed on acid-free paper. ∞

Printed in Canada

10 9 8 7 6 5 4 3 2 1

In memory of Frankie,
and of our parents, Chris and Anto

CONTENTS

THE STATE

INTRODUCTION

Motivating the Argument

FOR A CENTURY OR MORE, competing states or polities have claimed and controlled most of the surface of the earth; the only exceptions are international waters and some areas of wilderness.[1] While it has taken millennia for the network of states to extend over the whole planet, and while that network is consistent with continuing shifts in the distribution of power and territory, it looks now like an arrangement that is destined to survive, at least in the absence of massive shocks. It might be disrupted or undone by catastrophic climate change, by a large meteor strike, by a rampant plague, or by a nuclear world war. But short of such a radical shock, the state system is likely to stay around for the foreseeable future.

The status quo is stable for at least three reasons. First, no people can hope to live without a state in their territory; in the absence of a state their land would surely be taken over, perhaps as a protectorate, by one or another rival regime. Second, no regime is so strong that it can hope to drive others to extinction and establish itself in sole possession of the earth. And third, the distrust between peoples is likely to block the formation of a binding, sustainable contract in support of a global government.

The states that constitute this stable network are all coercive, territorial regimes in which an individual ruler or a ruling group exercises power over other residents, asserting the right to act for them in maintaining interstate relations. But otherwise, those regimes vary enormously in how they are organized, how they treat their subjects, and how they behave toward other states.

---

1. I use "state" and "polity" as synonyms, following a different usage from some others, such as Collins and Lawford-Smith (2021).

The inescapability of the worldwide state system means that the future and welfare of our species—and perhaps that of others too—depends on how states perform. It is only if we can recruit states individually and collectively to the service of human flourishing that we can hope to deal with climate change, pandemic threat, chronic deprivation, and the eruptions of inhumanity that seem to come with our genes. The ideal of justice within peoples and between peoples continues to capture the human imagination. But we can hope to advance along the path to justice only if we can steer the state onto that road.

This is a challenging demand, for the state or polity is an institution with a very mixed record. While it has often been a force for domestic order and welfare, and sometimes international accord, it has just as often enabled the few to lord it over the many, legitimated xenophobia within and without its borders, and given a license to violence and war. Can we really expect it to be able to serve the cause of justice? Is it up to the task?

The Role and Potential of the State

Yes, it is, at least when there is a rough balance of power between rulers and their subjects: between decision makers and decision takers. The rulers must not be so powerful that they can ignore the interests of the ruled. And, a less prominent possibility, they must not be so powerless that there is disorder and strife among those they rule. Barring such developments, so this book argues, there is a role or function we can expect the state to play, and a set of distinctively political desiderata that we can hope it will satisfy. If it plays that role—and only if it plays that role—it will have the potential to advance the cause of justice, whether it actually does so or not.

The state that plays this role will satisfy what we may describe as the ideal of statehood or, to be more exact, the ideal of modern statehood. And depending on how well it meets the demands of the role, it will satisfy the ideal to a lesser or greater degree. While statehood is compatible with justice, as we shall see, it does not make such high demands. The balance of power under which it can be realized does not require an inclusive democracy, for example, or any significant degree of civil liberty or social security. As interpreted here, indeed, that balance does not even preclude stratification among decision takers, so that only the upper echelon hold any power against rulers. Although the ideal of statehood is not high-flown, however, it still makes a range of significant demands on the state and supports the ascription of a variety of important powers.

The theory of the state—specifically, the modern state—that is offered here is realist, then, in two distinct senses. It is historically realist in assuming that the state will endure through the foreseeable future, contrasting on that front with the idealism of traditional anarchists like Peter Kropotkin (1902). It is normatively realist in arguing that although the state need not satisfy a moral ideal like that of justice, it should satisfy a political ideal that reflects the function it will have if there is even an approximate balance of power between rulers and ruled.

The theory answers in those ways to the aspiration for a realist political theory of the kind endorsed by Bernard Williams (2005) and the many thinkers he has influenced (Leat 2010). Although less demanding, the requirement for a rough balance of power is an analogue of what Williams describes as the basic demand of legitimacy on the state. As he looks for the general shape that a state ought to assume, on political rather than moral grounds, if it is to be minimally legitimate, so we look for an account of the general shape it ought to assume, if it is to reflect a minimal balance of power between decision makers and decision takers.

The book offers a theory of the role of the state in the first chapter of part I; specifically, of the state where rulers and ruled enjoy a rough balance of power. Many states are outliers on this count, with rulers who are powerful enough to practice brutal repression or so powerless that they fail to achieve effective control. An implication of the theory is that such regimes are not proper states but failed or failing counterparts. If they still count as states, that is only in the sense in which the heart that has ceased to pump blood is still a heart.

These states count as outliers because they fail to serve the function ascribed to the polity. But are they likely to be statistical outliers too: that is, empirically atypical? Yes, insofar as the balance of power required is not very demanding; the state may exist without anything like an equality of power between rulers and ruled, or indeed within the ranks of the ruled themselves. Such a balance has often been achieved in history and is routinely achieved today. Indeed, it looms as a prospect that threatens every state where the ruling clique try to rule only for themselves.

Where the opening chapter of part I offers an account of the role ascribed to the state, the remaining two chapters argue that if it is to do as well as possible by that role—if it is to realize the ideal of statehood fully—the state should meet two further desiderata. The functional state should be organized as a corporate agent to pursue its role, but ought at the same time to be composed out of decentralized, mutually constraining units.

The book goes on in part II to argue that, contrary to some common doctrines, the functional state will have the potential to deliver three important benefits. Contrary to an absolutist form of statism, it will be able to give its people collective, countervailing power; contrary to a radical libertarianism, it will be able to recognize and honor significant rights on their part as individuals; and contrary to laissez-faire theory, it will have the capacity to intervene productively in the market economy.

As these remarks indicate, a major reason for wanting to have a theory of the state is that it is required for developing a relatively realistic picture of what we may expect to be able to achieve by way of justice. But, while the focus on justice remains in the background of the discussion, the theory developed may be of interest in legal and political theory more generally, and across a range of the social sciences. It is a striking feature of work in these fields that while much has been written on the history, economics, and dynamics of states, there has been little work on the theory of the state in the sense in which we pursue it here.

In discussing the various issues raised by the function and potential of the state, I frequently draw on the arguments of historical figures like Jean Bodin, Thomas Hobbes, John Locke, Jean-Jacques Rousseau, and Immanuel Kant. I do this because they are the sources of arguments that remain current and important today and because they often offer the clearest, most challenging statements of the arguments. But while I situate those thinkers in the context of their times, this is not a work of intellectual or political history. I focus on the idea and institution of the state that first emerged in modern times—in Europe, from about the sixteenth century on—and that has assumed its distinctive form only in the last century or two.[2]

Three Assumptions about Role or Function

There are three assumptions that we may expect to be satisfied by anything that is to count as a function of the state. While that function must consist in a particular effect that the state has in the lives of its members, no effect can count as part of its function unless it meets the constraints encoded in

---

2. On the framework of ideas and influences within which the practice and idea of the modern state arose, the outstanding source is Quentin Skinner's (1978) magisterial study of *The Foundations of Modern Political Thought*. On the challenges that the emerging state raised for established thinking about natural law, see Brett (2011).

those assumptions. And if none of the effects it has meets the constraints, then we must give up on the idea that the state as such has a distinctive role or function.

The first assumption is that the function of the state or polity is an effect that it brings about robustly over a certain range of possible variations in the society; it brings about the effect regardless of such variations, at least when they preserve the required balance of power. These variations allow the population to be large or small, for example, culturally uniform or diverse, as they are and have been in many states. And they even allow that those who are ruled in a state may be divided or stratified, as they have been in many regimes, with only one subclass accounting for the required balance of power in relation to rulers; those outside that class, distinguished by gender, ethnicity, or whatever, will typically be subordinate to its members.

This last variation means that a state may count as functional even if those it serves directly—its citizens proper, as we may describe them—are not inclusive of the population as a whole. They may be restricted to the barons with whom King John signed the Magna Carta; to the propertied, mainstream males who dominated the more progressive states in modern Europe; or to men alone, as remained the case in even progressive, nineteenth-century democracies. But there is an important point to notice here. That the function of the state is one that it can play whether the citizenry is restricted or not means that it cannot be a discriminatory effect like that of supporting the subordination of an underprivileged class. The state may support that subordination in a stratified society but, by our first assumption, that cannot count as part of its function; it is not an effect that the state will bring about robustly, since it won't bring it about under the social variation where the citizenry are inclusive.

The second assumption about the role or function of the state is that it is one that the state will play only when the officials who run it—the rulers and their appointees—act as their offices in the state require them to act. This means that in searching out the role of the polity, we must take corruption among public authorities—that is, a failure to enact their offices properly—to be absent or limited. If the polity has a function in the lives of its citizens, after all, then presumably it will discharge that function only when those who run the organization meet this constraint.

The third assumption we make about the role or function of the polity is that it is not just an effect that the state contingently generates—not, for example, a contingent benefit that it happens to provide for its citizens—but one that has a special explanatory role. This is grounded in the more general assumption that no effect that an institution generates will deserve to be called a role or function that it plays unless its occurrence helps in some way to explain the existence of that entity.

There are three ways in which an institutional effect might meet this explanatory condition. The institution may have been intentionally designed by its creators for the generation of that effect. The institution may have been selected for that effect in past competition between societies where it was present and societies where it was not. Or the institution may be likely to survive a variety of possible problems in virtue of having that effect; the effect may explain why it exists as a relatively resilient feature of the society: why it enjoys an enduring rather than an ephemeral presence there.[3]

To anticipate later argument, the role assigned to the state under the theory defended here is an effect of the third variety. It is an effect that might be expected to keep the state resiliently in place, even if its presence were not required by the state-bound character of the world. Given that state-bound world, it is an effect that may be expected, at least so long as citizens retain a balance of power with rulers, to keep the state in a shape that is suited to producing the effect: to stop the state from devolving into the form of an outlier regime.

Exploring the Role of the State

The method we adopt for exploring the role of the state has a genealogical character. It runs a thought experiment that explores what would be likely to transpire in a world without a state—indeed a world, as we shall see, without even conventions, norms, or laws—where the protagonists are human beings like us and the circumstances allow an approximate balance of power among many members, if not among all. The aim is to see whether a state would be likely to appear and survive in such a world, without any miraculous or lucky trigger: whether in that sense its appearance and survival would be robustly rather than just fortuitously likely.

If the thought experiment is run under appropriate constraints, and if it turns out that something recognizable as a state or polity would reliably materialize there, then that prompts an obvious question. What effect does the state generate that might account for the robust likelihood of this development? If

3. On this conception of function, and for a suggestion that it was endorsed among classical functionalists like Émile Durkheim, see Pettit (1996).

we can identify an effect or set of effects that meets the constraints for counting as a function, then that will direct us to the function that the state discharges in the counterfactual model. And that will then give us at least a hypothesis about the state in the actual world: namely, that its role or function parallels that which it has in the model. The degree to which the hypothesis is plausible will depend, as we note in chapter 1, on how well the counterfactual world is taken to model the actual one.

While a suitable genealogy, if it were available, would deliver this reward, there is no guarantee that it will be available. The thesis defended is that there is indeed a suitable genealogy available—one that identifies a plausible function for the state in the model—but that is a claim supported by our thought experiment, not something that had to be true. For all we might have guessed in advance, nothing like a state might be destined to appear in our counterfactual world. Or the state that was destined to appear might be one that does not live up to what we might have hoped; it might be a purely repressive regime, for example, incapable of advancing the cause of justice.

The genealogical methodology is routinely used in philosophy, as we shall see later. But it is also employed in social science. It figures prominently, for example, in the approach traditionally adopted among economists for identifying the role and nature of money (Menger 1892). We shall look at this approach to money in chapter 1.

The book develops a counterfactual genealogy of the state or polity, building on the genealogy of law developed by Herbert Hart (2012) in his classic study from the early 1960s (Pettit 2019b). It starts from a world where power is roughly balanced among at least a privileged class of members and argues that a state would emerge and endure there in virtue of the intelligible, unplanned adjustments that individuals would be robustly likely to make to their circumstances.

A state would appear and survive in that counterfactual world, so the story goes, because of supporting a benefit for those individuals. And that benefit points us to a role that the actual state properly plays. That role is, first, to establish or enforce a coercive, territorial regime of law under which its citizens, whether they be an inclusive or privileged class, know what they can do with legal impunity and legal protection; and second, to entrench or safeguard that regime against internal and external dangers, such as dangers of collapse or colonization.

This account suggests that if the state plays that role, then it will prove relatively resilient; it will preserve a character that continues to support the function, provided the balance of power between rulers and ruled is not disturbed.[4] The idea is that under that proviso the complaints and protests that functional failures would elicit among citizens, or the anticipation of such complaints and protests on the part of rulers, would be likely to keep the state more or less true to its function.

This view of the function of the state does not entail that if rulers—say, a single individual or family or clique—were very powerful relative to others in the society, still they would be inclined to introduce a functional state. And it does not entail that if the rulers in a functional state developed such a preponderance of power, say because of a new military or informational technology, then they would continue to ensure that the state serves its proper function. Those rulers might be led to hold the state to its function for fear of protests among the ruled. But then again, they might not: the attractions of power for members of the ruling clique might lead them to opt for brutal repression.

The Plan of the Book

The three chapters that form part I of the book offer a picture of the role of the state and its demands. Chapter 1 develops the genealogical argument and offers support for a law-centered account of the function of the state. But the state, as we shall see, may serve that function more effectively or less effectively, and that observation leads into the argument of the following two chapters. Chapter 2 holds that the state will play its allotted function better insofar as it incorporates fully as an agent or agency and acts reliably, across different scenarios, for a stable set of ends. Chapter 3 goes on to maintain that nevertheless its function also argues that it ought to assume a decentralized form, materializing in the interaction of mutually constraining subagencies.

While part I gives us a picture of the nature of the state, and how it should be organized to serve its purpose best, the three chapters in part II address in turn three questions related to the potential of that polity. Can the functional state grant countervailing powers to its people or citizens collectively? Can it countenance significant rights on the part of its individual citizens? Can it satisfy the requirements of an autonomous market economy? The issue in each case is whether it can follow that course while discharging its function properly.

---

4. This condition requires more than that the state will continue to exist in some form, such as a repressive one. Its continuing to exist in some form would be ensured in any case by the considerations reviewed earlier that entrench the state system worldwide.

The three questions are raised by familiar doctrines in political philosophy, which we may describe as statism, libertarianism, and laissez-faire theory. Chapters 4, 5, and 6 defend affirmative answers to the questions, arguing in turn against those doctrines. First, the citizenry will have considerable, collective power, constitutional and extra-constitutional, in any functional polity—indeed, in any polity whatsoever—and may have it in a greater or lesser measure. Second, citizens will enjoy significant rights against one another, officials included, in any functional polity and, those rights being institutional rather than natural in character, they may vary in their scope and in the security they provide. And third, the functional polity will assume a constructive, interventionist role in any modern market economy, although the role it assumes may be more or less extensive, more or less radical.

The function ascribed to the state in chapter 1 will hardly prove surprising, since it has long been ascribed to the polity in different intellectual traditions. Those who are less interested in the genealogical argument presented for the ascription of the role may prefer to focus on the claims in the remainder of the book. They may find more interest in the argument that that function supports the case for an incorporated, yet decentralized, polity, and that it does not deeply limit the potential of the state in the respects examined in the later part.

Back to Justice

The properly functional polity may fall well short of justice, but the ideal of statehood that it embodies is still significant. While the functional polity serves only the citizens well, the citizenry it serves may be inclusive, and even if they are not inclusive, the state cannot be required by its function to support the subordination of noncitizens. How will the functional polity serve its citizens? By establishing and entrenching laws that enable them to tell how they may act with legal impunity and under legal protection. It will provide this service more reliably to the extent that it is incorporated enough to make the laws determinate, yet decentralized enough to guard against the danger of capture by private interests. Thus, the fully functional state should give each citizen a reliable, determinate zone of legal security, however limited it may be, within which they can decide on how they want to live their lives.

How does the ideal of statehood so interpreted relate to that of justice? Broadly in the way that the ideal of prudence relates to that of morality. As the demands of prudence on an individual are a subset of those of morality, so plausibly the demands of statehood are a subset of those of justice. As the demands of prudence are conditions that an agent must satisfy to count properly as a person—or at least an intertemporally connected person—so the demands of statehood are conditions that the state must satisfy to be properly a state. And as the demands of prudence may be satisfied in different degrees by an individual, so a state may satisfy the demands of statehood in different degrees.

But not only does the ideal of statehood square in this way with the ideal of justice; it also directs us to the range of questions that a theory of the just state should surely consider. How broad should the category of citizenship be? How deep should be the security that the law provides for citizens in relation to one another? How deep should be the security that it provides in relation to those—those other citizens, as we assume—in public office? And how should the state behave in relation to the peoples of other states, presumably as part of an international community?

Our account of statehood in this book should serve, then, to orient discussion of what justice requires of the state. But it should also emancipate the discussion from some traditional barriers, which are discussed in part II. Arguing that statehood is not challenged in the manner envisaged by absolute statists, right-wing libertarians, or laissez-faire thinkers, the account of statehood opens up questions that those doctrines would shut down. How far does justice require that the citizenry should have collective powers against the state? How far does it require that individual citizens should enjoy significant rights against one another and against the state? And how far does it allow or necessitate intervention in the market economy?

While postponing discussion of justice for a companion volume, it may be useful, for the record, to sketch the view that our account of statehood foreshadows. In a just state, according to that view, all adult, able-minded, relatively permanent residents

1. should count as full citizens, with special provision for individuals outside those categories: say, for children, for certain atypical adults, for refugees and temporary immigrants;
2. should be equally provided with a deep enough security against one another's power of interference to be able to relate to one another—in a common phrase, to look one another in the eye—without reason for fear or deference on that count;
3. should share in such an equal and adequate system of control over the state that they also enjoy deep enough security against the government of the state to be able to look on personally unwelcome initiatives as just tough luck, not the work of an alien will;

4. should be able to require their polity to work toward an international order that enables the people of every state, consistently with preserving the global commons, to enjoy as much security as possible against other states and bodies;

5. and should be able to require their polity to work for other ends that, like international order, are goods that attract a high enough level of popular support to count as common goods and that are unlikely to be otherwise available.

The view of justice outlined in these points fits with what I have elsewhere described as a neo-republican theory. That theory is distinctive in taking incorporation as an equal citizen under a state to be essential for anyone's enjoyment of justice and in treating global justice as essentially dependent on the relationship of states to one another. It connects with the long tradition of republicanism insofar as it makes freedom fundamental for justice and takes freedom to require security against the will of others: the absence of domination. And it connects further with that tradition insofar as it takes the required security to be needed both to combat private domination—that of other citizens or corporate bodies—and to guard against public domination by the authorities who act in the name of the state. Thus, the theory of the state developed here may be viewed as a prologue to a neo-republican theory of justice, although I hope that it may also appeal on other grounds.[5]

While the theory foreshadows such a theory of justice, however, it remains realist, as we saw, in the two senses associated with the way of thinking that Bernard Williams (2005) advocated. It is historically realist insofar as it presupposes that justice can be achieved only by the state. And it is normatively realist in arguing that independently of moral ideals like that of justice, the state has to satisfy functional norms of its own, at least on the assumption of an approximate balance of power between rulers and ruled: this, as mentioned, is a weaker analogue of what Williams calls the basic demand of legitimacy. Satisfying those functional norms, the state need not be a weapon in the arsenal of an elite; it can in principle be mobilized for the good of its members and of humanity as a whole (Pettit 2017).[6]

---

5. For my own conception of neo-republican justice within the state, see Pettit (1997; 2012; 2014; 2015a). And for my view of its implications for global justice, see Pettit (2014, chap. 6; 2015b); see too Laborde and Ronzoni (2016). More generally, see Lovett and Sellers (forthcoming).

6. I am grateful to Nic Southwood for drawing my attention to the connection with Williams's political realism. For a discussion of realism in relation to republicanism, see Pettit (2017).

Acknowledgments

I worked through the material of the book in graduate seminars at Princeton in Fall 2018 and Fall 2021 and learned enormously from the continual, constructive interrogation of the participants, some students, some visitors; I cannot name them all and must simply acknowledge my debt to them collectively. I wrote up much of the material at the Australian National University, where, in an ideal research environment, I benefitted from many discussions with my colleagues and students there. And I took a raft of ideas from the anonymous reviewers of the manuscript at Princeton University Press, as well as from my editor, Rob Tempio. My thanks to all for forcing me to defend the lines taken on various issues and for their many observations and suggestions. And my special thanks, as always, to Tori McGeer, who continues to be the mainstay of my life.

PART I

The Role of the State
and Its Demands

1

The Function of the Polity

IF THERE IS a function that the state or polity serves in the lives of its members, what is it? That is the question addressed in this first chapter. The discussion of the question falls into six main sections. The first introduces the methodology of reconstruction or genealogy that we follow in seeking to identify a function for the state. The second and third begin that genealogy, explaining in turn how conventions and norms might be expected to emerge under plausible social conditions. The fourth continues it with a genealogy of law, which is modeled on that developed by Herbert Hart (2012) over fifty years ago. And then the fifth and sixth sections move on to the emergence of the state or polity proper.

The fifth extends Hart's genealogy of law, arguing that any regime of law that is going to prove enduring over the sorts of scenarios that have appeared in modern history will give rise to something that deserves to be described as a polity or state. And the sixth argues that the function of the state, as it appears under this genealogy, is to stabilize, on the domestic and international front, a system of law by means of which it provides a palpable benefit for citizens— perhaps all subjects, perhaps only a subset—securing them in their relations with one another. We describe this function of the polity as nomothetic, from the Greek words for law, *nomos*, and for something that is put in place, *thesis*; in doing this, we assume that the laws put in place are beneficial in the required manner.

The notion of state or polity is distinct from the notion of government (Crawford 2006, chap. 1). In this work, the government will generally refer not to the state as such, but to the body of authorities or officials who run its business. This body does not just encompass the domain-general authorities in legislative and executive office, who are often taken to constitute the government in ordinary parlance. It also includes the domain-specific officials in the judiciary and in various government agencies as well as the citizenry when they are recruited to public service, as in juries, citizen assemblies, and referenda. The state is the entity in whose name all such agents and agencies operate.[1]

1.1 Genealogy and Reconstruction

Identifying the Function of the State

Modern states come in a variety of forms, developed and underdeveloped, democratic and nondemocratic, parliamentary and presidential.[2] But is there a single function that we might assign to the typical modern state, assuming its officials act as they are supposed to? Is there an effect that might keep the state true to a form suited for its production, robustly across a range of variations in its circumstances, or at least a range of variations in which rulers and ruled share in a rough balance of power?

This chapter describes a methodology by which we can explore the question and argues that there is indeed reason to assign such a role or function to the state. Since that function may be satisfied to a lesser or greater extent, the following chapters then go on to explore how the state might better discharge its function and what its function allows—what potential it gives the state—on a variety of fronts.

The Genealogical Methodology

Imagine a prepolitical world with creatures like us living in a situation broadly like ours, where there is a rough balance of power across members. Would a state be robustly likely to arise in such a prepolitical world, emerging as the

---

1. In some absolutist theories, as we shall see, a distinction is made between the sovereign holder of state power—usually the legislator or legislature—and those in government, as it is usually put, who act at the behest of that sovereign. We will follow this restriction of the concept of government to nonlegislative authorities only in the discussion, mainly in chapters 3 and 4, of absolutist theories.

2. For a philosophical introduction to the idea of the modern state, see Morris (1998); for a more sociological account, see Poggi (1990); for an analysis of the various ways in which the state is conceived in legal and political theory, see Lawford-Smith (2019, chap. 2); and for an overview of different theories of the state in the history of thought, see Vincent (1987). On debates within the theory of international law as to what is essential for statehood, and whether or not it requires recognition within a system of states, see Crawford (2006). On the varying conception of the state and its relationship to the Crown and other bodies in British legal thought, see McLean (2012).

unplanned result of intelligible adjustments to circumstances? If it would, is there an effect it generates that explains its appearance and might deserve therefore to count as a function it serves?

The idea behind the thought experiment is that if a state emerges in our counterfactual narrative and if it really resembles the state as we know it, then that gives us reason to take it as a model of the actual state. And if the state in the counterfactual narrative has an effect that satisfies the constraints on being a function, then that supports the hypothesis that the state in our world serves a similar function: this, at any rate, so long as the balance of power envisaged in the narrative obtains in the actual world.

We mentioned three constraints that an effect or set of effects would have to meet if, assuming a rough balance of power between rulers and ruled, it is to count as a function of the state. First, that it is associated with the state in no matter what form that institution takes, so long as there is a rough balance of power between rulers and ruled. Second, that it is associated with the state only when officials avoid corruption and act according to the requirements of their roles. And third, that it explains why the state exists: at the least, why it is attractive enough to command the resilient allegiance of citizens, whether or not the citizenry is a restricted body.

A thought experiment of the kind envisaged is well suited to enabling us to identify a function for the state that fits these constraints. It will naturally fit with the first constraint insofar as it assumes a pre-political balance of power, restricted or unrestricted, and may be realized in a range of different ways. It will fit with the second insofar as the narrative takes it for granted, as it naturally will, that the officials of the emerging state will follow their briefs. And it will fit with the third insofar as the evidence provided for why the state would be robustly likely to emerge—that it serves the effect cited—would naturally explain why it would also be robustly likely to survive. Thus, if we can construct a thought experiment of the kind envisaged—a conceptual or philosophical genealogy, as we may call it—then we will be in a position to identify a function for the state in the counterfactual model. This will support the hypothesis that the function of the actual state is similar to that of the state in the model insofar as the counterfactual world resembles the actual world.

There is no advance guarantee, however, that the thought experiment will work out to our tastes, directing us to a suitable function for the state, counterfactual or actual. It might turn out as we run the thought experiment that nothing like a state would make a reliable appearance. Or it might turn out that while something like a state would reliably emerge and endure, it would not do so in virtue of a congenial, justice-compatible effect or function. For example, the effect might be that of enabling those of a domineering mentality to exercise power over those of a more timid disposition. Such a genealogy would debunk the state, as Nietzsche's (1997) nineteenth-century genealogy of morals sought to debunk ethics. By the argument developed here, however, there is a persuasive genealogy that vindicates the state rather than debunking it in that fashion; it identifies a function for the state that would enable it to be an instrument of justice.

The sort of counterfactual genealogy pursued is quite distinct from the historical genealogy that looks at how the notion of the state operated in actual societies over different periods (Skinner 2009). It argues in the spirit of a thought experiment that human beings like us would face salient problems in a suitable prepolitical society; that they would likely adjust to them in a variety of ways; and that an unplanned result of such adjustments would be the appearance and survival of an institution that resembles the modern state. Building on that narrative, then, it would identify an effect or function to explain the emergence and endurance of that institution in the counterfactual world. And that would provide a candidate for the function that the actual state may be taken to play.

Although not often recognized as such, philosophy has frequent recourse to this sort of genealogical or reconstructive methodology (Pettit 2019a).[3] Edward Craig (1990) invokes it to give an account of the concept and nature of knowledge, Bernard Williams (2002) to provide an elaboration of the ideas and practices associated with truth and truthfulness, and I have relied on it myself to provide a genealogy of ethical practices and concepts (Pettit 2018a). But a particularly clear example of the method appears in economics, in the standard way of explaining the role of money.[4]

An Analogue: The Genealogy of Money

The genealogy of money begins with an imaginary barter society in which people seek to trade with one another for the commodities or services they require. The members of this society will face obvious problems, for no matter

3. For a very useful overview and discussion of the methodology, see Queloz (2021).

4. For a classic source of the genealogy of money that the text elaborates, see Menger (1892). That the barter society imagined really is imaginary is argued by Graeber (2011); he would argue that however useful in other ways—specifically, in identifying a function that money serves—it is not a good indication of how money actually emerged in early societies.

how well resourced someone is, they may have nothing to trade that is wanted by those who can meet their needs. But there is a way out of this difficulty that is likely to materialize regardless of various contingencies.

It will become salient at a certain point, so the standard account goes, that one or another commodity—perhaps gold or cigarettes or cattle, for example—is particularly attractive for most people. And at that point everyone with access to that good will be able to use it, or to use suitable IOUs in the commodity, to purchase what they want: if others do not want the good for themselves, those with whom they can trade will likely want it; and if those with whom they can trade do not want it for themselves, those with whom they in turn can trade will probably want it; and so on. Thus, everyone will have a motive to try to obtain that commodity, using it as a means of making purchases. It will serve a role that would lead us, in our language, to describe it as money.

Something serving people's interest in making exchange possible would be likely to emerge in our counterfactual scenario across a range of possible scenarios. It would appear regardless of which commodity came to play the role: gold or cattle or cigarettes, for example; regardless of how quickly or slowly it came to be recognized in common that many people want that commodity; and regardless of a variety of other obstacles that might be expected to obstruct the development. It would be likely to appear robustly over most such contingencies, even if communally disruptive shocks like a civil war or a widespread collapse of trust would undermine it. The important point is that it would appear, not by the sort of fortuitous contingency invoked in the traditional just-so story, but regardless of how things might transpire on a wide range of fronts.

If money would reliably emerge in circumstances akin to those that prevail in our society, then it can plausibly be relied upon to survive in those circumstances. The interest served by money that would make it into a reliable emergent in the counterfactual scenario would make it also into a reliably continuing feature there. And as this is true of that imagined scenario, so it is likely to be true of the actual world it models; money will have an enduring rather than a merely ephemeral presence among us.

The resilience of money in the counterfactual context, and by analogy in the actual, is explained by the effects money will have in enabling exchange and in serving associated roles that a medium of exchange is bound to serve. One of these is to provide a common currency in which to put prices on different commodities and services and compare them. And another is that of enabling people to build up their trading resources or wealth, provisioning themselves against future need.

The effects that give money its robust likelihood of survival, whether in the counterfactual or actual world, constitute its function, in a readily intelligible sense of that word. The function of money will be to provide a medium of exchange, a metric of price and a means of accumulating wealth. It may not have been designed or selected to serve that effect, as in some accounts of how an effect can get to count as a function. The effect will count as the function of money insofar as it is robustly likely to keep money in existence, making it into a relatively permanent feature of the world.

A common view today is that the effect of a certain type of institution can count as its function only if it was designed intentionally to have that effect or was selected as a survivor in a historical process of competition by the fact of having that effect (Elster 1979). But there is every reason to single out as functions any effects that make the continued survival of an institution robustly likely, even in the absence of actual design or selection. It was arguably in this sense that classical sociology and anthropology argued that a variety of institutions have functional effects that it is important to identify, because of how they make their bearers likely to be enduring rather than ephemeral. And in that sense of function, it is clear from the genealogy that money has the function of serving as a medium of exchange and, as a result, a metric of price and a means of storing wealth.[5]

Insofar as a genealogy enables us to identify the function of money, it will also enable us to form a view about its nature and origin. The nature or essence of money will be to facilitate exchange and the like, we can say, whether in one or another form; it will constitute a functional kind. And while the genealogy may not enable us to say much about its actual origin—a point emphasized by some (Graeber 2011)—it will at least teach us this negative lesson: that while it may have appeared as the result of an inventive social contract, or as the result of some such fortuity, it would probably have appeared even in the absence of that development. That it would have been robustly likely to appear in that way, absent the development that actually brought it onstream, is enough to point us to a function that it plays: an effect that will give it an institutional resilience.

5. For an argument that the great social scientists in the functionalist tradition may have been looking for features that promise to have an enduring rather than an ephemeral presence, see Pettit (1996).

Toward a Genealogy of the State

Our aim here is to do for the state what this sort of genealogy does for money. The analysis of money suggests that we should follow this sort of recipe in developing a genealogy of the state.

1. Imagine a counterfactual world with parties like us and circumstances relevantly like ours, where the target to be explained, be that money or the state, is missing: it hasn't yet appeared among our counterparts.

2. Identify problems that those parties would face, and the individual, unplanned adjustments, if any, that they would be robustly likely— likely, independently of contingencies like brute luck or brilliant initiative—to make in response.

3. Investigate the likely effects of those individual adjustments as they evolve in waves, with earlier adjustments leading to later ones, and see if they would lead to the emergence and endurance of something like the targeted institution.

4. If it turns out that such an outcome would be robustly likely—that is, likely independently of fortuities—then that is presumably because of a beneficial effect of their adjustments for the individuals involved.

5. That effect will count as a function served for those individuals—and plausibly for us—by the target institution, money or the state, and will support related claims about its functional nature and its possible origin.

Following this recipe, our goal here is to conduct the required thought experiment and see if something like a state or polity might emerge and survive in the same robustly probable manner as money. If we can show that the members of a prepolitical society satisfying plausible conditions would come to form and sustain a suitable political organization, without any planning or design, then that ought to enable us to identify a function that the state typically serves in that scenario and point us to a function that the state may serve under similar conditions in the actual world. This will be an effect that would keep the state faithful, robustly over certain variations of circumstance, to a form capable of realizing that very effect, and that would stop it from assuming a nonfunctional form.

If the genealogy gives us an image of a function that the state serves, of course, it will tell us also about its nature: that the essence of the state, regardless of its form, is to ensure fulfilment of that function. And it will communicate something about the actual origin of the state: that however it originated—perhaps because of someone's ingenious insight into how useful such an institution would be—it need not have emerged in that way: had no one had such an insight, for example, still it would have been robustly likely to appear in a manner like that described in the genealogy.[6]

The story envisaged for the state may call to mind the narrative presented in contract theories of the kind exemplified in the work of Thomas Hobbes and John Locke in the seventeenth century and Jean-Jacques Rousseau in the eighteenth. But the resemblance is only superficial. On an emergentist story of the sort that we seek, the adjustments required for the appearance and survival of the state must be, not just likely, but robustly or resiliently likely under suitable conditions. On a contractual story, the initiatives required of individuals entering an agreement with one another do not have to be robustly likely, or even likely at all; they may be presented as the product of fortuitous insight and alignment.

When the emergentist story tells us that a certain effect or set of effects makes the state robustly likely to appear and survive under certain conditions, it directs us to a function that the state serves in such conditions. When the contractual story invokes the benefit that might make the state sufficiently appealing for people to agree to enter or support a contract, it does no such thing. It tells us about how a state might appear or might have appeared and does not direct us to a feature that would be robustly likely to prompt its emergence in the absence of any explicit contract.

The contractual narrative has the character of a just-so story about how possibly the state might come into existence in a counterfactual scenario or might have come into existence historically. The emergentist narrative at which a genealogy aims contrasts sharply with any such just-so story, as it looks for a reason why under certain conditions the state is likely to appear, regardless of a range of contingencies: regardless in particular of whether things facilitate the formation of a political contract. It is because of this difference that, unlike the contractual story, it can aspire to identify something that might count as the function of the state.[7]

---

6. Thus, the line adopted on the function of the state is not jeopardized by accounts of the historical origins of the state that take a rather different form from that of the counterfactual genealogy. See, for example, Clastres (1987), Scott (2017), Graeber and Wengrow (2021). I am grateful to Paul Patton for raising this issue with me.

7. Contractual theorists like Hobbes and Locke are anxious to suggest that it was robustly likely that the contract to which they trace the state would have taken place. Given the

There is also another way in which contractual theories differ from emergentist or genealogical accounts, and it may be useful to mention it here. Contract theories, however they differ from one another, must all assume that prior to forming a polity people have access to something like a concept of the state and that they contract with one another to form a body that answers to that concept.[8] The theories offer an account of the state that would resemble an account of money in which people are taken to understand what money is prior to establishing such an institution and then, given that understanding, agree with one another to take steps that would bring the institution into existence. A theory of emergence avoids this problem by explaining how the concept and the practice could have coevolved in a single development.

Thus, the genealogy of money explains both how people would come to treat a certain commodity as a medium of exchange and how at the same time they would view and name that commodity as something fitted to those roles. In doing this, it makes sense both of how the practice can be concept-dependent, requiring people to conceptualize the commodity appropriately, and of how at the same time the concept can be practice-dependent, emerging only in tandem with the practice.[9]

As the genealogy of money makes sense of the interdependence of practice and concept in that case, so a genealogy of the state should make sense of a parallel interdependence. Starting from a world where people have neither political concepts nor political practices, it would explain how concepts and practices would be robustly likely to coevolve as the unplanned result of people's adjusting to various problems. And in doing that it would offer us a story about the

---

organizational challenge of forming a proper contract, however, the claim is implausible. Hobbes might reply that while a contract "by institution," as he calls it, is implausible, all he needs is the contract "by acquisition" that might occur, for example, in the course of conquest. Pettit (2008a) defends a reading that makes this reply relevant, if not persuasive, casting the contract by institution, however imaginary, as useful for illuminating the nature of the state, in the way that knowing how a circle might have been constructed by a compass illuminates the nature of a circle.

8. Or at least they must assume that contractors must have some related concept of what they want to achieve together.

9. The idea of a theory that serves these two goals is already evident in the work of David Hume (1978, 3.2.2), the eighteenth-century philosopher, on the institutions of promising and property. Hume (1994) explicitly rejects the notion of political contract and consent in favor of something like emergence, but as we note later, he doesn't offer a genealogy of the state similar to his genealogy of promising and property.

emergence and endurance of something like that state, directing us to a function that the state serves.

The Genealogical Starting Point

If a genealogy of the state is to play the part envisaged, then it must begin from
a suitable starting point. To begin with, the psychology ascribed to the protagonists and the conditions under which they operate must be familiar and
plausible. If their psychology was very different from ours, or their conditions
were extremely improbable, then however reliably a state-like institution
would have emerged among them, it could not be expected to have a similarly
reliable presence—a corresponding durability—among us. Whatever function it would serve in their society, then, there would be little reason to think
that it serves that same function in ours.

To make the starting point of the genealogy psychologically plausible, we
need to postulate that, like most human beings, the protagonists are moderately self-regarding in the goals they pursue, moderately rational in the beliefs
they form about how to reconcile and realize their various goals, and mutually
dependent in a manner that leads to some convergence in their goals and cooperation in their efforts. That they are moderately self-regarding allows them
to be altruistic on various fronts, requiring only that they tend, as human beings generally tend, to give priority to benefits for them and theirs. That they
are moderately rational allows them to display the sorts of biases and heuristics that can lead anyone astray (Gilovich, Griffin, and Kahneman 2002); it
requires only that they are unlikely to stick with strategies that repeatedly fail
and frustrate them. And that they are mutually dependent means that they are
likely to work together for common benefits in the manner that is characteristic of human beings (Tomasello 2014).

But what is required to make the conditions in which the protagonists operate suitably familiar and plausible? Given that states seem to have emerged
only in the wake of the agricultural revolution, we should postulate that the
counterfactual society envisaged has the settled character of an agricultural or
post-agricultural world in which different societies would inevitably compete
for territory (Scott 2017). And given that the human world has never been one
of unlimited abundance, with manna falling regularly from heaven, we should
postulate that the society is one where relative scarcity obtains. But what must
we assume about the power of our protagonists relative to one another, given
that we aim to look for a role that an emerging state may play when there is a
balance of power, however imperfect, between rulers and ruled?

Given that aim, we must assume a corresponding balance of power among the members of the society from which the genealogy starts. But we can hardly assume that power must be equally shared among individuals in that society, since that would hardly be realistic; in any case, it would limit the significance of any lesson the genealogy teaches for the actual world. If we are to be realistic, we should assume either that power is more or less equally shared in the society—that can hardly be ruled out—or that it is more or less equally shared among a subclass, in particular one that is too large to constitute a ruling clique on their own.

This disjunctive assumption will work for us only if it is plausible that there is an effect for which the relevant members of the society would be led to cherish an emerging state under either disjunct: that is, whether power were shared among all or only among such a subclass. That raises a pressing question, however. If the effect is one that we might expect to appeal to members under the widespread equality assumed in the first disjunct, it cannot be discriminatory in character. But, to go to the second disjunct, why would the members of a powerful subclass settle for a state that did not serve them in a discriminatory way?

There are two plausible assumptions about the starting point of our genealogy that explain why an elite subclass would not necessarily seek a discriminatory state. First, that the subordination of others to the elite is established by culture and tradition, independently of the state, and does not require political reinforcement. And second, that it is the empowerment of members of the elite relative to one another, not their empowerment vis-à-vis subordinates, that is likely to make something like a state attractive to them.

These assumptions being plausible, we can work with a genealogy that leaves it open whether the group that shares power relatively equally in our starting society—the group that will presumptively figure as the citizens of an emerging state—is inclusive or not. The state that emerges in a society where that group is not inclusive may very well go on to adopt discriminatory policies, buttressing the subordination of others. But under the assumptions with which we are working here, the effect that makes it appealing in the first place, and that may deserve to count as its function, need not involve any such discrimination.

The one society that is ruled out by our disjunctive assumption about the distribution of power is one in which a single individual or family or clique has a near monopoly of power, whether for cultural, economic, or military reasons. And the probability of such a society existing prior to the state is low, if only for the reason Thomas Hobbes (1994b, 13.1) registers, when he says that in a prepolitical society "the weakest has strength enough to kill the strongest, either by secret machination, or by confederacy with others that are in the same danger with himself."

Summarizing this discussion, then, we must start in our quest for a genealogy of the state with a prepolitical society of moderately self-regarding, moderately rational, and mutually dependent agents. And we must take those individuals to operate under conditions of agricultural settlement, relative scarcity, and an approximately balanced distribution of power, whether the balance is achieved among members as a whole or within a restricted class.

Drawing on that starting point, we go on in the remaining five sections to propose a genealogy of the state. The genealogy developed explains the appearance, not just of the state, but of the conventions, norms, and laws associated with life under a state. Some like Hobbes suggest that the state comes first, and those rules later. On the account we defend, however, they emerge first and the state only later. Hence, we begin with a genealogy that applies to them and extend this later to include the state.

The second and third sections describe the initial stages of our story, providing a genealogy of conventions and a genealogy of norms, and then the fourth, drawing on the work of Herbert Hart, builds on those accounts to provide a genealogy of laws. The fifth section extends that genealogy to explain the appearance and development of the state or polity in two stages: first, in the rudimentary form it may take under circumstances sufficient to elicit conventions, norms, and law; and then, in the form it will take under pressures associated with modern society. The sixth section completes the chapter with an account of the function of the polity that the genealogy supports.

The function ascribed to the state, specifically to the modern state, is that of individually securing its citizens against one another under a regime of law that it safeguards against internal and external dangers. This nomothetic function, as we described it earlier, falls well short of requiring the state to pursue justice. But it certainly makes the state into an entity that can increase in justice, by any of a variety of benchmarks. It will increase in justice, by almost any standard, insofar as more and more members are admitted to the status of equal citizens and that status is progressively enriched in various ways. It may be enriched by giving citizens more determinate and expansive protections against other citizens and against those in office; we shall assume, for simplicity, that it is only citizens who serve in office, whether permanently or on an elected or rotating basis.

In developing the genealogy of the state in this chapter, and in detailing its implications in the chapters that follow, we shall often speak for convenience as if all the protagonists in the genealogy enjoy relatively equal power and play relatively similar parts in adjusting to problems and thereby giving rise to the state. This need not be misleading, provided we remember that the points to be made can be translated into a narrative where the protagonists are members of a privileged class who enjoy a balance of power among themselves.

1.2 Reconstructing Conventions

Coordination Predicaments and Conventions

In the Hobbesian version of contract theory, it is assumed that prior to the polity or state—prior to the contract that brings the commonwealth into existence—there are no lasting agreements among human beings and no established rules, not even conventions governing day-to-day exchanges. The condition of nature, as he calls it, is a war of all against all, and in the absence of a polity there is nothing to determine "what is to be called right, what good, what virtue, what much, what little, what *meum* and *tuum*, what a pound, what a quart, etc." (Hobbes 1994a, 29.8).[10]

Hobbes's claim may have been accepted in the eighteenth century by Jean-Jacques Rousseau and even perhaps by Immanuel Kant, who was greatly influenced by Rousseau. But it was certainly rejected by their contemporary, David Hume, as indeed it had been rejected by John Locke in the previous century. And with good reason. It requires only a few plausible assumptions, as David Lewis (1969) has shown, to explain why and how at least a certain range of social practices would emerge in any population of interacting human beings.

This is the range of practices that he describes as conventions. These arise in situations where people generally prefer that some regularity be established among them in their interactions but are relatively indifferent about which should do so. Thus, everyone wants there to be an established rule of the road but is indifferent between a rule that prescribes driving on the right and one that prescribes driving on the left.

There are bound to be coordination predicaments like this in any society. In such a predicament it will be in everyone's independent interest to act

---

10. There were earlier thinkers, no doubt, who tended toward this Hobbesian view. According to Benjamin Straumann (2020), Polybius was an example from the second century BCE.

according to the same pattern as others: say, travel on the same side of the road or assemble at the same place for meeting or use the same gestures as tokens of peace or affection. Suppose that two people act on the same pattern in any example of such a scenario, satisfying their different preferences. It will then be true, first, that each will fare worse by departing unilaterally from the pattern and, second, that each will fare worse if the other departs unilaterally from it.[11] This means that if there is a salient means available, whereby they can converge on the same pattern—a means salient to each, saliently salient to each, and so on—then that will cue them to conform.

Adjustments and Regularities

But will there always be a salient means of coordination available? Lewis assumes that in general there will. Natural inclination may make it salient that smiling rather than snarling is a way to indicate goodwill; the central position of the crossroads may make it a more salient place to meet than anywhere else; and contingent precedent may make it salient that driving on the right is the safer option to take on the road.

In the presence of such salience triggers, then, we may expect to see a cascade of coordinating adjustments as different pairs or larger groups of people find their way to resolving coordination predicaments. In each case the adjustment will be one such that over time each party in the pair or group will conform to it, and expect others to conform, in future interactions. The expectation that others will conform should help to explain the very conformity expected: each will prefer to conform, after all, so long as others do so.

As one or another pair or group successfully identifies a coordinating adjustment, that is likely to be obvious, or become known, to others. And as that happens, it will provide a precedent that others may be triggered to follow. There may be several precedent solutions, of course, but since individuals will often move between groups, there is bound to be pressure to settle on just one within any unified community. Thus, we may expect that for any general sort of coordination predicament, a regularity in the favored adjustment will emerge across the society.

The dynamic described so far involves two stages, each of which is taken to be likely regardless of contingencies. First: the appearance of coordinating

---

11. The first condition means that that outcome is a proper Nash equilibrium, in decision theory terms, the second that it is also what Lewis (1969) calls a coordination equilibrium.

adjustments by the members of this or that group in one or another predicament. And second: the emergence of a regularity across the society, as one or another type of adjustment, such as driving on the left or the right, catches on generally across the population.

While Lewis does not treat these stages as distinct, he accepts that a regularity will certainly emerge and he identifies such a regularity as a convention. Insofar as we are inclined to use our own word "convention" for that sort of regularity, the emerging regularity satisfies most of the assumptions that surround the word in our ordinary usage. And an examination of what is involved gives us an indication, however preliminary, of the function of such a convention: to resolve potential coordination predicaments.

Recognition and Regulation

The two stages distinguished in the genealogy so far—adjustments and regularities—are robustly likely to be followed quickly by two more: recognition of the regularity as a matter of common awareness and, to introduce an idea only implied in Lewis's own account, the use of the regularity in regulation: that is, in people's instruction of newcomers as well as the young and in their correction of those who offend. For mnemonic purposes, we might say that there is going to be an ARRR or A-triple-R pattern: adjustment followed by regularity, recognition, and regulation.

The regularities that constitute conventions will be recognized as matters of common awareness, given that everyone has evidence of their existence, given that it is evident to everyone that everyone has this evidence, given that this in turn is evident to everyone, and so on.[12] It is likely in each case that everyone believes in the existence of the regularity, believes that everyone believes in its existence, believes that everyone believes that everyone believes in its existence, and so on indefinitely. The indefinite progression need not be a problem, since people do not have to form a positive belief about the issue raised at each level of the hierarchy. All that is required is that each should be disposed to give a positive answer, should a question be raised at any level in the indefinitely progressing hierarchy and should they be able to comprehend the question.

---

12. That this sort of repeating evidence is sufficient for the appearance of common awareness is defended in Lewis (1969). I do not address the need for refinements to the argument, or to the conception of common awareness presupposed, as the line of the book is unlikely to be sensitive to them. See Lederman (2018).

Given that conventions are recognized in common awareness, people should be able to have a word or concept—something like our word "convention"—in which to identify any such regularity. And such an expression would serve an important role. For it would enable participants in a convention to invoke it as a way of doing things to which any outsider or child—indeed anyone at all, including themselves—must conform, if they are to get along with others and gain acceptance in the community. At this point the convention can become a guide for instructing and correcting others and indeed for self-regulation. It will constitute a rule in the familiar sense of something that can be "consulted by those whose behavior is being assessed" (Brandom 1994, 64).

That a convention serves in guiding or regulating people's behavior does not require that people actively consult it as they go along, explicitly registering what it requires and acting for that reason in accord with it. They may act generally out of sheer habit, or an independent motive, in conforming to the convention, say of driving on the right. But the convention will still play a guiding role insofar as they would be quickly alerted to what it requires if their habits or motives let them down, prompting them to drive on the wrong side of the road. Any failure to conform would be likely to raise a red flag. And insofar as that would prompt them to correct the failure, they may be said to be guided by the rule. They are regulated by it virtually, so to speak, rather than actively; their desire to conform is there in standby control, ready to intervene if their independent inclinations do not do the job.

It is hard to see how regulation by a convention could occur in the absence of the concept of a convention and of cognate concepts like those of conforming to a convention and acting in an accepted manner. Prior to such regulation, the regularity in behavior might well be established, but it would come about behind people's backs, as it were, not as a pattern that they could identify and exhort one another to track. They would conform to the regularity, to be sure, but not out of a desire to do so as such; they would not properly follow the convention. Conformity would be generated under the motor of a wish, now in this instance, now in that, to adjust in a suitably coordinated way to others. But it would not be steered by any sense of the general pattern involved or of the costs associated with breaking it.[13]

---

13. By Lewis's own account, the appearance of a word to designate a given item would have to involve a convention as well. But linguistic conventions might evolve simultaneously with other conventions. And while the use of such a linguistic convention in instruction or correction would have to invoke a word like "meaning"—"the meaning of the world precludes that

These comments help to explain why conventions would be robustly likely to emerge in any community, quite independently of a polity or state, and of why their emergence as devices of instruction and correction would involve the simultaneous appearance of concepts and practices. The practice is going to be concept-dependent in the sense that it could hardly materialize as a regulated pattern in the absence of the concept. And the concept will be practice-dependent in the sense that there would be nothing for it to identify in the absence of the corresponding practice.

What Lewis offers us in his account of conventions is a good example of a genealogy in the sense explained earlier. By his account, relatively rational individuals routinely confront one another in coordination predicaments without conventions to guide their individual responses and adjustments. The argument is, first, that they would find it rationally appealing to rely on inclination, salience, precedent, or whatever to identify what they each expect the other to do in any such interaction; second, that insofar as those indicators pointed them in the same direction, the people's reliance on them would give rise to regularities that deserve to be described as social conventions; third, that people would recognize those regularities as matters of common awareness, identifying them as conventions; and, fourth, that they would give those regularities a directive or regulative role.

The regularities explained within this genealogy will fit many common assumptions about conventions, in our usage, so that we will surely be happy to apply the term to them. But the genealogy also serves to identify a function for conventions in resolving coordination predicaments. And it thereby implies that conventions are a functional kind, united by the role they play rather than how they are composed, and that they need not have originated, as in the Hobbesian story, in an episode of joint contractual planning.[14]

Internalization and Ratification

There are further stages to be added to this genealogy that Lewis himself does not explicitly mention. The first, implied in his account, is that in the community he describes it is bound to be the case, not just that everyone wants to

---

usage"—there is no reason why such a word might not coevolve with linguistic conventions in general; there need be no vicious circularity involved.

14. There are regularities that we might describe as conventions that may not answer to Lewis's account. But many certainly will, and the lesson of his account is that those conventions are a significant social kind that serve an important function in people's lives. See Pettit (2019a).

conform to a convention given that others are conforming, but also that every-one is going to want that everyone should indeed conform.[15] Introducing a term that has more significance with norms, as we shall see, the convention will be internalized by everyone in the community. But that being evident to all, evidently evident to all, and so on, it will surely be recognized as a matter of common belief. It will be manifest to all that the convention is internalized in that sense. And this manifest internalization opens a novel possibility for the regulative use of the convention.

If a convention is manifestly internalized, then anyone in the society can speak for all without fear of contradiction in saying: that's the thing to do, that's the approved way of acting, where the qualification "around here" is under-stood. They effectively claim the right, speaking for the community, to tell the person what to do, be that individual a newcomer or child or offender. This marks a contrast with their stance in instructing the other about what to do, on the explicit or implicit assumption that that person will want to avoid a failure to coordinate. In highlighting the appeal of avoiding such a failure, they give the other prudential advice; in speaking for all, they give that per-son an unqualified order, albeit in the name of the community, not in their own name.[16]

The contrast here is described by Hobbes (1994b, 25.2–3) as a divide between offering counsel and giving a command. "Counsel," he says, "is where a man says, Do, or Do not this, and deduces his reasons from the benefit that arrives by it to him to whom he says it." "Command," by contrast, "is, where a man says, Do this, or Do not this, without expecting other reason than the will of him that says it": the will, in this case, of the community.

This development marks an important shift in the genealogy of conventions and is paralleled, as we shall see, in the case of norms and laws. The convention may come into existence on the basis of the strategic self-interest of members: their interest in coordinating successfully in certain predicaments. But once it is manifestly established and internalized in society, it will allow anyone to speak without fear of contradiction for the group, enjoining members to con-form: that is, to conform, period, not just to conform provided they want to avoid coordination problems. Members will continue to have a self-interested

15. This is implied in Lewis's view that a convention, as mentioned in an earlier footnote, would constitute a coordination equilibrium as well as a Nash equilibrium.
16. On the notion of speaking for another, or indeed for oneself, see the discussion in section 2.2.

reason to conform, of course, but the convention will enjoy the authority of a communal instruction, not just that of a prudential maxim.[17]

Even this development is not the end of the story. If a convention is manifestly internalized and available for anyone to enjoin categorically in the name of the community, then its availability in that role is itself robustly likely to be recognized as a matter of common awareness; it will be evident to all, evidently evident to all, and so on. Thus, the convention will gain the status of a regularity that the society, as a matter manifest on all sides, requires members to abide by; if you like, it will count as a socially ratified mode of behavior. And with such ratification, of course, it may appeal to members, not just as the prudent or strategic thing to do, but as the right—the socially right—way to act.[18]

In the original, simpler story of emergence, we saw that the genealogy displays an A-triple-R pattern: adjustment, regularity, recognition, regulation. The further, robustly likely developments that we have just tracked display an I-triple-R pattern: internalization, recognition, regulation, and recognition-cum-ratification. The same pattern, as we shall see shortly, appears also in the genealogies of norms and laws. And in those cases, as in this, it gives strategic maxims the status of social dictates.

1.3 Reconstructing Norms

Many regularities in social life are collectively beneficial in the way conventions are beneficial. But unlike conventions they are often individually burdensome. People may all prefer that some such regularity should materialize in a certain domain rather than having no regularity at all, as in the case of conventions. But conforming to the regularity will be burdensome so that each may prefer that while others uphold the regularity, they themselves get away with

---

17. This genealogy of conventions, like that of norms and laws, can be further enriched with the help of the idea of commitment, introduced in the next chapter. The person who speaks for a group makes a commitment that binds others in the group, should they not object. And the member of the group who does not demur at the manifest expectation that they will conform to a regularity makes a personal, if virtual, commitment to conformity. On these matters, see Pettit (2018a; 2019b).

18. The motivational transition here has parallels. While prudential motives may lead people to look for friends, for example, they will naturally give way, once a friendship is formed, to the natural incentive to do well by that friend. Prudential motives may lead people to generate conventions but give way, once a convention exists, to a simple desire to conform to the convention as to a ratified way of acting.

not doing so; while others bear the burden of conformity, they themselves get a free ride. Social regularities that are individually burdensome and invite free riding—and this, despite being collectively beneficial in the relevant group—may be described as norms rather than conventions (Ullmann-Margalit 1977).[19]

The focus here is on norms that govern relationships between people who enjoy a balance in their mutual power, and that are collectively beneficial from their point of view; the parties involved need not be inclusive of all: in a divided or stratified society, they will be members of the most privileged group. They include norms against deception, infidelity, and violence and, assuming property conventions, a norm against theft. A paradigm case is the norm of truth-telling. Everyone will do better if everyone tells the truth than if only some or none do so. But equally, everyone will be subject to the temptation to free ride, benefitting from the information others provide without giving information—say, about the location of food—that they might do better to keep to themselves.

Norms raise a problem for the emergence story sought in our genealogy because of being individually burdensome. If conformity to a norm is individually burdensome, however collectively beneficial, it will often be in the interest of individuals to free ride and break that norm: to seek to share in the collective benefit provided by general compliance with the norm without having to bear the burden or cost of complying themselves. And so, the norm can remain in place only if other members of the society respond to defectors in such a negative fashion that defection is relatively uncommon, and compliance is general enough to establish the norm as a social regularity.

The Enforcement Dilemma

One way in which individuals might respond negatively to defectors is by recognizing their actions as offenses against a beneficial regularity and sanctioning them intentionally for offending. Were the members of our counterfactual society to take this line, then they would assume the role of enforcers of the relevant norm, where enforcement might consist in rebuking or shaming or punishing offenders.

19. A norm might be collectively beneficial in either of two senses: by benefitting individuals directly and the group indirectly, as in a norm of truth-telling; or by benefitting the collectivity directly and individuals indirectly, as in a norm supporting a social result like the mitigation of climate change. We focus on norms in the first category and comment later on norms in the second.

But the idea that individuals might be prepared to enforce a norm has come in for serious criticism. The economist James Buchanan (1975, 132–33) presents a particularly sharp version of the challenge. Enforcement, he assumes, is going to be costly for the enforcer: at the least it is likely to take time or cause embarrassment. And that means that if people are so self-interested that it is necessary to enforce the norm against them, they are likely to be too self-interested to enforce it against others. Why would they enforce a norm against another, for example, when they have no special interest in the conformity of that other: when they are not in the position of the victim and not implicated in the victim's fortunes?

On this account, the idea of spontaneous enforcement, as Buchanan puts it, confronts a dilemma. If enforcement of a norm is needed—if people, including the protagonists in our genealogy, are so self-interested that they don't spontaneously comply—then it won't be available. And if it is available— if people are public-spirited enough to be prepared to enforce the norm— then it won't be needed: people will be public-spirited enough to conform spontaneously.[20]

This dilemma is sometimes rejected on one of two grounds. First, that enforcing conformity is likely to be less costly than conforming, enforcing enforcement less costly again than enforcing conformity, and so on (Sober and Wilson 1998). Or, second, that there is psychological evidence to the effect that people have been selected to want to enforce established norms against others (Fehr and Gächter 2002). Even if such mechanisms are in place, however, there is another device, long recognized in tradition, that would explain why the enforcement dilemma is not a general problem and why, therefore, we should expect certain norms to emerge in our genealogy, without the need for a state.

The Economy of Esteem

Suppose that I, a protagonist in the genealogical narrative, seek to lessen the burden of truth-telling and mislead you on a given occasion: I tell you that the fruit on the hill is still not ripe, hoping to keep it for myself. When you discover my deception, you will conclude that I cannot be relied upon to tell the truth about something like this, when I have an incentive to lie. And under plausible assumptions, that means that you are less likely to rely on me in

20. For further discussion, see Brennan and Pettit (2004, chap. 14, sec. 2).

future, and less likely to prove reliable in turn. You will impose a cost on me as a result of my defection, but you will do so not out of a desire to enforce a related norm, but out of concern for your own welfare. The cost is that I will be unable to rely on you with confidence in future exchanges of this kind—we may assume that there is an indefinite number of these in prospect (Pettit and Sugden 1989)—and I will be unable to get you, when I wish, to rely on me. My reputation with you will have fallen, and I will consequently be at a serious disadvantage in dealing with you in the future.

This being so, a concern for my reputation as a truth-teller may well be enough to get me to prove generally reliable in my exchanges with you. And in the same way a concern that you should expect me to keep promises, to avoid violence, or to respect property may be enough to get me to display such collectively beneficial patterns in our dealings. And as I will be concerned to earn this reputation with you, so I will be concerned to earn it with everyone with whom I am likely to continue to interact on a regular basis.[21]

For all this strictly suggests, the reputation I am seeking as a member of the society might be restricted in your case to a reputation for behaving cooperatively with you, in the case of a second person a reputation for behaving cooperatively with them, and so on with each of those with whom I interact in a relevant way. But being able to identify me by look or name or whatever, each will be likely to see how I interact with others and will naturally think that as I deal with the others, so I will deal with them. That being manifestly so, I will want to have a reputation for being cooperative with just about anybody with whom I interact. I will want to have a reputation for being generally disposed to avoid deception, infidelity, violence, theft, and the like: for having the standing dispositions of honesty, fidelity, peacefulness, and respect for property.[22]

As this is likely to be true of me, so it is likely to be true of all. And the idea that it is true of all connects with the traditional doctrine that one of the most dominant concerns in human life—and presumably in the life of the protagonists in our narrative—is the desire to enjoy the good opinion of others, and to

21. The elements in play up to this point prompt the emergence of tit-for-tat regularities, as in the pathbreaking analysis by Robert Axelrod (1984). The points we go on to register as essential to the economy of esteem, however, put novel elements in the picture.

22. Why might I not be reputed, not to have this disposition, but rather the disposition to act with the aim of getting others to think I have it? Perhaps because of a feature of human psychology, commonly known as the fundamental attribution bias. This "candidate for the most robust and repeatable finding in social psychology," according to E. E. Jones (1990, 138), consists in "the tendency to see behavior as caused by a stable personal disposition of the actor when it can be just as easily explained as a natural response to more than adequate situational pressure."

avoid their bad opinion: in particular, to enjoy a reputation for virtue and to avoid the disesteem or shame that a lack of virtue, or a proneness to vice, would trigger.

Adam Smith (1982, 116) put the doctrine with particular force. "Nature, when she formed man for society, endowed him with an original desire to please, and an original aversion to offend his brethren. She taught him to feel pleasure in their favorable, and pain in their unfavorable regard." But even if the desire to attract the good opinion of others is not built into our nature in that way, it is likely that people will want to enjoy the good opinion of others for the instrumental effect that it is likely to have on how those others treat them.[23]

Assuming that I care about the opinion or esteem in which I am held by others, I will not just have a motive to tell the truth myself or to live up to any presumptive standard; I will also have a motive to draw the attention of others to someone who has let me or anyone else down: in effect, to criticize offenders in gossiping about them. By doing this, I will presumably earn some extra esteem for myself. I will give others reason to expect me not to fail in the same way as the person I report on, since such a failure would impose not just the ordinary reputational cost, but the cost of being cast as a hypocrite; it would mean, in an ancient metaphor, that I could be hoist by my own petard.

As I will have a motive to gossip in this way about those who breach beneficial patterns, so everyone else will have such a motive too. And, as this becomes a matter of common awareness, the power of the esteem motive in social life will grow. Each of us will realize that how we treat others in any exchange will not only determine our reputation with the parties and witnesses to the interaction but also affect the opinion in which we are held by many others in the society.

The Appearance of Norms

The protagonists in our narrative are not only likely to be attracted to winning esteem, and to be repelled by the prospect of disesteem. Two further assumptions are also likely to hold. One is that they will be unable to secure

23. For a nice introduction to the traditional belief in the power of esteem, see Lovejoy (1961). And for other treatments, drawing on many different cultures and approaches, see McAdams (1997), Brennan and Pettit (2004), Appiah (2010), Liebert (2016), and Origgi (2018). Even if the concern for having a good reputation with others appeared among our own forebears on the basis of instrumental reasoning, it may also have come to be genetically assimilated, with natural selection disposing us to seek it, thereby guarding against failures of reasoning (Crispo 2007).

themselves against the scrutiny of others in their behavior: they will be generally exposed to the possibility of others recognizing how they behave, forming attitudes of esteem or disesteem in response, and communicating those attitudes to others. And the other is that they will be able to recognize that they can be esteemed or disesteemed in circumstances where others do not say or do anything in response to their behavior. Despite the absence of anything like an enforcing sanction, it will be obvious in many situations that others will think well or badly of them—and will form attitudes of acceptance or aversion—depending on how they act.

When these plausible assumptions are satisfied, there is every reason to think that notwithstanding the enforcement dilemma, various norms like those against deception and infidelity, violence, and theft will emerge and endure among our protagonists.

As the esteem motive will get me to tell the truth, keep promises, avoid violence, and respect property, so it will provide the same motive for others in our narrative. And so corresponding regularities are bound to emerge across the society. Each will be motivated to conform to those regularities by a desire for the esteem of others or an aversion to their disesteem. Those others may do nothing in the way of intentional enforcement to elicit this conformity; just by being there, manifestly in a position to register how each behaves, they will serve as unintentional enforcers.

The esteem motive may not be strictly necessary to support conformity in this way. Other mechanisms, including a brute habit or a degree of virtue, may fully account for people's conformity. But the presence of the esteem motive will at least serve as a backup to help guarantee that even if the other mechanisms fail, still the conformity will continue. The appeal of esteem may support conformity to the regularities in the virtual manner that we identified in discussing a parallel possibility with conventions. Thus, while someone generally tells the truth or keeps a promise out of habit or virtue, the failure of such a factor to activate might raise a red flag, trigger the concern with esteem, and ensure that they still tell the truth or keep the promise.

By our earlier account, conventions are regularities with which almost everyone conforms and expects others to conform, where this expectation helps to explain the conformity: this, because everyone prefers to conform so long as others conform. The regularities targeted here, by the emerging account, are of a distinct but parallel kind. They are regularities such that almost everyone conforms with them; almost everyone expects conformity to attract esteem, nonconformity disesteem; and that expectation helps to explain the conformity: this, because almost everyone seeks esteem and shrinks from disesteem.[24]

The story told so far explains why the protagonists in our genealogy will be led in the economy of esteem to adjust to situations where free riding is tempting and give rise to regularities that rule out deception, infidelity, violence, and theft. Those stages correspond to the first two steps in the A-triple-R pattern that we noticed with convention—those introducing adjustment and regularity—although not yet recognition and regulation. But the last two steps will also be paralleled in the full genealogy of norms.

Suppose that a collectively beneficial regularity like that of nondeception, nonviolence, or the like materializes in the society. That the regularity holds will be evident to all, evidently evident to all, and so on. And for that reason, it will be recognized as a matter of common awareness within the society.

Once a norm becomes a matter of common awareness, of course, it will be possible for participants to have a term or concept in which to designate it. And, as in the case of a convention, such a way of speaking and thinking will enable them to invoke the regularity as a way of doing things that everyone should abide by, on pain of rejection by others in the society: on pain, at the limit, of being effectively ostracized, as word spreads of their disposition to ignore the regularities or to free ride opportunistically. Thus, they will be able to cite the norm in instructing others—and indeed themselves—about how it is in their interest to behave.

Not only will members of the society be able to use the norm to regulate others in that manner, they will also have a motive for doing so, even when their own well-being is not at stake. The individual who explains to an outsider or child or offender that this or that mode of behavior is how things are done in the local society can expect to be esteemed by third parties for exhorting others to conform to the regularity; after all, such exhortation will presumably reinforce a pattern that is generally attractive. Thus, the economy of esteem can provide a special reason for why norms might assume the role and status

24. For an earlier version of the conception of norms developed here, see Pettit (1990) and Brennan and Pettit (2004). Something close to the current version, although without the emphasis that we give below to the regulative role of norms, appears in Pettit (2008b; 2015c; 2018a, chap. 2; 2019b). This notion picks up points made in a variety of approaches. See, for example, Hart (1961), Winch (1963), Coleman (1990), Sober and Wilson (1998), Elster (1999), Bicchieri (2006), Shapiro (2011), and Bicchieri (2017). For an approach that takes the notion of the normative to preexist norms but is otherwise reconcilable with that adopted here, see Brennan et al. (2013).

of properly regulative rules: devices of instruction and correction. And, to take up Buchanan's challenge, it can make sense of why individuals should be willing to enforce those rules in that regulative mode.

This completes the A-triple-R genealogy of norms: mutual adjustments in predicaments involving truth-telling and the like give rise to regularities across the society; those regularities are recognized as a matter of common awareness, and they are then invoked in social regulation. All of the norms surveyed, however, involve social regularities that scale up pairwise regularities: this, in the way the social regularity of truth-telling scales up the bilateral regularity in which one person tells the truth to another. But there are norms that do not have this special feature, such as the norm requiring that everyone in a group, or in the society as a whole, should contribute to some common good. Does our genealogy explain how such a collectively beneficial, individually burdensome norm might emerge in the society imagined?

It does not offer us a four-stage breakdown of how such a regularity might emerge and assume the status of a norm. But in explaining how the individuals in the society will live under an economy in which each seeks the esteem of others, it enables us to make sense of why social norms of the targeted kind might also appear. Whenever there is something that is recognized as a common good across the society, and as a good that can be generated only by the combined efforts of individuals, there will be positive esteem for anyone who is seen to make a contribution, and as the number of contributions rise, disesteem for anyone who is seen to fail (McAdams 1997; Brennan and Pettit 2004, chap. 7). Thus, to the extent that contributory efforts and failures are discernible, we may expect corresponding regularities to emerge, to be recognized in common awareness, and to be invoked in mutual regulation and self-regulation.[25]

Our story about the robustly likely development of norms, and presumably their robustly likely survival, directs us to the function that they serve in the counterfactual world of our narrative, and indicates that the corresponding norms in the actual world may serve a similar function. That function, of course, is to enable people to achieve a collectively beneficial result, establishing norms that serve everybody positively, despite the free-riding temptation that

---

25. It is worth noting that the tit-for-tat mechanism cannot explain such norms itself, for it does not operate reliably in multiperson as distinct from two-person groups. If only one party defects in a multiperson setting, it will not usually be in the interest of the others to retaliate since the defection will not have imposed a significant cost. See Pettit (1986).

each is liable to experience. Whether in the counterfactual or actual society, that collectively beneficial effect is going to explain, via the economy of esteem, why the norms promise to be resilient realities, fit to survive a range of contingencies and challenges.

As we have characterized them so far, the norms established under the economy of esteem satisfy only the A-triple-R pattern that we identified in the case of conventions. It remains to see that they will also satisfy the richer I-triple-R pattern displayed by conventions and that they will gain the authority of social dictates. Before we turn to that topic, however, it is worth noticing some categories of norms that are excluded by our focus so far.

A Restriction of Focus Noted

There are three categories of norms that fall outside this focus. These are worth noting for a number of reasons, including the fact that they too lend themselves to being explained by an esteem-based story of the kind that we have told. They show that the economy of esteem may not always serve a generally welcome purpose.

First, the story we have told can be extended to explain the emergence of certain norms within any society, even one of equals, that are beneficial for members of a particular subgroup but harmful for the society as a whole. These will include norms of honesty among thieves, for example, and partisanship among politicians. Hume (1994, 24) directs us to how the story applies in this sort of case. "Honour is a great check upon mankind," he says. "But where a considerable body of men act together, this check is, in a great measure, removed; since a man is sure to be approved of by his own party, for what promotes the common interest [of the party]; and he soon learns to despise the clamors of his adversaries."[26]

Second, apart from norms that govern relationships between those of relatively equal power in any society or class, there are bound to be norms governing the relationships in a divided or stratified society between those in an alpha class and the members of a beta, or indeed any subordinate class. It may well

26. A more difficult task is the explanation of norms that like those of revenge or dueling may govern everyone in a class of relative equals, not just those in a particular party, but may serve them badly from a detached point of view. For an illuminating discussion that also draws on the economy of esteem, see Appiah (2010). And for a helpful, independent explanation of such norms, see O'Connor (2019).

be that the interests of the individual beta, including their interest in esteem, will often be best served by subservience and deference to the individual alpha. And it may be that the adjustments beta members individually make, as well as the adjustments of their alpha counterparts, will become regularized in the society, recognized as regular patterns, and invoked in instruction and correction. Nothing in our story about norms is meant to gloss over that bleak possibility.

A third restriction of focus in our treatment is less obvious but even more noteworthy. As we have seen, people in our imagined society will tend to conform to collectively beneficial norms—and indeed invoke them in regulation—because of thinking that others approve and will esteem them for complying, disesteem them for defecting. But what we should now notice is that people may be mistaken in ascribing such attitudes of esteem and disesteem to others. The ascription may be a misperception on the part of each, even a misperception that is registered as a matter of common belief. While no one really wants others to conform to the regularity, in other words, it may be that each believes that as a matter of common awareness others do want this: that they esteem conformity and disesteem defection. That is going to be enough to ensure that the regularity will come to obtain and be invoked as a prudential maxim, even though no one thinks it is beneficial, let alone collectively beneficial.

Consider an example of this possibility. A group of students who regularly go drinking together may each drink more than they wish, even exhort one another to that level of drinking, because of the mistaken belief that otherwise their fellows will hold them in disesteem; they may uphold a norm out of "pluralistic ignorance" about the attitudes within the group (Miller and Prentice 1994; 1996). This ignorance may appear even when there is a salient and feasible alternative to the norm in question, such as drinking less or drinking according to personal preference; when many members of the group each prefer that this should be the general pattern; and when, as a result, they do not actually disesteem those who breach the established pattern or esteem those who conform (Pettit 2008b).

Notwithstanding these three sorts of limitation, however, we shall continue to focus here on norms that are collectively beneficial in a more straightforward way. These are norms that are collectively beneficial for members of the society as a whole or at least for members of the most privileged class if the society does contain different classes. We shall see why this focus is justified early in the fourth section.

From Internalization to Ratification

Returning now to collectively beneficial norms, we shall see that not only does their emergence satisfy the A-triple-R pattern we identified in the case of conventions, it is also robustly likely to satisfy the I-triple-R pattern as well: that of internalization, recognition, regulation, and recognition-cum-ratification.

For a norm to be internalized among the members of the group, by our earlier account, it must be the case that they each generally prefer that the established pattern obtain rather than no pattern at all or rather than any salient alternative. We just saw that some norms, such as the drinking norm in our example, may appear despite the fact of not being internalized in this sense by those who sustain them. The students in that case do not prefer that everyone should drink to the established limit but would prefer that each drank according to preference or to a lower limit instead.

The fact that collectively beneficial norms are manifestly of benefit to each is going to ensure that they are internalized. This will certainly be true in the case of norms like those of truth-telling, fidelity, and nonviolence that generally provide the same benefit for each. But what of norms of property, given that some individuals are likely to own less than others and be less happy with those norms?

Even in such a case, by contrast with the case of the drinking norm, everyone may prefer that everyone conform to the norm rather than not. Once it is established, a property norm will be the only feasible regularity available: it will be susceptible to reform only in the unlikely event that people act together for its reform. And general conformity to the norm will have an appealing feature that is likely to elicit an overall preference on the part of each that the conformity should remain general, with almost everyone conforming. It will mean, once established, that each can form reliable expectations about how they and others can act without fear of objection or hindrance; it provides for the coordination of expectation among the parties, where such coordination is clearly beneficial for everyone.[27]

When the pattern of overall behavior that a norm introduces has a feature that makes conformity with it appealing in a general way, then we may say that it is accepted among those to whom it appeals. Many may prefer that another norm should obtain in its place, as in the case of property, but this attractive feature will give them some reason, over and beyond a prudential concern

---

27. The drinking norm introduces the coordination of expectations too, but by assumption coordination in that case is not particularly attractive to anybody.

with reputation, to conform. Its presence will mean that they do not conform just out of the desire to gain esteem or avoid disesteem, but also, at least in part, for the benefit that general conformity introduces. The fact that a norm is accepted in this sense, however reluctant the acceptance, makes it extremely likely that it will be internalized. If there is a feature of the order established by the norm that makes it attractive for just about anyone, then it will presumably make it attractive to them that everyone should conform; if they do not, the order that appeals will cease to obtain.

Let us assume, then, that in the world of our narrative, the parties will all accept an established norm, finding conformity with it to be appealing in a general way, and that they will therefore internalize it. Once that state of affairs is in place, it is likely to be evident to all that it is in place, evidently evident to all that it is in place, and so on. Thus, the acceptance and internalization of the norm is likely to be recognized as a manifest feature of the society; in other worlds, the acceptance and internalization of the norm will be recognized as a matter of common awareness.

Once norms get to be manifestly accepted and internalized in this way, of course, to rerun a lesson that we drew with conventions, that will enable any party in the narrative to invoke them in instructing children and newcomers and in correcting offenders. In instructing others to follow a norm, by our earlier account, an individual need only be advising or counselling them about how they must behave if they are not to be shunned or ostracized: if they are not to suffer a prudential cost. But given the manifest internalization of the norm, such a person can speak for all without fear of contradiction, in saying that that is the approved mode of behavior: it represents the behavior approved by the society, not just by the speaker alone. They can assume the authority of the community in directing newcomers and offenders to conform, period; they need not recommend conformity provisionally on the person's caring about how they fare in prudential terms.

But the fact that anyone can speak for others in this way without fear of contradiction is itself going to be evident to all, evidently evident to all, and so on. And that has an important implication. If it is a matter of common awareness that no one would attract objection for claiming to speak for all in presenting conformity to a norm as a social requirement, then it is going to be a matter of common awareness that the norm is supported by all. And that is to say, in our terminology, that it has a ratified status in the community.[28]

28. That certain norms enjoy such ratification does not require that the parties involved think in moral or ethical terms about the relevant norms. Individuals may ratify the norms only

In this transition from internalization to ratification we see the second-wave pattern that we identified in the genealogy of conventions: the I-triple-R pattern linking internalization to recognition, to regulation, to recognition-cum-ratification. In the first wave of the genealogy of norms, the parties are taken to invoke a norm in prudential counselling, to use Hobbes's term, recognizing and conveying that it is in the strategic self-interest of the addressee to conform. In the second wave of the genealogy, we see how the norm will get to assume the extra status of a social dictate, as the parties come to require conformity in the manner of a command supported by the community.[29]

1.4 Reconstructing Laws

From Norms to Laws

Conventions and norms may clearly exist in any society without being matters of law. But what would be involved in their becoming matters of law? And might laws emerge within our counterfactual model, in the absence of a polity or state?

In *The Concept of Law*, first published in 1961 and now a classic of legal theory, H. L. A. Hart (2012) tells a story about how this would happen (Gardner 2013). He provides a genealogy of how laws might plausibly arise that begins at the point we have reached in our own narrative, and we may develop that story by drawing, with just a little amendment, on the genealogy he presents.

Hart assumes a relatively equal balance of power among all the protagonists in his story, and he focuses only on norms that are collectively beneficial for the inclusive group, especially norms that are important enough in governing the relations between members to call for regimentation and reinforcement (Hart 2012, 195). We need not assume such a universal balance of power here, although we shall continue to speak for convenience as if there were such a balance. We assume only, as explained earlier, either that there is such a relative equality of power among all or that there is a privileged group of inhabitants among whom such equality prevails.

Hart takes it for granted in his genealogy that the norms that call for legal regimentation and reinforcement—more on why they do so in a moment—are the collectively beneficial norms that play a role in protecting residents in

---

on the basis that they think of them as requirements that the community imposes on its members; they need not subscribe to any more general criterion of assessment. For an account of how they might attain a moral viewpoint, see Pettit (2018a).

29. For an earlier exploration of such stages in the likely evolution of social norms, see Pettit (2019b).

relation to one another: in giving them security in their interactions. Norms that have this status will include those that guard people, for example, against violence, coercion, deception, theft, and the like. In building on Hart's genealogy, we allow for the possibility of division or stratification in the society. And so, we shall assume that the norms that call for legal support are those collectively beneficial norms that protect citizens in relation to one another—the concept of citizenship will appear only after law, of course—whether the citizenry encompass all residents or only those in a privileged class.

Norms in this category call for legal support insofar as law is required to secure citizens in a domain where security is needed: namely, in their relations with one another. But that consideration does not apply with various other norms, so that they will not call for the same legal support. These will include norms in a divided society that bear on how the members of other classes relate to one another. And they will include norms of the kind that we distinguished earlier in noting a restriction in our focus. Thus, for want of a collective benefit to the citizenry, the norms without need of legal support will include norms that are beneficial for members of a subgroup among the citizens but harmful for the citizenry as a whole, norms in a divided society that govern the relations between citizens and noncitizens—citizens will not require protection on that front—and norms that are not accepted and internalized in the society.

Primary and Secondary Rules

Hart (2012, 88–89) supposes, without offering a genealogy of their emergence, that in almost any society, collectively beneficial, individually burdensome norms like those against deception and infidelity, theft and violence, are bound to emerge and endure. And he takes it that, like any general norms, they will dictate people's rights and duties vis-à-vis one another: they will constrain how each may treat others under those norms and how each may expect to be treated by others.

Hart (2012, 86) describes these norms as primary rules, arguing that they are regularities with which "the general demand for conformity is insistent and the social pressure brought to bear on those who deviate or threaten to deviate is great." He holds, in line with our discussion of the economy of esteem, that this "social pressure may take only the form of a general diffused hostile or critical reaction which may stop short of physical sanctions."

But why should a regime of primary rules give rise to developments that usher in a regime of laws? Why should they call for legal regimentation and

THE FUNCTION OF THE POLITY 47

reinforcement? While generally endorsing Hart's answers, we cast them here as answers to questions raised about our counterfactual world.

Hart argues, in a manner reminiscent of Locke's *Second Treatise of Government* (1960), that there are three problems that the members of any society governed by such collectively beneficial norms would be likely to confront. And he maintains that individuals would be likely—in our terms, robustly likely—to adjust in response to those problems after a pattern that introduces a legal regime. Where Locke thinks that contract would be required to remedy such problems, however, he holds that the parties in his narrative would make adjustments on a spontaneous, unplanned basis without the need for collective discussion or contract.

According to Hart, the first problem with a regime of norms is that they would be uncertain or indeterminate; it would often be unclear what exactly the norms were or what implications they supported. The second is that they would be static, lacking the flexibility required for covering the new circumstances arising from changes in culture or technology. And the third is that they would be inefficient in leaving it up to alleged offenders and would-be victims to agree on whether this or that norm was breached in some interaction and on what recompense or retaliation should be implemented.

In response to these problems, the members of the society would be likely to improvise solutions, he suggests, relying on the salience of certain procedures, the prominence of certain individuals, or the existence of certain precedents, to determine the approach to take. The responses might initially be ad hoc, with some prominent individual or body presuming to pass judgment in this or that case, without objection from others, or with someone proposing without objection that a salient process or procedure should be employed. Such responses would be likely to consolidate over time, establishing patterns or routines—secondary rules, in Hart's terminology—for dealing with the different issues arising.

As Hart envisages this development, the adjustments made in response to the three problems, now in this case, now in that, would determine what the norms are, when that is needed; how they are to be amended to cope with changed circumstances; and how alleged infringements are to be decided and, by extension, how convicted offenders are to rectify things or be otherwise sanctioned: if reputational pressures do not constitute sufficient sanctions, the procedures may allow also for other penalties. These regularities of adjustment he describes respectively as rules of recognition, rules of change, and rules of adjudication.

Once such regular patterns are established, of course, they are liable to be recognized in common awareness and then to be invoked in regulation, if only by those who are deputed to implement them. Thus, we find once again the A-triple-R pattern of adjustment, regularity, recognition, and regulation. The regularities are described as secondary rules by Hart precisely insofar as they are required to organize the framing, updating, and application of preexisting, primary rules: to resolve the problems of indeterminacy, inflexibility, and inefficiency that those rules would raise.

A Legal System

The appearance of secondary rules to govern the development and application of the primary rules or norms, providing remedies for the problems raised, would take us, Hart (2012, 94) says, from a prelegal into a legal world: the "three remedies together are enough to convert the regime of primary rules into what is indisputably a legal system." The remedies would establish a set of procedures and a range of personnel to pronounce on what the norms are, to amend those norms to fit new circumstances, to determine when violations have occurred, and to identify and implement the measures, if any, that are required to deal with offenders. Their function would be to remedy the sorts of problems identified, regimenting and reinforcing the system of collectively beneficial social norms.

The remedies might do this, of course, in a very simple manner, rather than in the complex fashion of an advanced society. But even in that case, they would take us from a society of informal conventions and norms to one where at least some of those regularities are identified, applied, and administered on a public basis. And in Hart's view the patterns regimented on that basis— the primary rules—as well as the patterns involved in regimenting them—the secondary rules—are good candidates for being described as laws. Thus, he takes his argument to show that, like conventions and norms, laws would emerge in the targeted society on an unplanned basis: in particular, without planning by the officials of a preexisting state.

The secondary rules introduced in this picture will count as decision-maker laws that determine how officials ought to be appointed and what they are required, permitted, or forbidden to do in the exercise of their various offices. The primary rules, once given a legal status, will count by contrast as decision-taker laws, as we might say: laws that constrain how people in general ought to behave, whether they hold office or not. The category of decision-taker laws will include not just primary rules, however, but also laws that are introduced in amendment or extension of those rules by decision makers. Where the primary rules are presumptively beneficial for all, these new laws may not be; they may reflect more partial interests, as the officials established under the secondary rules flex their lawmaking and law-changing muscles.

Regular, decision-taker laws will enable individual citizens to know how they generally stand in relation to one another and in relation to those officials—by assumption, citizens themselves—who are licensed by decision-maker laws to take charge of the law in general: to shape decision-taker laws and perhaps also to change the decision-maker laws themselves. Wherever there are laws of these two kinds, there are bound to be associated rights and duties. Decision-taker laws will give a range of general, relatively determinate rights and duties to all citizens, and decision-maker laws will give a range of relatively determinate special rights and duties to officials.

Together, those two bodies of law will enable everyone to know, at least in broad terms, where they stand in relation to others. They will know what, on pain of legal sanction, others may claim of them in their identity as citizens or as officials: what duties they have toward others. And they will know what they may claim of others in the civic and official roles those others occupy; what rights they have against others.

From Internalization to Ratification

Hart (2012, 88–89) assumes, plausibly, that since the primary rules are collectively beneficial guidelines for society at large, the laws that formulate them will attract what he describes as the internal point of view in the society he imagines. Without going into the interpretation of what exactly he means, we can equate this with their being accepted and internalized in the sense explained earlier. Having a beneficial feature, those laws, like the norms they express, will give each party a reason to conform over and beyond the fear of any sanction, reputational or otherwise: a reason, as we put it, to accept the laws. And they will therefore give each a reason also to prefer that everyone should conform, since general conformity will be essential for generating the appealing benefit: in other words, they will give them a reason to internalize the laws.

Why identify the internal point of view with acceptance and internalization? According to Hart (2012, 86) the fact that the primary rules attract the internal point of view explains why "the general demand for conformity is insistent." And the general acceptance and internalization of those rules would certainly have that same explanatory effect.[30] It would mean that people abide by the laws for a virtue that they see in them, and not just because there are "grounds for a prediction that hostile reactions will follow" any breach of the laws (Hart 2012, 84).

So much for the laws corresponding to primary rules. Will secondary rules and the laws formulating them be internalized in the same sense as the primary? Hart assumes that at least the officials will accept and internalize them in that way, as they guide their own behavior by them and use them as guidelines to assess the behavior of others. They will take themselves to be operating by generally attractive procedures that they each prefer every official to follow.

While it is certainly plausible that individuals in our imagined society will generally accept and internalize the collectively beneficial primary rules, and the corresponding laws, there are grounds for wondering whether they will internalize secondary rules, each preferring that the officials follow them. And there are similar grounds for wondering whether they will internalize the novel decision-taker laws that officials can introduce under the power given them by secondary rules. Both the secondary rules, and the laws introduced under those rules, may serve some individuals or groups better than others, and not be collectively beneficial in the straightforward manner of primary rules.

For reasons rehearsed in discussing the internalization of norms, however, we may expect the protagonists in our narrative to accept and internalize secondary rules as well as primary rules and also, short of extremes, to accept and internalize the new decision-taker laws introduced under those secondary rules. Once they are established, those rules and those laws will have the attraction of enabling people to coordinate with one another, by supporting reliable expectations and eliciting aligned actions. This coordinating role will be a feature that provides each with a potentially significant reason, given the absence of feasible alternatives, to prefer to conform to those regularities rather than not—that is, to accept them—and to prefer that others should conform as well: that is, to internalize them. And to that extent the laws will be accepted and internalized widely, if only reluctantly; they will merit the internal point of view, on our interpretation of what this involves.

30. For an argument that looking at the genealogy of primary rules, as Hart conceives of them, makes it possible to understand just what an internal point of view involves, see Pettit (2019b).

We may assume, as we did with conventions and norms, that the fact that any laws enjoy internalization will be recognized in common awareness, being evident to all, evidently evident to all, and so on. Returning to a point made with conventions and norms, that means that when anyone instructs or corrects others under those laws, they can speak for the society, enjoining conformity in the name of the community. Thus, in recommending conformity to children, to newcomers, and to offenders, they will not just offer prudential or strategic advice to the effect that conformity is the best self-interested policy: that if they break the law, they will be sanctioned. Speaking for the community, they will issue a categorical directive to conform; in Hobbes's terminology, they will give a command rather than offering counsel.

To the extent that this is true of decision-maker laws—secondary rules— and of the novel decision-taker laws introduced under them, the regularities introduced by the laws will enjoy the status of social norms as well as a legal status. Independently of their legally enforced status, they will be regularities such that conformity attracts esteem, nonconformity disesteem; regularities that establish an order with a general benefit that prompts acceptance and inter- nalization; and this being manifest, regularities that can be invoked to an instructive or corrective purpose in the name of the society. Decision-taker laws that answer to primary rules may reinforce existing social norms. But these novel laws will engender or elicit social norms to support them: the regularities they generate will enjoy the status of norms as well as laws.

At this point we can see that like independent conventions and norms, laws will materialize in the imagined society under an I-triple-R pattern, not just the A-triple-R pattern characterized earlier. Not only will anyone be able to speak for the society in supporting the law. It will also be a matter of common recognition that that is the case, so that the laws involved will assume a com- munally ratified status; they will command allegiance, not just as strategic maxims, but as social dictates. The internalization of the laws will materialize and be recognized; this recognition will support anyone in regulating others categorically to conform to the law; and that in turn being commonly recog- nized, the laws will count as regularities ratified within the community.

This observation enables us to respond to a misgiving that is sometimes raised about Hart's genealogy. Even some sympathetic readers have held that the account fails to explain the fact that when a regime of law is in place, then members of the society will take the law to rule categorically on how they ought to behave, and officials will represent it as having the mission of provid- ing such guidance. The idea is that Hart does not explain either why people will think that the law gives them categorical reasons to behave in this or that manner, not just reasons conditional on their prudential ends; or why officials will represent the law as having the goal of pronouncing on what people ought to do, in that categorical mode.[31]

We have a ready, parsimonious response to this challenge. Given that decision-maker and decision-taker laws will be manifestly internalized by each, if only in a reluctant way, they can be invoked by anyone, especially officials, as identifying approved modes of acting, and can be seen in that light by individuals overall. And given the fact that they can be invoked in this way is itself going to be a matter of common awareness, the laws will count as enjoying collective ratification. They will not represent directives for how best to satisfy a certain prudential end, or indeed any discretionary goal. Without yet being designated as moral imperatives, they will have the general imprimatur of the people and will be perceived and promulgated as categorical imperatives for any member of the society.[32]

1.5 The Emergence of the State

The Polity Is Not the Producer of Law

The genealogy traced so far shows that starting from an imagined society in which there is a relatively equal balance of power among all members, or among the members of a privileged subset, we can expect a rich development. First, that collectively beneficial conventions and norms will emerge and endure among them; and second, that these will give rise, under the adjustments elicited by problems of indeterminacy, inflexibility, and inefficiency, to a regime of laws: a system of suitably internalized and ratified rules. The lesson taught by the genealogy is that the members of such a society will be in a position, in response to the emerging practices, to use legal concepts to describe

---

31. Scott Shapiro (2011) formulates the challenge raised in one way, Joseph Raz (2003) in another, David Plunkett (2013) in yet another, but the differences are not relevant for the purposes of the discussion here. Plunkett offers a very useful overview of the issue.

32. Shapiro (2011) argues that in order to respond to the challenge we should go beyond Hart and treat laws not as the unplanned byproduct of mutual adjustment and coordination but as elements in a jointly endorsed plan for the organization of the law; in doing this, he draws on Michael Bratman's planning theory, elucidated more recently in Bratman (2014). On a reading that would cast the planning required as a social contract, this offends against parsimony. But it might be construed as postulating just that people or officials follow the rules involved, once they have emerged, in the way they might follow a plan (see section 4.3 below).

those practices, to give expression to the duties the practices impose and the rights they establish, and to recognize that such obligations and entitlements hold with collective ratification.

According to the methodology outlined in the first section, this genealogy offers us the following attractive hypothesis. That in speaking of the conventions and norms and laws under which we ourselves live—presumptively, live as equals before the law—we are using the same concepts as the story's protagonists and referring to the same social realities. And, correlatively, that in speaking of our rights and obligations under that dispensation, particularly under our regime of law, we need not be invoking anything more mysterious than what the participants in the genealogy might invoke.

In sketching a way in which a regime of conventions, norms, and law—for short, a legal regime—might come into existence, the story gives us a plausible account of the function such a regime will typically play among us. By that account, the function of conventions is to enable us to avoid coordination predicaments, the function of the sorts of norms targeted to guard collectively beneficial regularities from free-riding problems, and the function of laws to make it possible to transcend problems of indeterminacy, inflexibility, and inefficiency that norms on their own would raise.

Since it does not posit the existence of a polity or state as a precondition for the developments charted, the genealogy gives the lie to the sort of picture proposed by Hobbes, which we mentioned earlier in the chapter. There is no reason to think that a law-bound society could come into existence only because of the initiatives of an independently established polity or state. And there is no reason to think that in speaking of the rights and duties under law of the protagonists in our genealogy we are presupposing the existence of a state to which they are in some way bound.

The Polity as the Precipitate of Law

But if the polity does not figure in this picture as something that has to go into the production of law, it does plausibly figure as a precipitate whose existence is guaranteed by the appearance of law (Lovett 2009). Or at least by the appearance of law among people who are bound by the agricultural practices of harvesting crops and domesticating animals to remain territorially settled over an extended period (Scott 2017). The state will be a precipitate of such a regime of law insofar as the operation of the regime entails the existence of a skeletal state.

If a regime of law comes into existence, according to the genealogical narrative told so far, then it establishes a set of practices under which various individuals assume authorized roles in relation to others, whether permanently or temporarily, where those roles are distinctively political in character. The roles require such officials to define a set of laws and, in applying those laws, to grant citizens their legal rights and to hold them to their legal obligations: to treat them on the impartial lines established by the law. Decision-maker laws are secondary rules that establish and constrain officials in their roles and that enable them, operating under those laws, to take charge of the decision-taker laws—at base, the primary rules—that apply to all citizens, whether the citizenry be inclusive or not. Indeed, the officials may also be given charge of the decision-maker laws insofar as they are enabled to do so—perhaps under certain limitations—by those laws themselves.

In the counterfactual society imagined, then, there will be certain temporary or enduring authorities whose job it is to say what the laws are, perhaps setting them out in written form. There will be other authorities to say how the system of laws should be changed to deal with novel circumstances. There will be yet others to determine when someone has offended against the laws and to determine the recompense or sanction required. And there will be others again to ensure, if necessary, that the offender does provide that recompense and does suffer that sanction.

Whether these authorities involve different individuals, or the same individuals under different hats, it should be clear that they will discharge the three sorts of roles associated with the polity in thinkers as diverse as Aristotle (1996), Locke (1960), and Montesquieu (1989). One is the legislative role of establishing what the law is and how it should be changed. Another is the judicial role of determining when a law has been broken and how the offense should be sanctioned. And a third is the executive role of implementing associated requirements: at a minimum, that of imposing the remedies and sanctions prescribed by judicial authorities.

Should we conclude that the bare existence of a regime of law should be taken to ground or ensure the existence of a polity, at least in a relatively settled society? Perhaps we should, in a very thin sense of what a polity is. The sort of institution that serves to maintain a regime of law, identifying regular, decision-taker rules under decision-maker practices, can be taken to constitute a rudimentary state, albeit one lacking many of the features that we currently associate with the polity. The state in this sense need not be reliably coercive, for example: it may take the pressures of social esteem to be sufficient to enforce the laws; and it need not have a well-defined territory of the sort claimed and defended by every modern state.

But, while the sort of body implied by a legal regime may not constitute a state in the familiar sense, there are reasons to think that under circumstances that have generally obtained in recent centuries—and that may have obtained in some cases before (Morris and Scheidel 2009)—the authorities in such a regime would be pushed into making adjustments that will give rise to the modern sort of state with which we are acquainted. Arguably, these circumstances will force a rudimentary state into becoming something that is close to the modern state, as we generally understand such a state. They will put flesh and muscle on the skeletal state inherent in a regime of law.

There are four problems, parallel to Hart's three problems of indeterminacy, inflexibility, and inefficiency, that modern circumstances will raise for the officials and citizens of a rudimentary state in our counterfactual scenario. And, as will become apparent, these will elicit adjustments that have the effect, not necessarily planned by anyone, of bringing a familiar sort of polity or state into existence. In developing this genealogy of the state, we go beyond assuming merely that the participants in our story live under conditions of moderate scarcity with a relatively equal balance of power among at least the members of an elite. As mentioned, we assume that people live in a settled society of the kind that the agricultural revolution introduced quite early on. And we assume that states will multiply and threaten one another, forcing each to take on a self-defensive profile.

The resolution of our four problems, as will be evident, requires a signal extension of the role of executive authorities. Such officials will not only be needed, as in the rudimentary state, for implementing judicial decisions as to what services offenders should perform, or what sanctions they should suffer. They will also be required, to anticipate the discussion, for making the regime effectively coercive, for suppressing or denouncing rival sources of coercion, for identifying and policing the borders of the jurisdiction, and for defending the territory against the possibility of invasion from outside.

The Compliance Problem and the Need for Coercion

The regime of law envisaged so far might not be coercive. The legislative authorities might see laws merely as signaling general expectations; the judicial authorities might simply make recommendations as to what an offender ought to do in putting things right with the victim or the victim's family; and the

executive authorities might intervene only to help determine a suitable recompense or negotiate an acceptable sanction. Something like this might have
happened, for example, in traditional small societies.

This is bound to change, however, in a society that grows in population as
agricultural practice and industrial development are bound to make possible.
A noncoercive, esteem-based regime would certainly collapse in the presence
of offenders, whether they be officials who offend against decision-maker laws
or citizens of any stripe who breach decision-taker laws. Indeed, it would likely
collapse even in the presence of a belief on the part of the law-abiding that
there were offenders of that sort who could free ride on their own efforts:
make suckers of them, as the common metaphor has it.

Assuming that they are not offenders themselves, the authorities in the
regime to which the genealogy of law leads will make corrective adjustments
in response to problems of official corruption, regular lawbreaking, and the
like. The legislative authorities are likely to support the laws promulgated with
penalties designed to encourage compliance, and the judicial authorities will
be disposed to impose penalties on convicted offenders. And of course, the
executive authorities will ensure that any legislatively or judicially nominated
penalties are put into effect, where this is probably going to require the establishment of an enforcing and policing body. Those authorities, moreover, will
naturally be required to advertise the commitment of the regime in these
respects.

These adjustments will give the laws envisaged a coercive cast, as the authorities present them to members of the society as regulations that must be
obeyed, on pain of sanction. And, plausibly, the authorities will have to impose
those laws with the same coercive force on all, not just on those who are likely
to offend: it is hardly going to be possible, after all, to identify potential offenders in advance.[33] The need for this encompassing form of coercion will be
buttressed by the necessity of taxation. In any sizeable society, an effective
system of law is going to cost money, money is going to be most readily available via taxation, and taxation is certainly going to require a coercive state.

We have presented our arguments on this as on earlier points, as if it can be
assumed that there is a universal balance of power among the members of the
society. What if one group is more powerful than others and only its members

---

33. None will be allowed to claim a special status, then, not even those—presumptively, a
large majority—who are spontaneously averse to breaking the law. For an argument that most
people obey the law without focusing particularly on the associated penalties, see Tyler (1990).

gain protection as citizens under the law? How might we expect the law to treat those outside the citizenry? Presumably the law will impose duties suited to their status on those in the less privileged class or classes, as it will impose duties on citizens proper. But the rights it gives those individuals may presumably fall short of the rights of citizens.

The Competition Problem and the Monopoly Claim to Coercion

As the problem of compliance is bound to push laws into a coercive mode, so a problem with competition is likely to create a pressure for the authorities in our imagined society to claim and assert a monopoly on the use of coercive force. Suppose that there were two sets of legal authorities in the society, or that the presumptive authorities were continually undermined by a covert, mafia-like organization that dispensed its own version of legal justice. That sort of competition would undermine the possibility of a stable legal regime, as almost all political theories acknowledge (Nozick 1974). Thus, one group of authorities would have to drive out the other, establishing its monopoly on the use of legal coercion: in effect, the sole right to exercise force in imposing the law. Or the two groups would have to come to an arrangement whereby each enjoyed that sort of monopoly in its own domain. One group would have to conquer, or the two would have to divide.

The solution by conquest is likely to be the more reliable. But the competition problem will prompt such a solution only to the extent that one side has the physical and cultural power to impose it on the other. And sometimes therefore a solution by the division of power is the only possibility. In large parts of medieval Europe, for example, the secular and ecclesiastic authorities represented and imposed rival systems of laws, illustrating a solution by division rather than conquest, albeit one that often gave rise to conflict (Canning 1983).[34] The ecclesiastical authorities wielded power and jurisdiction in ecclesiastical precincts or over ecclesiastical personnel, the secular wielded power and jurisdiction in other cases.

In early modern times, particularly after the Reformation in the sixteenth century, this problem came to be resolved by conquest, with the secular authorities assuming monopoly rights over the framing and application of all

---

34. Indeed, for much of that period, the secular authorities were themselves divided, at least in Germany and Italy, with the Holy Roman emperor enjoying a limited jurisdiction over the republics and princedoms ruled by more local officials.

domestic law. The religious divisions within countries forced those authorities to develop their power in the attempt to establish domestic peace. And of course, the conflict that often appeared between countries also prompted a growth in the powers of secular governments.

The solution by division is unlikely to provide stability, since the rival authorities will almost certainly struggle with one another for a greater share of power, as indeed happened in medieval Europe. Thus, we may presume in our counterfactual model that the legal authorities will try to solve the competition problem by rejecting rival claims to exercise coercion legitimately and by eliminating or corralling those who make such claims.

The Permeability Problem and the Need for Territorial Definition

The legal regime derived in our genealogy begins to look worthy of being described as a state insofar as it assumes a coercive form and claims a monopoly over the right to legal coercion. But for all we have said so far, that regime need not have a determinate territory or jurisdiction. People living under the regime may be able to move at will beyond the reach of its laws. Or at least they may be able to do so, when they are not hemmed in by mountains or seas or tied down by dependence on the land, family ties, linguistic restriction, or the sheer difficulty of moving elsewhere. This problem together with the problem of protection considered next argue that the state is likely in our genealogy to become territorial as well as coercive.

If many residents were able to move elsewhere, the permeability of its borders would make a legal regime ineffective. Offenders from within would be able to escape sanction by fleeing the power of the authorities, thereby undermining faith in the law. By the same token, offenders from without would be able to make incursions at will and to commit offenses with impunity. And random movements of population would be liable to jeopardize the economy of esteem and the infrastructure of social norm that is essential, plausibly, for the stability of the regime. Should they materialize as prospects, these dangers would prompt the legal authorities to establish and police their borders, marking the beginning and end of their jurisdiction. It would be close to unintelligible if they failed to do this, since a failure would jeopardize the system that they run.

We saw just now that in Europe it became possible for the secular authorities to establish a monopoly claim to the use of legal coercion, restricting the rights of the church, only after the Reformation. The circumstances that would force legal authorities to establish borders materialized in Europe in the same modern period. From the seventeenth century on, people developed the material and cultural resources that made mobility possible and often appealing, at least for the well-off. They gained geographical knowledge, learned portable skills, and had access to reliable means of transport. And with these developments, they were able to move without difficulty between different regimes. In such circumstances, it would be important for the legal authorities in any regime to establish and police its borders.

Assuming that such modern conditions obtain in the society targeted in our narrative, the authorities will feel bound to take steps to establish and enforce the borders of their jurisdiction, claiming the territory within. Only by taking such steps will they be able to guard against the permeability problem, preventing domestic offenders from fleeing or outside offenders from operating as opportunistic raiders.

The Protection Problem and the Need for an International Profile

Still, even the creation and policing of borders would still leave another problem in place for the authorities in any legal regime under circumstances that materialized frequently in medieval and modern times, especially in Europe. This last problem is that those who run other regimes, particularly more powerful ones, will seek to extend their writ into its territory. There are many incentives that might motivate such aggression: for example, the desire for more or better land, the prospect of mineral resources, easier access to the sea, or the wish to extend a favored creed or culture.

This problem, like those preceding, will be bound to elicit an appropriate response from the legal authorities in our counterfactual regime. The potential hostility of other regimes will lead them to assume a military profile, establishing defenses against invasion and perhaps, at risk of generating a vicious spiral, making retaliatory or even preemptive strikes. The authorities will have little choice but to take this step, say by organizing a militia or a military, and using that power to strike against potential enemies or invoking it as a threat to negotiate a truce or a treaty.

The pressure to assume an international profile of this kind, advertising a capacity to defend against aggression and threatening aggression in retaliation or preemption, may be the most important factor that will drive our rudimentary state to begin to look like a familiar polity. For if each regime in a network of states begins to establish such a defensive-aggressive profile, the pressure will increase for each state to go one step further in that protective effort. And with this increase of protective efforts on the part of each, the network will become ever more embedded; it will begin to resemble the worldwide network of states that dominates the earth today. The historian Charles Tilly (1975, 42) says that "war made the state and the state made war." The remark will be as likely to hold in our genealogy as in the actual world.

The natural extension of this problem of protection, of course, will be for the state to go beyond military threat, defensive or offensive, to assume a diplomatic role. It will make sense in terms of both cost and safety for the officials of the regime to try to establish treaties of nonaggression with other states and perhaps even a multilateral form of understanding: the rudiments of an international order and international law.

1.6 The Function of the State

The State Proper

Think now about the legal regime that not only solves problems like Hart's, establishing a rudimentary state, but also responds appropriately to the four problems listed, including those that became historically pressing in modern times. It will constitute a nomothetic state, authorizing legislative, judicial, and executive officers to act in its name. It will enable decision-making officials

- not just to resolve indeterminacy, inflexibility, and inefficiency in law; but also
- to impose the law coercively on all citizens;
- to assert a claim to a monopoly right on the use of coercion;
- to introduce and police the territorial boundaries of the jurisdiction; and
- to establish a defensive-aggressive profile in relation to other regimes.

As we think about the coercive, territorial institution that will emerge out of such changes, we must grant it the name of the state. The claim is intuitively plausible and, as we shall see later, fits with a long tradition of thought in political philosophy, in legal theory, and even in social science. According to our genealogy, this nomothetic body will be robustly likely to emerge among relatively rational, interdependent parties living a settled, non-nomadic existence under conditions of moderate scarcity and of an approximate if restricted balance of power. And as it will emerge reliably under those conditions, so it will reliably endure.

The reason it will endure is that it provides an important benefit for those who have the status of citizens. Whether the citizenry be inclusive or not, the state will give them a degree of legal security against other citizens, including those in public office, albeit not perhaps the high degree that justice might require. And being coercive and territorial, it will entrench the regime against internal and external dangers. Providing each citizen with such an entrenched zone of security, it will enable them to make certain choices with some degree of impunity and protection.

Let the state proper provide such security and the effect is likely to give it a stable hold on the allegiance of the citizenry. The state is likely to remain in place, then, so long as rulers continue to exercise power effectively and do not gain the preponderance of power that would enable them to be brutally repressive. Under that condition, indeed, it is likely to remain in place resiliently—robustly over other contingencies—retaining the character that makes it possible to secure its citizens domestically and internationally. If the state ceased to ensure such security, however, there is little reason to think that it would retain its hold on the affections of its citizens and to continue to elicit their support.

This story about the state that would emerge in our counterfactual model suggests that in its proper form the actual state may be taken to have the same characteristics. Operating under conditions where there is an approximate, if restricted, balance of power, it will give citizens the same sorts of benefits as those we have described. It will establish a regime of law in which they enjoy a certain security against other citizens, including those in office, and it will entrench that regime against dangers from within and without.

Repressive and Ineffective States

This account of the state proper allows us to see why a repressive regime should count as an outlier form of the institution, barely deserving of the name of state. Such a regime might rule by laying down ad hoc, case-by-case decisions; by laws that it honored as much in the breach as in the observance; or by laws so manifestly inimical to the interests of many citizens that they are not accepted or internalized. And in any such case, it would fail to provide the benefit ensured under a proper, nomothetic regime.

Because the laws in a proper state will generally attract acceptance and internalization, on the account given, we can say that the regime itself will enjoy acceptance by the citizenry. Whatever the faults that citizens see in the laws, they will each have good reason to comply, and to want others to comply. The laws will enable them to form reliable expectations of what they and others may do with impunity and protection, thereby achieving an attractive level of mutual coordination, and will give them reason to prefer that everyone should conform rather than not. Even when this holds, of course, citizens may still conform with the laws on the basis, in part, of coercive sanction; the important point is that that fear of sanction will not be the only reason they have for compliance.

The decisions of a repressive state will not have the same attraction and will not gain acceptance and internalization in the same sense. If decision making is ad hoc or arbitrary, the decisions will not give citizens the knowledge of where they stand in relation to other citizens and to officials that might enable them to benefit from a coordination of expectations. And if the decisions do introduce laws but ones that are repulsive rather than attractive for many people, the coordination of expectations that they ensure will not provide a compensating benefit. In such a regime, all or many citizens will comply with the decisions of rulers on the basis simply that otherwise they will be exposed to sanction; they will be kept in line by intimidation alone. In its most extreme form this state, if we can use that word of it, will constitute a reign of terror.

Where a repressive state is an outlier for the reason that it fails to provide any ground, or at least any attractive ground, for mutual coordination, the ineffective state, as we described it, counts as an outlier because while it may promise to provide such a ground for coordination, it does not deliver on that promise; it does not really enable citizens to know where they stand in relation to one another. Unlike the repressive regime, it may aspire to deliver the benefits secured by a proper state, but it does not live up to that aspiration.

Identifying the Function of the State

If the provision of citizen or civic security is the effect that explains why the nomothetic state would emerge and endure in the counterfactual world—that is, endure in its nomothetic form—then in our terms it constitutes the function of that state and of its counterpart in the actual world. The role of this state, on the individual front, is to provide security for citizens under a coercive, territorial regime of law that gives them rights and duties vis-à-vis one another and vis-à-vis officials. And its role, on the society front, is to stabilize that system in face of dangers like internal dissension or corruption and external infiltration or aggression.

The function the nomothetic state serves in supporting civic security presupposes a class of citizens who enjoy a more or less equal status before the law, where the citizenry need not be inclusive of all intuitively eligible residents. That function remains in place, no matter how restricted or extensive the class of citizens. Thus, while the modern, nomothetic state may have emerged with a restricted citizenry—and while only a restricted citizenry needs to be assumed in our genealogy—its function does not preclude the extension of the citizenry to, for example, all adult, able-minded, relatively permanent members of the society.

To allow that the citizenry may be exclusive of some residents, as we noted, is not to say that its exclusion of those members is part of the function of the state. By the account offered, the law and the state will appeal to those in the privileged class insofar as it regiments and reinforces norms that protect them against one another both as citizens and as officials. It is others in their powerful class that will represent a danger for each, and it is those others with whom it will be profitable to secure good relations. Thus, the state need not serve its citizens by reinforcing their power over a subordinate class. Going back to our genealogy, the state that emerges there will appeal to citizens for the protection it provides against those with whom it is needed, and in the domestic case this means against other citizens, however inclusive that class, not against those who are already subordinate and relatively powerless.

Of course, the state may often be recruited, and has historically been recruited, to reinforce the subordination of noncitizens to a restricted citizenry. But by our account such an initiative is not required by the function of the state as such; it is not implied in the ideal of statehood. Does the ideal of statehood require, at the other extreme, that the state in a divided or stratified society provide protection for noncitizens against citizens? Here too the answer is negative. As the ideal of statehood does not require that citizens be secured against the subordinate, so, alas, it does not require that the subordinate be secured against citizens.

The function of the state not only allows the citizenry to exclude some members of the society; it also allows the security provided for citizens, whether against one another or against officials, to be incomplete. For all that the functionality of the state requires, citizens may have only few and fuzzy rights against one another—the law may leave a good deal of leeway in how civic relations are allowed to develop—and may have only few and fuzzy rights against citizens in office: the law may not require officials to be selected by citizens, for example, and may give officials a great deal of unconstrained discretion. In this respect, as in the extension of the category of citizens, functionality or statehood requires much less of the state than the demands of justice might do.

Although we allow that the citizenry may not be inclusive of all residents in a polity, and although we allow that the laws may not give substantive rights even to citizens, we shall assume that the rights and duties that citizens enjoy under the laws are at least the same for all. To that extent the citizens will be equal before the law. But equality before the law does not imply equality in other dimensions too: say, in wealth or influence or dignity. And, consistently with the law, some may be able to take advantage of such privileges to intimidate others and extract a degree of subservience.

The Nomothetic State in Intellectual Tradition

Conceiving of the state in nomothetic or law-related terms, and emphasizing the security it ensures for citizens, involves a double contrast: first, with conceiving of it in power-related terms that would allow the repressive regime to be a proper state; and second, with conceiving of it in justice-related terms that would require the law to meet high standards of inclusion and protection. The connection with law makes the nomothetic state rich enough to mark a contrast with the repressive regime. But since the law that it establishes may be restricted to a privileged class of citizens and may not give them some rights that justice intuitively demands, the nomothetic state remains impoverished in comparison with the sort of just state that we might reasonably seek.

In taking this line on what is required for an organization to deserve the name of a state in the proper sense, we join a long tradition in political thought. According to that tradition, a state must not just exercise power over the people of a territory but create a law that confers legal rights and duties on at least a significant class of those individuals. Aristotle (1996, bk. 1, 7; 3, 6) supports that idea in *The Politics* when he distinguishes constitutional rule from the rule of a master, without yet supposing that every constitutional form of rule is just. Rousseau (1997b, 1.5.1) does so when in *The Social Contract* he distinguishes ruling a society, even ruling a society badly, from subjugating a multitude. And Kant (1996, 296–97, 409, 461) supports it in various works, when he assumes that the state essentially involves a system of law—a "civil" condition—distinguishing this both from a regime of brute force and from a state whose laws introduce a "rightful" form of government.[35]

Even Hobbes goes along with the nomothetic assumption that the state must operate by law. While he insists, in an absolutist vein, that the sovereign

---

35. On Kant, see Waldron (2006, 196–97) and Ripstein (2009).

ruler can change any laws at will, he does still acknowledge that, assuming the law has not been changed, the sovereign must abide by it in dealing with citizens or, in his term, subjects. "If a subject have a controversy with his sovereign," he writes, "grounded on a precedent law, he hath the same liberty to sue for his right as if it were against a subject, and before such judges as are appointed by the sovereign" (Hobbes 1994b, 21.19).

The security that the functional, nomothetic state gives its citizens may be equated, in a traditional phrase, with *salus populi*: the safety of the people. This is a goal assigned to the state by many traditional thinkers, starting with Cicero, the Roman lawyer and philosopher of the first century BCE. Speaking of the main officials of the state, Cicero (1998, 152) says that "to them the safety of the people shall be the highest law"; *salus populi suprema lex esto.* The safety of the people can be taken to involve their individual security under a suitable regime of law—a regime that resolves the problems of indeterminacy, inflexibility, and inefficiency—and the stability of that regime on internal and external fronts. It requires nothing more or less than the individual and collective safety of the people.

The ubiquity of the *salus populi* principle in Western thought is highlighted by how Hobbes (1994b, introduction) makes use of it. Absolutist though he is about state power, he still takes "*salus populi* (the people's safety)" to be the "business" of the commonwealth. He says that "the safety of the people" is a goal that the sovereign, as a matter of natural law—in effect, self-interest—ought to promote. And in view of the benefits that he thinks that the nomothetic state would bring, he takes the goal to encompass such benefits too: "by safety here is not meant a bare preservation, but also all other contentments of life, which every man by lawful industry, without danger or hurt to the commonwealth, shall acquire to himself" (Hobbes 1994b, 30.1).

The assumption that the state proper has a nomothetic goal survives, unsurprisingly, among contemporary legal and political theorists. Hans Kelsen (1992, 99), the twentieth-century German jurist, casts the polity in this mold when he characterizes it as a legal system in which there are "certain organs—whose respective functions reflect a division of labor—for creating and applying the norms forming the legal system." He thinks of those organs of government as unifying the regime and maintains that "when the legal system has achieved a certain degree of centralization, it is characterized as a state."

To take this line on the polity may appear to break with the empirical assumption, in Max Weber's (1946, 77) words, that "one can define the modern state sociologically only in terms of the specific means peculiar to it, as to every political association, namely, the use of physical force." But he employs the notion of legitimacy in adding that on this approach, "a state is a human community that (successfully) claims the monopoly of the legitimate use of physical force within a given territory" (78). And while he immediately explains that "legitimate" in this context means "considered as legitimate," he suggests that being considered in that way means being licensed in broadly a nomothetic manner: by the traditions of the society, the charisma of those in charge, or the rule-based character of the regime (78–79).

To restrict the concept of the polity to a nomothetic regime is not only faithful to the Western tradition of political philosophy; it also mirrors a general feature of states in the long history of political order (Fukuyama 2011). A state will cease to be nomothetic when it systematically favors those in certain families or networks of acquaintance, and does not establish a discipline of impersonal law, however restricted to one class of members. But the non-nomothetic regime in which a family, mafia, or clique dominates others can elicit disaffection and resistance. And perhaps for that reason political regimes have often sought to depersonalize their rule, defining membership or citizenship firmly, and establishing a law before which all citizens can hope to enjoy an equal, if inadequate, level of protection.

We can see this commitment to depersonalization in the examination system whereby Chinese emperors exercised their power via a disciplined mandarin class, selected on the meritocratic basis of scholarly success (Elman 2002). And we can see it also in the way that the Ottoman sultans relied on a janissary system where office could not be inherited (Fukuyama 2011). In each case the regime was designed to achieve the sort of result associated with an established legal system.

The Demands of Nomothetic Function

Consistently with arguing that the role of money is to serve as a medium of exchange, a metric of price, and a means of storing wealth, there is room to ask about whether there are ways in which money might play this role more rather than less effectively. And consistently with arguing that the role of the state is to establish and entrench a regime of law under which citizens enjoy a realm of individual security, there is room to ask whether, short of achieving justice, there are ways in which the state might be organized to realize that end more effectively.

The following two chapters address two distinct modes of organization that might be expected to achieve this result. The claim in chapter 2 is that if the state is to give its citizens maximally determinate security under the law, then it had better incorporate as a group agent, establishing a single voice behind which officials can rally in acting for the state and under which other citizens can have a precise sense of where they stand. But in apparent qualification of this theme, chapter 3 then goes on to claim that despite incorporating as a unified body, the state ought to operate under a decentralized mode of organization in which officials can check and balance one another; otherwise, it is going to be less reliable in delivering individual security to its citizens.

By this account, incorporation and decentralization are functional desiderata on the state, not requirements that it has to meet. Where the functional state must meet the specifications outlined in this chapter, it may fail to meet these two desiderata. Having discussed them in the second and third chapters, we look in the final three chapters at three alleged limitations on how the functional state may perform, arguing contrary to some familiar doctrines that it is not blocked from granting collective powers to its citizens, from acknowledging significant rights on their part as individuals, or from intervening productively in the market economy.

The approach taken in this and the following chapters parallels what Ronald Dworkin (1986) describes as a methodology of constructive interpretation (see too James 2005; Sangiovanni 2008). Applied in the political area, constructive interpretation would identify the institution of the state, presumably independently of whether it is just or not; provide an interpretation of the purpose that it promotes at its best; and then look at the institutional ways in which that goal might be promoted even more effectively. We have relied on a counterfactual genealogy, rather than interpretive intuition, to give us an account of the function or purpose that the state serves at its best: that is, by our account, when there is a rough balance of power between rulers and ruled. And now, in the second and third chapters, we explore ways in which the state may be organized to promote that function better.

2

The Polity Incorporated

EVERY STATE CAN BE said to do various things in the name of its residents, so that there is a prima facie case for taking it as an agent (Runciman 2000b). But as we shall see, while the state may have to be a corporate agent in some sense, it may or may not be properly or fully incorporated. The members who have power within it—the citizens in a functional state—may or may not be organized as a polity to operate as an agent on the pattern, for example, of a commercial corporation, a trade union, or a university. Should the state operate as a fully or properly incorporated agent, then, if it is to be effective? In particular, should the functional state operate in that way if it is to discharge its function as effectively as possible?

The chapter explores this question in five sections, arguing on functional grounds that the polity ought to incorporate fully, establishing an effective single agency to operate in the name of its citizenry. In the first two sections of the chapter, we lay the basis for exploring the question, looking in the first section at the general concept of agency as it applies in any system, biological, mechanical, or social; and in the second, at human agency in particular and at the features that make it distinctive. Those sections lead into the third where we show how individuals may incorporate as an agent with distinctively human features and argue that any functional polity will incorporate in that manner. We show in the fourth section, however, that consistently with serving a nomothetic function the state need not be incorporated fully as an agent. And then in the fifth we identify three reasons why it should incorporate as fully as possible; full incorporation, as we shall see, would require the state to satisfy rule-of-law constraints, to guard against allowing its agencies to go rogue, and to make it capable of being held to account as a responsible agent.

The discussion of agency in the first two sections introduces independently important, somewhat complex matters. But it provides essential background for introducing the idea of a corporate agent and will be important, not just in developing the argument in this chapter, but in looking at the case for the decentralized state in chapter 3, in discussing the role of the collective people within the state in chapter 4, in considering their individual rights against the state in chapter 5, and in looking at the distinctive nature of commercial corporations in chapter 6.

In presenting the argument of this chapter, we continue to write as if all of those who might count by any criterion as members—or at least adult, able-minded members—are full citizens, enjoying the same rights and duties. But that is only a presentational convenience and is not strictly necessary to establish the conclusion, as we shall note at various points. The citizens of a functional regime, for all the argument requires, may or may not be a group inclusive of all potentially eligible members.

2.1 Basic Agency

Introducing Agency by Example

Rather than address the abstract question as to what conditions we would expect an agent of any kind to satisfy, it may be better to start from presumptive examples of systems that count intuitively as agents and systems that do not. There are biological organisms like trees and plants that are certainly not agents; and of course, there are others, like animals, that presumably are. There are mechanical artifacts like telephones and computers that are not agents and, again, there are artifacts like robots that may be. And equally, there are social groups like the residents of this or that postal code that are not agents as well as social groups like corporations that surely are. What is it that distinguishes the agents or agencies in each of these cases from the organisms or artifacts or groups that are non-agential?

In order to answer the question, it may be useful to start with a particular example (List and Pettit 2011, chap. 1). Consider a simple robot, and the features that would lead us to call it an agent. I put a small box-shaped mechanism on a large table in front of you. It has a little camera-like lens at the end of a stalk protruding from the front and swiveling slowly up and down, left and right; it has wheels that make it capable of directional movement; and it has levers or arms on either side that make it capable of manipulating other objects.

With bottles arranged in upright positions at different places on the table-top, the mechanism behaves as follows. Whenever a bottle is put on its side, the lens fixates on it, the wheels take the mechanism toward the bottle, and then the levers manipulate it into an upright position. With that done, the robot renews its stationary position, with the stalk swiveling to and fro until it fixates on any other bottle that is put on its side and goes through the same routine. And when all the bottles are upright, it continues the swiveling but remains otherwise at rest.

Perhaps as a result of a natural, biologically based disposition, we are all disposed to see an entity of this kind as an agent, adopting what Daniel Dennett (1987) calls the intentional stance toward it.[1] We identify a purpose or purposes that it pursues—in the robot case, to set the bottles upright—across situations that vary in different ways: say, in the size and shape, the direction and distance, of the bottles. And we take it to pursue its purpose in a manner suited to the specific situation in which it acts.

To cope with such situational variations, the robot will have to register or represent the features of any situation where it is to realize its purpose, and let those representations shape the way it approaches its task in that situation. And to ensure success it will have to form representations as to how it is doing; it will have to register how near the bottle lies, how wide it must stretch its arms to grasp it, and at any moment how far it has raised the bottle toward the perpendicular. To say that it must form representations of such features of its situation and its efforts is just to say that those features must reliably elicit certain changes within it and that the changes must dispose it to adjust its behavior appropriately—adjust it so as to raise the bottle—in response to the features at issue.

The Characterization of Agency

This example suggests that to count as an agent a system like the robot has to satisfy three conditions. It must have purposes, whether inbuilt as in this case or capable of emerging or changing over time. It must have representations of the environment relevant to its purposes and of its own performance in pursuit of those purposes: states that update with changes of environment or purpose. And it must be disposed to behave in a manner that realizes its purposes, according to its representations; those representations must shape the emerging behavior, signaling available opportunities for pursuing them, for example, and providing feedback on how existing efforts are going.

1. That the disposition is innate is supported by Heider and Simmel (1944).

To count as an agent, of course, a system like the robot need not be fool-proof. There will almost certainly be conditions, which it makes independent sense to see as disruptive, such that in their presence it malfunctions or under-performs. Thus, it may be fooled by the hologram of a bottle on its side, and it may often knock a bottle off the table if it is very near the edge. But in normal or nondisruptive conditions the system must form its representations reliably and act reliably for the achievement of its purpose in response to those repre-sentations. It will not count as a proper agent if it merely happens to form accurate representations and to act according to them in pursuit of its pur-poses. It must do this robustly over an open range of possible variations in its internal configuration and its external context.

Thus, it is only insofar as the robot would respond appropriately, more or less regardless of the number or size or makeup of the bottles, and of their posi-tion or the time of day, that we are entitled to think that it registers and re-sponds to the general fact that a bottle is on its side. And it is only insofar as it responds appropriately more or less regardless of how exactly the bottle reg-isters with it—regardless, for example, of the exact angle at which the bottle presents to the lens—that we are entitled to ascribe the purpose of putting any such bottle upright. If it performed appropriately only under more demanding specifications, then we would have to alter the purposes or representations we ascribed.

The ascription of intentional states like purposes and representations—if you like, desires and beliefs—is appropriate, on this account, because it identifies a general pattern in the robot's behavior that we may expect to obtain more or less robustly over certain changes in the particularities of context and configura-tion. The robot does not put bottles upright, only provided certain particulari-ties obtain; and of course, it does not put them upright, only in a hit-or-miss way. Thus, when you learn that the robot put a bottle upright because of reg-istering that it is on its side, you may not learn much about the precise features of the bottle that causally triggered the reaction, or about the precise electron-ics within the robot that mediated it. You learn, rather, that regardless of the form taken by such triggering or mediating details, the robot would have moved to put the bottle upright; it would have done so robustly over many possible variations in those details.

How robust do we expect the intentional attitudes and actions of an agent to be? With any agent, and certainly with one as simple as the robot, we make assumptions about the domain within which it can form representations and realize purposes; we assume, in the case of the robot, that the domain is confined to bottles positioned vertically or horizontally on a table and presented under appropriate illumination. What we expect is that the agent will be reliably capable of registering any feature relevant to its assigned purpose in that domain—say, any bottle on its side—and will be reliably disposed to respond so as to realize that purpose. This expectation will enable us to counterfactualize about the system, declaring for example that while it acted to raise a bottle lying on its side in the northwest corner, it would have acted to raise any bottle that lay on its side, regardless of where it lay.

The reliability we expect in anything that counts as an agent requires us to assume that how it represents things to be, and how it uses its representations in pursuing its purposes, is due to its own organizationally structured processing. It will not be an agent if, like a remotely controlled drone, it performs appropriately but only under the influence of wirelessly communicated instructions. And it will not be an agent, if it does not do any processing in response to different situations but has been predesigned by an ingenious, fantastical planner to respond to any situation possible, as to a mechanical stimulus, with an appropriate response: that is, a response that a proper agent might make.[2]

The Characterization Generalizes

The upshot of these observations is that a system will count as an agent just to the extent that, in intuitively normal conditions:

1. it behaves so as to realize certain purposes according to certain representations
2. robustly over many variations in internal configuration and external context
3. and in virtue of its internally organized processing.

With any candidate agent, the crucial requirements are that it be organized to form representations reliably in response to evidence and to act reliably for the execution of its purposes according to those representations. In a phrase,

2. The requirement of organizational structure would deny the status of an agent to the marionette controlled from Mars, which Christopher Peacocke (1983) imagines. And the requirement of organizational processing would rule out Blockhead, so called: the system, imagined by Ned Block (1981), that is fitted by its near-omniscient designer with a table to determine appropriate behaviors—that is, behaviors that seem to give evidence of suitable purpose and representation—in all possible circumstances. See Jackson (1992).

the system must be evidentially and executively reliable. It must form eviden- tially suitable representations and act in an executively suitable manner, ro- bustly over a range of variations in its context and configuration. Its reliability on these fronts constitutes what we naturally think of as forms of rationality: evidential or theoretical rationality on the one side, executive or practical ra- tionality on the other.

With this characterization in hand, it should be clear that a variety of ever more complex systems may count as agents. The robot has only one purpose and pursues that purpose on the basis of passively realized representations. But even simple animals are much more sophisticated. First, they pursue many different purposes—equivalently, they have many distinct desires— and select the purpose to be pursued—the intention to be formed—on the basis of their own needs and the opportunities provided by the environment. Second, they form reliable, directive representations—beliefs, as we call them—on the basis, not just of a single modality like the robot's lens or eye, but also of other sensory modalities, of memories in any modality, and of rational inference from the information thereby available. And finally, they often make experiments in search of information about their environment— in search of further beliefs—as when the fly seeks, now this route, now that route, out of the flytrap.

2.2 Human Agency

Interpretation and Self-Interpretation

Whether uniquely or not among animal species, we human beings achieve further complexity insofar as we form and act on reliable representations or beliefs, not just about the actual here and now, but also about things at a spatial distance, things in the past and future, and things that are merely possible. But there is another, more basic respect in which we differ from the sorts of agents considered so far; this is more basic insofar as it helps to explain many of the other ways in which we achieve a distinctive level of complexity.

In interacting with robots and with other animals we are confined to inter- preting their purposes and representations, their desires and beliefs, looking from outside at the behavioral patterns they display over a range of scenarios. But we human beings don't just wait for others to look at the behavior we display and to assign attitudes to us on that basis. We meet our interpreters halfway, inviting them to ascribe this or that attitudinal or intentional profile to us. We use natural language to reveal our attitudes to others, purporting to be competent in identifying those attitudes and truthful in conveying them.[3]

This difference would be relatively insignificant, if we had no better access to our own beliefs and desires than the access that others have by means of scrutinizing our behavior. If I could tell you what I believed or desired on the basis only of looking at how I acted, then that might be marginally helpful in shaping your interpretation of my attitudes, provided you took me to be a careful and truthful reporter. But it would not lead you to think that I had any special authority in conveying my attitudes and it might not prompt a different take from that which you would adopt with a purely mute agent, robotic or biological.

It is sometimes suggested that if we do not have to rely on looking at our behavior in the manner of an outside observer, that is because we can rely on a sort of inner observation; we can put an inner eye to work in what is often described as introspection. But it is doubtful how far inner observation can help to explain my ability to know what I believe or desire to do (Shoemaker 1996). And even if there were such a capacity, it would not give self-knowledge a special authority: presumably I am as liable to be misled by introspective evidence—and this in a way that cannot be checked against the evidence registered by others—as I am to be misled by behavioral.

But there is a different reason why we human beings can come to know at least some of our own attitudes. This consists in the fact that we are able to make up our minds in certain domains about what to think or seek or do and that we have a capacity in that exercise to know what it is we come to think or seek or do; we have a sort of maker's knowledge, as distinct from an observer's knowledge, of our attitudes in the relevant domains. To understand corporate agency, we need to provide an initial sketch of this special human capacity.[4]

The Basis of Self-Interpretation

In order to understand the special authority that you or I enjoy when we interpret our attitudes to others, we need to take a little detour into the philosophy of language and mind. The first thing to mark in this detour is that if

3. As noted earlier, Bernard Williams (2002) offers a genealogical defense of why it should be natural for creatures like us to demand such sincerity or competence from one another.

4. In exploring the approach here, I draw heavily on material in Pettit (2016a; 2018a; 2024). The line taken connects closely with the set of approaches in which a person's knowledge of the attitudes they hold is said to depend on their practical, attitude-forming ability rather than their epistemic access to their own minds. See, for example, McGeer (1996, 2008), Moran (2001), and Boyle (2009).

language is to be functional or reliable, making its survival in the history of our species intelligible, then two conditions must be fulfilled. It must be, first, that we can make assertions in which, on the basis of evidence available, we give presumptive information to one another; and second, that when you or I make a careful, truthful assertion about how things are—say, about where there is fruit to be found or game to hunt—then in general we will have a belief to that effect: an evidentially reliable representation designed to direct behavior in an executively reliable way. This may be a belief that preexisted our assertion, or it may be a belief that comes into existence as we think about what it is appropriate to assert in view of the evidence available.

If there were not this general sort of congruence between our careful, truthful assertions and what we believe, then our assertions would be of no use to others in indicating how they should expect us to behave and, assuming our beliefs are careful and competent, how things are in the environment about which we hold beliefs. The congruence need not be perfect, of course. Sometimes a careful judgment may not catch, so to speak; it may not give rise to the belief, at least not to a reliable belief. Thinking about probabilities you may judge that the gambler's fallacy is a fallacy—that a run of reds does not increase the probability of a black—but that may not really change your belief; you may still be disposed in the excitement of the casino to bet heavily on black after a long run of reds.

The general congruence between assertion and belief will be manifest to all of us. Thus, since we will be able to act out of a desire to determine what it is appropriate to assert sincerely to others on some issue, we will be equipped to act out of a desire to form an appropriate belief on that issue. Or at least we will be equipped to do this if there is evidence enough available to support the assertion and, in parallel, the belief that would normally go with it.

We can exploit this congruence between assertion and belief by raising questions for one another and gaining useful information from the answers provided. In domains where evidence is available to another, posing questions will enable us, assuming the other's sincerity, to extract answers that tell us about how that person believes things to be and, assuming the other's competence and sincerity, how things are likely to be in fact.

As we can raise questions for one another, however, so we can raise questions for ourselves; and as we can each answer the questions of others, evidence permitting, so we will often be able answer our own questions. In answering the questions of others, we express our judgments, as it is said, in the sincere assertions we make; that is what makes the assertions sincere. In answering our own questions, we will make judgments for ourselves that we need not express in words. By making a judgment in either mode, public or private, we learn what belief the evidence available supports—a belief that we ought rationally to hold in view of the evidence—and assuming that we are sensitive to that evidence, we learn what belief we actually hold.

We may or may not have held that belief before consulting the evidence in this way. If we did, then the exercise will have brought that belief to light and reconfirmed it evidentially. If we did not hold the belief previously, the exercise will have enabled us to extend our beliefs, and presumably to gain new information, as we might have done by posing the question to another.

Making Up Our Minds

Pursuing this sort of exercise, we can intentionally raise a question for ourselves as to whether this or that is so—say, a question as to whether there is fruit to be found on the hill—survey or recall the evidence at our disposal, and let it push us into assenting to the appropriate proposition: into making the appropriate judgment. And in virtue of the congruence alleged, we can take those same steps with an intentional view to forming or at least reconfirming the belief. By doing this, as it is often said, we can make up our mind about what to believe. We can take charge of our belief-forming habits, no longer relying only on the automatic updating to which, for all we know, other animals may be restricted.

As language means that we must have the capacity to make up our minds in the case of belief so the same is true in the case of desire and other attitudes. Assume that any type of scenario is going to attract me in virtue of having properties of a manifestly attractive kind: say, holding out the prospect of being fun or pleasing a friend, of resolving some predicament fairly, or just of satisfying a relatively idiosyncratic taste. Under that assumption, we can make up our minds about what to desire between various possible ways things might be—say, between vacationing in the mountains or at the sea, between having a more equal or a more prosperous world—by making a judgment on how they compare in such desiderata.

When we make up our mind about such a general scenario in this way, we remain open to changing our mind should further desiderata surface on one or another side. And in that case the sort of qualified desire we form is, in ordinary terms, a preference. The judgment about the desiderata leads us, as we say, to decide about what to prefer: to decide on our preference ranking among the alternatives.

Where preference is one form of desire, intention is another; or at least it is an attitude that disposes the agent in the manner of a desire to pursue this or that purpose. Intention can form only in relation to certain sorts of scenarios, however: mutually exclusive, jointly exhaustive alternatives, as they appear to be, in an actual or foreseen choice that we take to be within our control. And intention must dispose us in an unqualified way to take the option targeted: unlike a preference, it does not operate under a proviso on our part that novel desiderata do not surface and give us pause (Bratman 1987; Holton 2009). When we make a final judgment that a particular option scores over others in a choice—that it does so, period—then we decide on what intention to form.

In intentionally seeking to form preferences or intentions—desires, in one or the other sense—we set out intentionally to determine the desiderata present in different options, and to let them weigh with us in eliciting desire or intention. We valorize those desiderata in a manner that parallels the way in which we valorize evidence when we let it prompt judgment; we judge that something is fun or fair, for example, without detaching ourselves from that concept, employing it in a scare-quotes sense (Smith 1994, 66–71). Language would not be functional in the absence of congruence between judgments and beliefs, including beliefs of the kind in play here about the distribution of desiderative properties. And equally, it would not be functional in the absence of at least a high degree of congruence between desiderative judgments and the attitudes of desire—preference or intention—that they typically serve to prompt.[5]

Knowing and Communicating Our Minds

The fact that we can make up our minds about various attitudes means that we have access to a special sort of knowledge about what, in relevant cases, we believe or desire or intend. Suppose, as argued, that when we make a careful judgment that p—say, when we truthfully and carefully assert that p—it will normally be the case that we believe that p. Suppose, as also argued, that when we exercise care in making a judgment about the desiderata present in rival

5. To keep things simple, I have concentrated on desiderative judgments, where all that is required of the properties ascribed is that they manifestly attract the agent. A similar point will presumably go through with normative judgments where it is required in addition or instead that the properties impose an obligation of some kind on the agent—perhaps prudential or legal or moral—to act accordingly. See Pettit (2018a).

options, and in valorizing them on a certain pattern, we will not only form the corresponding belief but also form the preference or intention that they elicit. And suppose, finally, that all of this is a matter of common awareness, with the evidence being there for all to see, with the evidence that it is there for all to see also being there for all to see, and so on.

In that case, we are going to be in a position to know that we believe that p just in virtue of knowing that we judge that p: we assent to that proposition. And we will be in a position to know that we prefer or intend to X just in virtue of knowing that we judge that X-ing scores over relevant alternatives in its desiderata. Our understanding of what it is to assert carefully and sincerely that something is the case, which is implied in being able to speak with others, will give us an understanding of what it is to judge that something is the case. And recognizing that we are making appropriate judgments, we will know that all going well, we must therefore have the corresponding dispositions to action: in effect, attitudes of belief or preference or intention.

This means that when it comes to the purposes and representations that govern your actions, I will be able to rely, not just on looking at your behavior as I might look at the behavior of a mute animal, but also on what you have to say for yourself. Or at least I will be able to do this, if I have reason to believe that in communicating your purposes or representations, you are speaking carefully and sincerely in a common language. But is there going to be reason to think this? Yes, assuming that you are concerned about your reputation for reliability in living up to your word.

To see that the reputational motive will have particular force when it comes to communicating your attitudes to me, we need to think about the forms that such communication may take. Broadly speaking, they may take the form of reports on those attitudes—reports that you make about your-self as you might make them about another—or commitments to the attitudes involved.[6]

Suppose you have made up your mind on some matter of belief or desire, whether at the time of speaking or on a more enduring basis. You might report on that attitude, as you might report on the attitude of another, by

---

6. The argument that follows applies only to speech acts that communicate a belief or desire or intention such that any failure to act as the attitude requires of me is likely to be salient to others. Thus, it will not apply to acts that communicate only finely probabilistic beliefs, only idle desires, or only highly conditional intentions. To anticipate the argument in the text, such speech acts are unlikely to be more expensive than reports and unlikely to be any more credible.

self-ascribing it in words such as "the evidence is that I believe such and such or desire so and so." If you are going to retain the reputation for being a truth-teller—if you are going to conform to the truth-telling norm—then here as in any report you will need to be careful and truthful about what you say. But you will be able to retain your reputation even when you speak falsely— even when you fail to act later as the ascribed attitude would require—if you have a plausible excuse: an explanation for the mistake that lets you off the reputational hook. One excuse might be that you got the evidence wrong— you were misled about your own mind—and another that the evidence changed since you made your report: you changed your mind.

This raises a problem for the credibility of the self-report. By contrast with reports about the shared world, it will be relatively easy to excuse an error in this case by saying that you were misled about your mind or by claiming that for whatever reason you changed your mind since you spoke. And that means that the self-report is not going to make others very confident that you will act as required by the attitude you ascribe to yourself. They will be able to see that you can get off the hook so easily that your words are cheap and do not offer any solid grounds for confidence that you will live up to them in action.

It will be possible for you to get over this problem, however, by committing to the attitudes you ascribe rather than reporting them as you might report the attitudes of another. Commitments come in two forms, which we may describe as avowals and pledges. They can offer others greater assurance about the attitudes ascribed by making the ascriptions more expensive and credible than self-reports.

Take avowals first. You can convey a belief, such as that the fruit on the hill is ripe, not by reporting it—that would be very unusual—but by asserting simply that that is the case. This is because saying that p expresses the belief that p, indicating that you have made up your mind that p. You can convey a desire in the same manner—say, a desire to eat the fruit—by saying that it would be nice to taste those apples or pears or peaches again. And you can convey an intention to go find the fruit by saying, for example, that there is nothing to beat that alternative.

In conveying your belief or desire or intention in such a manner, you indicate that you have made up your mind on the matter. And in doing that you deny yourself the possibility of invoking the misleading-mind excuse in the event of not living up to your word—not displaying the attitude ascribed. The message will be that you did not rely on any evidence, whether of an introspective or behavioral kind, but spoke on the basis of having knowingly exercised your practical capacity to make up your mind. You deny yourself the misleading-mind excuse when you do this for, not having consulted evidence, as your words imply, you cannot have been misled by it. In such a case, as we may say, you avow the attitude rather than just reporting it.[7]

The avowal will be more expensive than a report—and will count as a form of commitment—insofar as it exposes you to a greater risk of having to pay a reputational cost, should you not live up to your word. Assuming that you willingly or voluntarily chose to avow rather than report the attitude, there is a straightforward sense in which you willingly or voluntarily took on that extra expense. And in that case, I have a powerful reason to think that you must have guarded against having to pay that cost. You must have taken pains to form the attitude carefully and to convey it truthfully.[8]

This explains why we should routinely use avowal in communicating our attitudes. By undertaking the expense of avowal, we make ourselves more credible to one another and raise the chances of being able to establish ongoing exchange and collaboration. It should be no surprise, then, that we take one another to avow attitudes rather than just reporting them even when we make what look on the syntactical surface like reports: even when we say, for example, that we believe there is fruit on the hill, that we would love to eat it, or that we intend to go in search of it. To indicate that we are just reporting on ourselves, we would have to resort to excessively cautious phrasing, as in saying that we think our belief or desire or intention is such and such but cannot be certain: the evidence, so we imply, is not clear.

Once we see the importance of avowal in the self-interpretation of human agents, we are positioned to understand why people should also employ a further mode of commitment in conveying their attitudes. When you avow an intention to do something—say, to meet me on the hill at dawn—you cannot invoke the misleading-mind excuse to get off the reputational hook, but you can readily excuse your nonappearance by saying that you changed your mind. This alerts us to a further possibility, however: that in such a situation you might make the communication of your intention even more expensive and more credible by also foreclosing the possibility of invoking that excuse. This is what you will do if you pledge the intention to be there: if you pledge or promise to join me.

7. For a generally congenial account of avowal, see Bar-on (2004).
8. There is a discussion of voluntariness in chapter 4.

As you will have opportunity and reason to avow various attitudes, so you will have opportunity and reason to pledge various intentions. You will have the opportunity insofar as you recognize that even if the desiderata of going to the hill at dawn lose their grip on you, the desideratum of showing that you are a person of your word—that you can be relied upon when you pledge to be there—may be motivation enough to maintain the intention and act as you pledged. And there will often be good reason to avail yourself of that opportunity, taking advantage of the fact that the payoff associated with keeping a pledge—that it will prove you to be a person of your word—can make it rational to do just that.

This opportunity will be available only with intentions, however, since the idea of maintaining a belief or desire—at least a desire associated with independent desiderata—because of the attraction of proving faithful to your word is barely coherent. A belief maintained for such a reason would not be sensitive to data in the way that belief requires. And a desire maintained for such a reason would not be sensitive to independent desiderata; it would not be like the desire to go mountain climbing at dawn that is associated with the attraction of early light or heavy exercise.[9]

When you avow an attitude, you do so as an alternative to merely reporting the attitude; and when you pledge an intention, you do so as an alternative to merely avowing or reporting it. You commit voluntarily or willingly to paying the cost of not being able to invoke a misleading-mind or a changed-mind excuse in the event of failing to live up to those words. You bet on your voice reflecting your mind and you stake your reputation on that voice proving to be reliable. You speak *for* yourself in the first person rather than just speaking *about* yourself as you might speak about another.

Because commitment in the sense explained amounts to betting on yourself to act on an attitude avowed or pledged, it belongs in the first place to the interpersonal or social context. It is hard to see how the notion could achieve relevance and utility, after all, without the social pressure that individuals will often feel to convince others about how they think or what they seek. But with the notion in place, it is also possible for any individual to self-commit: to make a resolution about the attitudes they will display rather than viewing themselves in observational mode. The cost of their failing to live up to a resolution will not be as serious as the cost of failing to live up to a commitment to another but it will still be significant. The individual who fails to keep a resolution will

9. It might then count as an impulse, a compulsion, or the like; see Pettit (2018a, chap. 3).

naturally berate themselves for the failure, seeing it as another might see it in holding them responsible.[10]

Conversability and Personhood

Our earlier considerations about language show that it enables us to make up our minds individually, and to do so in a way that is intelligible to others under shared standards. A good way of expressing that lesson is to say that language makes it possible for us to be conversable agents. Conversability in this sense has three aspects.

First, it enables us to make up our minds individually on the basis of intentionally researched and considered data or desiderata that are recognized as relevant on all sides; it gives us an important kind of autonomy. Second, it enables us to see one another as intelligible agents who can be influenced by data and desiderata; it makes us addressable, as we might say. And third, it enables us to speak for ourselves in an expensive, credible manner; it makes us into commissive creatures who can hold one another to account.

In one of his most original and important contributions to philosophical psychology, Thomas Hobbes (1994b, chap. 16) argues that as an agent of this conversable, inevitably commissive kind you deserve to be described as a person. The word "person," he reminds us, derives from the Latin *persona:* literally, the mask through which an actor in ancient times would speak, where the mask indicates the character that the actor represents or "personates." Hobbes suggests that in speaking for your attitudes in the manner of a conversable agent who is committed to those attitudes, you are inviting others to ascribe the corresponding character to you. And you are doing so in a way that binds you, on pain of reputational loss, to keep faith with your words, proving to have the persona that you assume.

The case for identifying the conversable agent with a person does not just rest on Hobbes's etymology, of course. The autonomous, addressable, and commissive character of conversable agents gives them features that we associate with personhood in ordinary exchange. Persons, we assume, are autonomous agents who can make up their minds about what to think. Persons are addressable agents who can help one another to make up their minds, presenting suitable data or desiderata for consideration. And persons are

10. Hobbes (1994b, chap. 26.6) downplays the significance of self-commitment, arguing that since binder and bound are one, "he that can bind can release."

commissive agents who can avow various attitudes and pledge their intentions, accepting that they will be held to account for whether they live up to those commitments.[11]

This connection between personhood and accountability is particularly worth underlining. When you and another each speak for yourselves, as in avowals or pledges, you allow and effectively invite one another to hold you responsible for your words, blaming or censuring you for any failure to live up to them. Or at least you do so in the absence of certain unforeclosed excuses, such as the practical excuse that you broke a leg. And when you rely on one another's avowals and pledges, you each do so because of understanding that you can hold one another responsible in turn: that you have a right to blame and censure another for any failure on their part, expecting that this is likely to guard against similar failures in the future. Thus, the concept of personhood is tied up closely with the practice whereby you and others can hold one another to account. As John Locke (1975, s26) describes the concept some decades after Hobbes's discussion: "It is a Forensick Term appropriating Actions and their Merit."[12]

Being a person in the sense introduced requires having relationships with other persons to whom you can bind yourself, inviting them to ascribe the conversable, committed image—the persona—to which you try to measure up. You learn what it is to be a person in learning, with this practice of mutual commitment, how you are able and disposed to perform: what sort of being in that respect you are. As you can learn to self-commit because of knowing what it is to commit interpersonally, of course, so you will naturally learn to see yourself, in your intrapersonal dealings, in the same way; you will recognize yourself as an essentially commissive being. You will learn to see yourself in a manner that others will see you: as an agent for whom commitment is inescapable, and who is required by nature to make only commitments you can keep and to keep whatever commitments you make.

You are a person, on the story emerging from these considerations, insofar as you can and do generally regulate yourself so as to display the character that you project both for others and—this is what distinguishes personation from

11. For a fuller defense of the view of personhood sketched here, see Pettit (2020) and especially Pettit (2024, lecture 6).

12. Carol Rovane (1997) usefully emphasizes this Lockean theme. In *Group Agency*, Christian List and I describe this notion of the person as functional or performative rather than moral. See List and Pettit (2011, chap. 8).

impersonation—for yourself. You may occasionally fail to live up to your commitments and fail in a way that allows no unforeclosed excuse. And of course, you may even fail to limit yourself to feasible, coherent commitments. But if you are not to exit the pale of human interaction—if you are not to lose your claim to be a properly minded subject—you must be able to depict such failures as contingent departures from form, not par for the course. You must persuade us, and you must persuade yourself, that those failures do not define you—that when you displayed the failures, you were not yourself—and that you are robustly capable of avoiding and, where relevant, rectifying them.

On this account, operating as a person is a work in progress, not a fait accompli. It involves the sustained attempt to keep your spontaneous, psychological nature in line with your assumed, social character. To be a person you must be able, at least over the long run, to let the mind you display answer to a coherent voice and to let it answer reliably to that voice, regardless of the noise created by random inklings and impulses. This discussion of personhood may not seem very relevant to our concerns in this book, but it provides a background, as we shall soon see, for the question of whether corporate agents can count as persons.

2.3 Corporate Agency and the Polity

Basic Group Agency

Can groups of independent agents combine to form higher-level agents or agencies? It certainly seems that nonhuman animals can do this, coalescing spontaneously into aggregates that display at the group level the robust patterns associated with agency. The possibility is presumptively realized in the colony of ants, the swarm of bees, even perhaps the shoal of fish or the flock of birds; in each case, we can ascribe evidentially reliable representations and behaviors that are executively reliable in channeling the group's pursuit of certain purposes. But can human beings combine to form group agents of a corresponding kind? Can they incorporate, as we say? Can they form themselves into bodies—the Latin for "body" is *corpus*—that can count as agents in their own right?

When nonhuman animals combine to form group agents, the members presumably respond in a spontaneous way to local cues, as when each bird in a food-seeking flock tends to veer toward any likely source of food yet tends at the same time to stay within a certain distance of its nearest fellows. In other words, they constitute group agents on the basis of more or less automatic responses to individual stimuli (Couzin and Levin 2015).

There may be cues of a local kind that operate in a parallel way on us in crowds, without our necessarily being aware of the effect, as sociologists have sometimes claimed. But most of the human groups that present as candidates for the ascription of group agency cannot plausibly form on that basis. Thus, none of us thinks that companies, churches, political parties, or voluntary associations, come into existence in the same spontaneous way as flocks of birds or shoals of fish.

This is backed up by the fact that there is considerable evidence to suggest that it was only in the high Middle Ages that such entities came to emerge in Europe, and that their emergence was dependent on their being conceptualized as bodies that could claim various rights and that incurred corresponding responsibilities. More on this below and in chapter 6.[13]

Human Group Agency

How can companies and churches and other such groups of individuals come to constitute agents? How can they instantiate at a group level the purposes and the representations of an agent and the ability to pursue those purposes according to those representations? How can they do this in virtue of their own organization, not for example by dint of direction from outside? How can they do it robustly over variations in their internal configuration: for example, over changes in and of the membership? And how can they do it robustly over variations in the external contexts where they act: over changes, for example, in the opportunities and obstacles they confront?

Hobbes's theory of human agency gives him the key to resolving this question. While there is much that is missing and mistaken in his resolution, as we shall see in the next chapter, the basic idea is insightful and illuminating.

In virtue of being a conversable agent, you can display your agency by publicly committing to evidentially supported beliefs and desires, and by robustly responding as those attitudes require to various contingencies of circumstance. Hobbes argues that in the same way a group of individuals can achieve

13. This account of the appearance of corporate bodies is supported broadly by a variety of authors: for example, Woolf (1913), Duff (1938), Canning (1980), and Kantorowicz (1997). For an argument that corporate bodies also existed, and were suitably conceptualized, in ancient Rome, see Malmendier (2005).

agency by establishing a voice that commits them as a body to certain attitudes and then, when they operate as members of the group, by robustly responding in this or that circumstance as those attitudes require. The voice will enunciate the attitudes of the group, making up the group mind as to what purposes to espouse, how to take things to be in any situation, and how to pursue those purposes in that situation. Being pledged to follow that voice, the members will reliably enact the attitudes enunciated when they act in the name of the group.

How might a set of people establish a voice to speak for them in this way and to direct their behavior in the name of the group? They need to identify a voice to follow, as a matter of common awareness between them.[14] And as a matter of common awareness, they need to pledge with one another to play whatever part is required of them by that voice in their role as members: to enact the attitudes, in the manner required, that that voice enunciates. Depending on circumstance, they may be required as individuals to discharge this or that task in the name of the group. Or they may be required to discharge a task in collaboration with some or all others. Or they may be required just to go along with what others are individually or collaboratively required to do. The members must authorize the common voice by giving it a directive role, and they must each live up to the words issued in their collective name by that voice.

Where might the members of a group find such a voice to authorize in this way? Hobbes envisages two possibilities. One is that it may be the voice of a single decision-making individual who is selected as spokesperson for the group. Another is that it may be a voice that is generated by a procedure to which different individuals contribute, as in setting up a decision-making committee.

This second possibility raises the question as to what social procedures might be used to generate a common voice—a reliably coherent common voice—that the membership could follow. But that is a question on which Hobbes goes astray, and we return to it in the next chapter. For the moment, we may assume that there is no problem about where the voice to be authorized by the membership comes from. That voice may be the voice of an individual or a committee or, as we shall see, a voice generated under a procedure to

---

14. Is common awareness strictly required? Perhaps something weaker would do: say, that each is aware of what others are doing. But common awareness is certainly present in the cases of interest to us, so we need not go further into this question.

which many contribute and in different ways. Hobbes himself only envisages the possibility where an individual or committee—a committee of the few or the many—speaks for the group. But for the moment we may put aside that aspect of his views.

The Polity as a Corporate Agent

Hobbes thinks that there are many group agents in any developed society, holding for example that a company of merchants counts as a corporate agent (Hobbes 1998, 5.10). As he sees things, the members in such a case authorize an individual or committee as their spokesperson, agreeing to rally behind the spokesperson's presumptively coherent voice, letting it determine how they should behave. In the case of a company of merchants or any such private grouping, Hobbes (1994b, 16.14) thinks that they authorize the voice only under a "limit in what, and how far" they may be spoken for. Thus, with an individual spokesperson in charge—a powerful CEO, we might say—"none of them owneth more, than they gave him commission to act"; none of them pledges to follow that voice if it goes beyond the agreed limit, speaking *ultra vires*.

But if the members of such a private corporation can constitute a single agent by recognizing and rallying behind a single voice, it should be clear that the same can be true in the case of a polity. Hobbes (1994a, chap. 27.7) suggests that the possibility of a state organizing itself as a corporate agent, on the model of a company of merchants, had escaped his predecessors: it "hath not been taken notice of in the body of a commonwealth or city."[15] This claim to originality, as we shall see shortly, was mistaken. But the important point is not that he was taking up an older tradition in maintaining this view. Rather it is that on the voice-first view of agency, illustrated in the case of the individual human being, there is no block to recognizing corporate agency and to seeing that the polity itself, whether it be functional or not, may constitute an agent.

Hobbes (1994b, 16.14) not only recognizes the possibility that the polity should be a corporate agent; he thinks that as a matter of fact the polity cannot fail to be an agent of that kind. Moreover, he holds that the polity will be a

---

15. While he thinks that the concept of the state as a group agent is analogous to the concept of a group agent like a company or other private association, Hobbes maintains that it is only in virtue of the existence of a state that such associations can form.

special sort of corporate agent, in which the members are required to confer "authority without stint" on the individual or committee that speaks for them; they cannot put any limits on the power—the sovereign power—of their spokesperson, be that an individual or committee.

There is little reason to agree with Hobbes that the spokesperson in a state, particularly an individual spokesperson, should have authority without stint.[16] The important point for us in the Hobbesian theory, however, is that by that account every state or polity, especially every state or polity that counts as functional, will constitute a corporate agency on a par with other group agents.

In every functional state there will be a voice, operating under decision-maker laws, that enunciates presumptively accepted and internalized decision-taker laws and, subject to a constraint introduced in the next chapter, that may play a similar role with the decision-maker laws themselves. That may be the voice of a supreme spokesperson or sovereign, as in a Hobbesian monarchy. Or it may be a sovereign voice that is generated procedurally, depending on the issue addressed, by a single committee, by a network of interacting committees, or even by the citizens themselves. We look at those possibilities in the next chapter, breaking with Hobbes's view of the non-monarchical state: the state, as he thinks of it, that is ruled by a committee rather than an individual.

Insofar as the polity is organized around a personal or procedural voice, the citizens will rally around that voice, whether in official roles or not, taking the laws it enunciates to bind them individually as decision takers and to allow or require them, if they are decision makers, to take appropriate initiatives under decision-maker laws. Those initiatives might involve framing the law in the legislature, interpreting it in judicial or administrative contexts, or assuming an executive role in acting for the state on the domestic or international front.

When the individuals in a functional polity rally around the voice of the law in this sense, then they will satisfy the conditions for constituting a group agency. They will act as a group to realize the various purposes formulated in the state's laws and policies, doing so reliably over variations both in how they are affected as decision takers by the pursuit of those purposes and in what the pursuit requires of them as decision makers. They will display an individual

---

16. His reason for thinking this is that no contract is valid, by his lights, unless there is an agent or agency to enforce it; the social contract between people in the state of nature is valid because it gives enforcement power to a sovereign; and that enforcer cannot be expected to enforce any limitation on its own power (Hobbes 1994b, 18.4). See Pettit (2008a, chap. 8).

pattern of action and acquiescence that ensures, on the voice-first view of agency, that they together constitute a unified corporate agent.

Corporate Agency and Personhood

We saw that you, an individual human being, count as a person for Hobbes in virtue of being a conversable and therefore commissive agent: someone who can speak for yourself and assume responsibility in relation to others. By this reasoning, a corporate agent will count as a person too: specifically, in common terminology, a legal person. And Hobbes embraces that conclusion. He says that insofar as they are represented—that is, spoken for in the way you speak for yourself—a "multitude are united by covenants into one person civil." And so, he is prepared to describe "companies of merchants" as "civil persons" and to speak of the polity, as many of those who later follow him will speak of it, as "the person of the people."[17]

As in the individual case, the ground for thinking of a conversable, commissive body as a person is plausible insofar as personhood is linked with that body's capacity to make up its mind autonomously, to be addressable by other persons, and to make commitments to others and be held to account for living up to those commitments. Bodies of this kind are bound to be able to speak for themselves as conversable agents, bound to be capable of making avowals and pledges in which they commit to one another as well as to individuals, and bound to have the capacity to prove faithful to their commitments and fit to be held responsible. They are bound, in Hobbes's favored word, to personate: to hold out an image of who they are, inviting others—other individual and corporate persons—to rely on their living up to that persona.

It is plausible for these reasons to regard corporate agents as persons on a par in that respect with individual human beings. But to cast them in that light is not necessarily to think that they have or should have the rights of individual persons. We return to that issue when we discuss the ontological status of commercial corporations, and of corporate bodies in general, in the final chapter.

17. These quotations come respectively from Hobbes (1994a, chap. 20.1), Hobbes (1998, 5.10), and Hobbes (1990, 120). Hobbes's view of corporate personhood is somewhat more complex than these remarks suggest; for a fuller discussion, see Pettit (2008a, 72–75) and Skinner (2002b). For a contemporary defense of the view that the state is a person, see Wendt (2004); see also Erskine (2003) and Tanguay-Reynaud (2013).

The Medieval Origin of Hobbes's Ideas

While we have taken Hobbes as the source of this approach to the idea of corporate agency, and of the agency of the state, it should be said that his argument fits well with an older, medieval tradition. In that tradition too, a corporate body—in the contemporary Latin term, an *universitas*—was held to come into existence via the representation of the membership by an individual or council. Thus, in 1354, Albericus de Rosciate could say that a collegial agent, "although it is constituted out of many members, is still one by virtue of representation"; it is a unity in the sense that is implied in the word *universitas* (Eschmann 1946, 33n145).

The theme sounded in this remark dominates the work of legal theorists in the fourteenth century, such as Bartolus of Sassoferrato and his pupil Baldus de Ubaldis, who make much of the way represented groups, including the represented people of a city, can figure as corporate agents (Woolf 1913; Canning 1983). Thus, arguing that the *populus liber*, the free people of a city republic, is a corporate agent, Baldus explains that this is because "the council represents the mind of the people": *concilium representat mentem populi* (Canning 1987, 198).

Not only did the medieval thinkers have a theory of the corporate agent and the state that anticipated Hobbes. They also used the notion of the person to characterize a corporate body. In 1246 Innocent IV, a lawyer who had recently become pope, argued in a missive addressed to the members of the University of Paris that while a corporate body or *universitas* is a person, it is not a natural person. Rather, in a phrase that he inspired, it is a *persona ficta*: in one translation, a fictional or pretend person, in another a real but artificial person.

Innocent's main purpose was to insist that because of being just a *persona ficta*, the corporate body did not have a soul and so could not be excommunicated and condemned to hell; this issue had previously been unclear in ecclesiastical practice (Eschmann 1946, 29–36; Kantorowicz 1997, 305–06). But whether taken to be a fictional or artificial person, the corporate body would not have a soul, and could not be excommunicated. Thus, Innocent's document opened up the question as to which sort of person it is: a pretend person or an artificial person.

This question gave rise to a big division in medieval thought. Philosophers like Thomas Aquinas argued that the corporate body was a person or agent only in a fictional or pretend sense (Eschmann 1946, 11). But lawyers such as Bartolus and Baldus took the view that it was a real, if artificial, person (Canning 1980). The driving issue may have been the question as to how far such a body could be held responsible, and the lawyers were anxious to insist that it could certainly be held responsible in human law.

The legal view prevailed in political and public discourse, giving rise to the notion of the legal person. And it was a version of that view that Hobbes defended with his characteristic brio. His main novelty may have been to insist that the reason it is appropriate to present a corporate body as a person is that like individual persons, corporate agents are conversable, addressable, and commissive. They come into existence only in virtue of their members allowing themselves to be spoken for and acquiescing in whatever is avowed or pledged in their common name. They are personated by that authority, in his vision of things, in the way that you as an individual personate yourself.[18]

Despite this novelty, however, Hobbes was wrong to claim, as we saw he claimed, that he was the first to liken a commonwealth to a corporate body like a company. The claim that a city-republic could be a corporate agent was explicitly used by Bartolus in the mid-fourteenth century to argue an important point in international law: that such a republic still had a prince or king and was protected from interference—particularly, from the interference of the Holy Roman emperor—because of the accepted legal principle that in his own territory a local king is emperor: *rex in suo regno est imperator sui regni*. Bartolus's argument was that a city republic, being ruled by a rotating, representative council, is a corporate agent like a guild or university; that as a corporate entity of this kind it counts as a person; and that as a person it can itself be a king or prince. In a famous remark, he maintained that in a city republic like his own city of Perugia, the organized citizenry is *sibi princeps*: a prince unto itself.[19]

2.4 The Polity without Full Incorporation

Law without Full Incorporation

Our extended discussion of agency and personhood, individual and corporate, will be of importance at various later stages in the argument of this book. But its point in the context of this chapter is to provide us with the tools for looking at the question of whether the functional polity, in the sense articulated in

18. For a useful, comprehensive account of the history of thinking about the person under law, although one that overlooks the role of Hobbes, see Beran (2020).

19. For background to these brisk claims, see Woolf (1913), Canning (1980; 1983), and Ryan (1999). I describe the required council as representative and rotating on the basis that for Bartolus the members of the council in a *regimen ad populum*, a popular regime, are selected *secundum vices et secundum circulum* (Woolf 1913, 180). For a related translation of *secundum vices et secundum circulum*, see Jonathan Robinson's version (Bartolus 2012, line 337). I am grateful to Daniel Lee for his advice on this issue.

chapter 1, should assume the full dress of a corporate agent.[20] The question is whether the citizens and officials of a nomothetic state should operate to the fullest extent possible as a single agent. We continue to assume that officials will be citizens themselves, whether they hold office for a period or on a permanent basis.

Insofar as a state is nomothetic, its officials will follow certain decision-maker laws in laying down a body of decision-taker laws, and perhaps in changing those laws themselves. Won't that body of decision-maker and decision-taker laws constitute a single voice that can be said to direct the relevant members of the society in the manner envisaged by Hobbes? And doesn't that mean that the functional state or polity is bound to be a fully incorporated agent under which citizens pursue together the purposes encoded in its laws?

It certainly means, as we have seen, that the functional state must be incorporated as an agent. But it doesn't mean that it must be fully incorporated in that way. It will fail to be fully incorporated insofar as the voice speaks equivocally rather than univocally or attracts less than universal conformity. It is quite possible for a state to rule by law, thanks to suitable decision-maker procedures, without that law achieving the univocal content or eliciting the universal obedience associated with full incorporation; it might establish authorities that do not guard appropriately against incoherence in the law.

It is readily intelligible why universal obedience to its voice might fail to materialize under an otherwise well-organized functional polity. It will not fully materialize insofar as there are recalcitrant agents or agencies within the state. That recalcitrance might show up in a failure on the part of officials to discharge their roles in the manner or to the effect that decision-maker law requires of them. And of course, it might appear in a failure on the part of some citizens to fall in line with the demands of any decision-taker laws or of most citizens to fall in line with the demands of some.

But while it is readily intelligible why the law of a functional state might fail to elicit universal obedience, it may seem hard to understand how it could fail to have a univocal content. The polity that emerges under our genealogy, after all, would have to be organized to resolve the three problems of indeterminacy, inflexibility, and ineffectiveness that necessitate law, on Hart's account. So how could it resolve those problems but fail to speak with a single,

---

20. For an argument that it is important to consider whether the contemporary state is a corporate agent, see Runciman (2000a).

unambiguous voice? The answer is: because of a failure on the part of the different agencies that emerge in response to those problems to achieve uniformity across their rulings: to realize the sort of integration prized by Ronald Dworkin (1986).[21]

We devote the remainder of this section to illustrating failures of integration before turning in the final section to a functional argument for the relatively full incorporation of the state. This makes the case for a degree of incorporation that would establish a more or less univocal voice for citizens to rally around and would attract something close to universal obedience among those citizens, in particular among those in public office.

Athens and Failures of Integration

Athens in the fifth and fourth centuries BCE exemplified a functional regime that fails in precisely this manner.[22] The reforms of Callisthenes in Athens of the late sixth century built on the earlier reforms of Solon to shape a set of arrangements that served to give ordinary people a great deal of power over their rulers. Although it operated under arrangements that appointed most officials by lot, it fully deserved the name of a democracy in the etymological, Greek sense that the *demos* or people enjoy a good deal of *kratos* or power (Ober 2008b).[23]

21. Dworkin (1986) maintains that in order to achieve integration in their judgments—and perhaps to guide their enterprise as a whole—judges must invoke moral constraints as well as social facts and, contrary to legal positivism, that those constraints help to determine the law; for a positivist response, see Hart (2012, postscript). The approach taken in this book may fit more naturally with the positivist claim that whether something is the law is fixed by social facts, including perhaps the fact that the courts, à la Dworkin, make such and such moral judgments. But there is nothing about the approach that is inherently inimical to the antipositivist position.

22. I am enormously indebted in the discussion that follows to advice received from Melissa Lane. She drew my attention to Danielle Allen's (2000) claim, supportive of the interpretation I offer, that ancient Athens embodied a rule of judgment—impartial but inevitably ad hoc judgment—rather than a rule of law. This claim is maintained also by Adriaan Lanni (2006) and supported, albeit in modified form, by Josh Ober (2008a); see too Ober (1999). For a different reading, see Harris (2006) and Canevaro (2017).

23. Cammack (2019) offers a somewhat different view on the meaning of "demos" and "democratia" from that of Ober. For an overview of democracy in classical Athens, see Hansen (1999) and Carey (2017); and for a recent argument about the structure of lawmaking, see Canevaro (2013).

Athens was divided into ten tribes under Cleisthenes's reforms, and the lottery system ensured, year by year, that these were equally represented in the executive council or *boule* of five hundred, in the judicial panel of six thousand from which members of different courts or *dikasteria* were drawn, and in the ad hoc committees of lawmakers or *nomothetai* that were periodically assembled, in a reform of the late fifth century, to consider whether to change the law. The only body that was not filled by lot was the assembly of all citizens—the *ecclesia*—that met close to once a week; this regularly attracted over five thousand of the thirty thousand or so full citizens.[24]

Law played a central role in Athens, and it was surely in recognition of the sort of role it was given there that Aristotle (1996) could associate rule by law with rule by reason. But laws were relatively few in Athens and, after the late fifth-century reform, they were not easy to change, let alone expand. Legislative change required, first, the agreement of the assembly of citizens (the *ecclesia*) to a special request for an amendment to be considered; second, the selection by lot of about one thousand citizens (the *nomothetai*) to give the issue consideration: these were drawn from the judicial panel of six thousand; and, third, a decision by those individuals, in the course of a single day, as to whether the law should be amended or not. Thus, legislative change could not occur at the behest of the *ecclesia*, let alone the wish of the *boule*; those bodies played mainly executive roles.

The restriction on the number of laws meant that their interpretation in any instance was left to the courts (the *dikasteria*). For trials, these were popular bodies of up to five hundred members that were selected by lot from the larger judicial panel established in an annual lottery. While their members swore fidelity to the law, they inevitably enjoyed a great deal of interpretive leeway under Athenian decision-making procedures. They were not bound by the precedent of other court judgments, for example, and were not subject to review of any kind.

How you were judged under Athenian law, then—under what interpretation, the law was applied to you—was up to the particular group of jurors selected for your trial. Indeed, whether you were exposed to a trial—whether you were prosecuted in accord with the executive procedures of the state—itself depended not on the suitably constrained judgment of a public prosecutor, but on whether one or another citizen was willing to take you to court.

24. For a useful overview of such Athenian institutions, see Carey (2017, chap. 4).

The lottery system, together with the number of citizens involved in any court, would certainly have helped to ensure that the citizens who appeared as defendants were treated impartially, as their civic status required. But the absence of constraints on how the courts operated—and on the operation of certain executive officials—would have meant that while every citizen was equal before the law, as a nomothetic regime requires, the interpretation of the law that applied in any individual case depended on what group of individuals happened to make the judgment.

The Athenian decision-making system was certainly designed to establish a law that was as uniform as possible across cases, so that the polity would speak to citizens with a single voice. But it operated on a basis that led people to acknowledge that full uniformity could only be a matter of aspiration. This appears in the oath that every juror was required to swear in Athens of the period. While it commits the juror to abide by the laws, it recognizes that on many issues the laws are silent and that in those cases the juror should seek to be impartial.[25]

> I shall vote according to the laws and the decrees of the Athenian people and the Council of the Five Hundred, but concerning things about which there are no laws, I shall decide to the best of my judgment, neither with favor nor enmity. I shall judge concerning those things which are at issue and shall listen impartially to both the accusation and defense. I swear these things by Zeus, by Apollo, by Demeter. May there be many blessings on me if I keep my oath, but if I break it may there be destruction on me and my family. (Scafuro 1997, 50)

Even if our characterization of Athens is not strictly accurate, it should demonstrate the possibility that a polity that plays the role envisaged by Hart, even one that aspires to having a system of uniform law, may not succeed in incorporating fully behind the voice of decision-taker law: the voice that is meant to dictate what is expected of each citizen, and no doubt of any noncitizen residents. It may support the primary rules of the society, resolving the issue of their identity by providing a list of laws, it may allow for the possibility of changing those laws where needed, and it may have a means of determining in each individual case whether an offense has occurred and what recompense or sanction is due. Moreover, it may do this in a way that treats citizens

---

25. Thus Sara Forsdyke (2018, 205) writes, "While the rhetoric of the courts in the fourth century often articulated the ideal of the Rule of Law, the Juror's Oath both reinforced this ideal and acknowledged its impossibility."

impartially, recognizing their civic status as equals. Yet it still may not support the uniform sort of law that we would normally expect in a fully incorporated polity: a law that all can pledge to try to follow and obey.

Thus, a state like classical Athens was not a body fully incorporated to establish and impose domestic, decision-taker laws. There was no single body of law that it was organized to identify in general terms and interpret uniformly across judicial and executive forums. Athens may have aspired as an agent to reliably enforce and entrench a regime of law in accord with reliably formed representations of the different cases where that purpose is relevant. But it did not have the decision-making institutions necessary for fulfilling that aspiration in applying decision-taker law.

To say that Athens was not a fully incorporated agent, however, is not to say that it was not a corporate agent, period. It was not fully incorporated to the extent that at a certain level of administration or adjudication, the interpretation of its domestic law was systematically exposed to a diversity of interpretations. It was incorporated in a significant measure, however, to the extent that failures of uniformity were limited to that level and that the state aspired to speak with a single voice up to the margin at which chance kicked in.

Hart recognizes that the sort of problem we have been looking at arises also in the common-law courts with which he was familiar, since they inevitably have to exercise a certain discretion when they close gaps in statutory and customary law. The courts, he says, treat legal rules as "standards to be followed in decision, determinate enough, in spite of their open texture, to limit, though not to exclude, their discretion" (Hart 2012, 147). But he thinks that despite the discretion they enjoy, "the English system of precedent" can push the courts toward establishing more or less uniform interpretations of such open-textured rules, "making them as determinate as any statutory rule" (135). It is the lack of anything like a rule of precedent that systematically exposed the Athenian *dikasteria* to failures in the uniform interpretation of law.

The problem illustrated by Athens involves a failure on the part of the judicial branch to operate with an interpretation of law that is uniform across its different courts. But the same sort of problem may also occur, of course, within the executive branch insofar as its agencies vary in the interpretation of the laws they implement or one and the same agency varies in its interpretation over time. Here as in the judicial case, there is a need for checks like the law of precedent that would enable citizens to know where they stand under the law. This sort of failure is particularly threatening in a contemporary state, where agencies multiply in the attempt to cope with ever more complex problems.

The sort of judicial failure illustrated by Athens was realized also in Rome, another broadly nomothetic regime, because it too left much of the interpretation of its laws to relatively popular courts that were not bound by precedent. But Rome would also have faced a salient prospect of executive failure since it allowed for the enactment and implementation of a growing body of laws. It did so, moreover, on the basis of a mixed constitution, as it was described by the great admirer and historian of Rome, Polybius (2011, bk. 6), writing in the second century BCE. This would have complicated the task of keeping the law uniform, as it put competing individuals and bodies into decision-making positions; we return to that issue in the next chapter.[26]

Because decision-taker law was not uniformly interpreted under the decision-making procedures in Athens and Rome, it did not represent a voice in which the state speaks in a systematically uniform manner. But the Athenian and Roman models do not represent the only way in which a functional polity might establish a suitable regime of law yet fail to achieve a univocal voice. Another possibility is that which materialized in many medieval European countries after the rediscovery of the corpus of Roman Law at the end of the eleventh century; the relevant lawbooks had been compiled over five hundred years earlier under the eastern emperor, Justinian.

The popes used the newly discovered law as a frame and a model within which to set out canon law and to claim ecclesiastic jurisdiction across Europe. It was mainly because of the ascendancy that Roman law thereby achieved that the first European university was established in Bologna in the mid-1100s. The secular authorities across Europe followed the papal lead, regimenting their legal systems and their jurisdictional claims on Roman lines—often in conflict with Church authorities—and relying on the newly emerging universities for the training of their clerks. This development would have been reinforced by the fact that the Roman law served a useful, coordinating function in negotiations between different regimes.[27]

The upshot was that the interpretation of the law on the part of judicial and executive officials may have been governed as much by the diverging opinions of scholars as by the dictates of local legislators. This source of complexity,

26. There are many excellent accounts of the institutions of republican Rome. For a collection of useful studies, see Flower (2014); the overview of Roman institutions (50–51) is especially useful.

27. For a useful overview of this period of change, see Berman (1983). For background on views about the polity in this period, see Skinner (1978).

even confusion, would have been exacerbated by the existence in many countries of local courts and administrations. The complexity would have made it
impossible for the law that ruled in European regimes of the period to constitute
a fully uniform voice. If there was an exception to this pattern, that was probably in the cities of northern Italy where, as we saw, thinkers like Bartolus and
Baldus took a city republic to be a corporate agent. These cities may have been
small enough and disciplined enough for the application and implementation
of the law across different forums to have been relatively uniform.

2.5 Why the Polity Should Incorporate Fully

We turn finally to the question of whether the functional polity should incorporate as fully as possible. Should it constitute a single agent, organized in such
a way that, ideally, those who act in its name do so under a voice that has a
univocal content and elicits universal obedience among its members? Should
it be organized so that those who act in its name cannot intrude their own
goals or judgments but are bound to enact only corporately endorsed attitudes? Should the goals it espouses and the judgments it passes—and hence
the actions taken in its name—be constrained to follow a constant or at least
a smoothly evolving pattern across the different scenarios where it operates?

In addressing these questions, we focus only on the functional or nomothetic state; the repressive state may also be fully incorporated, but incorporation
might take it even further from the functional ideal, not bring it any closer. It
should be clear that classical Athens, a broadly nomothetic state, is not fully
incorporated since it is organized around a voice that speaks with a discordant,
inconsistent voice in its courts. And it should be clear that a state may be
broadly functional in the same way yet operate in the presence of recalcitrance
and disobedience among many of its officials or other citizens.

There are three salient reasons why the state should be fully incorporated
if it is to operate to the best functional effect. The first is the need for the state to
be so organized in its decision-making that unlike classical Athens or Rome it
can speak with a univocal voice in the decision-taking laws it lays down.
The second and third reasons derive from the need for the univocal voice of the
polity to elicit universal obedience, especially among certain officials. Of these,
the second is the need for the state to be organized so that powerful bodies
like the police and the military are obedient to a corporate voice. And the third
is the need for the state to be organized so that others can rely on it to live up
to the commitments it makes, whether in the domestic or international

context; this requires those who make commitments in its name and those who are called upon to enact the commitments to answer to the same voice and march to the same drum.

In meeting the first of these three needs, the state will be an agent with a single voice, avoiding inconsistency in its laws. In meeting the second, it will be an agent with a single will, curtailing any rogue elements in its ranks. And in meeting the third it will be an agent with a single identity that can credibly assume responsibility over time for what it says and does.

The first of these needs connects directly with the requirement on the functional polity to establish a regime of law in which the citizenry enjoy security in relation to one another. The other two needs each connect with the requirement on the functional state to entrench that regime against internal and external dangers. The need to guard against a rogue police or military and the need to make the state accountable within and without its borders are both relevant to entrenching the regime of law against dangers on those fronts.

The aim in this discussion is to show that the state will fulfill its function better just to the extent that it fully incorporates as an agent, meeting these three needs. The point is to display the functional case for full incorporation, holding this out as an ideal of statehood, not merely as an elevated wish or an ideal of justice. We will not say very much on how the state can most effectively incorporate, however, and satisfy the three needs considered. That would require empirical investigation and modeling—it would be an exercise in institutional design—and is not a goal that we can hope to advance here.

The Need for a Single Voice

The failure that we illustrated in the case of Athens, and in the other cases mentioned too, reflects the lack of a single voice. The Athenian polity is incorporated in some degree, since it establishes decision-making authorities and procedures that recognize and support the prospect that decision-taker laws will be interpreted uniformly across cases. It fails to achieve full incorporation, however, insofar as it falls short of ensuring such uniformity; it allows different agents of the state—different courts or *dikasteria*—to give different verdicts on similar cases, so that the state may not speak with a single voice.

A fully incorporated state would enable citizens to know where they stand in relation to one another much more effectively than an incompletely incorporated state like that which classical Athens illustrates; it would help to ensure that the law is uniformly understood across legislative, judicial, and executive agencies or, at the least, that the law is not exposed systematically to diverse interpretations. That the state is incorporated on this front means that it will address its citizens with a single voice, formulating and applying decision-taker laws that allow them to know how they should behave if they are not to fall foul of that law and how they may expect others, on pain of legal sanction, to behave toward them. That law will identify their rights and duties as citizens, in their dealings both with one another and with those in office.

When the nomothetic state is incorporated as an agent in relation to its citizens, it will give the power of a unified voice to the law: it will put the law in itself, rather than the law as authorities choose at will to interpret it, in charge of how citizens are allowed to behave. Where any nomothetic regime requires impartiality in how a standing law applies to citizens on judicial and executive fronts, the single-voice constraint also requires uniformity in how the law is interpreted in those forums.

Establishing a uniform law, it should be stressed, is quite consistent with deep and widespread forms of injustice; it would do little or nothing to transform a functional regime into a just regime. Classical Athens is often hailed as an ideal insofar as it was designed to restrict the emergence of an elite among the citizenry, but it denied citizenship to the majority of adult, able-minded residents—all women and male helots—and its laws did not protect individuals from abject poverty and dependency. Giving the law a single voice would have made that city-state into a more functional polity, reducing the inconstancy in interpretation of the law, but it need not have done anything to improve the regime on such other fronts.

All that the single-voice constraint requires is that decision-taker law should be properly integrated. Or at least it requires that that law should be generated under decision-making procedures that allow for integration in response to evidence of failure. Such routines would bind decision makers in sites of legislation and administration by suitable constitutional and administrative law and would bind the courts by suitable procedural laws. To take the judicial case as an example, let one court interpret the law in a first way, another in a second, as in classical Athens, and there would be grounds for the defendant to appeal, say under a rule of precedent. And the fact that that is so would give each court an incentive to keep its interpretations in line with those of others: certainly, with those of other courts at higher levels in the chain of appeal.

There are different ways, as we shall see in the next chapter, in which a regime might meet this desideratum. What is bound to be required of any such polity, however, is that it should impose decision-maker constraints on officials that help to ensure uniformity in the interpretation and application of the law by different authorities. There should be such constraints in place that we may judge of those authorities, not only that there is a coherent law that judicial and executive authorities are bound to apply impartially, but that they are bound also to apply it under a more or less uniform interpretation. In any situation where they fail to interpret the law uniformly, there will be grounds for contestation by relevant parties and some hope of correction within the system. It will not be true, in any significant measure, that the authorities are able to change the law as they go along.

The first reason why the state ought to incorporate fully is that the fully incorporated nomothetic state would give citizens a more determinate sense of where they stand, thereby fulfilling its function better; it would enable citizens to properly know their rights and duties in relation to one another and in relation to officials. Even the elite citizens of a polity as admirable as that of classical Athens would not have enjoyed this boon. Assuming the system worked well, they would have known that they were equals before an impartial law. But they would also have realized that two contingencies affected the chance of whether they would be found guilty, should they commit an offense against public law.

The first contingency is that the chance of conviction depended, even in the case of what we would call a criminal offense, on whether someone chose to charge them with the offense; there might be no one like the victim of an offense in private law, who had a motive to bring a case against them. And the second contingency is that the chance of being found guilty depended on how the law dealt with them in the event of their coming before the courts: in effect, on who happened to be selected as jurors and how those jurors exercised the discretion they enjoyed.

This discussion, and that which follows, suggests that whether the state operates as a fully incorporated body that speaks with a single voice is an on-off matter. But this is a convenient simplification. We saw that every agent is required to pursue its purposes reliably, according to reliably formed representations, only under normal conditions. But consistently with enabling it to perform as a corporate agent—even as an agent we would treat as fully incorporated—the procedures established in a polity may be contingent on the satisfaction of a larger or a smaller set of normal conditions. And in a corresponding sense, the polity itself may be a reliable agent to a greater or a lesser degree: its reliability may depend on things being favorable on a wider or a narrower front. This consideration will be of relevance later: for example, when we discuss the merits of a presidential versus a parliamentary system in the next chapter.

We have said little or nothing about the institutions that might help to give a single voice to the nomothetic state. But, as Hart indicates, a rule of precedent would certainly help to resolve the problems raised by judicial interpretation. More generally, the single-voice desideratum will be satisfied to the extent that the rules governing decision-making authorities are manifest, determinate, and resistant to opportunistic alteration by any officials. This argues for insulating those rules against easy alteration, whether by means of a written constitution or in deeply laid convention and tradition. And it argues for introducing checks and balances of the kind discussed in the next chapter, which would empower different agencies to monitor and constrain one another. But we cannot pursue that argument here. It must be enough to recognize where institutional design is needed; pursuing such design would take us beyond the remit of the book.

The Rule of Law

Giving the state a univocal voice connects closely with the ideal of a rule of law. What the rule *of* law requires, in effect, is that the state should not only rule *by* law, and be incorporated to that extent—not only should it be nomothetic, in our sense—but also give a univocal voice to that law, achieving a fuller degree of incorporation as a ruling agent (Tamanaha 2004).[28]

The rule of law is usually articulated as a set of formal constraints that decision-taker laws should satisfy (Fuller 1971; Waldron 1989; 2016b). We may follow this tradition, while acknowledging that the ideal has no hope of being realized unless it is embedded psychologically in people's hearts and sociologically in their behavioral habits (Krygier 2016).

Rule-of-law constraints derive from two basic demands. The first demand is that the discretion of individual decision makers in framing, altering, or interpreting decision-taker laws should be reduced as far as possible; individuals should not be able to impose law at will, and perhaps in their personal favor, rather than in the interest of the citizenry as a whole. And the second demand is that the vulnerability of decision takers to the power of decision makers— their vulnerability to the laws that those authorities impose—should also be

28. I am grateful to Eliot Litalien for points he raised about my discussion of this topic.

reduced as much as possible. In each case the degree of reduction required may be taken to be fixed by what is needed for the state to serve its function optimally, not by what is needed under this or that ideal of justice.[29]

Adopting this line, we can formulate rule-of-law constraints as specifications of these two demands. The rule of law, we can say, is designed:

A. to reduce the discretionary power of individual decision makers
   a. in framing the laws: the laws should be general in character;
   b. in changing the laws: they should be relatively stable over time;
   c. in interpreting the laws: they should be uniform across agencies; and
B. to reduce the vulnerability of individual decision takers by enabling them
   a. to know the laws: the laws should be promulgated and accessible;
   b. to understand the laws: they should be clear and intelligible; and
   c. to follow the laws: they should be prospective, coherent, and feasible.[30]

The idea of a rule by law argues in itself that law should be general and stable, and that it should be known, understood, and capable of being followed; let any of those conditions fail and it is not clear that law would properly serve the role envisaged in a nomothetic regime. But if the nomothetic regime is not fully incorporated, then it will certainly fail to satisfy the requirement that the law be uniformly interpreted across the legislature, the judiciary, and executive agencies. And failing in that way, it will also jeopardize the capacity of decision makers to support only general and stable laws, and the capacity of decision takers to know the laws, to understand those laws, and to follow them.

Requiring the polity to speak with a univocal voice in the laws it enunciates and enforces—requiring it in that respect to be fully incorporated—will rectify this shortfall and enable the nomothetic state to establish a rule of law. Not

29. These demands echo the core idea in traditional discussions of the rule of law: that it should not be a rule of will. In a slogan associated with James Harrington (1992) in the mid-seventeenth century, the empire of law should not be an empire of men (Lovett 2012).

30. Lon Fuller (1971) famously identifies eight constraints of the rule of law: that laws should be general, promulgated, prospective, intelligible, coherent, feasible, stable, and congruent or uniform across agencies; all eight are captured in our six constraints. He thinks of them as requirements of morality—the morality of law, as he describes it—whereas from our viewpoint they are design specifications on a functional regime of law. This construal of them fits well with the line taken by Herbert Hart (1965) in a review of Fuller's book.

only will it remain appealing, as in the ideal of a rule by law, that the law should be general and stable, and be capable of being known, understood and followed; the polity will be able to respond to that appeal, ensuring or helping to ensure that the law speaks with a single voice.

Thus, we may expect the fully incorporated state to satisfy all the rule-of-law constraints, supporting the capacity of citizens to know where they stand vis-à-vis one another, including vis-à-vis officials. It will give them a clearer idea of what they may and may not do with legal impunity and legal protection, enhancing the security that they enjoy under the law. This polity may not be fully just insofar as it does not make the citizenry inclusive or does not give citizens an appropriate range of security. But it will give them more than the best that would have been available, for example, in classical Athens or republican Rome.

One final comment. While the decision-making procedures under a rule of law should ensure that those in office satisfy the various constraints listed, generating and imposing suitable decision-taker laws, those procedures do not have to be unchangeable themselves; they may allow for at least partial amendment, as we shall see in the following chapter.

The Need for a Single Will

The second argument for why the state ought to incorporate fully is connected to the role it must play, not in establishing a regime of law, but in stabilizing that regime against dangers from within and without the society. The polity needs to elicit universal conformity among those powerful officials and official bodies that are established to combat those dangers. It must impose a single will on them, not allow them to act at their own discretion.

The internal danger to any polity is the collapse of the system due to non-compliance with the law on the part of regular citizens, on the part of corrupt officials, or among any who seek to overturn the government without regard to decision-maker rules. For the polity to domestically entrench the regime of law—ideally, the rule of law—it must ensure that the law criminalizes relevant forms of deviance and dissension; it must create a body with the capacity to uncover deviance or dissension; and it must enable that body to use coercive force against offenders, where that is required, and to bring them before the judicial authorities for sentencing and sanction. That body will constitute a police force that guards against the breaching of decision-maker or decision-taker laws.

But a police force that is designed to identify and arrest presumptive of-fenders against the laws will have enormous powers within the polity. It will be required to have a means of surveilling and combatting other citizens and officials, being set apart in that respect from others in the domestic society. And its power will be all the greater for the fact that while officials in the force will be as prone as any other officials to corruption, any corruption within their ranks is likely to be particularly difficult to combat. Corrupt police will know the best ways of avoiding detection, and even if their corruption is detected, others in the force may be loath to pursue them: they will be tempted to close ranks. The age-old question will arise. *Quis custodiet ipsos custodes?* Who will guard against the guardians themselves?

The main external danger to any state comes from exposure to invasion and associated forms of intimidation by bigger and better resourced regimes. This creates the need, as already registered, for the polity to protect its borders and opens the prospect of aggression and war. In such a situation the polity will need to establish a military force of some kind: a force that serves it externally in much the way that a police force will be required to serve it on the internal front.

The same question that arises for the police arises also with the military that is established to guard the borders of the polity and to protect it against infiltration or invasion by another state. Traditionally, the problem raised by having a standing army was taken to be much more pressing than that raised by having a powerful police force; this, no doubt, is because policing devel-oped as an institution only in recent centuries. European political thinkers and historians embraced a lesson they drew from the collapse of the Roman Re-public: that it was due to Rome's retreat from reliance on a citizen militia to reliance on a relatively established army. The lesson led the American found-ers, for example, to establish "the right of the people to bear and keep arms"; this is grounded, as the Second Amendment to the Constitution puts it, in the assumption that "a well regulated militia" is "necessary to the security of a free state."

Suppose that those operating within a police or military force can take initiatives and pursue projects at their own discretion. Suppose that like the jurors in ancient Athens they are called upon to behave impartially and virtu-ously in pursuing their duties but are not appropriately constrained by the decision-maker rules binding officials of that state. Suppose, more specifically, that they are unconstrained to the point that how they operate on any occasion depends in great part on their own will or discretion, or on the will or discre-tion of those in charge within their ranks.

Under those assumptions, the police or the military may clearly take the law into their own hands. Citizens—even citizens who constitute an elite within the society—will be individually exposed to the discretionary, unpredictable will of the police. And they will be collectively exposed to the discretionary will of a military that could launch a coup d'état if at any point things were not being done to their taste.

Curtailing the discretion of Athenian juries to ensure a uniformity of response to similar cases will require the polity to incorporate more fully, as we saw earlier, with its decision makers on the courts constrained to advance only corporately authorized ends by corporately authorized means. The same lesson applies here. While a police or military force is certainly going to be needed, the state will have to incorporate to the point where their decision-making power can be exercised only for corporately approved ends and under corporately approved procedures. It cannot allow the police or the military to have the discretion of an independent collection of agents, bound at most by the sort of oath that Athenian jurors were required to take. It must constrain the police and military as fully as possible so that they pursue only duly endorsed purposes according to duly endorsed judgments on how those purposes are best served. It must ensure that when those forces act, it is the polity itself that acts by their hands.

Putting this in other terms, the polity must become an agent that implements a single will in dealing with the dangers of deviance and dissension, infiltration and invasion, rather than offloading that task to relatively independent and potentially inimical bodies. It must be so well organized that we can treat it as the agent that operates when the police or military exercise their powers. It must be so well organized that those forces act, when they act, not just in the name of the polity but at its bidding rather than their own discretion. Like other decision-making authorities within the polity, they will ideally have to act under such constraints or instructions that we can see them as enacting the single will of the state.

In concluding this discussion, three qualifying remarks. A first connects with the previous discussion of the way in which the state that fully incorporates to realize the first aspect of its function, will thereby satisfy the ideal, as it is widely understood, of a rule of law. As incorporation to ensure a single voice for the law will require the polity to satisfy something like this ideal, so will incorporation to guard against the police or the military becoming rogue entities. Were the police or the military to have rogue power, then that would undermine the rule-of-law aims of restricting the discretionary power of decision makers and reducing the vulnerability of citizens to decision-making power.

A second comment is that incorporation is never likely to be perfectly complete, and a degree of discretion is likely to remain with the police and military, or with other decision-making authorities, under any feasible constraints. This is tolerable insofar as evidence of any use of the discretion that is taken to jeopardize the equal standing of citizens, however lawful it may currently be, is liable and even likely to trigger a corrective response by the system: a response that makes that sort of discretion illegal or at least that curtails its availability.

The third qualification needed echoes one made in the previous discussion. While it is relatively easy to argue that a functional polity ought to incorporate the police and military effectively within its organization, that argument says nothing on the issue of institutional design that it raises. How is the polity to achieve this result: how is it to guard against the guardians, incorporating the police and military more fully within itself? This is an issue with which contemporary polities continue to wrestle, whether out of a wish to be functionally effective or to achieve some ideal of justice.[31]

The Need for a Single Identity

The final argument for why the polity should fully incorporate derives, like the second, from the role it must play, not in establishing a regime of law, but in entrenching that regime against dangers from within and without the society. If the functional state is to play this role as effectively as possible, then it must enable those with whom it makes contracts to rely on its commitments, whether those contractual partners be domestic entities like corporate, professional, or associational organizations, or external entities such as other states, international agencies, or multinational corporations. It is only if it can make credible contracts that it will be able to employ contractual means for the purpose of guarding against many domestic and international dangers.

In order to make itself into a reliable partner in such contracts, the functional state must ideally operate with a single identity or character, assuming

---

31. The decentralization of the incorporated state for which we argue in the next chapter might be a useful device for curtailing the power of the police or the military; it would divide those bodies into subagencies that might be expected to be able to check and balance one another.

only commitments it can live up to, and living up to all the commitments it makes. It must be fully incorporated in such a way that one and the same voice is enunciated by those who make commitments and enacted by those who are bound by the commitments. Assuming that those who enunciate the commitments conform with decision-maker law, and can claim to speak in the name of the state, those who are called on to enact those commitments must conform to that same law, living up to the commitments, if they can claim to act in the name of that state. Let them fail regularly to do this, and the state will be unable to make credible commitments over time and can scarcely count as a cross-temporally enduring agent.

How can the state ensure that its voice will be constant and effective on these fronts, so that it can display the identity of a single agent between commissive and enactive episodes? The issue is particularly important and difficult on the external front since international bodies like other states will often pose the most serious dangers for its stability. We shall concentrate almost entirely on the external issue here, for the domestic issue, as we note later, can be resolved in a relatively straightforward manner.

If the state is to mitigate external dangers, the decision-making authorities may have to be capable, when necessary, of waging war in protection of its borders. But if they are to achieve peace of a robust kind—if they are not to live in the precincts of war, to echo a phrase from Hobbes—then they must also be able to establish treaties of peace with other willing regimes and to subscribe to any feasible international order that allows for the settlement of disputes. And so, they must be able to undertake the commitments that such initiatives involve.

When individuals undertake a commitment, as we saw earlier, they communicate an attitude in a more expensive and therefore credible manner than is strictly required; they convey it in a manner that exposes the communicator to a special cost in the event of their not displaying the attitude conveyed. Thus, the person who avows a belief or a desire will communicate that attitude more expensively and credibly than if they had just reported it, for they will not be able to invoke a misleading mind to excuse a failure to live up to it. And the person who pledges an intention to do something will communicate that attitude still more expensively and credibly insofar as they will be unable to invoke either a misleading mind or a changed mind in excusing a failure.

Making a commitment may require nothing more of an individual than avowing and pledging an attitude, since it will be manifest to all that if the person fails to enact the commitment and is unable to excuse a failure, then that will be very costly for them. It will compromise their status in the economy of esteem—their reputation for honesty, fidelity, and the like—and undermine their aspiration to perform as an enduring person with a single identity or character. Indeed, the same may also be true of the commitments made by private corporate agents within a society or even across societies. The corporation that reneges on a contract, for example, will run a serious risk by doing so since the bad reputation it will thereby incur may inhibit other agents, individual or corporate, from doing business with it.

Even among such individuals and corporations, of course, the reputational expense of avowal and commitment may not be taken to suffice in every case. In particularly important contracts, the parties will often register the arrangements they make in law, exposing themselves to legal redress as well as reputational damage, should they fail to stand by their words.

How is the polity to make the words uttered in its name, as in entering a treaty or subscribing to certain international regulations, suitably expensive and credible? How is it to make them costly and credible enough to convince others to rely on those words, as they might on the words of an agent with a single continuing identity? More generally, how is a polity going to establish the infrastructure of reliance and trust with other states—and ultimately its integrity as a self-identical body—that is needed for economically and socially beneficial relationships with them (McLean 1999; 2004)?

This raises a great difficulty for states because those who speak for the state at any time are likely to involve different individuals and bodies—even a different government—from those that speak and act for the state later. The words of the authorities in any period will be credible only to the extent that it will be manifestly expensive for those who act later to fail to live up to the words given.

Such a failure will certainly be expensive for the state itself, because of the reputational concerns or economic costs it triggers, or because of some form of redress written into the original contract: say, a form of redress that the state can ignore only at the cost of retreating to a warlike stance. Such a legally agreed form of redress may be determined, under prior agreement, by the states or other bodies entering the contract. And it may well involve the recognition of some agency as entitled to pass judgment on the failure and on the penalty appropriate for failure.

But many international treaties and arrangements are likely to be made in the absence of a recognized adjudicator or a recognized form of redress for contractual failure. Here it is only reputational concerns or economic costs that can operate to give credibility to the words of those who speak for the state, giving them the status of spokespersons for an entity with a single continuing identity. And even if there is a recognized adjudicator and form of redress, reputational and economic considerations will always remain relevant and important. After all, those who act later for the state may prove willing to defy any legally agreed, even enforced, attempt at redress.

The lack of an agency powerful enough to impose legal redress on an offending state marks a big difference between the problem of how to make the state externally accountable and the problem of how to make it accountable in dealing with domestic bodies or individuals. If the state is decentralized, then a domestic agency within the state itself may be empowered to call any other state agency to account for breaching a legal contract with some corporate or individual agent within the jurisdiction. We shall be looking at arguments for why the state should be decentralized in the next chapter, and one relevant consideration is that this would enable the state to be a credible party to domestic contractual arrangements.

Returning to the international case, however, it is noteworthy that neither a formal arrangement nor the presence of informal sanctions can guarantee that a state will remain faithful to the international commitments that it makes. This is particularly so when states change government, whether under a constitutional process or not. The incentives of those in a new government may be different from those of the old and may even include an incentive to do things differently from the predecessor and to renege on many of its promises. When this is manifest on all sides, a government will be unable to make a credible contract in the name of the state, only in its own name. But if things were always as uncertain as that, then the ability of states to engage credibly in mutually beneficial arrangements would be severely hampered. There would be little prospect of establishing a firm international law, of making treaties to set up international or regional agencies, or of entering long-term country-to-country treaties.

These considerations underline the importance of organizing the functional state in such a way that it can boast a single identity as an agent over time and make credible international commitments. If its commitments are to be credible then it had better be clear that there will be a serious loss attendant on any later government for not living up to those commitments: that is, for not assuming the responsibilities of the state in whose name it purportedly acts. And it had better be the case that, presumptively for fear of that loss, the later government will reliably act on the commitments made earlier in the state's name.

Thus, if it is to ensure the credibility of its commitments, the state must be organized so that others in the international world can plausibly expect that later authorities will assume responsibility for commitments made by the authorities at an earlier time: say, in an electoral regime by a different government. There will be cases where the later authorities can credibly provide excuses for why, despite acting for one and the same state, they cannot be expected to fulfill the commitments made by some predecessors. But they must not be able to dodge responsibility by citing an irrelevant excuse or by pretending that no excuse is required. The organization of the state must preclude this dodge, else the state will be unable to make any credible commitments at all.

To say that the state must be organized in this way is just to say that it must be incorporated in a suitably full measure in its relations with other states and other international bodies. It must be organized so that when its representatives speak in its name, then it is truly the state as a corporate agent that speaks through them and it is truly that self-identical agent that is obligated, on pain of one or another sanction, to act as they pledge it will act. In other words, it must be that their words plausibly bind later representatives to act correspondingly in the name of the state. There must be a single self-identical body for which the relevant agents and agencies act, despite a change of government or just the lapse of time.

We saw previously that the state can operate with a single will only insofar as the more powerful decision-making individuals or bodies, such as the police and the military, are brought under the discipline of a single directive voice and are blocked from going rogue. A parallel lesson holds here. The state can be an accountable agent, capable of engaging other international or indeed domestic bodies—it can count as a body with a single identity over time—only if the temporally separated decision makers that enter and enact commissive arrangements are also subject to the discipline of one and the same voice. Let the later authorities have the power of going rogue—let them cease to be constrained by the voice of their predecessors—and the capacity of the state to secure the benefits of long-term contracts will be reduced.

It is not just the distinction between the authorities who speak and the authorities who act that can create problems for the incorporation and accountability of the state. A single body may be responsible for making a commitment at one time and living up to it at another and yet fail to match its words with its actions. An example might be the case where the U.S. Congress allows the executive to adopt policies requiring it to incur debts in the name of the country but refuses at a later point to raise the debt ceiling and make it possible for the executive to honor the country's debts. That that can happen, say because a particular party wishes to put the governing party at an electoral disadvantage, is a sign that the decision-making rules are inadequate; they allow the United States to say one thing and do another: to act as if there was not a self-identical body represented by the Congress in its earlier words and the Congress in its later deeds.

How should a state be organized so that it can operate as an accountable or responsible agent among others, gaining from the benefits of peace and commerce? This takes us back to the challenge of institutional design that we are setting aside here. As issues of institutional design arise with bringing the police and the military under the discipline of the polity, so they arise in this area too. There is no easy way to guarantee that the decision makers at any one time can effectively bind those at a later time or even to guarantee that the self-same decision makers will resist short-term pressures and incentives to break faith with the words they themselves gave before. And yet there is hardly any more important demand that a state must satisfy if it is to exercise its proper function.

These observations complete our inquiry into the question raised in the chapter. Because of considerations about the nature of agency—basic, human, and corporate—we have seen that if the state is to serve its function effectively, it will have to incorporate fully as an agent. If it is to establish a regime of decision-taker law that enables people to know where they stand, it must incorporate so that the courts and other decision-making agencies speak with a single voice in framing and interpreting the law. And if it is to stabilize that regime against internal and external dangers, it must achieve a high degree of obedience to that voice, especially among those citizens who serve as officials.

This need for stability requires the state, first, to incorporate under a single decision-making will so that the police and armed forces are limited to pursuing corporately approved ends by corporately approved judgments. And that need requires it, second, to incorporate in a way that testifies to a single identity, so that its decision-making representatives can bind themselves and their successors credibly, whether in entering beneficial treaties with other states, in subscribing to a beneficial international order, or in making contractual arrangements on the domestic front.

3

The Polity Decentralized

THE DISCUSSION in the first chapter identified the function of the state with domestically and internationally stabilizing a system of laws under which its citizens—possibly, only a subset of its members—enjoy a certain security in relation to one another and in relation to officials: their rights and duties under the laws enable them to know where they stand in those relationships. The function, in a classic phrase, is the promotion of *salus populi*: the safety of the people, domestic and international.

The discussion of the last chapter argued that there is a strong case for the functional polity to incorporate as an agent in the fullest measure possible. By fully incorporating in this way, it can give law a uniformity of interpretation across different authorities—a univocal voice—enabling citizens to know where they stand in relation to one another and to officials: this, in accord with the ideal of a rule of law, as distinct from just a rule by law. Moreover, by fully incorporating as an agent, the polity can also ensure universal conformity to its voice, especially among agents whose role is to stabilize the regime of law against internal and external dangers. Thus, it can establish policing and military forces to serve in this role without letting those forces act at their own discretion rather than the corporate will. And it can discipline representatives so that the domestic and international commitments made in its name are reliably enacted and count as the self-representations of a continuing, identical body.

But while letting the functional state incorporate fully has these undoubted advantages, it also poses a danger. Full incorporation may enable the citizens who collectively run that unified state—those in government—to enjoy a level of power that they can use, should they wish, to neglect the demands of office and act predominantly in their own interest. They will have charge over a *Leviathan*, in Hobbes's image, and may be able to run it in the service of their own purposes, passions, and prejudices.

Lord Acton was drawing on a long tradition, ultimately a republican one, when he said that all power tends to corrupt, and absolute power corrupts absolutely (Pettit 1997, chap. 7). His observation suggests that, if we want the state to serve its natural function, we need to guard against the extra power that the officials of a state may gain with full incorporation. And that concern takes us to the topic of this chapter.

The question that faces us is how to guard against the danger that power will be misused in the organization of the state: how to ensure that decision-maker laws will protect the citizens of a state against the power of the authorities. The argument pursued is that decentralizing the state—making its organization polycentric—should help to meet the problem. It promises a system of decision-maker law that requires the government to operate via relatively independent agencies that check and balance one another's power. In a phrase with a long republican pedigree—it goes back two millennia—the proposal is to organize the state around a mixed constitution or framework.

Having just argued for the need to incorporate the state as a single agent, denying independent discretion to various organs or agencies of the state, it may seem like a turn-around to put the case now for dividing up the polity in a polycentric manner. But that is not so, as will become clearer over the discussion that follows. We shall see that to organize a state in a network of mutually checking authorities, individual or corporate, is not to prevent it from being a single corporate agent, so long as those authorities implement a univocal voice. The state will remain fully incorporated if the authorities are forced to overcome their differences and to act as a single agent in discharging the function of the state.

This position will seem particularly controversial in view of the argument for sovereignty developed in the absolutist tradition of Jean Bodin, Thomas Hobbes, and Jean-Jacques Rousseau. Arguing that every state—in effect, every state that is incorporated fully as an agent—must be organized around a single sovereign power, these thinkers maintain that this arrangement is inconsistent with the mixed constitution or polycentric regime. While their argument for sovereignty is broadly on the right lines, by the account defended here, it does not rule out organizing the state in a decentralized manner. And there is good, functional reason to seek to organize it in that way.

Why give such attention to figures like Bodin, Hobbes, and Rousseau? Partly for historical reasons, partly for philosophical. While they were mistaken about the feasibility of a polycentric state, it was they who first showed that if the state is an agent, then it must have a single sovereign. And while dated in various ways, their arguments are more systematic than anything to be found among contemporary opponents of the decentralized state. That opposition is most clearly represented by those neo-populists who defend autocratic, electoral democracy, arguing against allowing agencies like statutory bodies or public-interest movements to hem in the elected government of a state.[1] We agree with neo-populists when they say that the state must embody a single sovereign agent but reject their view that a polycentric constitution would rule out the possibility of having such a sovereign (Pettit 2022).

This chapter falls into five sections. In the first section, we set out the idea of the polycentric or mixed constitution, distinguishing the forms of decentralization it may impose, and explain why decentralization is desirable. In the three sections following, we argue that decentralization is not only desirable but feasible, and feasible even in a fully incorporated state that is organized around a single sovereign. Then in a short fifth section, we look at the radical and moderate forms that a decentralized or polycentric state may assume, associating these two forms with presidential and parliamentary systems, and argue in favor of the moderate.

3.1 The Polycentric Constitution

The Polycentric or Mixed Constitution

Assume, plausibly, that every aspect of political activity, legislative, judicial, and executive, is relevant to establishing the law: this, by way of formulating it, as in the legislature, or interpreting it, as in judicial and executive decision making; as we shall see later, this assumption is qualified by absolutists, who prioritize the legislative aspect. On that assumption, polycentric organization may come about by one or more of three familiar devices; these are not the only modes possible, as we shall see in the next chapter, but they are the most familiar.

The first device is a relatively sharp separation of power between some or all of the three branches of government, legislative, judicial, and executive, requiring them to coordinate with one another in determining the precise content of law. The second involves a sharing of power among different

---

1. The neo-populist tag may be used to distinguish this group from those populists who argue that there is room and need within the existing constitutions of many democracies for establishing more centers at which popular inputs to decision making can be made. On neo-populism, see Mueller (2016), Urbinati (2019), and Krygier, Czarnota, and Sadurksi (2022).

individuals or bodies in any one of these branches, as in a bicameral legislature or a hierarchical court system. And the third is the outsourcing of some of the powers of any branch, usually the executive, by giving independent, presumptively impartial agencies an effective, if not conclusive, influence; examples of such agencies might be an electoral commission, a bureau of statistics, or a central bank (Tucker 2018; Sunstein and Vermeule 2020).

The proposal to separate the legislative, executive, and judicial authorities came into prominence in the work of the Baron de Montesquieu (1989), the early eighteenth-century author of *The Spirit of the Laws*. But for Montesquieu the separation of powers was tied up closely with the idea that the powers separated should themselves be shared among many hands, so that he embraced the first two of our three devices. Both are aspects of a regime of mutual checking among public authorities that he took to be necessary to ensure that the law is not abused by the authorities. His general principle is that to protect against abuse, "power must check power by the arrangement of things," because "it has eternally been observed that any man who has power is led to abuse it; he continues until he finds limits" (Montesquieu 1989, 155–56).

This principle led Montesquieu (1989, 164) to praise "the fundamental constitution" in England where he argued that various autonomous powers—for example, the Commons, the House of Lords, the Monarchy—check one another to the point where they "are forced to move in concert," not in the way that might have been most attractive from any one perspective. His view had an enormous influence within England itself and on those who designed the U.S. Constitution in 1787.

Montesquieu's influence showed up in the growing domestic enthusiasm for the British way of separating and sharing power: the British constitution, as it was commonly known (Lieberman 2006). That influence is manifest in William Blackstone's *Commentaries on the Laws of England*, published in the 1760s. For Blackstone (2016, 103) "the true excellence of the English government" consists in this: "that all the parts of it form a mutual check upon each other." The influence of Montesquieu is also palpable in the U.S. Constitution, and in the *Federalist Papers*, written in its support, where he is frequently cited and figures as "the celebrated Montesquieu" (Madison, Hamilton, and Jay 1987).

But Montesquieu was not the first to invoke the desirability of separating and sharing the powers of a state among distinct agents or bodies. Writing in the second century BCE, Polybius (2011, bk. 6) praised a similar dispensation in Rome and argued that it was that arrangement—that mixed constitution, as he described it in an older Greek idea—that made the Roman Republic so successful and stable. This characterization of Rome was appropriate, insofar as Roman law was made and interpreted in a process of interaction between independent bodies.

Only members of an elite could hold public office in Rome and belong to the senate. But to hold office they had to be supported by annual election in a popular participatory body: the tribal or centuriate assembly. And while only those holding public office could propose measures for legislation, those measures could be established as laws only if they were not vetoed by the tribunes of the people and were supported at a meeting of one of the popular bodies. Again, when it came to the implementation of the laws, this was done by the public officials, with the advice of the senate, but in each kind of executive office, power was divided between several individuals: at the top of the hierarchy, for example, between two consuls.

Polybius's characterization and celebration of Rome was endorsed by Cicero (1998) and other Roman authors in the following century. His idea of the mixed constitution became central for the broadly republican tradition that influenced thinkers and activists in medieval and Renaissance Italy, seventeenth-century England, and eighteenth-century America and France. These thinkers all took republican Rome as a model for organizing the polity, relying on Polybius's characterization of a regime where different bodies, often representative of different sectors among the citizenry, provide checks and balances on one another's behavior.[2]

The mixed constitution, although not always under that name, came to be hailed by a range of later republican writers such as Niccolò Machiavelli (1997) in sixteenth-century Florence, James Harrington (1992) in seventeenth-century England, and of course the American founders in the eighteenth century (Madison, Hamilton, and Jay 1987). All were defenders of the idea of a constitution that disperses power among many hands. Montesquieu (1989, 39) was deeply influenced by this republican tradition of thought as he almost certainly was by Polybius himself: "judicious Polybius," as he describes him.

The separation and sharing of power were seen as different sides of this dispersion of control within the broad tradition of support for the mixed constitution. The third idea of outsourcing power is a more recent development

---

2. I ignore the disputed question of how the notion of the republic connects with that of the state in Roman, medieval, and Renaissance usage. Among recent writings on the issue, see Skinner (2009), Hankins (2010), Nelson (2010), Kharkhordin (2010), and Vatter (2014).

in political practice and, while it is not associated with any one thinker, it too has been generally taken to implement a dispersion of control that guards against political abuse, in particular incompetence and corruption among other officials. For our purposes, we may regard it as a natural extension of the idea of dispersing power that the mixed constitution epitomizes (Pettit 1997).[3]

The Absolutist Opposition

The idea of a mixed constitution came to be strongly opposed, however, by Jean Bodin and Thomas Hobbes in the sixteenth and seventeenth centuries. They both thought of the polity as a corporate agent that must be organized around a single center of authority and power: a sovereign, to use the term—in French, *souverain*—that Bodin popularized. This aspect of their views is quite attractive, as we shall see. But what is not attractive is that they took the belief in sovereignty to entail a rejection of the mixed constitution that Rome was taken by republicans to exemplify; they thought that such a constitution would make the polity dysfunctional. They were sovereigntist in endorsing the need for a sovereign, as we shall understand sovereigntism here, and absolutist in tying the acceptance of sovereignty to a rejection of the mixed constitution.

The absolutist notion of sovereignty with which we shall be concerned is distinct from the idea of sovereignty that is often invoked in contemporary discussions of the sovereignty enjoyed by First Nations in countries like Australia and Canada, prior to colonization by European powers (Ivison 2020). Those nations certainly enjoyed sovereignty in the sense that the laws and customs of each nation established the rights and duties of individuals living in their sphere of control. And their sovereignty in this sense—if you prefer, their jurisdiction—was certainly taken from them in an unjustifiable use of force by colonial powers. But the First Nations did not enjoy sovereignty in the absolutist sense in which that would have required a single organized state, and it is that state-centered conception of sovereignty that is at issue in our own discussion.

3. For a useful account of the institutions of Rome, see Flower (2014). For further discussion of the ideas of the separation of powers and the mixed constitution, see Gwyn (1965), Vile (1967), Diamond (1978), and Franklin (1991); for an account of parliamentarism, an important aspect of the British version of the mixed constitution, see Selinger (2019); and for a good contemporary example of its being put to use in political and institutional design, see Braithwaite (1997).

While Bodin and Hobbes were the outstanding figures in the absolutist way of thinking, their hostility to the mixed constitution was maintained with similar intensity in the rather different style of political theory presented in the eighteenth century by Jean-Jacques Rousseau; we shall concentrate here on the theory he advanced in *The Social Contract*, published in 1762. We will be looking at the positive views of all three thinkers about sovereignty in the next section, but it may be useful here to describe their opposition to the mixed constitution and to put that hostility in historical context.

On St. Bartholomew's Day 1572, there was a widespread massacre of Huguenots in France, and it exemplified the killing, destruction, and chaos that threatened to materialize in the wake of the new, post-Reformation divisions in religious affiliation. One of the people it certainly scared was Jean Bodin, a French legal and political thinker. Already the author of a well-known treatise on historical methodology, he published his signature work of political theory, *The Six Books of the Commonwealth*, four years after the massacre, in 1576. The main thrust of the book was to defend a novel, absolutist conception of the power of the commonwealth or state, and specifically of the sovereign agent that holds that power: by his view, that could be a monarch but also an elite committee or even a committee of all the citizens. He must have found the notion of an absolute sovereign attractive for its promise of justifying a degree of political power that could suppress civil war and ensure a stable peace.[4]

Born in the late 1500s, Thomas Hobbes shared with Bodin a concern for a stable political order and a fear of where religious and related forms of dissension could lead. Tutor to generations of the wealthy and influential Cavendish family, he developed his political ideas in the context of such dissension, which was associated in England with the deep-running hostility between king and Parliament. This led to civil war in the 1640s, culminating in the execution of King Charles I in 1649, which was followed by a decade of republican government before the Restoration of the monarchy in 1660. Like Bodin, Hobbes argued strongly in favor of an absolute sovereign, be that an individual or committee, and like Bodin he thought that such a degree of sovereign power was essential to combat resistance and secure a stable peace.

Both Bodin and Hobbes agreed that the sovereign could be a committee: an elite committee as in an aristocracy, or an inclusive committee as in what they each chose to call a democracy. But they strongly favored the individual

4. On Bodin, see Hinsley (1967; 1986), Franklin (1973), Grimm (2015), and Lee (2016; 2021); and for general background, see Skinner (1978, vol. 2).

sovereignty of a monarch. Writing at a very different time, Jean-Jacques Rousseau followed them in the assumption that the sovereign would have to enjoy absolute power but, taking a stand for a more or less popular polity, argued that the only plausible sovereign is a committee of the whole citizenry (Rousseau 1997b, 1.4.4). He went along with Bodin and Hobbes, then, for very different reasons from theirs: not out of fear of anarchy and chaos, but rather because of a distaste for anything other than an intuitively popular regime.

Whether the sovereign is an individual or a committee, the important thing for all three thinkers is that power must reside in a single location. Political power must be vested, they thought, in an individual or corporate agent; it cannot be fractured among different authorities, as in the mixed constitution. Let a state become polycentric, they suggested—let it adopt a mixed constitution—and it will cease altogether to be a functional state; it will be "not a state," Bodin (1992, 105) comments, "but rather the corruption of a state." This commitment required them to think, therefore, that there is a single sovereign to be found in every effective polity. This exposed their view to empirical checking, and Bodin sought to defend it empirically by seeking to demonstrate, case by case, that every effective state involves a single sovereign.

Two softening assumptions, shared with later absolutists, made it relatively easy for Bodin to meet this empirical challenge. One, hardly plausible in contemporary states, is that the sovereign need control only legislation, since the legislative branch of government can monitor and shape the judicial and executive decisions taken in interpreting the law it formulates. The other is that a sovereign need not exercise power actively; it can do so by staying in the wings, relying on what we earlier called a virtual or standby form of control over how those entrusted to make laws actually perform.[5] Relying on assumptions like these, Bodin (1992, 105) argued that even Rome, the supposed exemplar of the mixed constitution, was actually ruled by the people, insofar as they were permanently poised to gather in one or another assembly for lawmaking purposes.

Bodin, Hobbes, and Rousseau took their belief in the need for an absolute, legislative sovereign to rule out any arrangement that disperses lawmaking

---

5. Richard Tuck (2016) argues that the distinction between sovereignty and government, common to Bodin, Hobbes, and Rousseau, made it possible to introduce a broadly majoritarian idea of democracy as a feasible ideal. On this ideal the people in any period would constitute a sleeping sovereign that may not actively endorse existing law but that does so virtually: while being in a position to revise any law on the books or in customary use, it does not choose to do this (Tuck 2016, 266–67).

THE POLITY DECENTRALIZED   121

power among many hands in the manner of the mixed constitution. They particularly criticized this in the rhetorical trope associated with the Greek idea of the mixed constitution as one that has monarchical, aristocratic, and democratic elements. Even Polybius played with this trope, arguing loosely that the consuls in Rome represented monarchy, the Senate aristocracy, and the committees of the people democracy (Polybius 2011, bk. 6). All the absolutists fulminate against such mixture, maintaining that it would break up the corporate agency of the state into different, conflicting subagencies.

But while all the absolutists express or simulate dismay at the idea of the mixed constitution, none of them makes a serious attempt to look at how power might be dispersed within a polity without depriving the state of its capacity as an agent (Franklin 1991). They derided the notion rhetorically rather than challenging it in argument. The tone was already set by Bodin (1992, 92). "The first prerogative of sovereignty," he says, "is to give the law to subjects. But," he then asks in disbelieving, rhetorical mode, "who will be the subjects and who will obey if they also have the power to make the law?"

Hobbes (1990, 16) derides the mixed regime as "mixarchy" and opines against it in a similarly unargued vein: "If the king bear the person of the people, and the general assembly bear also the person of the people, and another assembly bear the person of a part of the people, they are not one person, nor one sovereign, but three persons, and three sovereigns" (Hobbes 1994b, 29.16). And accentuating the note of mockery, he maintains that the mixed constitution makes the state into something like "a man that had another man growing out of his side, with a head, arms, breast, and stomach of his own," adding that if this man "had another man growing out of his other side," then "the comparison" would be "exact": there would be three elements corresponding to monarchy, aristocracy, and democracy (Hobbes 1994b, 29.17).

In *The Social Contract* Rousseau (1997b, 2.2.2) supports this mockery of a polycentric arrangement with a variation of his own. Comparing theorists of the mixed constitution to Japanese conjurors, he says that "they turn the Sovereign into a being that is fantastical and formed of disparate pieces; it is as if they were putting together a man out of several bodies one of which had eyes, another arms, another feet, and nothing else."

The Appeal of a Polycentric Regime

The basic appeal of polycentric organization is caught in the medieval Italian principle: *ubi multa consilia, ibi salus populi*; where many councils exist, there is the safety of the people (Waley 1988, 39–40). The idea is that if there are many different points at which any law or policy is to be examined, presumably with a view to how far it is collectively beneficial and coheres with the overall body of laws and policies, then the chances of its failing in such a respect are reduced. Failure might come about through incompetence or corruption on the part of authorities, and the idea is that increasing the gauntlet of checks that any measure must pass ought to reduce the danger of failure on the part of any one authority.

Increasing those checks, however, may itself pose dangers of a different kind. Where specific bodies or officials do not themselves have control over the overall outcome, this may lead to negligence since, as it is said, everybody's business is nobody's business. And where they each have a vested interest, it may lead to zealotry and gridlock, with some officials or bodies sticking out for the result that they themselves happen to favor. We shall return to such issues toward the end of the chapter when we look at the case for moderate rather than radical decentralization. For the moment, however, we look at the dangers that decentralizing the state can help to reduce, not at the dangers it itself can create.

To see the basic functional argument for polycentric organization, it is necessary only to reflect on the benefits that different modes of decentralization generate in securing citizens in the individual enjoyment of equality before the law, enabling each to know where they stand in relation to one another and to officials. The measures of separating, sharing, and outsourcing political power promise, each in their own way, to deliver a benefit on this front, guarding against the danger of incompetence or corruption.

Consider the separation of power first. To appreciate the attraction of this sort of measure, think about how lawmakers and executives would be able to perform, if there were no separation between the power they wield and the power of the courts in determining whether their laws or policies satisfy suitable constraints. Let those in charge of formulating the laws be in control of how the laws are interpreted judicially and executively, and they will find it correspondingly easier to breach the constraints associated with the rule of law. It will enable them to avoid constraints that keep laws general and prospective rather than letting them target particular groups, for example; constraints that make laws into publicly promulgated edicts rather than allowing them to be used in covert exercises of power; and constraints that prevent them from being vague enough to be used, now in this context, now in that, for favored, private purposes.[6]

6. These considerations argue not just for the independence of the judiciary, but also for some system of judicial review. Such a system would not necessarily resemble that in the United States, where appointees serve for life and are nominated in good part for their appeal to the

We saw that there is also a less salient, but no less important, benefit that the separation of the judiciary from the executive and legislative branches can confer. It can enable those branches to make or endorse credible contracts between the state and domestic bodies or individuals, thereby enabling a high degree of internal stability and prosperity. Those other parties can be sure that the state will be held accountable, so that its contractual commitments are credible, insofar as the agencies that make a commitment in the name of the state can be held to account by other agencies of the state—for example, the judiciary—if they fail to live up to their words. They can be held to account in that way just to the extent that the judiciary enjoys a certain autonomy in relation to the executive and legislature: just to the extent that there is a separation between those powers.

Moving on from the separation of powers, consider now the devices for sharing power within any branch. Within the legislative branch the sharing of power might come about via bicameralism, via the veto of the administration, via the veto of a constitutional court, or via federation. Within the executive branch it might come about via federation or via the outsourcing mentioned below. And within the judicial it might again come about via federation or, more generally, via measures like the law of precedent and the exposure of courts to appeal in higher tribunals. In each case, this sharing of power would guard against incompetence or corruption in one of those forums, making it harder for officials at any single site in the system to operate in a sloppy or self-serving manner.

Outsourcing power, to move to the third polycentric device, is usually motivated by one of three considerations: the need to have bodies that provide reliable information on government performance such as a bureau of statistics or a budget office; the need to have independent invigilators of those in government such as financial auditors, departmental inspectors, and commissioners charged with making specific inquiries; and the need for independent, impartial agencies such as electoral commissions and central banks to take charge in areas where other, often elected, authorities would have a conflict of interests (Tucker 2018; Sunstein and Vermeule 2020).

Outsourcing power to such informational, invigilating, and impartial bodies—such domain-specific authorities—promises to guard against salient dangers of corruption and incompetence in government. In the absence of an independent bureau of statistics or budget office or source of economic data, those in power would be in a ready position to hide their failures on such

---

government of the day. And it would be restricted to ensuring that decision-maker laws operate appropriately, meeting rule-of-law constraints for example. See Hickey (2019; 2023).

fronts. In the absence of auditors to keep tabs on the financial transactions of officials, those in office might well use public funds for private or partisan purposes. And in the absence of an electoral commission to determine electoral boundaries in wake of population changes, legislators and executives could adjust them, at whatever cost to the equality of citizens as voters, with a view to personal or party advantage.

These modes of decentralizing the state are bound to be reinforced in the presence of an established constitutional framework; an inclusive, electoral system that enables those in domain-general offices, legislative or executive, to be exposed to collective challenge; and a system that allows individual or organized groups of people to contest the proposals or actions of government—with full information on government performance—in channels as various as the courts, the media, and the streets (Pettit 2012; 2014). This means that even functional considerations as distinct from considerations of justice make a case for a constitutional, electoral, and contestatory democracy. We shall not dwell on that case here, however, recognizing that while they might be a source of beneficial decentralization, those measures may not be as functionally important as other, more traditional forms.

The Hobbesian Alternative

It may be useful to underline the contrast between the polycentric way of coping with the power of the state and a distinct argument, exemplified in Hobbes's work, as to why people need not be worried about the power that an incorporated state would give to the authorities in charge and, ultimately, to the sort of sovereign Hobbes envisages. On his view, the authorities may be able to undermine the security that law is supposed to provide for individual citizens, free of the checks that a mixed constitution would provide. But still, he claims, ordinary citizens need not have to worry about living under such a power.

A first ground on which he holds this is that life under a powerful set of authorities is more acceptable than the only alternative he contemplates: a state of nature—a war of all against all—in which "life is solitary, poor, nasty, brutish and short" (Hobbes 1994b, 13.9). We may not concern ourselves with this argument, however, since there is little reason to think, as we saw in chapter 1, that the absence of a state would leave people ungoverned by conventions and norms.[7]

---

7. The view we take is similar in this respect to Locke's position in his *Second Treatise of Government*, albeit he tells a contractual story rather than a story of emergence; we discuss his views in chapter 4.

A second reason why Hobbes is complacent about the power given to the sovereign is more interesting, offering a nice counterpoint to the reasons invoked in support of polycentric organization. He holds that any sovereign may be expected to deal reasonably well with citizens, since otherwise they might resist authority and choose to live outside the law.[8]

By Hobbes's view it is rationally obligatory and morally permissible— permissible in self-interest or natural law—for individuals to resist the efforts of the sovereign to hurt them, even hurt them in punishing breaches of the law; thus, he says that no one can enter a contract that denies them the right to resist (Hobbes 1994b, 14.29). Since this is strictly consistent with the sovereign's having the right and power to impose the law, however, Hobbes (1994b, 21.15) holds that this permission need not frustrate "the end for which the sovereignty was ordained": namely, in Cicero's words, "the safety of the people" (Hobbes 1994b, 27.3).

It will not frustrate that end, provided that the sovereign is prudent and does not force too many to live as outlaws. While others may be expected to rally behind the sovereign in punishing one or two defectors—in this case the sovereign's "actions are avouched by them all, and performed by the strength of them all, in him united" (Hobbes 1994b, 18.4)—they will be less and less reliable, the more outlaws of this kind there are. And so, by Hobbes's (1994b, 30.20–21) reckoning, the sovereign should be expected in prudence to be careful not to alienate too many subjects, and to prove a beneficent presence in people's lives. In this sense, as he says, "the good of the sovereign and people, cannot be separated."

Hobbes's argument that the sovereign has to be cautious about not getting too many people offside led his contemporary, Bishop Bramhall, to describe Leviathan as a "rebel's catechism" (Curley 1994, 142). What Hobbes justifies, however, is scarcely radical and was frequently justified in the eighteenth century as a benevolent despotism. He argues, in effect, that while the power that the authorities may enjoy under a state allows despotism, still despotic authorities will have reasons of prudence to be benevolent toward their citizens.

8. It may seem that Hobbes (1994b, chap. 18.6) also relies on a third consideration: viz., that it is impossible "to do injury to oneself" and that the sovereign cannot do injury to an incorporating member. But an "injury" in Hobbes's language means a wrong, not in natural law—this would be an iniquity, in his terminology—but in virtue of a prior contract: an injustice, as he often says. And under his social contract, the sovereign has power without stint so that there is nothing the sovereign could do in the enunciation of law that would count as a wrong. The point is clear, when Hobbes goes on to add that "they that have sovereign power may commit iniquity, but not injustice or injury in the proper signification."

The discretionary power that Hobbes would grant the authorities in a state—ultimately, the sovereign—is the sort of power enjoyed today by the authorities of many nondemocratic regimes and indeed of autocratic democracies also. What to think, then, about the Hobbesian argument that such power is acceptable to the extent that the authorities can be expected for reasons of prudential self-concern to be benevolent in exercising their power?

The argument assumes that if you are exposed to the unchecked or discretionary will of another—in the seventeenth century usage, the arbitrary will of another—that is not going to be a problem, so long as the person or body in question has any reasons not to hurt you, whether they be reasons of prudence or virtue. But this flies in the face of common sense and long tradition. If you are subject to the power of such a master, then however benevolent they may be, it is their will that is in charge, not yours. And that is already an offense against your interests. You may be able to act as you wish, given such benevolence. But you will be able to do so only if the master remains happy to let you act that way: in effect you will depend on the master's permission for doing anything you choose to do.

This complaint about subjection to a master, even a benevolent master, is associated with the republican tradition from Polybius and Cicero to Machiavelli and Harrington, and to a raft of eighteenth-century authors. It applies not only to the individual and private master, but also to the citizen in relation to the state and its authorities. And it directs us to a functional argument, not just an argument of justice, for decentralizing the state and keeping the authorities in check.

In a polity where officials have discretionary power, ordinary citizens will not know where they stand in relation to one another or to those officials. And this will be so, even if the laws are fine on paper. Subjection to unchecked authorities, however benevolent, will create an inhibiting reason for citizens to be cautious, cozying up to the officials or keeping out of sight. There would be no ground for such caution or cowardice, however, in the presence of polycentric protection; it would enable citizens to enjoy a totally different relationship with their rulers.

Think of how you would feel as a citizen in one or the other dispensation. Under the protective regime, you would be manifestly able to call on other authorities or other citizens in resisting an offending official or in retaliating against them; you would enjoy a power capable of countering their power. Under the prudential regime, you would be manifestly exposed to the official's abuse of power and could depend only on their long-term concern for themselves, or their inherent virtue, to damp any temptations to treat you badly. These would include the potentially powerful temptation, especially should you assert your rights under existing law, to show you who is boss.

The citizens of the regime with unchecked rulers could not know with any confidence where they stood in relation to one another and especially in relation to officials. Writing later in the seventeenth century, John Locke displayed a sensitivity to this point that Hobbes seems to have lacked. He argues there that it is vital to curb the power of a king over subjects, not just to give him an incentive not to misuse that power, but also on the grounds that otherwise the king may "make a prey of them when he pleases" (Locke 1960, s137). This gives nice expression to the thought behind the case for a polycentric state.

But it is one thing to hold that the polycentric organization of a state is desirable; it is quite another to show that it is feasible or possible. We shall argue over the next three sections that it is possible, even on the assumption that there must be a sovereign in any functional state. In the second section, we sketch the core argument shared among absolutist thinkers like Bodin, Hobbes, and Rousseau that every state must be organized around an individual or corporate sovereign and that it cannot therefore have a mixed constitution. In the third we provide an assessment of that argument, endorsing a somewhat revised version of their case for sovereignty but showing that it does not support their rejection of the mixed constitution. And then in the fourth section, we show that if a functionally effective state operates under a mixed or polycentric mode of organization, then it will have a sovereign, albeit one of a kind that traditional absolutists overlooked.

3.2 The Argument for Sovereignty

Behind the rhetoric of our three absolutists against the mixed constitution lay a general, innovative position on the nature of law and state. This was put with great force by Bodin, developed with extra sophistication by Hobbes, and given quite a novel twist by Rousseau. It may be useful in this section to summarize the form it took in these different thinkers as they used it to make a case for sovereignty and, as they thought, a case against the mixed constitution. We shall argue later, in the next section, that the argument for sovereignty is fundamentally sound but that it does not make a case against the mixed constitution; in that sense, we defend sovereigntism but reject absolutism.

In this summary, we abstract inevitably from some of the differences between the three figures, for the aim is to identify a line of thought that moved them in common rather than detail the thinking of any one individual. In this summary, we also concentrate on the more persuasive points made by them in support of the position taken, since the aim is to reconstruct an argument of a relatively persuasive sort rather than trace any idiosyncrasy or weakness in the reasoning of its earliest proponents. As we shall see in the next section, the argument, charitably construed, makes a sound case for the presence of a sovereign, with broadly the power they ascribe, in every functional state. We break with them, not on that point, but on the form that a sovereign may take.

There are six claims that are crucial to the sovereigntist argument, and it may be useful to set these out initially before looking in greater detail at each.

1. The function of the state is to establish a regime of laws
2. Laws are commands imposed on members of the society
3. As commands, laws presuppose an accepted, sovereign commander
4. This sovereign must be a proper agent, natural or corporate
5. And must be beyond legal and other forms of domestic control.
6. But may be bound by normative, contractual, and constitutive constraints

We now look at each of these claims in turn, indicating how the absolutists generally supported them and intruding some explanations of the way in which they understood them.

The Function of the State Is to Establish a Regime of Laws

The first sovereigntist claim is that the state is, in the terminology introduced earlier, a nomothetic body. This proposition passes in most of our sovereigntist authors without remark, figuring as a deep presupposition of their thinking. Thus, Bodin never addresses it, approaching the nature of the state and sovereignty, as we might expect of a lawyer, on the assumption that regimes he would have described as states or republics—mostly the terms were equivalent for him—are legal regimes.

Hobbes assumes in the same way, and without much explicit commentary, that having a state means living under laws. With the "Artificial Man, which we call a Common-wealth," he says, go "Artificial Chains, called Civil Laws" (Hobbes 1994b, 21.5). He argues that if the state or commonwealth is to establish peace among residents, as he assumes it will, then it must use laws to establish a common understanding of what each may demand of others and what each must deliver in return. The state will have to "come up with rules or measures" of a shared and public sort, he says, "that each man may know by them what he should call his own and what another's, what he should call just and unjust, honourable and dishonourable, good and bad; in summary, what he should do and what he should avoid doing in social life" (Hobbes 1998, 6.9).[9]

Rousseau takes it for granted in the same way as the others that the role of the state is to establish law but gestures at an argument that resembles, and may even echo, that of Hobbes. He assumes that if human beings are to live in peace and prosperity, then they must agree on what their reciprocal rights and duties are. And he holds that what the state does, at least if it acts properly, is to provide laws that can ground such agreement. "In the state of nature, where everything is common, I owe nothing to those to whom I have promised nothing. I recognize as another's only what is of no use to myself. It is not so in the civil state where all rights are fixed by law" (Rousseau 1997b, 6.3).

Laws Are Commands Imposed on the Members of the Society

It is important to understand the context in which Bodin made the second sovereigntist claim that laws are commands, bequeathing it to his successors. Roman law had come to be recognized in the medieval European world as the *jus commune*: the law endorsed by secular and ecclesiastical authorities (Woolf 1913; Berman 1983; Canning 1983; 1987; Loughlin 2010). This law was known from texts compiled in the sixth century under the sponsorship of the emperor, Justinian, which had been rediscovered late in the eleventh. Its precepts had come to be routinely invoked in interpreting or challenging local laws within European states; in negotiating differences between competing, often warring regimes, in particular the city-states of medieval and Renaissance Italy; and in determining the authority of the Holy Roman emperor in relation to such regimes and in relation to the pope.

Rejecting the notion of law as encoded in Justinian's texts, Bodin (1992, 38) opted for a view that would have been refreshingly straightforward if not entirely radical: it echoed some minor strains in medieval thought. "Law implies command," he says, and laws are imposed on subjects with the support, except when they are "permissive," of suitable "rewards or penalties" (Bodin 1992, 57). In putting forward this view, he dismissed the traditional aura and authority

---

9. As he puts it in *Leviathan*, they are "the rules, whereby every man may know, what goods he may enjoy, and what actions he may do, without being molested by any of his fellow-subjects" (Hobbes 1994b, 18.10).

surrounding Roman law, which had been treated almost like a sacred text—a set of deliverances subject to scholarly interpretation—that every secular or ecclesiastical authority had to acknowledge. Bodin may have been encouraged to turn his back on Roman law by his affiliation with a school of humanist scholarship that had begun to show that the Roman corpus of law was a potpourri of often conflicting opinions, derived from different periods in Rome's long history. The view of law as command must have seemed to him like a refreshing alternative.

The characterization of law as command was taken up with brio by Hobbes. It is "manifest," he says, that "law in general"—law, no matter by whom issued—is "command," and this opens the way for his definition of the law imposed by the state: "Civil law, is to every subject, those rules, which the common-wealth hath commanded him, by word, writing, or other sufficient sign of the will" (Hobbes 1994b, 26.2–3). In characterizing law as command, as we saw earlier, Hobbes contrasts it with counsel. Command issues from the will of the commander in a peremptory fashion—"for the benefit of him that prescribeth it"—where counsel is given on a prudential basis: for "the benefit of him, to whom the counsel is given" (Hobbes 1994b, 25.2–3).

Rousseau does not use the language of command in characterizing the law, but he does take the laws, like commands, to issue from will and to be experienced like commands as restrictions on the will of individual citizens. It is a "declaration" of "will" that "constitutes law," he says, lining up in that respect with his predecessors (Rousseau 1997b, 2.2.1). But where Bodin and Hobbes used this claim as part of a case for making the state strong enough to keep chaos at bay, Rousseau uses it to raise quite a different issue.

He assumes that it is an unquestioned good for any agent that they should not be bound to the will of another. He grounds this in the fact that "no will can consent to anything contrary to the good of the being that wills," and so must be averse to anything that would "shackle" it (Rousseau 1997b, 2.1.3). The laws of actual society do shackle people, he thinks, by contrast with their natural condition: "Man is born free, and everywhere he is in chains" (Rousseau 1997b, 1.1.1). But he takes it that some form of law is essential since, as we saw, law is needed by his lights to fix people's reciprocal rights and duties. Hence the problem on which he focuses is how to design things so that the will that is expressed in the law, and imposed on citizens, does not shackle or frustrate the will of those individuals.

This is a very different problem from that which motivated Bodin and Hobbes, but his approach to it assumes, as they assumed, that law has the form of a command: that it issues as a set of dictates from a ruling will. His response to the problem is to claim, famously, that if the sovereign is a majoritarian committee of all the citizens, and if those citizens vote in an appropriately disinterested manner—if they are not factionalized, for example—then the will expressed in law will be the general will, as he calls it: a will that exists within each citizen, side by side with their particular will.

As Commands, Laws Presuppose an Accepted, Sovereign Commander

There are two strands to the third claim in the sovereigntist credo. The first holds that if laws are commands, then there must be a commander at their origin: a figure whose will the laws manifest. It is this commander who constitutes the sovereign so that, as Bodin (1992, 92) says, "law is nothing but the command of the sovereign." And the fact that that commander uses laws to impose their presumptively unified will means that command cannot be divided: "Whenever one believes one sees sovereignty divided," as Rousseau (1997b, 2.2.4) urges, "one is mistaken."

The indivisibility that our three figures ascribe to sovereignty shows up in the mockery of the mixed constitution that they all endorse, usually targeting that idea in the rhetorical form in which it is a mixture of monarchy, aristocracy, and democracy. "If sovereignty is indivisible," Bodin (1992, 92) asks, "how could it be shared by a prince, the nobles, and the people at the same time?" And, as we saw, Hobbes (1994b, 29.16) derides that same model of political organization, suggesting that it would invest authority in "not one person, nor one sovereign, but three persons, and three sovereigns."

So much for the first strand in this claim. The second strand requires the commander or sovereign who dictates the law to be accepted, as our formulation has it, although that is not a word used by any of our three thinkers. In Hobbes and Rousseau, this constraint is associated with the contract between subjects or citizens that is needed to establish a sovereign de novo. For both, the state comes into existence with people agreeing among themselves to recognize some agent as sovereign, rallying in compliance behind the laws laid upon them by that figure, and thereby displaying their acceptance.[10]

---

10. While each thinks that entering the contract that establishes a sovereign must be a voluntary act, they differ on what this means. Rousseau appears to take a voluntary act in a relatively standard sense as one that is not taken for want of an intuitively acceptable alternative.

While Bodin does not invoke any such social contract, he is adamant that to be introduced as sovereign, an agent must be accepted in some standard, recognizable fashion by the subjects. Thus, he contrasts the usurper who seeks sovereign power "on his own authority" with someone who becomes sovereign "by way of election, or lot, or right of succession, or just war, or by a special calling from God" (Bodin 1992, 112). And he goes on to suggest that if the power of someone in office is often "called into question"—if in that sense it does not gain stable acceptance—then they do not really count as the sovereign (Bodin 1992, 115).

We return in the next section to two issues raised by the acceptance condition. One is how far acceptance should extend if we endorse something like the absolutist conception of sovereignty: whether it should be a requirement, not just of initial appointment, but of continued performance. The other issue is how exactly acceptance should be understood within an updated conception of sovereignty: whether, for example, it should be taken in the sense given to the term in chapter 1.

Even with those issues set aside, this absolutist claim about the sovereign who imposes the commands of the law contrasts with the claim that Herbert Hart (2012, 18) finds, at least "in substance," in *The Province of Jurisprudence Determined*, a classic text by the nineteenth-century jurist John Austin (1954). On Hart's reading of Austin, laws are also commands, but the commands are akin to the orders, backed by threats, that a gunman might use to coerce victims. The sovereign in this picture need not be authorized in contract or legitimized in any other way to issue commands and need not enjoy the acceptance of the citizenry in the assumption of that role. Paradoxically, the Austinian sovereign enjoys a less qualified and more absolutist form of power than the sovereign of the absolutists themselves.

This Sovereign Must Be a Proper Agent, Natural or Corporate

If the sovereign role is to issue commands, determining how they are to be carried out and checking whether they are successful, then as the fourth claim holds, the sovereign must clearly be a proper agent; they must reliably pursue

---

But Hobbes holds that acting out of fear in entering a contract—entering it for fear of the alternative—may still be a voluntary act (Hobbes 1994b, 6.54); see Pettit (2008a, 67–69). Voluntariness in that strained sense is still consistent with acceptance in the sense we gave the term in chapter 1, so long as submission appeals not just for reasons of fear alone, but also for the associated prospect of a stable peace.

certain purposes in accordance with reliably formed judgments about how best to do so. The overall purpose for our three sovereigntists will be to make laws for the citizenry. But this purpose, so they hold, encompasses a range of judicial and executive purposes as well.[11]

Bodin (1992, 59) is absolutely explicit on the range of concerns, and the variety of purposes, that the business of legislation is going to give the sovereign. "This same power of making and repealing law includes all the other rights and prerogatives of sovereignty," he holds, "so that strictly speaking we can say that there is only this one prerogative of sovereignty, inasmuch as all the other rights are comprehended in it." Those rights give the sovereign control, not just over judicial decisions, but also over any executive functions that are identified in law.[12]

Hobbes defends a similar point of view. Focusing on the sovereign's control over the judiciary, he argues that the judicial interpreters of the law—the same point would apply to the executive—should be subject to the sovereign as to "the supreme judicature" and not be allowed to alter the law intended by the sovereign in any way. He stresses that "it is not the letter, but . . . the authentic interpretation of the law (which is the sense of the legislator), in which the nature of the law consisteth," and argues on that basis that its interpreters should be appointed and presumably controlled by the sovereign or legislator (Hobbes 1994b, 26.20).[13]

---

11. Hobbes (1994b, 26.4) seems to have thought of legislation, not just as laying down general rules, but also as issuing quite specific edicts. Bodin (1992, 52) contrasted laws with edicts, and Rousseau (1997b, 4.2.7) insisted in *The Social Contract* on the need for laws to be general. See Tuck (2016, 132–34). What is important for all is that the interpretation of the law should not be determined by independent courts or, as with medieval Roman law, by independent scholars. As Hobbes (1994b, 26) says, "When question is of the meaning of written laws, he is not the interpreter of them, that writeth a commentary upon them."

12. The other rights he goes on to list are "declaring war or making peace; hearing appeals in last instance from the judgments of any magistrate; instituting and removing the highest officers; imposing taxes and aids on subjects or exempting them; granting pardons and dispensations against the rigor of the law; determining the name, value, and measure of the coinage; requiring subjects and liege vassals to swear that they will be loyal without exception to the person to whom their oath is owed."

13. On the grounds that in espousing the making of law as an end, the sovereign must also espouse the means required, Hobbes (1994b, 26) argues further that the sovereign must assume, not just "the power of supreme judicature," but also that "of making war or peace by his own authority; or of judging of the necessities of the Commonwealth; or of levying money and soldiers," and so on.

Rousseau (1997b, 3.2.3) follows Bodin and Hobbes in taking legislation to be the distinctive business of sovereignty and in sharing their assumption that in pursuing this project properly the sovereign will also take charge of the "application of the law." He is not as sensitive as the others, however, to what taking charge is likely to involve, suggesting merely that it requires the sovereign assembly to appoint judicial and executive officials to apply the law (Rousseau 1997b, 3.7.4). We can only assume that he would have taken this power of appointment, at least ideally, to give the assembly sufficient control to guard against misinterpretation of its laws.

While the three sovereigntists are agreed that in this sense the sovereign must be a proper agent, controlling for the discharge of a range of duties, they differ on the form that the sovereign may assume. Bodin and Hobbes think that the sovereign may be a natural individual like a monarch—one selected under a monarchical line of succession—or a corporate body like a relatively elite or inclusive committee of members. And both think that that agent may exercise its controlling role in a partially or wholly active way or in a wholly virtual or standby manner: that is, by stepping back and assuming the part of a standby or sleeping sovereign (Tuck 2016).

Bodin and Hobbes describe a state with an individual sovereign as a monarchy, describe the state with an elite committee in sovereign power as an aristocracy, and, giving the term a novel sense, cast the state that is ruled by a committee of all its citizens as a democracy. Thus, according to Bodin (1992, 90), in a monarchy "a single individual has the sovereignty"; in a democracy, "the whole people, or the greater part thereof"; and in an aristocracy, "the lesser part of the people." And that approach is faithfully followed by Hobbes (1994b, 19.1). When the sovereign "is one man, then is the Commonwealth a monarchy; when an assembly of all that will come together, then it is a democracy, or popular Commonwealth; when an assembly of a part only, then it is called an aristocracy."

In taking this line, Bodin and Hobbes not only rule out the possibility of a sovereign established by a mixed constitution, but also offer a novel construal of democracy, which is the only popular or inclusive regime they take to be a functional possibility. Whether or not they were aware of the fact, this construal is different from the original Greek understanding in which, as we saw, any regime counts as a democracy—even a mainly lottocratic system like Athens—if it gives considerable power to ordinary people (Ober 2008b). Their innovation in that regard made democracy—and, by their lights, any popular regime—look infeasible, as they probably wished. Their construal of the ideal led even progressive thinkers to distance themselves from what they called democracy down to the early nineteenth century when the word slowly came to be applied to various representative, usually constitutional systems.[14]

Rousseau takes a very different line on the possible forms of sovereignty, as we noted earlier. He assumes, as Hobbes had assumed in his earlier works, that in the emergence of any polity the individuals involved will first have to assemble as a body and then face the choice of determining whether to remain the sovereign or to transfer sovereignty to a monarch or aristocracy.[15] And then he argues that as an individual who "gives himself gratuitously" into the hands of another individual, abdicating his will and his freedom, "is not in his right mind," so an inclusive assembly that gave up its sovereignty would abdicate its will and freedom and be "a people of madmen" (Rousseau 1997b, 1.4.4). Assembled in an inclusive body, the citizenry can and should take expert advice, seeking to be collectively informed as well as individually impartial, but it must retain its right to make up its own mind: "the people cannot divest itself of this non-transferable right, even if it wanted to do so" (Rousseau 1997b, 2.7.7).

Does Rousseau embrace democracy, then, in the Bodin-Hobbes conception? Not quite, since he does not think that the sovereign assembly should apply its own laws, as that conception would allow. He denies that the popular sovereign might operate wholly on a standby basis, since he requires the people to assemble at periodic intervals to oversee legislation (Rousseau 1997b, 3.13.1). But he also denies that it might be wholly active, intervening in adjudication and administration as well as legislation. He thinks that members of the assembly must make decisions, as in legislation proper, only about its "subjects in a body and their actions in the abstract, never any man as an

14. The Bodinian conception explains the hostility to democracy in Federalist 10, for example. "The two great points of difference between a democracy and a republic are: first, the delegation of the government, in the latter, to a small number of citizens elected by the rest; secondly, the greater number of citizens, and greater sphere of country, over which the latter may be extended" (Madison, Hamilton, and Jay 1987). And it is equally present in James Mill's (1978, para. 24) famous essay on government, first published in 1819, where he objects to democracy, among other counts, on the ground that "a community in mass is ill adapted for the business of government"; he opts for a representative system that he casts as an invention of his own time, not a traditional ideal.

15. This assumption is made by Hobbes in works prior to *Leviathan* in 1651: for example, *De Cive*, published in 1642 in Latin, and soon translated into French. In this, as in much else, Rousseau was almost certainly influenced by the early Hobbes; apparently, he did not read *Leviathan*.

individual or a particular action" (Rousseau 1997b, 2.6.6). On the grounds that otherwise they may be affected by "the influence of private interests"—they may cease to be disinterested—he says that they should have no role in applying the laws they make: "it is not good that he who makes the laws execute them" (Rousseau 1997b, 3.4.2). At most, presumably, they should exercise a virtual, hands-off form of control in the domain of legal application.

Although Bodin, Hobbes, and Rousseau differ on the forms that sovereigns and states may assume, however, and although they differ on the precise form that an inclusive sovereign power should take, they are united by one very distinctive assumption to which we turn in the next section. This is that when an inclusive or elite assembly constitutes the sovereign, it will do so by organizing a majority vote on each issue that comes before it, with provisos to govern the case of ties (Hobbes 1994b, 16.15–17). The assembly will let the majoritarian voice speak for it, with members rallying behind that voice in compliance with what it requires of them as citizens or officials.

Bodin is quite specific that in a democracy, at least when it operates in active mode, decisions are inevitably made by majority vote, so that a majority may impose a law that a minority opposes.[16] Thinking of the commonwealth as a group agent that needs a sovereign voice to represent it, Hobbes (1994b, 16) echoes the thought in his distinctive register: "If the representative consist of many men, the voice of the greater number must be considered as the voice of them all." For Hobbes this majority voice must be licensed by a unanimous agreement or contract to let it do so. And on this same basis Rousseau (1997b, 1.6.3) too takes it that in his inclusive assembly members will follow the rule of majority voting: "The law of majority rule is itself something established by convention," in the unanimously supported social contract.

And Must Be Beyond Legal and Other Forms of Domestic Control

The fifth sovereigntist claim is probably the most distinctive, since it doesn't just argue for the existence in every regime of a single sovereign, individual or corporate; it also maintains that that sovereign enjoys what is often described as absolute authority and power. The claim puts the sovereign above the law and above the power of any other individuals or bodies in the society.

16. This is in book 2, chapter 7, which is not included among the chapters translated in Bodin (1992). See Bodin (1967).

Whether the sovereign be natural or corporate in character, our three figures insist that having the power to make and unmake law rules out the possibility of subjection to law. As Bodin and Hobbes both point out, such subjection would be inconsistent with the characterization of laws as commands. Bodin (1992, 12) makes the telling point: "Although one can receive law from someone else, it is as impossible by nature to give one's self a law as it is to command one's self to do something that depends on one's own will." Hobbes (1994b, 26.6) picks up the same point when he argues that no sovereign power, whatever the form, can be subject to laws established or endorsed by that entity itself. Thus, he says of a monarch that "having power to make, and repeal laws, he may when he pleaseth, free himself"; no one "can be bound to himself," he explains, "because he that can bind can release."

Perhaps because of following Bodin and Hobbes on this point, Rousseau (1997b, 1.7.2) is equally insistent that the sovereign is above the laws: "It is contrary to the nature of the body politic for the Sovereign to impose on itself a law which it cannot break." Thus, there is no "kind of fundamental law that is obligatory for the body of the people." The sovereign assembly of the people, as he puts it elsewhere, is "above judge and law" (Rousseau 1997b, 2.5.7).

But not only is the sovereign subject in this sense to no legal control, being unbound by any law that it prescribes or allows to pass. The sovereign by the account of our three figures is also beyond the control of any other individual or body—any would-be authority—in the state. Bodin (1992, 11) puts forward this claim as something that is intuitively unquestionable. "Persons who are sovereign must not be subject in any way to the commands of someone else," he says, since otherwise the sovereign would not be able "to give the law to subjects, and to suppress or repeal disadvantageous laws"; the sovereign could hardly exercise such a power, so the thought goes, if there were "persons having power of command over him."

Hobbes gives the same unqualified support to this idea but puts forward an interesting argument in its defense. If the sovereign is established by a unanimous contract on the part of individuals to submit to such a power, as he thinks, then to permit individuals to challenge the sovereign's exercise of the power would be to allow them to allege a breach of covenant. But, Hobbes (1994b, 18) urges, "if any one or more of them pretend a breach of the covenant made by the sovereign at his institution, and others or one other of his subjects, or himself alone, pretend there was no such breach, there is in this case no judge to decide the controversy: it returns therefore to the sword again."

The idea here is that if citizens could challenge the sovereign under the constitution of the commonwealth—if, in other words, the challenge was not to be decided by the sword, as in war—then there would have to be a third figure to judge or decide the challenge. In Hobbes's view there is no such judge to be had in the state, so challenges cannot be allowed: the sovereign must not be subject to contestation or control by any other individual or body. Rousseau (1997b, 1.6.7) follows Hobbes in this argument: "if individuals were left some rights"—presumably, rights of contestation—"there would be no common superior who might adjudicate between them and the public." Thus, "each, being judge in his own case on some issue, would soon claim to be so on all," and they would fall back into "the state of nature."

The sovereign envisaged by these figures, then, is not only above the law they issue or authorize. The sovereign is also superior to any other body within the polity. It lies beyond both formal and informal varieties of domestic control, enjoying what all of them are happy to describe as absolute power.

They emphasize the extent of this power in their different ways. Bodin (1992, 23) says that "the main point of sovereign majesty and absolute power consists of giving the law to subjects in general without their consent." Hobbes holds that the task of the sovereign in relation to subjects is "to keep them all in awe" (1994b, 13.8). And Rousseau (1997b, 2.12.3) treats it as an ideal that however "independent of all the others," each citizen should be "excessively dependent on the City"; in effect, that they should be unconditionally subject to the majoritarian will of the whole.

But May Be Bound by Normative, Contractual, and Constitutive Constraints

The conclusion of the absolutist argument is that within the polity there must be a sovereign at the origin of law, operating beyond domestic control, legal or otherwise: that is, beyond the grip of constraints that can be enforced against it regardless of sovereign consent. But this position supports the final claim: that the sovereign may be subject to constraints that define an ideal of performance so long as they are not enforceable; to constraints set up by mutual consent, as in a voluntary contract; and to constraints that an agent must satisfy just to count as sovereign. The sovereign power may be subject, as we shall describe these restrictions, to purely normative constraints, to contractual constraints, and to constitutive constraints.

That the sovereign may be constrained in a purely normative, unenforceable manner shows up in Bodin's insistence that the sovereign should not break divine or natural law. "But as for divine and natural laws," Bodin (1992, 13) says, "every prince on earth is subject to them, and it is not in their power to contravene them unless they wish to be guilty of treason against God." But this constraint is not enforceable against the sovereign, and it does not introduce a bond of the kind that Bodin wants to exclude.

Hobbes takes a similar line in arguing that the sovereign is subject to many of the laws of nature, as he calls them. "To the care of the sovereign belongeth the making of good laws," he says, explaining that a "good law is that which is needful, for the good of the people" (Hobbes 1994b, 30.20). This sort of care imposes a long range of duties on that individual or body: to see "that justice be equally administered to all degrees of people," for example, "to make a right application of punishments and rewards," and "to choose good counsellors." This restriction by the laws of nature, however, does not involve subjection to the will of another. Hobbes (1994b, 15.41) takes those laws to be "dictates of reason" that indicate to a person what is in their interest. Thus, if they require the sovereign to care for the good of the people, that is only because "the good of the sovereign and people cannot be separated" (Hobbes 1994b, 30.21).

Rousseau is less forthcoming on whether the sovereign is subject to normative, unenforceable constraints, but his overall picture commits him to that view. The sovereign exists in his account by virtue of being supported by the social contract that individuals make to submit themselves to the whole: this is "the act by which a people is a people," assembled under its own sovereign rule (Rousseau 1997b, 1.5.2). But to rule itself properly as a people, the assembly must embody the general will—a will that "is always upright and always tends to the public utility" (Rousseau 1997b, 2.3.1)—not the will of a self-serving faction. And that means that members of the assembly must vote in a disinterested manner. Specifically, they must vote on the basis of what "is advantageous to the State," not what is "advantageous to this man or to this party" (Rousseau 1997b, 4.1.6). But this requirement on the assembly of individuals who constitute the sovereign can only be a normative constraint, since there is no way in which others could force the assembly to satisfy it.

As our three figures agree that the sovereign may be subject to normative, unenforceable constraints, so they admit that the sovereign may also be subject to voluntarily undertaken, contractual constraints. Thus, "if a sovereign prince promises another prince to keep laws that he or his predecessors have made," Bodin (1992, 13) says, "he is obligated to keep them if the prince to whom he gave his word has an interest in his so doing": that is, if that prince does not implicitly or explicitly release him. And the same even holds if the sovereign enters a contract with a subject. Such a contract also "obligates the two parties reciprocally and one party cannot contravene it to the prejudice of the other and without the other's consent" (Bodin 1992, 15).

Hobbes also makes room for this possibility. As mentioned in the opening chapter, he argues that "if a subject have a controversy with his sovereign, grounded on a precedent law, he hath the same liberty to sue for his right as if it were against a subject, and before such judges as are appointed by the sovereign" (Hobbes 1994b, 21.19). The controversy, as he explains, may concern debt or lands or fines or whatever, where the right of the subject depends on the fact that the sovereign operates "by force of a former law, and not by virtue of his power"; this ensures that "the suit is not contrary to the will of the sovereign."

Rousseau does not explicitly hold that the sovereign assembly can enter a binding contract with individual members, although there is nothing in his view that would make that impossible; the assembly might contract with one of its members, presumably, to perform some task for the state: say, to construct a public building or run some public event. And he, like the others, would also be presumably open to the sovereign making a binding contract with other sovereigns, for the sake of peace; "with regard to foreigners," he says, the sovereign "becomes a simple being, an individual" (Rousseau 1997b, 1.7.2).[17]

Finally, all three of our sovereigntists imply that there are constitutive constraints that must be satisfied by any sovereign, as there are normative and contractual constraints to which they may be subject.[18] One constitutive constraint that they explicitly endorse, as we saw under the third claim, is that if the authority at the source of law is to count as sovereign then in its assumption of that role, it must be accepted by the citizenry. For Bodin, the sovereign

17. Hobbes might have a problem in defending this particular possibility, since he thinks that a party can make a valid contract with another only if there is an assurance on each side that the other will abide by its terms; at least in the case of a contract or covenant involving a promise of future behavior, that will require the existence of an enforcer in his view (Hobbes 1994b, 22.29).

18. For a similar view of the constitutive constraints to which a sovereign may be subject, although not the majority constraint we consider in a moment, see Loughlin (2010, 67–70). And for a contemporary assumption that there are constitutive constraints to which a sovereign may be subject, see Malcolm (1991, 21): "A constitution does not limit sovereign authority in the sense of opposing it and reducing it. What it does is to determine—that is, state the rules for—the ways in which that authority is exercised."

must be appointed under some accepted protocol and not "on his own authority." And for Hobbes and Rousseau the sovereign must be introduced under the terms of a unanimous social contract among individuals to submit to a common rule.

Apart from the acceptance of subjects, a further constitutive constraint that the sovereigntists all acknowledge, although only implicitly in this case, applies where the sovereign is a corporate body or committee. Not often noticed as a constraint, this consists in the requirement they impose that the committee, whether of an elite or of the whole, should operate by majority voting. Subject to arrangements for overcoming ties, the constraint requires that a majority should support every law that is passed, every decision that is made. The committee might agree to require supermajoritarian support for certain changes but if a majority wishes, they can set aside that requirement at any point.[19]

The assumption in our three figures is that there is no other way apart from majoritarian voting for the body to constitute an agent and a sovereign. Should the members act on less than a majority, so the idea goes, then it will not be the committee proper, and not the sovereign proper, that acts. The membership will have been displaced—its role will have been taken over—by those who break with the majoritarian way of doing things.

Is the individual sovereign, by contrast with the committee, bound in any parallel way for the absolutists? The question arises for Bodin and Hobbes but not for Rousseau since he rejects the idea of the monarchical sovereign. For Bodin at least, the answer is affirmative: the monarch is bound constitutively by an appropriate rule of succession and cannot nominate who is to succeed them after their death or, presumably, abdication. He thinks that the appropriate rule is one under which the successor, if possible, should be the "nearest male relative of the paternal line and without division" (Bodin 1992, xlv).

19. True, Rousseau (1997b, 4.2.10) suggests that on some issues supermajority support may be needed "to declare the general will." But this is a normative, unenforceable recommendation. Besides, it cannot be irrevocably imposed by the assembly on itself: if supermajoritarian support were unforthcoming, a majority of supporters could reject the recommendation at any point, citing the social contract, according to which "the vote of the majority always obligates all the rest" (Rousseau 1997b, 4.2.7). On this account, what Rousseau recommends is something like the practice of the U.S. Senate in requiring a special majority to introduce certain laws, where that requirement can itself be set aside by a majority vote. Unlike Rousseau, Bodin (1967, bk. 2, chap. 7) does seem open to the possibility that a committee might irrevocably require supermajoritarian support in certain cases, but he doesn't make anything of the possibility in his general theory and we ignore it here.

Perhaps because of recognizing the problems of succession in England of his time, Hobbes (1994b, chap. 19) holds instead that it is best if the monarch nominates in advance the person who is to succeed, laying down several rules that should operate in the absence of such a nomination. Thus, he acknowledges no constitutive constraint on the decisions the individual monarch may make that parallels the majoritarian constraint on the sovereign committee.

Constitutive constraints on sovereignty have a special significance because when they are relevant, they would constrain the extent to which the sovereign can change decision-maker laws. While the sovereign is assigned the power to change any laws it enunciates, that is strictly true only of the laws enunciated in accordance with constitutive constraints. Thus, the committee sovereign cannot amend the majoritarian constraint that absolutists recognize; any supermajoritarian rule it chooses to impose on itself, as we noted, may be rejected at any time by a majority.

We should notice a final complication raised by the constitutive constraints of sovereignty before moving on. For all the absolutists, a sovereign must be accepted by citizens or subjects in the assumption of a sovereign role. But must the sovereign continue to be accepted, once established in that role? Is this too a constitutive requirement? We shall argue that it should be a requirement of sovereignty under our revision of the absolutist conception, on the grounds that giving it that status would reflect the spirit of the approach. But it would license rebellion against a sovereign-turned-tyrant and that would not have appealed in traditional absolutist circles.

Bodin and Hobbes are explicit in ruling out rebellion, recognizing no doubt that to allow citizens to overthrow a sovereign-turned-tyrant would be to condone and even encourage civic chaos of the form they each feared.[20] They take acceptance to be necessary for any individual or body to assume a sovereign role. But each of them holds that if a previously accepted sovereign becomes tyrannical, presumably losing general acceptance, still they will remain the sovereign. Thus, Bodin (1992, 6) holds that "the tyrant"—plausibly, the sovereign turned tyrant—"is nonetheless a sovereign." And while Hobbes requires that the sovereign be established by a social contract, he does not think that they cease to be sovereign just because they begin to operate as a tyrant,

---

20. Insofar as they uphold this view, Bodin and Hobbes cannot treat it as a constitutive constraint on the state that it should rule by law, since tyranny might involve ad hoc, arbitrary decision making. But they obviously think of this constraint as quasi-constitutive, as we might put it: a constraint that is constitutive for the state in what they take to be the standard case.

contrary to his laws of nature; dismissing this idea, he says that the terms "sovereignty" and "tyranny" differ, not in extension, but only in emotional tone (Hobbes 1994b, Review and Conclusion Sect. 9).

What about Rousseau? Does he take continuing acceptance by the citizens to be a constitutive constraint that the assembly of all must continue to satisfy if it is to remain the sovereign? Or does he think, like Hobbes, that no matter how badly the assembly begins to rule—no matter how tyrannical it becomes—still the fact that it was accepted in the social contract means that it remains the sovereign in such a case?

The issue is challenging for him, since he faces a hard choice (Pettit 2016b). Let citizens be entitled to reject the sovereign in such a case—effectively, in what they believe to be such a case—and the state will be chronically unstable. Let them be prohibited from overthrowing a factionalized assembly, and by his own account the state will be oppressive; "the characteristics of the general will" will no longer be "in the majority," and there will no longer be "any freedom" (Rousseau 1997b, 4.2.9). But Rousseau does not address the issue and it is unclear what he would say.[21]

3.3 Taking Stock of the Argument

With this presentation of the absolutist argument for sovereignty, we can now turn to its assessment. We argue that with one crucial revision, it is intuitively compelling but, contrary to the belief of the absolutists themselves, that it does not make a good case against the mixed constitution.

We look in the first part of the discussion at the six claims involved, upholding sovereigntism under an interpretation that introduces a revised conception of the constitutive constraint of acceptance. This revision is meant to make the belief in sovereignty more plausible, not to make the claim defended about the mixed constitution any easier to defend; it is a charitable revision insofar as it is faithful to many strands in absolutist thinking. Having explored and accepted the six sovereigntist claims, we then go on to show that the absolutists

---

21. *The Social Contract* of 1762 suggests that he would recoil from the prospect of instability and agree that despite corruption a sovereign assembly may still count as sovereign: "if individuals were left some rights"—to contest the sovereign—"there would be no common superior who might adjudicate between them and the public" (Rousseau 1997b, 1.6.7). But he seems to take the opposite view in *A Discourse on Inequality* (1997a, II.45), written some years earlier, when he says that as soon as the "fundamental laws" that give power to the magistrates "are destroyed . . . everyone would by right revert to his natural freedom."

were nevertheless mistaken in two important respects: in their belief in the possibility of government by majoritarian assembly and in their rejection of the mixed constitution.

The First Three Sovereigntist Claims

The first sovereigntist claim is that the function of the state is to establish a regime of laws, rather than a regime in which government is conducted in ad hoc, case-by-case decision making. But that claim is implied by the nomothetic view of the polity with which we have been working and, since we have already argued for that way of thinking about the state, we do not need to say anything more in assessing it.

The second claim is that laws are commands imposed on members of the society. This may not be persuasive if it is taken to mean that all laws unconditionally prescribe or proscribe action. Many laws do not enjoin or forbid things in the unconditional manner of criminal statutes, to be sure, but make things possible by setting out how certain results are to be achieved. They dictate how a charge of tort may be brought, how a contract may be made legally binding, how something can be bequeathed or inherited, how a company may be formed, and so on.

Even laws of this enabling kind, however, give instructions on what individuals are to do if they desire the results specified; they represent hypothetical imperatives, if not commands of the ordinary kind. They are instances of command, in the sense in which, as we saw, Hobbes opposes it to counsel. Each is issued on the assumption that the only reason for obeying it is that that is "the will of him that says it": in the case of law, the will of the sovereign (Hobbes 1994b, 25.2–3). Thus, the recognition of enabling law does not argue against the claim, and we may let it pass.[22]

The third sovereigntist claim is that being commands, laws presuppose an accepted, sovereign commander. That there must be a sovereign commander follows straightforwardly. And that the introduction of this sovereign must be accepted is necessary if there is to be a difference between the regime of brute force, such as a criminal organization might impose, and a regular sort of state.

But as we noted already, this reference to acceptance raises two issues for us, if we are to think of endorsing something like absolutist sovereignty. The

---

22. Bodin (1992, 57) may focus on unconditional imperatives, however, since he implies that "permissive" laws, as he describes them, are not commands.

one bears on whether acceptance can be required, by way of a constitutive constraint, to extend beyond how the sovereign is appointed to how the sovereign performs. And the second bears on how acceptance can be understood in this context and, specifically, on whether it can be understood in the way we construed it in chapter 1. We shall argue that acceptance can be extended in this way, and that it can be understood in the manner of our earlier discussion, while remaining faithful to the spirit of the absolutist view.

We need to extend the acceptance requirement so that it constrains the performance as well as the appointment of the sovereign, if we are to put a plausible restriction on any individual or body that is to count as sovereign. We have acknowledged that a functional, nomothetic state that ceases to operate by law may still deserve the name of state, albeit an outlier state. But if we are to associate sovereignty with statehood proper—if we are to allow that a ruler who reigns by intimidation alone is not a proper sovereign—then we need to introduce an extended conception of acceptance. True, the extension requires a break with the opposition of absolutists like Bodin and Hobbes to rebellion of any sort. But it is needed to satisfy their common and deeper commitment to thinking of the state in benign, broadly nomothetic terms. Unless we introduce it, for example, we will lose "the great difference," in Rousseau's (1997b, 1.5.1) phrasing, "between subjugating a multitude and ruling a society."

But wouldn't this extension of the acceptance constraint put the sovereign under the control of rebellious citizens and thereby conflict with a core requirement of sovereignty? No, it would not. The reason, which will be more fully explored in the next chapter, is that the citizenry that might rise in rebellion do not exist as an established agent or agency that might enjoy continuing control over the sovereign. If they do rebel, then they will do so by teaming up to act together for that purpose. But the team they will form in such a case will come into existence only for that purpose, in an ad hoc response to a manifestly unacceptable level of performance by the sovereign. It will not enjoy the status of an agent or agency that might exercise control over the sovereign.

Turning now to the second issue raised, how should we understand the notion of acceptance in this context? The natural line to take is that the sovereign should be accepted in the sense in which, by the argument of chapter 1, the decision-maker laws needed for any legal system, together with the decision-taker laws that they are used to support, may be expected to attract acceptance. Many of those laws may favor some citizens more than others and not be endorsed enthusiastically in every quarter. But still, they will gain acceptance on all sides insofar as the order they establish has an appealing feature—say, that of enabling citizens to coordinate mutual expectations—and is not supported just on the basis of fear of those in power.

If the decision-maker laws of an established state are likely to be accepted in this way, then the sovereign they put in place will be accepted in a corresponding sense. Thus, the sovereign may be accepted on the grounds that the regime has a generally attractive property—that of coordinating their expectations of what they and others may do without let or hindrance—even when the acceptance is reluctant rather than enthusiastic. The role of that generally appealing property in motivating their acceptance means that while citizens may be partially motivated to obey the law by fear of legal sanction, they will not obey it out of fear alone. If they did then sovereign and state would rely merely on intimidation and, in an extreme form, would constitute a reign of terror.

On our revision of the acceptance claim made by traditional absolutism, then, the sovereign must be a power that is acceptably introduced and performs acceptably over time, where acceptance is understood in our minimal sense. The citizens must have at least a partial reason to abide by the sovereign's laws over and beyond the fear of incurring sanction or punishment. Even under the unrevised absolutist understanding of the acceptance condition, as we saw, the sovereign envisaged is very different from the gunman sovereign postulated by John Austin. The revised version marks the contrast sharper, as it does the contrast with the sort of sovereign envisaged in other authors.

A good example of such an author may be Carl Schmitt (2005, 5), who seems to be contemptuous of the idea of making the claim to sovereignty conditional on acceptance. The contempt appears on one reading of his famous mantra: "sovereign is he who decides on the exception"; sovereign is he, in other words, who decides on whether an emergency should be declared at any time and the constitution set aside. An army powerful enough to launch a coup d'état, if its commanders so wished, would be a sovereign under one construal of that account, although it might not enjoy acceptance in the community.[23]

One final comment. We argued earlier that if laws are accepted in the sense explained, then this likely means that they will be internalized, with citizens

---

23. David Dyzenhaus (2015, 346) is kinder to Schmitt, arguing that he held a view "ambiguous between the claim that the one who as a matter of fact decides on the state of exception is sovereign"—this is the reading adopted here—"and the claim that the sovereign, by virtue of his position as sovereign, is the one who gets to decide on the state of exception." See too Mueller (2003).

each coming to prefer that others conform as well as they. And as that internalization is recognized as something manifest to all, anyone will be manifestly able to invoke the law with the authority of the community, so that the law will be collectively ratified as a norm to which every member is subject. A similar point will hold of the sovereign that is accepted in the sense introduced here by the citizens at large. The sovereign's acceptance by the community will also get to be ratified by the citizenry, bearing out a remark of Herbert Hart's (2012, 76–77) that if there is to be a sovereign—he is himself a skeptic—then that can only be on the basis of accepted norms.

The Last Three Sovereigntist Claims

What, finally, of the last three of the claims made by our sovereigntists? The fourth claim that the sovereign may be a natural or corporate agent is unproblematic, at least when we abstract from the view that a corporate agent can only be a majoritarian committee; we criticize that view in the next section.

Skipping the fifth claim for the moment, the sixth claim is also unproblematic, since any sovereign is liable to be subject to normative, contractual, and constitutive constraints. The only aspect of the claim that is worth emphasizing derives from the revision proposed for the acceptance condition: that the sovereign should continue to be accepted by the citizenry in how they exercise power, not just have received their power under an accepted procedure. This revision means that the sovereign that becomes tyrannical and ceases to be accepted in even our minimal sense ceases to be a sovereign proper; it fails the constitutive constraint of acceptance. And it implies that ruling by law is also a constitutive constraint on sovereignty, a claim that fits with the general spirit of the absolutist approach.

We may turn, finally, to the fifth claim that the sovereign must not be legally or otherwise controlled within the polity. The sovereign in our conception is not only in charge of the legislative framing and the executive and judicial interpretation of the decision-taker laws. The sovereign is also in charge of decision-maker laws to the extent that this is allowed by constitutive constraints on the notion of sovereignty: for example, by the majoritarian constraint that binds the sovereign committee envisaged by the absolutists. As the source of decision-taker and decision-maker laws, the sovereign cannot be subject to those very laws; that would make it impossible for the sovereign to change them and would undermine the very notion of sovereignty. But as the sovereign cannot be subject in that sense to the laws, so the sovereign cannot be subject to any other power within the country: any other continuing agent or agency; such subjection would give that other power control over the law.

It is important to emphasize that the sovereign, on this conception, controls decision-maker as well as decision-taker laws, albeit within constitutive constraints. This is because the term "sovereign" is often used to refer to just the authority that is put in charge of decision-taker laws, under the decision-maker laws that are in force. A. V. Dicey (1982), the nineteenth-century English jurist, described that authority in Britain—the parliament, as he took it to be—as the legal sovereign. But recognizing that this authority does not itself dictate the terms under which it operates, he says that the political sovereign is the authority that controls those terms. Emphasizing the role that referenda can play in changing those terms, he takes the electorate in Britain of his time to be the political sovereign in the country.

Would this move fit with the traditional notion of the sovereign, and the line of argument adopted here? No, for two reasons. The sovereign to which the work of Bodin, Hobbes, and Rousseau directs us occupies simultaneously the legal and political roles that Dicey distinguishes. And the electorate that he takes to be the political sovereign is not the sort of corporate agent that could exercise control over decision-maker law. It does not have a purpose or purposes that it systematically pursues across different situations in the manner required for agency. The electorate may team up to act together, as occasion demands, but as we noted in discussing a rebellious citizenry, such an ad hoc collectivity does not constitute an agent; we return to the point in the next chapter.

The assessment of the argument for sovereignty gives us reason for holding, with absolutists, that there really must be a sovereign in every state, or at least every well-ordered, incorporated state. But we should turn now to assessment of the claim that makes them into absolutists, not just sovereigntists: their rejection of the mixed or polycentric constitution. They argue that while the citizenry in general may be involved via a majoritarian committee in governing as sovereign of the state, they cannot be involved in government in the fashion associated with the mixed or polycentric constitution; the state cannot be decentralized in that way.

It turns out that they are doubly mistaken on this front. The majoritarian sovereign and state is not a feasible institution—it cannot operate as a corporate agent—whereas the polycentric state is perfectly feasible. There is a problem that makes the majoritarian proposal unworkable and no such problem—and, on the face of it, no other problem—that stands in the way of the polycentric alternative.

The Failure of the Majoritarian Proposal

According to the absolutist view, the non-monarchical state has no option but to rely on something like an assembly or committee—perhaps a parliament, perhaps a cabinet—to provide the voice and the law around which citizens can incorporate. And that assembly or committee must form the corporate mind by majority voting among its members. As Hobbes (1994b, chap. 16.15–17) puts it, allowing that special arrangements may be needed to cope with ties: "If the representative consist of many men, the voice of the greater number must be considered as the voice of them all."

In taking this view, the absolutists were not on their own. Even in medieval times, the assumption among political thinkers is that "voting in the general assembly and councils is by numerical majority" (Canning 1980, 28). And John Locke (1960, s96) suggests in his *Second Treatise of Government* that the idea has a mechanical basis, arguing that with any sort of body, physical or social, "it is necessary the body should move that way whither the greater force carries it" and that in the case of a social body this greater force is revealed in "the consent of the majority."

It is a mistake to think, however, that any corporate agent, including the state, can have its voice and mind formed via majority voting in any assembly, elite or popular. Such a voice, as we know, must be reliably coherent if it is to play the guiding role required; it must be formed on such a basis that any evidence of incoherence is liable to prompt repair. But the striking thing about majority voting is that even in a committee of individually consistent members, it can support an inconsistent set of views over various issues. And if it supports such a set of views, it will do so with a mechanical rigor that would not allow for repair.

Suppose that a small governing committee of three members is the sovereign within a state. Suppose that members are committed not to borrow money or print money and not to allow a budget deficit. And suppose that over time, or perhaps at a certain juncture in time, they face votes on the following three issues: whether to hold taxes, whether to raise defense spending, and whether to raise other spending. In taking a line on such issues they would be implementing the law that gives them these powers and, we may assume, proposing a law to implement the policy adopted.

Suppose that each member has a consistent but different set of views on how to resolve these issues. The first person, a fiscally conservative hawk, thinks that taxes should be held, defense spending raised, and other spending reduced. The second, a conservative dove, thinks that taxes should be held, defense spending reduced, and other spending raised. The third—a chicken because of not wanting to take a stand—thinks that taxes should be raised and both forms of spending raised as well.

If the committee uses majority voting to determine the corporate view— their view as a sovereign group and hence the view of the state—then they will find themselves with a problem. A majority, Hawk and Dove, will support holding taxes. A majority, Hawk and Chicken, will support raising defense spending. And a majority, Dove and Chicken, will support raising other spending as well. If no money can be raised by other means, as we may assume, and the budget must be balanced, the committee will support an incoherent package of policies.

The package is captured in the bottom line of table 1, which reveals how the majority is driven by the votes of members to embrace an inconsistent set of policies.

TABLE 1

	Hold taxes?	Raise defense spending?	Raise other spending?
Hawk	Yes	Yes	No (reduce)
Dove	Yes	No (reduce)	Yes
Chicken	No (raise)	Yes	Yes
Majority	Yes	Yes	Yes

Majority voting is attractive to the extent that it makes the views of the committee responsive to the views of individual members. But it is unattractive in this sort of case, because it ensures that the committee's set of views, and the set of views they would present in the name of the state—the set of views they would want to embody in law—is incoherent and irrational. The members of the committee, then, confront a dilemma: a discursive dilemma, as it is has come to be called. They may opt for individual responsiveness; in which case they must give up on corporate rationality. Or they may opt for corporate rationality; in which case they must give up on individual responsiveness. They face a hard choice.[24]

24. The discursive dilemma is identified in Pettit (2001a; 2001b). It is a generalized version of the doctrinal paradox in legal theory; see Kornhauser and Sager (1993; 2004). See too List (2006).

The discursive dilemma will be there to threaten any majoritarian committee, not just a small committee of three members. And so, it will be there to threaten the aristocratic or democratic proposals put forward by our absolutists in explaining how government can be partly or wholly inclusive of citizens. Let the inclusive sovereign try to operate on the lines endorsed by Bodin, Hobbes, or Rousseau, and it is in danger of endorsing inconsistent policies at or over time. And if it is unable to operate other than by majority voting, then even a recognition by some or all members of this problem will not necessarily enable them to solve it.

It might seem that an obvious way to avoid the problem would be for the members of the governing committee to renounce majority voting in favor of some variant system. But it turns out that the feature of majority voting that causes the problem—its responsiveness on each issue to the views of individual members—gives rises to the same problem in every bottom-up system: every system for letting the judgment of the group on any issue be mechanically determined, bottom up, by the judgments of the members on that same issue. Or at least this is true of every plausible bottom-up system: every system, for example, that does not require unanimity among members. Not only will majority voting fail to guarantee the coherence-sensitivity required for corporate agency, then; such alternatives will fail in the same way.

This more general claim is grounded in a recent range of formal results. No matter the adjustments made, more or less any bottom-up system of voting capable of generating a corporate set of views—this, by contrast with an infeasible system requiring unanimity, for example—is liable to generate an inconsistent and irrational set of views. It turns out that there is an inherent tension between the requirement of individual responsiveness and corporate rationality.[25]

The Lesson of That Failure

The lesson of these results is, plausibly, that if a corporate body is to identify a consistent voice behind which members can rally and establish themselves as a single agent, then that voice cannot be formed by a bottom-up, individually responsive procedure of the kind that majority voting illustrates. No plausible

25. An early theorem is in List and Pettit (2002). For an informal review of results, see List and Pettit (2011); and for a collection of relevant, technical papers, see List and Polak (2010). The relation between these results and Arrow's impossibility theorem is discussed in List and Pettit (2004) and more fully in Dietrich and List (2007).

system can be responsive to individuals on each of a set of connected issues, be capable of generating a corporate set of views on those issues, and guarantee not to leave the corporate body with an inconsistent set of attitudes to stand by.

How might a corporate group like our committee form its judgments on issues like the three in the example, yet avoid bottom-up, individual responsiveness to the votes of members? There are many ways it might do this, but the most straightforward is what we may call the straw-vote procedure (List and Pettit 2011, chap. 2). Under this procedure the members would look on each vote they take as a straw vote—a vote not necessarily to be ratified—until they determine that it is consistent with the votes already taken. If it is consistent, they ratify the vote. If it is not, then they go back to the drawing board, identify the previous votes with which it clashes, and then decide on de-ratifying either the vote just taken or one of those other votes.

Applying this procedure in the example given, the members of our governing committee would balk at the vote that supports raising other spending, if that comes last. This vote is inconsistent with the votes already taken, for they cannot raise other spending while holding taxes fixed and raising defense spending. And balking at the inconsistency, the members would then have to review the three conflicting votes and decide on which it makes most sense, given their various aims, to de-ratify. They would have to decide between the consistent sets of views possible on the issues involved: most saliently, the consistent sets associated with the different parties. This review might lead them, for example to de-ratify the majority vote in favor of holding taxes and opt for a corporate commitment to raise taxes and, using the extra funds generated, to raise spending in both defense and other areas; it might lead them, in other words, to adopt the profile of judgment displayed by Chicken.

This procedure is not mechanical, since there is no saying where the review will take the group; they might equally have decided not to raise defense spending or not to raise other spending. And neither is it wholly bottom-up. For regardless of which consistent set of corporate judgments they decide to endorse, at least one of those judgments will not be responsive to most individual votes on the relevant issue. If they opt for raising taxes, for example, then the corporate judgment on that issue will not correspond to the majority judgment by Hawk and Dove to hold taxes.

In allowing for a review of where bottom-up voting leads them, the members introduce a top-down filter to modify the effect of the voting. It is top-down in the sense that it requires the members to move out of their roles as voters, operating individually from below, and look from above at where their votes are leading the group in aggregate. The bottom-up voting represents their contribution as authors in presenting candidates for corporate ratification. The top-down review represents their contribution as editors in making sure that the candidates presented constitute a satisfactory package.

The discursive dilemma supports the negative lesson that notwithstanding the traditional orthodoxy, majority voting cannot be relied upon to enable our committee to incorporate, giving them a sovereign voice around which they can individually rally. The simple straw-vote procedure supports a corresponding, positive lesson. This is that the essential component needed to get over the sort of problem raised is that the members should have some editorial means of ensuring that the candidates they generate as authors—or the candidates generated by any authors they license—constitute a consistent set. With this lesson in hand, we can return to the issue of whether a corporate agent might be organized in a polycentric way.

The Success of the Mixed Constitutional Idea

The straw-vote procedure is not itself decentralized or polycentric in character, but it indicates an easy way in which a polity might be organized in this pattern. For suppose that the state that is guided by a majority committee introduces a procedure whereby it makes proposals as author, but a distinct majority committee has the power as editor to reject or revise them. Suppose, in other words, that the voice and law around which officials and citizens are invited to rally is the product of two independent committees, one with the authorial role of generating candidates, the other with the editorial role of filtering those candidates to ensure they amount to a coherent package. The candidates proposed by the one committee and tested by the other might be candidates for the framing of law. This authorial-editorial arrangement is the sort of mixed constitution proposed by James Harrington (1992) in the seventeenth century; he thought that a senate ought to propose law, and a popular assembly decide on which laws to accept.

Our discussion should make clear that such a decentralized sovereign would be capable, contrary to what Bodin, Hobbes, and Rousseau claim, of generating a set of policies and laws that are reliably coherent. While the first committee might fail to achieve consistency in one or another regard, the second would remain sensitive to the failure and capable of putting the problem right. If the first committee voted as in the example given with Hawk, Dove, and Chicken, then the second committee would vote on how to resolve the inconsistency. In effect, it would likely vote on whether to endorse the pattern of voting endorsed by Hawk, or by Dove, or by Chicken.

The irony, then, is that while such a polycentric polity would be sensitive to the problem raised, and capable of solving it, the single majoritarian committee favored by the absolutists would lack both that sensitivity and that capacity. The decentralized regime could guarantee the coherence of the law, enabling the state to operate as a corporate agent, but the centralized constitution that absolutists support could not.

Decentralization in a corporate state may take many forms, as we saw earlier. There may be a separation of powers, as in most advanced democracies, where at least the courts are independent from the legislature and executive. There may be a sharing of legislative power, as when different bodies are involved in authoring the laws; of judicial power, as when a court is required to interpret the law under threat of appeal to a higher court; and of executive power, as when different officials or bodies are involved in determining the interpretation under which laws are implemented. Finally, there may be an outsourcing of power, as when the executive, for example, shares powers with various statutory officials or bodies.

No matter how decentralized a polity becomes in these ways, it should be clear that it may impose a discipline on what is to emerge as law parallel to the discipline that our simple polity of two committees, one authorial, the other editorial, would impose. A suitable discipline would help to ensure, first, that there is a single body of coherent law and, second, that that law is uniform across the different sites at which it is formulated and interpreted. All that is required is that the system should allow for the imposition of an editorial discipline on the candidates proposed or endorsed at different points.

That sort of discipline will be imposed by the possibility that any ill-fitting candidates will be rejected, whether by bodies within the same domain—say, in the same legislative domain—or by bodies without, as in judicial hearings or popular referenda. And it will be facilitated to the extent that the authoring body shrinks from rejection by the editorial, as legislators or administrators might shrink from rejection by the courts, or a lower court shrink from rejection by a higher, appeals court. That distaste for rejection would motivate the authoring body, so far as possible, to do its own top-down filtering and avoid being overruled by its editorial counterpart.

3.4 Sovereignty with Decentralization

While the polycentric organization of the polity is functionally desirable, supporting the idea of a regime of law under which citizens know where they stand, it is deemed infeasible in the tradition, epitomized by Bodin, Hobbes, and Rousseau, that emphasizes the need for a single sovereign in every state. But the strictly sovereigntist commitment in this tradition—the commitment to the need for a single sovereign—is distinct, as we have seen, from the specifically absolutist rejection of the mixed or polycentric constitution. And where the sovereigntist argument is compelling, the absolutist is not: the absolutist belief in the rule of a majoritarian committee is misconceived and the absolutist opposition to polycentric arrangements is ungrounded.

These last observations show, in the language of the last chapter, that there is no reason why a polycentric polity might not be fully incorporated. There is no reason why the decision-making procedures it establishes, empowering several distinct agents or agencies, should not be able to generate a relatively coherent pattern in the framing and interpretation of decision-taker laws. There is no reason, in other words, why this state should not speak with a single, univocal voice. Thus, to take the simplest example, a state that divided the business of framing law between two distinct bodies, one authorial, the other editorial, might be very successful in generating an internally coherent body of law.

Given that we have endorsed the sovereigntist argument, however, the challenge we now face is to explain where exactly the sovereign is to be found in such a functional, polycentric state. Where is the authority, individual or corporate, that stands behind the law, binding others without being bound itself? Where is the unmoved mover in the system? Where does the buck stop?

Where Is the Polycentric Sovereign?

The sovereign bearer of political power in the absolutist vision is always a particular individual or committee, whether that be an elite committee or a committee of the whole. The relevant members of the polity borrow the voice of an individual and authorize it as the voice they will follow, whether in the role of officials or citizens. Or they borrow the majoritarian voice—something constructed by a mathematical algorithm—and authorize it in the same manner. In each case, the sovereign is the speaker present in that voice. This voice dictates how officials are to operate under decision-maker laws, including how they are to operate if they amend those laws, and how citizens are to behave under the decision-taker laws that the officials duly frame and impose.

Turning now to the polycentric polity, the sovereign bearer of political power must operate in the same manner by a voice that carries ultimate weight for decision makers and decision takers. But what is the voice that officials and citizens of that polity rely on? If we can identify that voice, we will be able to identify the speaker or sovereign that is present in the voice.

Where the members of an absolutist democracy or aristocracy borrow the voice of a mathematical algorithm, relying on a majority procedure to identify it, the authorities in a decentralized body construct that voice as they go along. They do this in making the continual adjustments required to implement or amend their decision-maker laws and to employ those laws in determining the framing or interpretation of decision-taker laws.

Consider our simple two-committee model. And imagine, plausibly, that as the committees operate under the structure described—under those decision-maker laws—they anticipate one another's responses and begin to negotiate about differences. The to-and-fro pattern of negotiation between those bodies will yield decision-taker laws as the normal product of that negotiation. And the decision-maker laws may themselves be amended from time to time, as the committees follow those very laws in negotiating a change in the laws themselves; we may assume that this is allowed by constitutive constraints. Such an amendment might allow the authorial body to consult the editorial on certain matters, for example, or to rule on other matters without fear of challenge.

Under a simple arrangement like this, and under any more complex but still effective polycentric constitution, the voice that rules will not be a preexisting voice like that of the majority voice among citizens or indeed the voice of a monarchical individual. It will be a voice that materializes in the adjustments of the authorities within the system, evolving in a potentially unpredictable manner as negotiations take one direction or another. Who will speak, then, in the two-committee model as decision-maker and decision-taker laws are enunciated? Obviously, the group agent that is organized around that structure. In other words, the polity itself. Rather than parasitizing a preexisting voice, algorithmic or natural, the polity will construct what it has to say by following its decision-making routines in laying down the law: decision-maker as well decision-taker law.

If the voice of decision-maker and decision-taker law is the voice of the polity, considered as a corporate entity, then the sovereign in a polycentric state of the kind envisaged is nothing more or less than the polity itself.

Traditional sovereigntists recognized that the sovereign may be a corporate agent, but they were mistaken to reduce the corporate possibility to that of having a majoritarian committee in charge.

There is no difficulty in seeing how the polycentric polity can be a sovereign given that incorporation, as we saw in the last chapter, will allow it to be an agent. And, as it turns out, there is no difficulty in recognizing that it can satisfy the assumptions about sovereignty made in the sovereigntist tradition, as we have charitably reinterpreted it.

Thus, consider the first three claims made in the tradition. The polycentric polity will rule by the laws it lays down, both on decision-maker and decision-taker fronts; its laws will have the status of commands or instructions as to how individuals and domestic bodies should behave; and the polity itself will count as the source of such prescriptions: a source that is accepted within the society in the minimal sense required.

Turning to the fourth sovereigntist claim, the effective polycentric polity will be a corporate agent, as the tradition allows, but it will not constitute a democracy, or indeed an aristocracy, in the absolutist sense; it cannot be run, as we saw, by a majoritarian committee. Will it be a democracy in the original Greek sense? Will it be a polity in which ordinary people enjoy a lot of power? That will depend on several factors: how far the decision-making authorities have a permanent grip on office; how far the decision-taker rules allow for challenges from ordinary citizens; and how far the citizenry is inclusive of at least adult, able-minded, permanent residents. We return to connected issues in the next chapter.

Will the polity envisaged operate, as in the fifth claim, beyond legal and other forms of domestic control? The question cannot be answered without first considering the sixth claim, according to which the sovereign state may be subject to normative, contractual, and constitutive constraints.

The polity may reasonably be taken to be subject to normative constraints of democracy in its original, Greek sense: constraints of political justice on its decision-maker laws; or to normative constraints of social justice on its decision-taker laws; or indeed to normative constraints of global justice on how it performs internationally (Pettit 2014). It will also be subject of course to any contractual obligations it incurs, as in the international treaties it makes or under international laws to which it subscribes. And most strikingly of all, it will be subject to constitutive constraints of organization.

As the absolutist democracy will be subject constitutively to the majoritarian constraint, the polycentric will be subject to the constraints dictating the decentralized mode in which its decisions are made. Or at least it will be subject to decision-maker rules that it cannot amend under those rules themselves: under an article of amendment—effectively, a constitutive constraint—determining the possible ways in which those rules can be amended.

Returning to the fifth claim, is the effective, polycentric state going to operate beyond legal or other control? Yes, although not if such control is implied in the constitutive constraints that are built in under its mode of organization. Insofar as those constraints allow, the polity will be able to change any law it wishes, escaping control by existing laws. And to that same extent it will be able to resist the control of any other domestic agent. But it will be unable to change its decision-maker laws other than via a procedure of amendment that its organization allows. And it will have to allow domestic challenges to existing laws that decision-making procedures themselves permit.

This observation means that a polycentric polity organized under suitable rules may count as domestically sovereign, even though it allows for lots of checks and balances in its constitutive workings. The majority committee envisaged by our traditional sovereigntists may rule supreme but will still be unable to operate other than in response to the majority views of its members. There is no contradiction there since majority rule is built into its mode of operation. A similar lesson will hold, obviously, with any decentralized, polycentric regime. The mode in which it is organized will be constraining in the way that majoritarian organization will be constraining. But the polycentric mode of organization may allow a widespread pattern of internal checking within its ranks, as no one individual or body is given the right to operate at will; each is subject to checking under the organization—broadly, the constitution—of the polity.

Consistently with the state being sovereign, then, the authorities may be subject to checks on their power of the kind associated traditionally with the mixed constitution, and specifically with the separation, the sharing, and the outsourcing of power. And to that extent, the individuals and bodies involved in acting in the name of the state may be denied forms of discretion that would have enabled them to favor themselves or their friends. Thus, without undermining sovereignty, polycentric organization can enable a state to serve its function well, establishing a regime of law under which citizens know where they stand with officials and with each other.

There may seem to be an inconsistency in asserting at once that the decentralized polity may have the status and power of a traditional sovereign and that it can involve the bevy of constraints associated with a regime of checks and balances. But the inconsistency is merely apparent. For it is the corporate agent constituted by the polity that enjoys sovereign power, while it is only the individuals and bodies that act in its name who are subject to a demanding range of constraints: those associated with the procedures they must follow, according to decision-maker law, if they can claim to act in the name of the state.[26]

Finally, a note on how far the sovereignty of the polity extends into the international domain. The constitutive constraints on a sovereign polity that we have been discussing would limit but not dictate how it may operate in relation to other states or to external bodies. Ideally, however, we might expect states to enter contracts whereby they impose collectively beneficial limits on what they may individually do: on what they may do in peace and even war, for example, in diplomacy and trade, and in those domestic operations that impact on the welfare of people elsewhere. Sovereign states will be able to enjoy the fruits of their sovereignty, as individuals will be able to enjoy the fruits of their freedom, only under binding arrangements that prevent each from harming others and that further ends shared across different, even rival regimes, avoiding global bads and advancing global goods.[27]

The Category Mistake Made by Absolutists

We noted earlier that in their absolutist opposition to the mixed constitution, the sovereigntists resorted to rhetoric more than argument. It is as if they were all independently motivated to find fault with the idea. Bodin and Hobbes would certainly have been motivated to find fault insofar as they thought that a strong form of centralized rule is the only possible way of combatting the danger of religious dissension and civil war. But how could they, and how could Rousseau, have overlooked the salient possibility we have been documenting: that even under a decentralized mode of organization, the polity itself can count as the sovereign?

The reason is a shared assumption that the sovereign in a polity must be one of the individuals or bodies that have power within it: the monarch, or an

---

26. If the polity fails to deliver a social order that has some independent appeal among the citizenry—if it attracts compliance with its laws on the basis of fear alone—then the citizens will be entitled to rebel against their sovereign, however polycentric, by our account of the acceptance condition. But as noted, the citizenry in that sense will still not be an agency that controls the sovereign in a problematic way. To anticipate the next chapter, the rebellious citizenry will be the incorporating people, the sovereign polity will be the people incorporated.

27. These international aspects of sovereignty are deeply important, of course, but not relevant to our concerns here.

elite or inclusive legislature. But that conception is unnecessarily restrictive. It rules out the possibility that it is the polity itself that is sovereign: that the sovereign is the group constituted by the polycentric network of political players, individual and corporate, and not any one of those players.[28]

But why should they make that assumption? A good line on the puzzle is provided by a lesson taught by Gilbert Ryle (1949) in his classic book *The Concept of Mind*. Anxious to present the human mind as an entity that is not on a par with the subsystems at work within a human being but something that emerges from the interaction of those systems, Ryle tells a story that is instructive for our purposes as well as his.

A visitor is shown around the colleges of the University of Oxford, so the story goes, but being anxious to see absolutely everything, asks also to be shown the university itself. As Ryle assumed his readers would know, the request is misplaced, since the university is not an entity coordinate with the colleges but rather something superordinate that emerges from their interaction. It is constituted by the colleges insofar as they operate together to organize the admission, teaching, assessment, and graduation of students, so that the university is a corporate agent that lies ultimately behind those actions. What each college does in admitting or teaching students, or what they do together in arranging for student assessment and graduation, is done by the university. That corporate body is just a network or organization of the colleges, not a separate entity that a visitor to the colleges might want to see in addition.

Ryle uses this story to suggest that just as the university is made up of the colleges in organized collaboration, so the mind emerges from the organized collaboration of different subsystems in the human makeup: it is not an element within that makeup—not for example a *res cogitans*, in Descartes's phrase, that lurks within the brain—but something that emerges from those elements. The story suggests a parallel lesson for us. The sovereign in a state need not be one of the players in the legal system, as assumed by all our absolutists: it need not be a monarch, a legislature, or anything of that concrete kind. Rather, it may be a superordinate body that emerges from the interaction and cooperation of such individuals and agencies.

Ryle thinks that the visitor who wants to see the university, having already seen the colleges, commits what he calls a category mistake. A. N. Whitehead

---

28. Noel Malcolm (1991, 22) endorses at least the negative part of this lesson, arguing that the "idea that sovereignty inheres in a particular body or institution within the state creates all sorts of problems."

(1997, 51) describes the sort of category mistake relevant to our case as a fallacy of misplaced concreteness. It consists in assuming with a term under analysis that, if it has application in the actual world, the entity it designates must be of a relatively concrete kind. That is the mistake made, in Ryle's reckoning, by philosophers who think that the mind is a force within the person, operating like Descartes's *res cogitans* as a receiver of experience, a locus of belief, and a generator of intention and action. And arguably it is the mistake made by those legal and political thinkers who imagine that the sovereign must be an organ within the body politic, not something whose presence is guaranteed by the way those organs are networked to act together.

In his image of the ideal constitution, Immanuel Kant held a view of the sovereign very like the view adopted here. In that polity, he thinks, "the sovereign, which gives laws, is, as it were invisible; it is the personified law in itself, not its agent"; or, as he puts it elsewhere, "law itself rules and depends on no particular person" (Kant 1996, 294fn, 481). What Kant recognizes in this argument is that the sovereign need not be a concrete individual or body that goes into the composition of a state but something more abstract and intangible: an entity that exists in virtue of how the state is composed, not one of its components. This image of an abstract sovereign escaped our three absolutists.[29]

It is worth adding that it may also have escaped those in Britain and the United States who embraced the notion of the decentralized polity, from Montesquieu to the authors of the *Federalist Papers*. They tend to ignore sovereigntist theory rather than addressing it, and they would hardly have done this if they recognized the possibility of taking the decentralized polity that they favor to constitute the sovereign in any country. They do often use the word "sovereign" but not in the proper sense that we have targeted. Rather they use it only to characterize the power of a state in relation to other states, the power of a monarch within a state, or any power within a state—even a divided legislature—that has the final say in making decision-taker law: this is the legal sovereign, in Dicey's term, not the sovereign as such.[30]

29. This may not be true of those in traditions influenced by Kantian thought. In nineteenth-century France, the sovereign is often cast quite abstractly as the nation—more on the origin of this idea in the next chapter—and in Germany it often became identified with the constitution or law. See Grimm (2015).

30. Thus, in the divided power of Commons, House of Lords, and the Monarchy, Blackstone (2016, 41) says in the mid-eighteenth century, "is lodged the sovereignty of the British constitution; and lodged as beneficially as is possible for society."

An Analogue of the Decentralized Polity

It may be useful to emphasize in conclusion that there is nothing anomalous about thinking of the polity as an agent that emerges from the interaction of more concrete bodies. This is the image of the agent that has come to dominate the cognitive science of animal, human, and indeed robotic agency (Fodor 1983). As Ryle thought of the mind as a higher-lever precipitate of interaction between lower-level elements, so cognitive scientists think of the typical agent as the precipitate of an organized network of subagencies: as an agent distributed among those different centers.

For Descartes, everything done by a human agent is the result of the thoughts and volitions, the *pensées* and *volontés*, formed in the headquarters of the mind: the *res cogitans*, the thinking center. Contemporary cognitive scientists and philosophers tend to deny that there is any single place within the agent where bodily mediated perceptions and the like are processed, and instructions issued for the bodily realization of one or another purpose (Fodor 1983; Dennett 1992; Clark 1997). They maintain that you or I perform as an agent in virtue of the relatively independent operation of different modules in the nervous system, where these modules may be distinct by nature or become distinct in the course of training.

The perceptual module in virtue of which I perceive the stick as bent in water is insulated by nature from the module in virtue of which I form the perceptual judgment that the stick is straight; that's why the illusion stays in place. The performative module in virtue of which my fingers hit the right keys on my computer is insulated by training from the module whereby I reflect on the position of each finger; that's why I can type at a decent pace. While most cognitive scientists believe in such modularity to some degree, they vary on whether the mind is massively modular, as it is put, or only moderately so.

The polycentric idea is that an incorporated group can be organized in a similarly distributed way, moderate or radical, without ceasing to be functional. The state will be organized on a distributed basis to the extent that its attitudes, however avowed, pledged, or enacted, are determined by the independent contributions of distinct subagents or subagencies. Those attitudes will not materialize, as in a single committee or assembly, by the parties each following the same plan—say, one of voting on different issues—to identify the attitudes to be endorsed by the group. The different subagents will make their individual contributions on a basis specific to their briefs and procedures, accepting that the attitudes to be endorsed in the group are determined by how their distinct inputs combine under corporate constraints.

In defending the idea of a sovereign, decentralized state that operates as a single agent, we may be breaking with more standardized ideas in political thought, but we are not resorting to an exotic fantasy or anything of that kind. We are putting forward a view about the agential state—or by extension any corporate body—that fits with standard views in the theory of agency more generally.

3.5 Decentralization, Radical and Moderate

There are many possible variations in decentralizing a political system, as already indicated in the last section. But there is one dimension of variation that is particularly worth noting. This is the sort of variation that occurs between a presidential system like that of the United States, or various South American regimes, and a parliamentary system like that associated with Britain, Canada, Australia, New Zealand, and many European democracies.

The United States is the most prominent example of a presidential system, and Australia offers a usefully opposed example of the parliamentary alternative. As in America, there are two elected houses of parliament, a written constitution, a system of judicial review, a federation of relatively independent states, and the same sort of electoral, generally nonproportional arrangements. Like the United States, Australia is certainly a decentralized state, displaying separation, sharing, and outsourcing of power. But, as we shall see, it is not decentralized in the same radical measure.

One reason for giving the presidential-parliamentary divide attention is to combat the common assumption that the mixed or decentralized constitution is specific to the American presidential system and that parliamentary systems are not decentralized in the same sense: that they install a single will in power, usually cast honorifically as the will of the people. The first task is to clarify the differences between the ways in which they are each decentralized. Having clarified the distinction, we can then look at which mode of decentralization has greater functional appeal.

The main differences between the American and Australian systems, to focus on those exemplars, all stem from the different ways in which the head of the executive or administration is chosen. This is a figure in each country who has a good deal of discretion in selecting other members of the administrative team and who has effective power over what laws are passed: in

America by virtue of a veto power over legislation, in Australia by virtue of leading the party with parliamentary power. In the American system, the head of the executive—the president—is elected by the people just as members of the legislature are elected and has an independent, electoral source of authority. In the Australian, the chief executive—in this case, the prime minister—is elected by the members of the legislature from among their ranks, and does not have an independent form of electoral authorization (Linz and Valenzuela 1994).

Parliamentary Democracy in Australia

Since the Australian prime minister depends for remaining in power on retaining majority support in the legislature, there must be sufficient members within the lower house willing to give them support. These will mainly consist in a party or coalition of parties committed to making common cause in the prime minister's support over the term of the parliament, but they may also include some supportive members who reserve the right to vote occasionally against the administration. Thus, the prime minister must be at the head of a group—the party or coalition in power—that is collectively disciplined to act as a corporate agent. That party—the government, in common parlance—will have a high degree of control, not just over the executive that it keeps in power, but also over the legislature. Being a fixed majority, and having reason to make common cause with one another, the members will generally be able to decide together—in a separate caucus, as it is often described—on what laws to propose and pass.[31]

This control means that in the parliamentary system any proposed law or any proposed law-based policy will be authored in most cases by the corporate party in power. But authorship is only one form of control, as we know, being moderated in many cases—the exemplars are a newspaper, journal, or book—by an individual or body in an editorial position. Parliament, and the polity in general, occupies an editorial position in relation to the party that makes law-related proposals. And the distinctive thing about the parliamentary system is that while the governing party or coalition is a relatively unified author of laws

---

31. Although private members may have the right to propose bills in parliament, the government can almost always ensure, if it wishes, that they do not get a hearing or that their bills do not get accepted. Thus, the government retains control of legislation—standby control—in this case too.

and policies, there are several sites within the polity at which editors or would-be editors can assert themselves.

Editorial efforts may be sponsored and supported by the main opposition party in parliament, of course, or by members who reserve the right to vote against the government, and these will sometimes be effective. But significant editorial efforts will also be pursued outside parliament: say, by the various statutory authorities, including the courts, established under the written constitution or established convention; by public-interest movements or associations formed among the population; or by initiatives on the part of groups or individuals in the courts, in the media, or on the streets. The authorial role will be centralized in the legislature—and within one party or coalition in the legislature—the editorial role will be distributed more widely.

Presidential Democracy in the United States

It takes only a little reflection to see that the authorial-editorial divide is bound to assume a very different shape in the presidential democracy of the United States. In this case, there is no likelihood of a single party or coalition of parties assuming a corporate shape under the leadership of the president since members of the legislature will not have to make common cause to keep the administration in power. Members of the same party, perhaps with some individuals from another party, may converge in the attempt to pass certain laws together. But they will each have individual incentives, usually associated with local interests or the interests of rival lobby groups, that may keep them at loggerheads and render it difficult to make or indeed repeal laws. This is going to be particularly so, of course, when, as in normal times, no single party controls both houses of Congress and the presidency.

In this situation, it is practically inevitable that now one legislator or set of legislators, now another, will propose measures for legislation in the hopes of being able to muster majority support in both houses and, as the constitution requires, win the consent of the president. And it is inevitable that they will face editorial challenges, not just outside the legislature, but also within. The result, which experience bears out, is that in this system the authorial role can be assumed, although not always with much prospect of success, by any members of the legislature, not just by the majority party. And the result, equally, is that any authorial initiative that gains traction among legislators can be blocked or edited beyond recognition inside the legislature itself as well as outside. The authorial role will be distributed across the members of the legislature, not centralized in one party or coalition; and the editorial role will be distributed both inside and outside the legislature. Where the author-editor relationship is one-many in the parliamentary system, it assumes a many-many character in the presidential.

Proportionality and the Contrast between the Systems

These comments should make clear that where the presidential system exemplified by the United States is massively modular or decentralized, the parliamentary system exemplified by Australia is only moderately so. In the presidential system, there are many authors and many editors and so many distinct centers that must be integrated in the making of decisions: many veto points, as it is often put. In the parliamentary system there are also many editors or would-be editors. But there is only one effective author: the party or coalition in government.

Before moving on, we should note that in one respect this presidential-parliamentary contrast is overdrawn. The moderation in a democratic parliamentary system will be reduced—the system will approach the presidential extreme—insofar as the electoral system is designed so that the mix of views in the legislature and executive tends to be proportional to the mix in the population. Proportionality would be very poor if, for example, there were single-seat majority constituencies, with nonpreferential voting, since a party with 20 percent national support might be defeated in every single constituency. Proportionality would be much increased, and that party would gain roughly 20 percent of the legislature, if the system were designed differently: if, for example, there were an electoral system that operated, as in Israel, with a single, countrywide constituency.

If a parliamentary democracy is to be moderately as distinct from radically decentralized, then there must be a constraint on proportionality. In an extremely proportional system, there are likely to be many smaller parties. And with an increase in the number of parties, there is likely to be a tendency to multiply the number of potential authors of law and policy within the parliament—and, correspondingly, the number of potential editors—especially if the parties entering government do not commit in advance to the policies they agree to implement.[32]

32. Things will be worse again, of course, if the coalition of parties in government has to rely on the support of one or another smaller party outside the coalition to get any law through.

While proportionality would reduce the contrast on which we focus here, it has obvious attractions. It need not introduce the same uncertainty as the U.S. system about what policies are likely to gain legislative support, since the parties in a coalition may agree on policy commitments, if not at election time, at least before claiming government. And it does have the attraction, missing in any two-party or three-party system, that it enables voters to reflect their preferences more finely in the votes that they cast.[33] This may compensate in some part for the fact that since no party is likely to dominate the legislature, voters cannot bank on their preferred party's policies being implemented, if it wins power.[34]

Three Major Advantages of Keeping Modularity Moderate

In a radically modular regime like the presidential system of the United States—or like the highly proportional, parliamentary system in Israel—there are manifest incentives in place that are likely to lead to what we may call legislative negligence. As those proposing a bill seek to get a majority on side in each house of Congress, and to make sure the president will not veto it, there is a powerful incentive to add more and more clauses to win support for the proposal or to introduce clauses that gloss over differences. And this incentive can drive legislative proposals that are so long and so complex, or in some aspects just so vague, that their coherence with other laws and with the constitution is often in doubt.

This problem can motivate a negligence among legislators as to what they are proposing and, as often happens, a reliance on the agencies and the courts to sort out the mess. It is no accident that the judicial review of legislation, and

33. Although broadly nonproportional, Australia has a system of preferential voting that goes some way toward delivering this attraction. While enabling voters to express fine-grained preferences, the system does not introduce much proportionality in the lower House of Parliament, where constituencies are single-seat. It does introduce a degree of proportionality in the Senate, however, since the constituencies for that body are multiseat; they consist in the different states and territories in the federation.

34. The nonproportional parliamentary system, to anticipate the argument below, gives each voter a coarse choice between a few parties, compensating for the lack of options by the fact that they know the policies that any successful government is likely to implement. The proportional system offers a finer choice between many parties to each voter but fails on the other side of the ledger: at election time no one will be able to tell for sure what parties are likely to form government or what policies any winning coalition of parties is likely to implement.

of the interpretation of laws by executive agencies, plays such a prominent role in the United States. Since the courts will generally represent a final ruling on the interpretation of the laws, their officials—ultimately, the judges on the Supreme Court—will enjoy a degree of power that is hardly true to the spirit of the mixed constitution.

But as negligence on this front is a danger in a presidential system, so too is policymaking gridlock. As those voting on a bill are exposed to the influence of local or lobby pressure or tempted by a chance to exploit a bargaining advantage, they may be led to veto a measure that is important for the polity as a whole. Since no single agent, individual or corporate, will have to wear the responsibility for failing to deliver—everyone can blame someone else—they may each reject the perspective of the whole in favor of a more self-seeking viewpoint, thereby generating gridlock in policymaking.

The dangers of negligence and gridlock are much less threatening in a relatively nonproportional, parliamentary system like Australia's. With only one effective author of law, it is going to be easier in such a system to avoid these problems. The party or coalition in power will generally be able to get legislation passed, avoiding gridlock; after all, it will command a majority or near-majority in the legislature. And because of that manifest capacity, it will be held inside and outside parliament to an expectation that, avoiding negligence as well as gridlock, it should propose only clear and coherent laws. It will be subject to reputational incentives to exercise its legislative power effectively and conscientiously.

There is a third weakness in the presidential system, related to the problems of negligence and gridlock. Since laws are made in that system on the basis in each case of the backroom deal making required to garner majority support, no individual or party going to the polls will be able to make a firm promise that, if elected, they will put this or that policy into effect. And so, the electorate will have to cast their votes based on affiliation with very general principles—if indeed principles divide the parties—or more plausibly, because of a tribal identification with person or party. They will be unable to identify the rivals by credible, relatively detailed policy programs.

Things can be much better in a parliamentary system like that in Australia. Each potential government in a nonproportional parliamentary system, be it a party or tight coalition of parties, will be able to implement whatever laws it supports. And this being a matter of common awareness, the party or coalition will generally have an incentive to propose a program of legislation in advance and to seek to live up to it, should it win government. In that case, then, the voters will have a good idea of the legislative programs between which they are choosing. The laws and policies that eventually materialize will not be the product of backroom, postelection deals, or at least not to the same extent. Most of the deals that are done will materialize before the election, appearing in the electoral programs of the rival parties, and will be subject to the assessment of the voting public.

This characterization idealizes away from some obvious failings in the parliamentary system. These include the capacity of the party in government to hide divisions and tactics in the backroom of party caucusing, the temptation within that party to provide government support in the marginal seats where electoral dividends are more promising, and the pressure on any prime minister to make cabinet appointments that keep their supporters within the party happy, not necessarily appointments that reflect individual competence. While the account given idealizes the parliamentary system in neglecting these dangers, however, the idealization helps to highlight the differences with the presidential arrangement and the advantage of keeping modularity moderate in the parliamentary manner.

Three Incidental Advantages of Keeping Modularity Moderate

Apart from the three advantages mentioned, there are also three more incidental benefits that a parliamentary system promises. A first benefit is that if a single party, or even a coalition of parties, holds power, as in a parliamentary system, it is going to be more difficult for private-interest lobbies to influence what it does; they will not be able to focus, as in a presidential system, on covertly pressuring or persuading marginal members who can push things their way. The private-interest lobby will generally have to win over a whole party or coalition to its cause, not some marginal members, and will be usually unable to keep such efforts covert.

A second, incidental advantage of the parliamentary system is that local voters and activists will have little or no chance of driving national policy by considerations of purely local advantage or interest, since representatives will have to vote, as a matter of common awareness, with their party: they will have to keep faith with the governing majority, and not let more sectional concerns drive their vote. In his famous 1774 speech to the electors of Bristol, Edmund Burke (1999) warned against the possibility of a legislature degenerating into a "congress of ambassadors" where the members each seek to advance a distinct interest and pay little attention to the good of the whole. The parliamentary system would guard against that danger, the presidential would make it all too salient.

A third, incidental advantage of the parliamentary system is that representatives will be motivated, as the members of an effective government, to vote with a view to the best outcome that looks to be achievable. They will be less tempted than in the presidential system by the prospect of striking an appealing, expressive posture—say, a posture that will give them the high moral ground—at a potential cost to the welfare of people overall (Brennan and Lomasky 1993).

Take an issue like whether prostitution should be decriminalized and assume for argument's sake that decriminalization does make good sense: this, say, because criminalization puts prostitutes beyond the reach of public protection, and is liable to foster organized crime and to generate funds for bribing the police. In which sort of system is decriminalization more likely to occur?

My response, borne out in some measure by actual differences between Australia and the United States, is the moderately modular system. A government that operates as a corporate agent will be able to weigh the pros and cons, register the case for decriminalization, and act as a body in favor of decriminalization: this, at any rate, in the absence of organized opposition, say by a church. But when legislation depends on individual lawmakers joining an ad hoc majority to support it, each is likely to be more intent on not attracting a name for favoring prostitution than on seeing that the common interest is well served overall.[35]

We argued in the last chapter that the functional advantages of establishing a polity with a single voice, a single will, and a single identity argue strongly for having the state fully incorporate as an agent. Without questioning that argument, this chapter has enabled us to see that not any form of incorporation will do. If the state is to discharge its role in stabilizing a system of law under which its citizens enjoy security in relation to one another and in relation to officials, then not only must the state be a corporate agent; it must be a corporate agent that operates under a decentralized—ideally a moderately decentralized—constitution.

35. The discussion in this final section draws on many points made in the appendix, jointly authored with Rory Pettit, to Pettit (2010).

PART II

The Potential of the State and Its Dimensions

4

The Collective Powers of Citizens

CHAPTER 1 ARGUED that the functional state has a nomothetic or lawmaking role. The argument for this view is that it would have evolved—it would have been resiliently likely to evolve—under plausible circumstances as an agency with that function. It would have taken the shape of an organization that secures its citizens under a system of law, letting them know where they stand in relation to one another and to officials; and that stabilizes that system against domestic and international challenges. We have often written, for reasons of convenience, as if the citizenry were inclusive of all intuitively eligible members, and we will continue to do that in the remaining chapters. But the claims for which we argued in earlier chapters, like the claims to be defended in later, go through whether the citizenry is inclusive or not.

Chapter 2 argued that if the nomothetic state is to do well by the function it is ascribed under our genealogy of the state—if it is to secure members individually under a stable regime of law—then it should be organized as a fully incorporated body or agency. By properly organizing in a corporate manner under decision-maker law, it can make the body of law under which people operate as decision takers sufficiently uniform to serve as a reliable guide, constituting a proper rule of law. By organizing in that manner, furthermore, the state can stabilize the regime of law without exposing itself to the dangers of an independent police or military. And it can make commitments for which it can credibly assume responsibility, thereby enhancing its capacity to make profitable domestic contracts and, more important, to enter arrangements essential for international order and peace.

Chapter 3 began from the observation that a fully incorporated state is dangerous insofar as it gives officials greater opportunities for abusing power in their own interests or in those of their associates. How to guard against this danger? The obvious answer is by resort to separating, sharing, and

outsourcing the power of officials, as under a mixed or polycentric constitution. But such decentralization of the state may seem to ensure that it lacks a
sovereign of the kind that is essential in a properly incorporated state according to absolutist figures like Bodin, Hobbes, and Rousseau. The chapter argued
that while the traditional argument for sovereignty is compelling, at least
under an updated reading, it does not support a critique of the mixed or polycentric constitution. On the contrary, as we saw, the polity itself will be the
sovereign in any well-designed state, even a decentralized one; and if decentralization is moderate, it will avoid dangers like those of legislative negligence
and gridlock.

If the polity is sovereign in this way, being possessed of associated powers,
that raises a question as to how its citizens relate as subjects to that sovereign. The
custom in asking about this question is to cast the citizenry as the people, and
we shall generally follow that custom here; doing so fits better with traditional
and common usage. The definite article in "the people," like the definite article
in "the citizenry," is meant to indicate that it refers to people or citizens of the
state in question; it should not suggest that they necessarily constitute a
body—certainly not a corporate body—that can be treated as single entity to
which actions can be attributed in the third person singular rather than the
third person plural.

On the account of the state that we have adopted, there is always going to
be a sovereign in the polity: a source of decision-taker and decision-maker law
that operates beyond the reach of legal or other forms of domestic control.
Can the state, consistently with establishing a sovereign, grant countervailing,
collective powers to its citizens in their role as individuals? Can it allow citizens
who are disaffected or dissatisfied in some way to seek to get the sovereign to
change or even seek to remove the sovereign altogether? Can those citizens
enjoy such countervailing powers against the sovereign?

The question is important because it appears that no matter what role the
state gives citizens in constituting a sovereign, it is always liable to displease
some of them as individuals. Thus, even if the state consists in a majoritarian
assembly of citizens, as in Rousseau's picture, it may still do badly by members
of a minority, especially if it becomes factionalized. In recognition of that problem, as we saw, he proposes that the assembly should try to ensure that it is not
factionalized or otherwise distorted, so that "the characteristics of the general
will are still in the majority" (Rousseau 1997b, 4.2.9).

Despite the possibility of individual dissatisfaction, the absolutists claim
that in two respects the state is blocked from granting collective, countervailing

powers to its citizens; they defend a sort of statism on this domestic front. Their statism connects with the rejection of the mixed constitution insofar as that arrangement too would give ordinary people the power to act together in contesting what is proposed or done in the name of the state.

Under any constitution, any set of decision-maker laws, absolutists argue that there is a conceptual or logical reason, deriving from the notion of sovereignty, why the people cannot attempt to exercise power over the sovereign, whether in a large or small group: even, at the limit, in a group of one citizen. And they argue that while any given set of individuals might attempt in an extra-constitutional manner to restrict the sovereign—even to oust the sovereign in a revolution or coup—there is a conceptual reason why the people acting together could not do so; the very concept of the people or citizenry rules that out. According to the absolutist charge, then, the capacity of the state to grant its individual citizens collective countervailing powers, constitutional or extra-constitutional, is inherently limited.

We argue in this first chapter of part II against this claim that the state, in particular the functional state, is limited for conceptual reasons of these kinds from granting countervailing power to its people. Then in the following two chapters we argue on a similar pattern against claims that the state is limited in other ways. In chapter 5, we maintain that it is not metaphysically limited from granting individual rights to its citizens: not limited by the existence of natural rights that a coercive, territorial state would inevitably breach. And in chapter 6 we hold that it is not empirically limited from intervening deeply in the market economy that is likely to emerge among its people; it is not limited by the alleged need for such an economy to operate autonomously.

The argument in each of these chapters is not meant just to challenge the alleged limitation addressed but to defend a positive claim. The claim here is that the functional state must give people some collective powers and may give them many; in the next chapter that it must grant citizens some significant individual rights, and that it may give them rights of increasing significance; and in the final chapter that it must intervene to some degree in the market economy and that it may intervene to quite a high degree. What initiatives ought the functional state to take among those that it may take? That depends on how the initiatives serve to increase the functionality of the state, as we shall indicate in passing, but it mainly turns on how they serve the cause of justice, and that will not be addressed here.

This chapter is in three sections. In the first, we expound and criticize the claim that the people cannot try to curtail the sovereign under the decision-maker rules that establish that sovereign; their constitutional power is not restricted on this front, specifically not for any reason related to the concept of sovereignty. In the second, we expound the absolutist argument—echoed, in a related form, among some contemporary constitutional and democratic theorists—that the people cannot act together extra-constitutionally against their sovereign: that the very concept of the people prohibits this. Then, in the third section, we criticize that claim, showing why the people can have extra-constitutional as well as constitutional power.

The lesson of the chapter is that under the decision-maker rules of a functional state the people must have some constitutional and extra-constitutional power and that they may have either sort of power to quite a high degree: say, to a degree required by justice.[1] This claim may seem unsurprising, but discussing it will take us to some basic issues bearing on how we should conceive of the people—the people as subjects—and their relationship to their sovereign and polity.[2]

As in the foregoing chapter, there will be a strong historical aspect to the discussion, since the best and most influential statements on the opposing side are from Hobbes and Rousseau; consequently, we shall spend a good deal of time on their views as well as on related figures like Locke, Kant, and Sieyès. The discussion is not meant as a comprehensive contribution to the history of political thought, of course. Thus, we do not look at the views of classical, medieval, or Renaissance figures on related issues, and we ignore many important thinkers in later intellectual history, such as Bodin, Grotius, and Pufendorf: for our purposes, what they say is better said by the figures highlighted.[3]

1. The lesson is relevant to the functional state but, as will become apparent, it applies in some way to any state, even one that has become repressive. That marks a contrast with the lessons supported in the following two chapters, which bear only on the functional state.

2. Thus, the discussion connects with current debates about how to think about the people in politics. See Badiou and others (2016) for a set of essays, deconstructionist in general style, that review different senses in which the idea of the people has been invoked, and the different uses to which it has been put. See Canovan (2005) for a historically organized review of those senses and uses. And see Weale (2018) for a trenchant critique of the idea of the will of the people.

3. What Bodin says on relevant matters is better said by Hobbes and what Grotius and Pufendorf say does not engage so clearly with the distinctions on which the text focuses. See Tuck (2016, chap. 2) for an overview that supports this judgment.

4.1 The Constitutional Power of the People

The question as to what power the people can have under the constitution is effectively the question of what power the constitution can give them in relation to the sovereign; specifically, what power it can give them to try to shape how the sovereign behaves. This question presupposes a conception of the people as the several individuals that are subjects of the sovereign and state where, as always, we take the subjects to be citizens, whether citizens in an inclusive or elite sense.

In considering how much power the people can have in relation to their individual or corporate sovereign, it is important to be clear on how we understand the people or citizenry. At this stage, there are two points of clarification to make: that the people are not to be taken either in a restrictive sense or in a reified sense. In discussing the question of extra-constitutional power, we shall see, there are other important distinctions to make as well, but for the moment it will be enough to make these points about restriction and reification.

Against a Restrictive Conception of the People

As emphasized, the people are equated with the citizenry in our discussion, whether the citizens be an elite or inclusive body. But even on this way of taking the people, there is room for equating them with the whole citizenry or only with a part. Since it is quite common among traditional and even contemporary authors to restrict the people only to certain citizens, it is important to stress that we take them to encompass the whole citizenry.

The restrictive mode of representing the people or citizenry can be found in many prominent figures from the past. Thus, while Aristotle (1996) sometimes takes all of the citizenry to constitute the people or *demos*—all of those who are free under the law—he frequently restricts the people to the relatively poor citizens who make up the bulk of society (Cammack 2019). Again while Cicero (1998) sometimes takes the people to be all of those who live as citizens under the state, he often uses the phrase to refer to those who are not rich enough to belong to the elite, senatorial class; his usage reflects the fact that in republican Rome it was not the people alone who were taken to hold power but the people and Senate: *Senatus Populusque Romanus* (SPQR). The restrictive way of thinking also continued, side by side with the more encompassing sense, in medieval legal thinking, where *populus* could refer to all the citizenry or to "that part of the community which is distinguished from the *nobiles*" (Canning 1980, 10–11).

This restrictive use of "the people" continues in Renaissance texts, as when Machiavelli (1997) argues for letting the people—the common people—rather than the nobles take charge of ensuring liberty.[4] And this usage is maintained in other defenders of Roman republican ideals like James Harrington (1992) in the mid-sixteenth century. As already mentioned, Harrington argues for having an elite senate that would propose laws and policies and a house of deputies, representing the people, whose role would be to reject or ratify those proposals.

Harrington was faithful to the ideal of the mixed constitution in maintaining that the senate would serve as an authoring body, the house representing the people as an editorial one. This restrictive mode of referring to the people also went naturally with the received way of depicting the mixed constitution as one involving three elements, monarchical, aristocratic, and popular. If the phrase was also used in a more encompassing way among republican writers, it was as a synonym for all of those invested as citizens in the *res publica* or commonwealth.

A restrictive conception of the people still figures in contemporary discourse. It is maintained by those who follow Machiavelli in stressing the importance of empowering the people in the sense of the relatively disadvantaged against those in power (McCormick 2011; Vergara 2020). And, more saliently, it plays a central role in neo-populist movements, when leaders or would-be leaders inevitably claim to speak for the people: the real people, as they are sometimes cast. The people neo-populists have in mind are always tacitly taken to comprise, not all of those permanently resident in the country, not even all of those enfranchised as citizens, but only those who fit a certain template projected in the policies of the movement. They may be all of those who share a certain religion or ideology, ethnicity, or color, or just all of those who identify as outsiders to, and opponents of, a nebulous range of elites.

In speaking here of the people, we shall take the expression in an encompassing rather than restrictive way to include all the citizens of the society. The people or citizenry are not even restricted to those outside the offices of government, on the assumption with which we are working here. Those who serve in government will still have to live under government as subjects of

4. For a pro-Machiavelli defense of the utility of seeing the people in this restrictive way, see McCormick (2007; 2011).

decision-taker law, by that assumption, and may serve as officials only on a temporary basis.

Against a Reified Conception of the People

Apart from restrictive conceptions of the people, there is a second set of conceptions that we should also set aside. These are reified ways of thinking that turn the people into an impersonal sort of entity—a *res* or thing—denying them the dynamic capacity to act, whether separately or jointly. Where the restrictive mode of referring to the people—the nonelite people—is found in authors from almost all periods, certainly all periods in European history, this way of referring to the people came into common usage comparatively late, perhaps even as late as the eighteenth century.

On the reified way of thinking about the people, the phrase is used as a synonym for terms like "the nation," "the folk," "the community," and "the public," not for a group of individuals credited with the power of action, whether on their own or together. This conception depicts the people as an entity to which attitudes can be attributed, but not in the literal way in which they can be ascribed to an agent.

In this respect, the phrase operates in the same manner as an expression like "the market." We may say that the market is pessimistic or optimistic about the likely intervention of the central bank, that it has regained its senses after a bubble, and the like. And in the same figurative manner, we may say that the nation or the folk, the community or the public, has had enough of political squabbling or will not put up with the dithering of the government about one or another issue. But in neither case do we think of the subject or subjects to whom such attitudes are attributed as agents who, for example, might speak up and contradict us.

The people reified in this way are a more or less passive or plastic entity onto which interpreters, with few disciplinary constraints, can impose one or another profile of opinion. Those interpreters will include local and foreign commentators, of course. But they will also include individuals who aspire to public office and offer an interpretation of the mind of the public or community, the nation or the folk, in support of their particular political message.

Why would this way of thinking about the people have emerged only in the eighteenth century or so? One possible reason takes us back to Hobbes and Rousseau (Pettit 2008a). Hobbes had argued that language enables people to think in general terms, to reason about what follows from what, to perform properly as mutually responsible persons, and to establish group agents. Rousseau and Herder, and the romantic tradition they established, built on Hobbes's idea that language shapes the minds of its users to argue that, having its own language, every community is liable to have its own mode of thinking: its own distinctive mind-set or *Geist*. And with that development, the old term "nation" became freighted with new connotations. It came to depict the people, considered as a relatively passive and plastic entity: an entity with a mind that others can interpret but not a mind that it itself forms and enacts.

Writing at the beginning of the French Revolution, the Abbé Sieyès invoked this idea of the nation in depicting deputies of the new congress as representatives of the people but representatives that were not subject to the people's power (Pasquino 1998; Tuck 2016, 62–80). Sieyès (2003, 134–40) argues that while the nation is "a willing and acting whole," consisting of the inhabitants of "the forty thousand parishes" of France, it has to entrust the exercise of its will to others. Thus, when the people are said to act, it cannot be "a real common will that acts but a representative common will." As Sieyès views the situation, "extraordinary representatives," however selected, will act for the nation in setting up a constitution for government, and "ordinary representatives" will act under that constitution in running government. And, since neither can get the nation wrong, their will is the will of the nation. They can style themselves as national representatives but still claim the status of plenipotentiaries in giving expression to the attitudes of the nation.

As we shall set aside restrictive conceptions of the people that equate them only with a section of the citizenry, so we shall avoid the sort of conception that reifies the people, transforming them into something plastic like the nation. The issue we face here is how far the people in the sense of an encompassing, active citizenry can enjoy power, constitutional or extra-constitutional, in relation to the sovereign. In this section we concentrate on constitutional power, turning to extra-constitutional in sections 2 and 3.

An Argument Against Constitutional Popular Power

Can people have a power to challenge the sovereign, whether successfully or not, that is constitutionally established? Bodin, Hobbes, and Rousseau all defend a negative answer, which is hardly surprising. If the people have the power as individual or group agents to challenge the sovereign—if they have that as a right under the constitution—then the sovereign will lose its constitutional status as the sole source of law and government.

There is a distinctive argument in Hobbes and Rousseau, briefly mentioned earlier, that supports this view. Assuming that the sovereign is established by a unanimous contract on the part of individuals to submit to such a sovereign power, allowing individuals to challenge the sovereign's exercise of the power would mean allowing them to allege a breach of covenant. But, Hobbes (1994b, 18) urges, "if any one or more of them pretend a breach of the covenant made by the sovereign at his institution, and others or one other of his subjects, or himself alone, pretend there was no such breach, there is in this case no judge to decide the controversy: it returns therefore to the sword again."

The idea here is that if citizens could challenge the sovereign under the constitution of the commonwealth, then, absurdly, there would have to be a third figure—a supersovereign—recognized in the constitution to judge or decide the challenge. Arguing on the same basis against exposing the sovereign to challenge, Rousseau (1997b, 1.6.7) maintains that "if individuals were left some rights"—presumably, constitutional rights to contest the sovereign— "there would be no common superior who might adjudicate between them and the public." "Where interested private individuals are one of the parties, and the public the other," he explains elsewhere, "I do not see what law should be followed or what judge should pronounce judgment" (Rousseau 1997b, 2.4.6).

The line of thought in both thinkers is that it would be absurd to allow for challenges to the sovereign within the constitution of the society because that would open up a regress. Let it be possible for individual or group agents to challenge the sovereign and there must be a superior—a supersovereign—to judge on the challenge; let it be possible to challenge the supersovereign and that will require a sovereign at yet a higher level; and so on indefinitely. To stop the regress, there must be some uncontestable sovereign in place, and there is no reason why this should not be the sovereign at the very first level.

Kant (1996, 299) develops just this style of argument, probably under the influence of Rousseau.[5] He asks us "who is to consider on which side the right is," if people are allowed to make judgments about how the law should be interpreted "contrary to the judgment of the actual head of state." And he then argues: "Neither can make the decision as judge in its own suit. Hence there would have to be another head above the head of state, that would decide

---

5. As Richard Burke pointed out to me, it also makes a passing appearance in Adam Smith's *Lectures on Jurisprudence*: "To suppose a sovereign subject to judgement, supposes another sovereign" (Smith 2010, I.1.16). These were delivered in 1763, a year after the appearance of Rousseau's *The Social Contract*, but published only over a century later.

between him and the people; and this is self-contradictory." To grant another party the right to contest the head of state would be to give sovereignty with one hand to the head of state but to take it away at the same time with the other.

Since the sovereign ruler is never going to be omniscient, Kant (1996, 302) concedes, each subject should have "freedom of the pen" as a right: that is, "the authorization to make known publicly his opinions." But "the constitution cannot contain any article that would make it possible for there to be some authority in a state to resist the supreme commander"; and this, even should that commander "violate the law of the constitution" (Kant 1996, 462).

How does the ban on a constitutional right to challenge the sovereign appear in a state where the sovereign is the assembly of the people, as in the democracy that Bodin and Hobbes allow or in the majoritarian republic endorsed by Rousseau? Can they act individually or in groups to challenge the decisions of that sovereign assembly: say, decisions that they as a minority oppose? No, according to the absolutists, they cannot. People could not assume such a contestatory right under the constitution without denying the rights of their sovereign: they would be treating the sovereign, after all, as if it did not have absolute constitutional power. They might each contribute to the collective, sovereign authorship of the laws in such a regime, but outside the assembly they would not have any right as individuals or as groups of individuals to try to exercise an editorial role. What Kant (1996, 462) says of sovereigns in general will be true also here: "the sovereign has only rights against his subjects and no duties (that he can be coerced to fulfill)."

Assessing the Argument

This argument against the idea that a non-sovereign agent might exercise power against the sovereign, and do so as a constitutional right, may look unassailable. Let every state be assumed to have a sovereign in control, and let every sovereign be assumed to have supreme domestic power. It will then follow that the constitution or mode of organization that establishes the sovereign cannot at the same time give any other agents among the people—any individual or corporate agents—the right to exercise power over the sovereign.

There are two points to make in response to the argument, however. The first is that no matter what sort of sovereign a constitution establishes, it is bound to give people a by-product right—a spandrel right, as we call it—to civil disobedience and a right to forcibly assert the complaints and demands that such disobedience will communicate. The second point is that even putting aside civil disobedience, the argument will have little practical import—it will do little to rule out the complaints and demands that citizens may make as subjects—when the sovereign assumes a polycentric form and the state is decentralized.

The Right of Civil Disobedience

The notion of a spandrel right derives from architecture and has been extended to serve also in biology; it refers to a feature that is not designed or selected for its own sake but emerges as a by-product of other ends sought (Gould and Lewontin 1979). For our purposes, it is usefully illustrated in an example from criminal law.

Within common law regimes, the role of the jury in a criminal hearing is to determine matters of fact, not law. Thus, in cases where the facts are uncontested and the law is clearly against the defendant, the jury may seem to have no choice but to bring back a verdict of guilty. But that is not so. True, they may have no explicitly recognized right to do anything but report a guilty verdict. But still, notoriously, they may bring back a verdict of innocence, say because of thinking the law unjust; and of course, they will do so with impunity. In the accepted phrase, the jury may choose to nullify the law.

The possibility of nullification is not an intended feature of the common law but is an unintended and inescapable by-product of what the law is designed to do: to let a criminal defendant be judged by his or her peers. The possibility is a spandrel: a feature, like the spandrel in medieval architecture, that is the unplanned, but often cherished, by-product of features that were indeed planned. Those on a jury have the right to nullify a law, not by explicit design of the criminal justice system, but as a by-product of the rules established in designing it.

As the right of nullification is an unplanned right of juries in the criminal justice system, there is an unplanned right to challenge the sovereign that any constitutional system is bound to give to subjects. This is the right of civil disobedience: the right to openly break some of the sovereign's laws, openly accept the penalties that the offense incurs, and use that act to contest some law or laws imposed by the sovereign: perhaps the very law broken, perhaps some distinct law or policy.[6]

---

6. Does civil disobedience have to be nonviolent, as is often assumed (Lai 2019)? Not by the approach taken here: the important thing is that it is conducted in a manner that does not challenge the rights of the sovereign. Of course, it may be that if such disobedience is to be causally effective or ethically acceptable, it has to be nonviolent. But that is a distinct matter.

Such an act of civil disobedience does not reject the claim of the sovereign to be the sovereign—it presupposes the continuing constitution—since the offender accepts the penalty due as the legally appropriate response to their action. But nonetheless it does constitute a form of challenge to the sovereign and one that the constitution itself allows. Let the constitution establish a sovereign operating under decision-maker laws; let that sovereign use decision-making powers to lay down decision-taker laws; and let those laws identify the penalties for any knowledgeable, competent offender. It will follow, regardless of the wishes of those setting up the constitution, that subjects will be able to challenge the sovereign's decisions in acts of civil disobedience. And if the government follows the constitution, it will be unable to act in retaliation other than by imposing the penalties accepted by their challengers. Like jury nullification, civil disobedience will be available as a legally unquestionable right—as a spandrel right—within the community.

Will civil disobedience be available as an option under a repressive regime? In principle, yes. Wherever a government imposes its decisions coercively, be they ad hoc or lawlike, it will identify penalties for offenses and expose itself to civil disobedience. Any subjects will be able to manifest disagreement with a law or decision and, by voluntarily exposing themselves to the associated penalty, they will contest the decision but, in accepting the penalty, not challenge the right of the government to rule under the constitution. A repressive government may have a policy of punishing civil disobedience, not by imposing just the penalties that regular offenders would receive, but punishment of the most extreme form. If it does this, the extra penalties will not remove the right of civil disobedience but merely ensure that only the heroically brave will be ready to exercise it.

The Polycentric Sovereign

The second point to make about the argument under review is that it is less confronting, when it is considered against the background of a decentralized state, a polycentric constitution. Assume with Bodin, Hobbes, and Rousseau that the sovereign in the state must be a concrete individual or body: in practice, a legislator or legislature that lays down the law and selects and controls those who judge and administer it. If the sovereign is a single concrete agent of this kind—even if it is a majoritarian assembly of all citizens—and if the constitution is simply the arrangement under which that agent or agency is cast in the lawmaking role, then it is clear why the absolutists should have been led to think as they did. Such a concrete agent will be denied sovereign power by the very constitution that purports to grants it, if that same constitution gives the subjects of the sovereign a countervailing power to express complaints and act to impose their demands. No individual or body can be sovereign if it is subject domestically to checking or control by an independent agent, individual or corporate.

But if the absolutist argument is intelligible on the assumption that the sovereign is a concrete individual or body, it loses all its impact once we recognize that the sovereign may be an emergent entity of the kind we described in the last chapter. For such a sovereign may operate under a permissive constitution that allows citizens freedom of speech, association, and contestation. And when it does so, attempts by citizens to act in groups, or even on their own, in mounting challenges to proposals or decisions by government will be constitutionally allowed.

Those challenges may be made in the courts, on the media, or on the streets, and they may consist in formal claims, informal arguments, or disruptive demonstrations. But no matter what their form, they will assume the profile, under a permissive constitution, of would-be inputs to the decision-making process whereby the state forms its corporate mind. Regardless of whether the inputs are successful or not, they will count as constitutional attempts to shape how the state behaves from within.

It may be useful to contrast the situation that would obtain when the sovereign is a majoritarian assembly of citizens, as in Rousseau's ideal, and that which would obtain under a polycentric, liberal constitution. In the first picture, citizens will each have their say from within the sovereign assembly. But once the assembly has ruled, they will be denied the right to protest or challenge its decision. The situation will be exactly like that which would obtain if the sovereign were an assembly of aristocrats, in the old image, or indeed an autocratic monarch.

In the second, polycentric picture, citizens will have their say from within the sovereign polity insofar as they or their representatives play their part in the process leading up to a decision; playing their part may only mean choosing not to object, when they have a right to do so. But once a decision has been taken, whether by way of making a proposal or implementing a policy, ordinary citizens or indeed officials will retain the capacity to have a say in its reconsideration, seeking to force a change of tack on the state. They will retain that capacity insofar as they have the constitutional right to contest any decision as parties who share in the sovereign power of the state. Their exercise of that right will constitute the beginnings of a reconsideration—a recourse to second thoughts—on the part of the polity as a whole.

Let the sovereign be a polycentric entity, as we argued that the sovereign should be in making a functional case for decentralizing the state. It will follow immediately that disaffected or dissatisfied citizens will have a power of challenging sovereign decisions, even on the sovereigntist premises endorsed among absolutists. They will enjoy an ability to exercise some control over the sovereign because their control will be exercised from within.

How might people exercise this sort of internal control over the operation of the decentralized state? The possibilities are as numerous and various as the devices that democracies might explore, and have explored, in seeking to realize the democratic ideal of providing ordinary people or citizens with a great deal of power (Ober 2008b). They include giving people an electoral role in shaping the constitution by triggering or participating in a referendum, in standing for office, in campaigning for a candidate or policy, or just in voting; giving those who wish to use it a right to challenge what the government proposes or does within the courts, in the media, or on the streets; and giving those selected on a random basis a responsibility to discharge a certain task, as in contributing to a citizen assembly that is called to advise on how to resolve this or that issue.

The constitutional power of ordinary people that is illustrated in these modes is parallel to the power that may be enjoyed under a polycentric constitution by any independent authorities like judges, inspectors, auditors, and the like. The decentralized state or sovereign may be the ultimate center of power, but its power will reflect the separate powers of the different constituent agents and agencies among which it is shared. People or citizens in the appropriate sense are one such constituent part and may even be the most important part of all; this will presumably have to be the case in any system that measures up to the demands of democracy in its original sense.

These observations are meant to show that it is possible for people to be given constitutional power within a sovereign state, contrary to absolutist claims. But is it desirable that they should be given higher degrees of power? It is almost certainly desirable as a matter of justice, for giving ordinary people such power is likely to guard against the domination of ordinary citizens by officials (Pettit 2012; 2014). But is it desirable from the functional perspective adopted in this study? Would widespread citizen power be likely to enable the state to do its job better in securing individuals against one another and against officials?

It would be hard to argue just on functional grounds that the state should give ordinary people the full array of powers associated with democratic, accountable government. But the case for giving them some range of powers is as strong as the general case that we made earlier for some degree of decentralization in the state. Let the incorporated state be centralized around the operation of relatively uncheckable authorities and it will be unlikely to secure citizens in the functionally required manner against officials and against those whom officials may favor. That means, as we argued, that some decentralization is certainly appealing in functional terms. And under plausible circumstances the decentralization that appeals will include the ascription of considerable power to ordinary citizens.

4.2 The Issue of Extra-Constitutional Power

Another Question

We have seen that, contrary to an argument found in absolutist authors, and even in someone like Kant, people or citizens in an active, encompassing sense will inevitably have a constitutional right to mount complaints against the sovereign and help to shape law. True, they may not have an explicit, legal right to such a role if the sovereign is a concrete agent or agency distinct from the people. But they will certainly have the spandrel right of civil disobedience that is guaranteed as a by-product of any decision-maker practices or laws. And they will have an explicit as well as a spandrel right to shape the sovereign's decision making, if the sovereign emerges from interaction between various individuals and bodies, ordinary people included: if the people in that sense constitute a proper part of the sovereign, as it were, but are not identical with the sovereign.

This shows how the people can have constitutional power within a polity, as in regular democracies. In other words, as we might put the lesson, it shows that what works in practice, as illustrated in democratic, polycentric regimes, also works in theory: specifically, in the sovereigntist theory endorsed in the last chapter, according to which every polity must be organized around a sovereign power. We turn now, however, to a very different issue, and one that is of more than merely theoretical significance. This is whether the people, when they act together can use extra-constitutional power against their sovereign. Here too we shall see that they must have some such power, in principle if not in practice, and that under a suitable constitution they will have a much higher level of power, and indeed a power that is available in practice as well as in principle.

Before arguing for that claim in the next section, however, we look in this at an argument found among absolutists against the idea that the citizenry or people can act together extra-constitutionally to restrict or remove their sovereign. According to this argument, it is downright impossible for the people of a state, acting together, to have such power over their sovereign.[7]

The conclusion that the argument supports can be formulated in either of two ways. First, as a ground-level claim about how the people considered as subjects of the law cannot exercise power against the sovereign. Or, second, as a higher-level, metalinguistic claim about how the "the people" or "the citizenry," taken in an encompassing sense, cannot be coherently said to have exercised such power together against the sovereign: such a report, so the claim goes, would be conceptually incoherent. The absolutist argument is best presented as a defense of this metalinguistic claim, which turns on how properly to understand the meaning and referent of the expression "the people" or "the citizenry."

Most clearly formulated in Hobbes but reflected also in the work of Rousseau and Kant, the argument is that were the people to attempt to challenge their sovereign extra-constitutionally—were they to try to corral or undercut the sovereign's status in a violent or peaceful assertion of power—then whatever form that challenge took, it could not be coherently described as something authored by the people acting together. This claim is not the property of past thinkers alone for, as we shall see, something very close to it is maintained by those political and legal thinkers who hold that there is a paradox of constitutional regress. The absolutist, metalinguistic argument for the claim is structurally parallel, as we shall see, to an argument that continues to exercise an attraction among contemporary thinkers.

---

7. A subsidiary argument, which we ignore here, is that any attempt on the people's part to exercise such power, if that were possible or feasible, would be undesirable. All that would be achieved by an attempt on the people's part to exercise extra-constitutional power, so the line goes, would be to return the society to a prepolitical condition. In Hobbes's (1994b, chap. 18.2) language it would be to return the members of the polity to a state of nature and to "the confusion of a disunited multitude." In Kant's (1996, 300fn) it would be to replace them by a "mob," and to release the "horrors" of anarchy.

To see how the original argument goes, we need to look at how Hobbes, Rousseau, and Kant thought about the people. They made a distinction between the people or citizens of a state acting in their own name alone and the people or citizens acting as an incorporated, group agent. And they argued that in neither sense can the people be credited coherently with the extra-constitutional capacity to challenge together the sovereign's power. Following Hobbes's presentation, we shall look first at their picture of the unincorporated people; second, at their image of the people incorporated as a group agent; and then at the argument—we present it as a dilemma—that they use those pictures to mount against the possibility that the people might successfully exercise extra-constitutional power against the sovereign.

The Unincorporated People

As with so many themes in the discussion of statehood and related topics, Hobbes makes a signal contribution in the clarity of his distinction between the people in the unincorporated and the incorporated sense. He concedes that "the people" is sometimes used as an expression to refer to either but prefers himself to use the term "the multitude" for the people unincorporated.

The multitude are characterized by the fact that they cannot ever be said to perform an action together, according to Hobbes, although of course they may act individually. Nothing can be "truly called the action of the multitude," he says, "unless every man's hand, and every man's will, (not so much as one excepted) have concurred thereto" (Hobbes 1994a, 20.2): unless—a condition he takes to be radically unlikely—there is complete convergence on the end to be pursued and the means to be adopted. Even when they confront a common enemy, he thinks, individuals will typically fail to act as a single agent: "being distracted in opinions concerning the best use and application of their strength, they do not help, but hinder one another, and reduce their strength by mutual opposition to nothing" (Hobbes 1994b, 27.4). If this is not obvious, he thinks, that is because we are disposed "to take for the action of the people that which is a multitude of actions done by a multitude of men" (Hobbes 1994b, 11.20).

The members of a multitude are essentially disunited, on this view: "a number of men, each of whom has his own will and his own judgment" (Hobbes 1998, 6.1). And so, according to Hobbes (1994a, 21.11), they cannot make a claim as a body in the manner of a person: they "cannot be said to demand or have a right to anything." This lack of unity leads Hobbes to speak of the multitude as an "aggregate" or "heap" of agents, "a disorganized crowd" or "throng," and a disjointed or "dissolute number of individual persons."[8]

In adopting this language, he joins forces with a common royalist line of argument in England in the 1640s. Deriding parliamentary pretensions to recognize the sovereignty of the people, royalist critics had given a suitably unflattering image of the people as a multitude "in continual alteration and change." As one account had it, this body "never continues one minute the same, being composed of a multitude of parts, whereof divers continually decay and perish, and others renew and succeed in their places" (Morgan 1988, 61). Hobbes would have had to disagree with these royalists, since he held that such a multitude can act if it gets to be incorporated under a sovereign, even a parliamentary sovereign. But his image of the unincorporated multitude is otherwise very similar.

The multitude as it is characterized by Hobbes and others refers to the people considered independently of whether they are represented or incorporated. In that sense, so we shall assume, the multitude continues to exist even if incorporation takes place. Considered under their aspect as separate individuals, the people will be a multitude; considered under their aspect as an incorporated body, they will constitute a group agent.

As *The Social Contract* makes clear, Rousseau (1997b, 1.5.2) follows Hobbes in his views on the people. He thinks of the unanimous social contract, like Hobbes, as an act of incorporation—"the act by which a people is a people"—and casts it as "the true foundation of society." And he represents the people before such an act—even the people who are "enslaved to a single man"—as "an aggregation but not an association," as indeed a "multitude" (Rousseau 1997b, 1.5.1).

We may assume that for Rousseau, as for Hobbes, the multitude continue to exist after incorporation: they are the citizens considered simply as individual, unorganized individuals. But he is more sanguine about the life of the unincorporated multitude in the state of nature. In such a condition, Rousseau's human being is not locked into endless comparison and competition, unlike the individual in Hobbes's state of nature, but lives a relatively untroubled existence. "His soul, which nothing stirs, yields itself to the sole sentiment of its present existence, with no idea of the future, however near it

---

8. These phrases are employed respectively in Hobbes (1994a, 21.11), Hobbes (1998, 7.11), and Hobbes (1994b, 6.37 and 42.27).

may be, and his projects, as limited as his views, hardly extend to the close of day" (Rousseau 1997a, 143).[9]

The Incorporated People

We noted earlier that in the fourteenth century, legal theorists like Bartolus of Sassoferrato had already begun to argue that the citizens of a republic such as his own Perugia organized themselves under a representative, rotating council, like the members of a guild, and constituted thereby a group agent. As the membership of the guild might be taken to refer to the members individually or to the body they constitute, so Bartolus and his ilk happily used the Latin word *civitas* to refer to both the citizens individually and the state they constituted. In taking this line, they developed the idea that the people can exist, not just as a collection or multitude of individuals, but as an incorporated body.

If the notion of the incorporated people was in place from the medieval period, however, it was Hobbes who really began to make much of it. The incorporation of any set of individuals, as Hobbes conceived of the process, depends on their authorization of a spokesperson to speak for them as a group. And the sovereign is the spokesperson that the members of a political society authorize—in this case, authorize without stint—to speak for them as a commonwealth or polity, making avowals or pledges in their name.

On this approach, it is the people as individuals, the people as a multitude, who authorize the sovereign, unanimously acquiescing in being personated or spoken for by that individual or committee. But insofar as they incorporate under a sovereign, those individuals come to constitute a corporate body. And this counts both as the people incorporated and as the commonwealth or state. Like Bartolus he used the word *civitas* to refer both to the citizenry and to the state formed by their incorporation; as the word could refer to either, the equation of the people with the polity, the citizenry with the state, might

---

9. The difference between Hobbes and Rousseau on this point may not run very deep, as I have argued elsewhere (Pettit 2008a, chap. 6). Hobbes thinks of the state of nature as a condition after the appearance of language among human beings, holding that while language gave them a range of cognitive and social capacities, it led them to seek eminence or superiority in relation to one another; in effect, it precipitated a zero-sum game: a war of all against all, as he calls it. Rousseau also thinks of language as a mixed blessing since it helps induce in human beings a desire to prove themselves better than their fellows—*l'amour propre*—but he casts the state of nature as a condition prior to the discovery of language and prior to the zero-sum game that that would have introduced.

have sounded more natural to medieval and early modern ears than it does to ours.[10]

Whereas Bartolus thought that only the free people of a republic can exist as a corporate body, Hobbes took a very different line. He argued that in every state—every commonwealth or *civitas*—the people are incorporated, and the commonwealth just is the incorporated people. According to the earlier approach, the state can be the people incorporated and that people can be described as *sibi princeps*—a prince unto itself—only when a suitably constituted council speaks for them. According to the Hobbesian approach, the people are a corporate person even when an individual or elite committee plays the spokesperson role. And whether the arrangement is democratic, aristocratic, or monarchical, as he would put it, the commonwealth just is that incorporated people.

According to Hobbes (1994b, 16.13), it is the sovereign, whether a sovereign individual or committee, that gives unity to the commonwealth, since unity "cannot otherwise be understood in multitude." And so, if the sovereign ceases to play that unifying role, then two things happen at once on his theory. First, the commonwealth is "dissolved"; and, second, the members become once again a mere multitude in which, as in the state of nature, everyone is "at liberty to protect himself" (Hobbes 1994b, 29.23).

Thus, as Bartolus would have taken the *civitas* in the city republic to be at once the people and the state—the *populus* and the *res publica*—so Hobbes thinks that no matter what the constitutional form, the incorporated people just is the commonwealth. He is even willing to say that "in a Monarchy the subjects are the crowd"—that is, the multitude—"and (paradoxically) the King is the people" (Hobbes 1998, 12.8; cf. 7.8). "The sovereign," as he puts it elsewhere, "is the public soul, giving life and motion to the commonwealth; which expiring, the members are governed by it no more, than the carcass of a man, by his departed (though immortal) soul" (Hobbes 1994b, 29.23).[11]

The view of the relation between the incorporated people and the state is broadly maintained by Rousseau, although for him the sovereign has to be an

10. On this claim about Latin usage, and on the contrast with the usage in classical Greek, see Ando (2015, 8, 45). I am grateful to Daniel Lee for help on this issue.

11. There is an important debate between David Runciman (1997, 2000b, 2003, 2006), Quentin Skinner (1999, 2005), and Richard Tuck (1998, 2006) about the interpretation of Hobbes on these matters. For a brisk overview—and for a defense of the position sketched here—see Pettit (2008a, 162).

assembly of all citizens. He postulates a social contract of a Hobbesian kind, taking it, as we saw, to constitute "the act by which a people is a people" (Rousseau 1997b, 1.5.2). And he argues that that act "produces a moral and collective body made up of as many members as the assembly has voices, and which receives by this same act its unity, its common self, its life, and its will" (Rousseau 1997b, 1.6.10). This is a body with many facets, as he goes on to explain, being known from different perspectives as a republic or state or sovereign. As a corporate entity the associates "collectively assume the name *people*," and as individuals they constitute "citizens" and "subjects": citizens, in their role as members of the lawmaking assembly, subjects in their role as takers of that law.

Kant (1996, 324) echoes Rousseau in speaking of "the act of the general will by which a multitude becomes a people," recognizing that people exist prior to incorporation only as a multitude. But for him the act of incorporation consists just in people's acquiescing in whatever "civil constitution" happens to be established. And this acquiescence may take place, not in wake of a social contract of any kind, but under fear of a despot. It may materialize whether the state "began with an actual contract of submission as a fact, or whether power came first and law arrived only afterwards" (Kant 1996, 462); the social contract, he says, is only an "idea of reason," not something realized, however informally, as a matter of fact (Kant 1996, 296). Despite this difference, however, Kant goes along with Hobbes and Rousseau in taking the incorporated people to be nothing more or less than the polity itself.[12]

The Dilemma for Popular Extra-constitutional Power

The dichotomy between the unincorporated and the incorporated people as it is understood in Hobbes, Rousseau, and Kant generates a dilemma. And they make use of the dilemma to argue that the people cannot use extra-constitutional power against the sovereign: in metalinguistic terms, that it is incoherent to think that a body that deserves to be called the people can act against the sovereign.

If the people can act to restrict or replace the sovereign, they must satisfy two conditions according to the absolutist argument: first, they must be

12. For all of these thinkers, the incorporated people, established by a constitution, will survive as long as the constitution survives. In the same spirit Jed Rubenfeld (2001) argues that the people in control of the state at any moment after the formation of a constitution is the continuing people it establishes, not a particular generation.

capable of performing as an agent for one or another purpose; and second, they must be independent enough of the sovereign to be able to act specifically for the purpose of opposing the sovereign. The alleged dilemma consists in the fact, supported by our observations so far, that the people cannot satisfy the conditions of agency and independence at one and the same time. The people as a group are either unincorporated or incorporated, according to absolutists; there is no third possibility. And under either possibility, the idea of a people that might oppose or oust the sovereign makes no sense.

If they are unincorporated, to take the first horn of the dilemma, they will satisfy the independence condition, being capable of existing independently of the sovereign, but they will not satisfy the agency condition: given that unanimity is bound to elude them, they will be unable to act together in any cause, including the cause of rejecting or opposing the sovereign. And if they are incorporated, to take the second horn, the reverse will be true. They will satisfy the agency condition, having the status of a corporate body, but they will not satisfy independence; the people in this sense will just be the polity and will be able to exist and act only so long as the sovereign is there to make this possible: the sovereign, after all, is the spokesperson that enables them to constitute a corporate body.

The idea behind the argument for the first horn of the dilemma, under which the people are identified with the unincorporated multitude, is based on the assumption that if they are to act, they must have a set of procedures under which they coordinate with one another in endorsing shared attitudes and acting as those attitudes require; in the Hobbesian version, they must all recognize a suitably coherent voice as speaking for them as a group. But, as a matter of definition, the unincorporated people do not coordinate with one another under any constitution: they do not rally behind any guiding voice. And so, assuming unanimity is nigh impossible, it follows that the people in that unincorporated sense cannot perform an action together and cannot act, therefore, against the state and sovereign under which they live.

Turning to the second horn of the dilemma, under which the people are incorporated, the referent of "the people" is certainly capable of action, as we know. But the problem here is that the incorporated people will be identical with the polity itself and will be represented like the polity by the sovereign. That means that if the people act against the sovereign, they will act against the representer or personator that enables them to constitute an agent capable of acting. If they deny the sovereign this role, they will cease to constitute an incorporated body and will cease to be capable of action: they will return, as Hobbes (1994b, 18.2) would put it, to "the confusion of a disunited multitude."

Suppose, impossibly, that the people qua corporate body did remove their sovereign. This would amount on the Hobbesian picture to a sort of corporate suicide, in which the members take away the principle that gives them "life and motion." Although a mortal man in the case of a monarchy, the sovereign is the public soul, according to Hobbes (1994b, 29.23), and if that soul departs the corporate body, then the body will be as dead and undirected as "the carcass of a man," abandoned "by his departed (though immortal) soul."

The line that Hobbes takes here is upheld by Rousseau insofar as he also allows the people to act only insofar as they incorporate, by a unanimous vote, as a sovereign assembly. The fact that that is so entails that it would make no sense for the incorporated people to act against the state: the people in that sense would be the state.

Although he follows Rousseau in other respects, Kant is like Hobbes in admitting constitutions under which the people have little or no role in government. And he also follows Hobbes in deeming the notion of popular resistance incoherent. Indeed, Kant (1996, 464) explicitly invokes the metaphor of suicide, arguing that if the people do kill a head of state, as in the case of Charles I of England, then "it is as if the state commits suicide"—"a crime," he notes somewhat obscurely, "from which the people cannot be absolved."

Kant (1996, 300) argues that the will of the state—the will of the people "as a commonwealth"—is the will that is expressed in the laws. While he is often prepared, as we saw, to identify the sovereign with "the personified law," he insists that the ruler is "the organ of the sovereign," the sole authority in determining the will of the people, so that they "cannot and may not judge otherwise than as the present head of state wills it to" (Kant 1996, 462). The people "cannot offer any resistance to the legislative head of a state" and "has a duty to put up with even what is held to be an unbearable abuse of supreme authority" (Kant 1996, 464). As with Hobbes and Rousseau, he thinks that if members of the incorporated people were to resist the head of state they would cease thereby to be incorporated, becoming a multitude or "mob" (Kant 1996, 300fn).

Will the decentralization of the state, for which we argued in the last chapter, help us to evade this line of argument? No, it will not. The assumption that the people can exist only in an unincorporated or incorporated form will still give rise to the dilemma in the case of a decentralized polity. Considered independently of their incorporation under a suitable constitution—considered, in absolutist terms, as a multitude—the people will be unable to act. Considered as a body that is coterminous with the polity, they will lack the independence that might allow us to think of them as restricting or replacing the sovereign. Thus, we cannot appeal to decentralization to argue that the dilemma is not a challenge.

The Paradox of Constitutional Regress

The dichotomy of unincorporated and incorporated people has left a trace in democratic and constitutional theory, being implicitly invoked in a paradox that arises on premises like those in the absolutist argument. This is worth noting both because it is of inherent interest and because it reveals the extent to which contemporary thinking still operates within a framework established in early modern European thought.

It is taken for granted in much contemporary constitutional thinking, as in the tradition we have been examining, that an unorganized multitude—a populace without any constitution under which to incorporate—cannot act. The idea is that a condition for them to be able to act together is that the members endorse a constitution that would give them procedural guidelines for collective action.[13] That raises the issue, then, of whether they can act to revise or reject the constitution under which they live.

More specifically, the question is whether the people can do this outside the constitution. Suppose that the constitution itself does not allow amendment, or at least amendment of the kind they seek, not containing a clause that establishes the procedures under which they may do this. Or suppose that the constitution makes it excessively difficult to achieve the amendment sought, as when it requires the agreement of an unwilling official or an elite authority. Can the people act outside the constitution to make the desired change?[14]

On premises shared with absolutists, a range of constitutional and democratic theorists argue that they cannot. The people properly conceived are the constitutionally organized people, and it would make no conceptual sense to

13. For a recent challenge to this assumption, see Negri (1999).

14. It is worth noting, however, that opinions may vary on what is allowed, and what is not allowed, under a constitution. For readings of the U.S. Constitution on which constitutional changes may occur without following Article 5, the clause explicitly addressing amendment, see Amar (1988) and Ackerman (1991). And for an illuminating discussion of the grounds on which amendments might be taken as constitutional or not, independently of their fit with Article 5, see Macedo (1990, chaps. 4–5).

say that that people can act outside their constitution to revise or replace it. If the people seem to have acted outside the constitution for such a purpose, then it was not properly the people—it was not the corporate agent established under the constitution—that did so.

These theorists often focus on an implication of regress that follows, as they see it, from this position. The regress comes into view when we ask about how a people could have generated or ratified a constitution in the first place. If they produced a constitution from scratch, so it appears, then they must have done so under a preexisting mode of organization or incorporation: in effect, a preexisting $constitution_1$. And if they ratified a constitution proposed by some other group, then equally they must have done so by relying on a form of incorporation that only a preexisting constitution like $constitution_1$ would provide.

Where would that preexisting constitution or mode of incorporation have come from? And was it adopted by the people themselves as distinct from being imposed on them? If we think that it was popularly adopted, presumably at a yet earlier stage, then we are driven to postulate yet another constitution, another mode of incorporation, that was presupposed in that act of adoption: call this $constitution_2$. But was $constitution_2$ itself adopted by them? If it was, then that means that they must have acted under yet another mode or incorporation: $constitution_3$. The regress that this line of thought opens up suggests, paradoxically, that at some point the constitution under which a people would have acted cannot have been actively adopted by them.

This regress problem has been identified as an issue among constitutional theorists, particularly those interested in how far a people can be democratically self-governing, as well as among more explicitly democratic theorists. Frank Michelman (1999, 48) gives nice expression to the problem from the viewpoint of constitutional theory, when he argues that "constitutionalism—the endeavor to place government under reason expressed as law—inevitably means the establishment of some a priori fixed, non-negotiable, non-debatable set of concretely intelligible normative first principles." The lesson is that on pain of regress, there must be some constitutional arrangements—some procedures for lawmaking—that themselves lie beyond the range of negotiation: that is, beyond the reach of what the people themselves might choose to adopt.[15]

15. There are many versions of the problem raised in constitutional theory. For a collection of papers dealing with it, see Loughlin and Walker (2007); for a paper outlining some different versions, see Zurn (2010); and for a good statement of the issue, see Michelman (1999, chap. 1).

Jürgen Habermas (2001, 774) offers a classic formulation of the paradox from the point of view of democratic theory: "The constitutional assembly cannot itself vouch for the legitimacy of the rules according to which it was constituted. The chain never terminates, and the democratic process is caught in a circular self-constitution that leads to an infinite regress" (see too Habermas 1995). The problem is also raised by democratic theorists who ask about how the boundaries of different peoples can be legitimately determined.[16] Frederic Whelan (1983, 40) registers the paradox in that context: "Democracy, which is a method for group decision-making or self-governance, cannot be brought to bear on the logically prior matter of the constitution of the group itself."[17]

The paradox of constitutional regress derives from similar assumptions to those that generate the absolutist dilemma. The assumptions are, first, that if they are not constitutionally organized—not organized, as we may say, under a sovereign—then the people in a polity are incapable of doing anything. And second, that if their capacity for action depends on their being organized under a given constitution, with a given sovereign, then they cannot act extra-constitutionally to challenge or replace that constitution and sovereign.

While the premises inherited from absolutists drive the problem of constitutional regress, however, it is worth noting that at least one absolutist, Thomas Hobbes, would have argued that he escapes the problem. He would have agreed, of course, that the unincorporated people cannot act, short of a vanishingly improbable unanimity, and that the constitutionally organized people cannot act extra-constitutionally to reject or replace that constitution. But he

---

There is a good discussion of a parallel problem in the generation of law in Shapiro (2011, chap. 2).

16. On the approach adopted here, of course, we sidestep the boundary issue by taking states as a given and letting state borders determine the borders between peoples. The approach is broadly similar to that taken by Anna Stilz (2019, 24), who defends "a novel, endogenous approach to the question of 'who are the people?' On the endogenous approach, there is no Archimedean point for delineating 'peoples' outside our existing structure of political institutions." Where Stilz wants to develop ethical principles governing the relation between peoples, however, we ignore that project here.

17. Like Whelan, Sofia Näsström (2007, 625) provides a useful overview and treatment of the democratic issue, formulating it somewhat differently. "The persons who are supposed to confer legitimacy upon the people are trapped in an infinite circle of self-definition. They cannot themselves decide on their own composition."

would not have agreed that the people could not have acted to adopt a constitution, whether in generating a novel arrangement or ratifying a proposed arrangement.

This is because he holds that the situation of the original contract is precisely one where, remarkably, unanimity obtains. An action cannot be "truly called the action of the multitude," he says, "unless every man's hand, and every man's will, (not so much as one excepted) have concurred thereto" (Hobbes 1994a, 20.2). He suggests by the remark that if individuals unanimously support what a multitude brings about, then the multitude can be said to bring that about as an action. And of course he thinks that that is what would have happened in the original contract that took them out of the state of nature— the war of all against all—and into the polity. In that sort of case, he holds, "a multitude of men do agree, and covenant, every one with every one," to treat "all the actions and judgments" of the sovereign "as if they were his own" (Hobbes 1994b, 17.1).[18]

A Reductio Ad Absurdum

Absolutists and defenders of the paradox of constitutional regress are each faced with a problem to which the answer they must give is intuitively absurd. The problem is raised by the fact that there are many historically documented episodes of extra-constitutional shifts in which one and the same people appear to have changed their constitution or their sovereign. That happened in the United States when, by a procedure that was not previously validated, the 1777 Articles of Confederation were replaced by the Constitution drawn up in 1787 and adopted by the existing states. And it happened in England in 1688, when Parliament forced James II to depart and put William and Mary on the throne; indeed, it had happened in Hobbes's own time when the civil war led to the execution of Charles I and the assumption of sovereignty by Parliament.

What are we to say about these cases on the premises shared between absolutists and defenders of the paradox of constitutional regress? In the American case, it seems we must say that with the adoption of the new constitution, the

18. While a commonwealth may come about by acquisition or conquest rather than being instituted in a formal manner, Hobbes (1994b, 2) thinks the distinction is of little account: "This kind of dominion, or sovereignty, differeth from sovereignty by institution only in this, that men who choose their sovereign do it for fear of one another, and not of him whom they institute: but in this case, they subject themselves to him they are afraid of."

corporate body that we might have referred to as the American, incorporated people ceased to exist and that it was replaced by another body and another people, albeit one deserving of the same name. And in the English case, we must apparently say something similar: that with the advent of the new regime, ushered in without reliance on the old, one English people ceased to exist, and another people took its place.

These responses are counterintuitive to the point of being absurd. There is clearly a sense in which the same body of people survived in each instance and acted via representatives—agents treated by most citizens, at least after the event, as representatives—to implement a change of constitution and sovereign. We turn in the final section to a viewpoint under which we can explain why this does indeed make sense. Before we turn to that task, however, it is worthwhile looking at a very different conception of the state that emerged in the modern period in response to the absolutist argument. This is associated mainly with John Locke and still retains a hold in various quarters.

The Lockean Response to the Dilemma

The theories of the incorporated people that nurture the absolutist dilemma all assume that incorporation occurs by virtue of state formation, so that the incorporated people do not enjoy the independence from the state that a capacity to rebel would require. Let the state cease to exist, according to each of them, and the incorporated people will cease to exist as well; they will become a multitude and return to the state of nature. But there was a dissident tradition of thought that sought to break this linkage between the incorporated people and the state, and it deserves a mention in any typology of ways of conceptualizing the people. This, in its earliest form, was cast as the monarchomach tradition, which argued for the right of the people to combat—as in the Greek word, *machein*—the monarch or sovereign (Skinner 1978, vol. 2; 2002a, chap. 9).

Adherents of the tradition accepted that the people may exist in only two forms, incorporated and unincorporated. But they argued that prior to the appearance of a political sovereign, the people would have existed as a corporate body that was represented by a variety of prepolitical religious and social authorities. And because of that assumption, they maintained a defense of the right of rebellion.

The defense, broadly, was that a corporate people who live under monarchical rule must be presumed to have contracted in the past with that sovereign and his or her successors to rule over them on certain terms; and that if any monarch fails to act on those terms, the people are entitled to rebel and dismiss the person involved. The doctrine appealed in the late sixteenth century to religious dissidents such as the Huguenots in France, who were subject to persecution from the center. Its best-known expression was the book *Vindiciae, Contra Tyrannos* (Languet 1994), published in 1579, seven years after the St. Bartholomew's Day massacre.

Absolutists like Bodin and Hobbes opposed the monarchomachs strongly, seeing the proposal as a recipe for civil disaster. Their argument, in its Hobbesian version, was that it would have taken a proper, political sovereign to unite a multitude, rallying members around a directive voice; and that the multitude that preexisted the appearance of a sovereign monarch would not have had the organization required to enter a contract with that individual. The people in that sense cannot make a contract "as one party," Hobbes (1994b, 18.4) says, "because as yet they are not one person."

At the end of the seventeenth century, John Locke resurrected many themes in the monarchomach tradition, in particular the idea that the people are able and indeed entitled to rebel against a monarch who betrays their trust. And he did so in a way that is designed, consciously or not, to evade the Hobbesian line of criticism.

According to Locke's *Second Treatise of Government*, the unincorporated people in a state of nature do not live in a war of all against all but interact under a range of collectively beneficial norms and live in relative peace. He implies that such norms would spontaneously appear, reflecting the laws of nature, as he envisages them; these, unlike Hobbes's laws of self-interest, stipulate that "being all equal and independent, no one ought to harm another in his life, health, liberty, or possessions" (Locke 1960, s6). People in the state of nature, so he suggests, would each force others to conform to the laws of nature in dealing with them, thereby establishing those laws as social norms. This is because, on his picture, each "hath by nature a power, not only to preserve his property, that is, his life, liberty and estate, against the injuries and attempts of other men; but to judge of, and punish the breaches of that law in others, as he is persuaded the offence deserves" (Locke 1960, s87).

Why would people form a state in such a condition of nature? They would resort to having a polity—a polity without the sovereign power in which absolutists believed—only because of "those inconveniences of the state of nature, which necessarily follow from every man's being judge in his own case" (Locke 1960, s90). Locke's (1960, s87) polity is designed by its members to set up an "umpire," then, not an absolute monarch: specifically, to introduce "a common established law and judicature to appeal to, with authority to decide controversies between them, and punish offenders."

Despite these differences from the absolutists, Locke goes along with them in thinking that individuals leave the state of nature and become an incorporated people only by unanimously entering a social contract, explicit or implicit, to allow the community as a whole—this, as in the democratic assembly envisaged by Bodin and Hobbes—to act in the required role of umpire. And like those absolutists, Locke (1960, s132) holds that if the community exercises this role itself, it will constitute a "perfect democracy," and will operate—inevitably, as he thinks—by majority consent.

Locke holds that the people thus incorporated are very likely to outsource their umpiring power to officials who operate under this or that constitution, specifically to an elite legislative entity or person.[19] But at this point he breaks in a decisive respect with Bodin and Hobbes. For where they say that any such transfer of power must be irrevocable—else the transferee will not count as sovereign—Locke (1960, s149) holds that the legislative body or individual can be given "only a fiduciary power to act for certain ends." And that implies that the incorporated people may force changes on their lawmaker or lawmakers, as the monarchomachs held, if they abuse that power. As Locke says, "There remains still in the people a supreme power to remove or alter the legislative, when they find the legislative act contrary to the trust reposed in them": they can reclaim a power that is rightfully theirs.[20]

According to Locke, the people will exist and operate as a corporate agent just insofar as the majority speaks for them. He thinks this is inevitable, as already mentioned, arguing in his *Second Treatise of Government* that "it being necessary to that which is one body to move one way; it is necessary the body should move that way whither the greater force carries it, which is the consent of the majority" (Locke 1960, s96). In the normal course of events, the legislature established by majority consent in the past will retain the presumptive

19. This means, in effect, that there will usually be two covenants, one to form a community, the other to form a government. The two-covenant theory is often associated with the work of Pufendorf (2005) from earlier in the seventeenth century. But Pufendorf did not think of the first covenant as establishing anything like an incorporated agent; the community materializing in that covenant would not have a procedure like majority voting around which to organize. See Tuck (2016, 113–15).

20. The notion of the *vindicatio* in Roman law, echoed in the title of the monarchomach tract, *Vindiciae Contra Tyrannos*, encoded this notion of reclaiming one's property or, in the case of wrongful enslavement, reclaiming one's status as a free person. See Lee (2016, 150–51).

right to speak for the people. But if an individual plaintiff or plaintiffs have a complaint against this presumption that is shared and actively supported by a majority, then they are entitled to rebel against the legislature. And they are likely to achieve satisfaction if the "illegal acts" about which they complain "have extended to a majority of people" or are such that "the precedent, and consequences seem to threaten all" (Locke 1960, s209).

But the power or right of plaintiffs to seek to force changes on the legislature is unlikely to materialize very often, on Locke's view. Majority support for change is likely to be forthcoming, as he himself says, only if there is "a long train of abuses," with a "design visible to the people" (Locke 1960, s149). This is presumably because people will each be afraid of not gaining majority support in launching an individual protest, and perhaps suffering retaliation as a result; they may fail to gain such support, presumably, either because others do not have the same complaint in the same degree or because others do not want to risk retaliation if not enough people join the protest. And so, Locke sounds a note that ought to console the most timid, conservative souls. "Great mistakes in the ruling part, many wrong and inconvenient laws, and all the slips of human frailty, will be borne by the people without mutiny or murmur."

Does Locke show us a way beyond the absolutist dilemma? No, for two reasons, one formal, the other substantive. The formal reason is that what Locke defends is strictly a constitutional right to popular power, not an extra-constitutional one. On his picture, after all, the constitution that remains in effect, even after the appointment of an elite government, is one of popular majority rule, albeit a form of majority rule that operates normally on the basis of the assumption that the government has majority support. That constitution clearly allows the opposition that Locke countenances, so that strictly it presupposes the constitution in place rather than overthrowing it.

The substantive reason for not enthusing about the Lockean approach is that it is hard to take seriously the claim that the people remain an incorporated group quite independently of the government that speaks for them, when there are no procedures for assembling the people and determining the majority views on relevant issues. The disposition of the majority to air their views can show up only in extreme circumstances: only where a majority are outraged enough and fearless enough to muster against those in office and power. And so, it is hard to see how, in normal times, it could be taken to silence the presumption of government to speak for the people in a sovereign role.

Something akin to the Lockean approach was sometimes invoked by eighteenth-century political radicals, particularly in America, where it was used to justify the war of independence (Zuckert 1996; Tuck 2016, chap. 4). But if the role of the people in relation to the state is confined to the reserve power of majoritarian resistance or rebellion, at a potential cost to personal safety, then it is hard to enthuse about the approach as a response to the dilemma. It may represent the best response possible, on the assumption that there is an exhaustive dichotomy between the unincorporated and the incorporated people. But it clearly leaves much to be desired.

The approach defended in the next section goes beyond the dichotomy of the unincorporated or incorporated people with which Locke and these other thinkers worked. But the picture it supports can be seen as a cousin of the Lockean way of depicting things. While Locke is stuck with having to maintain that the people who might act against the existing constitution have to be already incorporated as a group, the approach we defend does not. And while Locke thinks that the bare possibility of armed rebellion is enough to show that the people retain power, our approach suggests that more is institutionally required to make such power accessible.

4.3 The Extra-Constitutional Power of the People

However old and distinguished its pedigree, the dichotomy between the unincorporated multitude and the incorporated polity offers a badly misleading perspective on the idea of the people. On the first account the people in a state are as diversely driven and directed as the sellers and buyers in a competitive market; we might think of them as capable only of disjoint actions. On the second, in Hobbes's own image, they are as unified and organized as a company of merchants: they are capable of proper corporate action. But we shall see that the people or citizens of a state often get to act together in a manner that carries them beyond the multiplicity of disjoint action without taking them to the unity of corporate.

They often perform joint actions, as we shall describe them, and there is a perfectly appropriate referent for "the people" offered by citizens when they act jointly to change their sovereign or constitution. This referent is a third alternative to the people in the disjoint sense of the multitude and the people in the corporate sense of the polity. In this third sense the people may indeed enjoy extra-constitutional power over the sovereign and state.[21]

21. Stephanie Collins (2019) distinguishes between collectives, coalitions, and combinations, looking at how far they can be properly ascribed obligations. Her distinction between

Disjoint Action and Corporate Action

When members of a multitude act disjointly they each pursue their own ends and cannot be said to do anything, or to aim at any welcome result, together; each of them, according to Hobbes (1998, 6.1), seeks to act by "his own will and his own judgment." In pursuing their own ends rather than a common end, then, individuals sponsor "a multitude of actions done by a multitude of men" (Hobbes 1994b, 11.20); and, short of an unlikely unanimity, there is nothing that can be "truly called the action of the multitude" (Hobbes 1994a, 20.2).

The paradigm case of a multitude of actions performed by a multitude of agents is offered in a market where the parties each seek to do the best that they can by their own interests, whether acting as sellers or buyers. It is worth noting that while Hobbes sees only chaos in the phenomenon envisaged here, however—while he takes the disjoint actions of participants to be more like a free-for-all—Adam Smith (1976) and others in the eighteenth century came to recognize that there may be an important pattern to be discerned in such a multiplicity of acts. They argued, in the now standard model, that if the market is open and competitive, then the actions of participants will drive prices down to the lowest level at which sellers can stay in business. Let any seller try to sell above that competitive level, so the argument goes, and they will find themselves without custom; there will be others in the market, or ready to enter the market, who will undercut them and attract their customers.

The actions of market participants will have this effect, under the accepted account, in a relatively mechanical way. The effect will materialize, not as the product of anyone's intention, and not even in a manner that anyone may have foreseen, but by a process that is not necessarily visible to participants. It will come about by "an invisible hand," as Smith (1982, 184–85) put it.[22] What is true of the invisible hand, on this account, is also true of the mechanism of esteem—by analogy, an intangible hand (Brennan and Pettit 2004, pt. III)—that operates on our earlier account to generate collectively welcome conventions

---

collectives and coalitions is broadly like that which we draw here between corporate agents and jointly acting groups. For approaches that make a similar distinction but differ in other ways, see Schwenkenbecher (2021), who defends a more individualistic theory of shared responsibility, and Pasternak (2021), who explores how far the responsibility of a state—a corporate agent—devolves on citizens.

22. Although the metaphor of the invisible hand is memorable, however, it collapses the distinction between a not necessarily seen hand, which is all that the argument supports, and a hand that is necessarily unseen: an invisible hand, strictly understood.

and norms. Where the invisible hand would enable self-serving actions to bring about a collectively beneficial effect, the intangible hand would enable self-serving motives to bring about actions of a collectively beneficial kind: actions supportive of collectively beneficial norms.

Hobbes overlooks the possibility that disjoint actions on the part of a multitude of individuals might have an effect that is welcome to all of those involved, whether as the result of an invisible or an intangible hand. But if he is mistaken on that account, he is surely right that disjoint actions, even actions that combine to produce a generally welcome effect, could scarcely enable a multitude to do something in concert, such as acting against the sovereign. Thus, the absolutist claim would seem to stand. If the people have an extra-constitutional form of power that they can use against the sovereign, this is not so in the sense in which "the people" refers to the multitude of people in a state.

If the people have such power and agency, on the absolutist dichotomy, then they can only have it as a body that is capable of corporate action. They would constitute such a body, by our earlier analysis, if they endorsed a purpose or range of purposes and established an organizational basis for reliably registering variations in their environment—say, obstacles or opportunities relevant to their purposes—as well the evolving impact of their interventions, and could act reliably for its purposes in accordance with those representations. But such a corporate body could not have the extra-constitutional power to act against the sovereign, since it would depend for its very existence on that sovereign.

If there is a sense in which the people can have extra-constitutional power, then there must be a way of reading the relevant expression—"the people"—in which the referent is neither a multitude of disjointly acting individuals nor an organization of corporately engaged members. We shall now see that there is indeed an alternative of this kind, in which the people act jointly but without constituting a corporate agent.

Joint Action

Although the market supplies the paradigm case of disjoint action—or at least the paradigm of collectively beneficial disjoint action—it also provides lots of examples of what we will characterize as joint action. Consider what the partners in some common enterprise do when they collaborate for mutual advantage: say, when an investor gets together with an engineer and a builder to construct a block of apartments that they can sell at a shared profit. Or, to take a very different case, consider what two or more participants do when they bargain with one another about a price at which a mutually desired trade is to be made, each seeking to get a competitive advantage.

In these cases, the agents act jointly for a common goal: in the first case, for a goal that requires them to cooperate, in the second for a result that is achieved only by competing in the bargaining exercise. Despite the difference between the cooperative nature of the first activity and the competitive character of the second, the pattern in their behavior contrasts sharply with the disjoint activity of individuals each seeking their own ends by their own means, even when this generates a commonly welcome result.

But the parties in these two examples also contrast with the individual members of a corporate body. They would constitute such a body, by our earlier analysis, only if they were organized to realize certain purposes robustly over variations in the external context and indeed in their own configuration. There is no such mode of organization present in these cases. The parties each adjust to achieve a common aim, whether that of investing profitably together or identifying a price acceptable on all sides. But they do so in a way that is tailored specifically to the situation and problem on hand, not in a manner that establishes a mode of organization that would give them a procedure for identifying what is to be done in a range of situations if they are to realize any one of their purposes. They act together for a shared end but only in a one-off or repeating type of situation; they are not organized on an enduring basis to adapt the pursuit of a purpose or set of purposes to changing situations.

A stock example of joint action that contrasts in the same way as the two considered with disjoint and corporate action is provided by those on a beach who respond quickly, without any prior organization, when it is manifest to all that there is a child in difficulty in the water, that they all wish to save it, that the only way to do so is to enact a plan of action suited to that situation, and that anyone initiating a feasible plan is likely to be joined by others. In such a situation it might be manifest, perhaps by virtue of one of them proposing it, that they can save the child by forming a chain into the water. And it is surely plausible that they might act jointly in that manner to effect the desired result. In doing so, they would not be acting disjointly like those in a market and they would certainly not be acting corporately like those who constitute a commercial company.

There is one sort of corporate body that is limited in the domain where it is equipped to act and may be mistaken for a group that acts jointly together, in the manner of the people on the beach. Thus, to stick with the same sort of case, consider the life-saving team that has a procedure for dealing with swimmers in different sorts of predicaments. This group may have only one purpose, but it will be organized to pursue that purpose appropriately in situations, however similar, that differ in ways that require the group in question to adapt appropriately; in these respects it is not unlike the robot we imagined that acts to put certain objects into an upright position. This sort of group will represent a limit case of incorporation, organized around procedures that give members a voice to follow as they confront, now a swimmer caught in a rip, now a swimmer suffering cramp, and now a swimmer in danger from sharks.[23]

The action taken by people in the beach example is the sort of joint action that the three partners in our construction enterprise take. They will be focused on a purpose, to be sure, but they may have no procedure for determining how to respond to evidence of environmental changes and no procedure for deciding in light of such evidence about how to adjust their behavior for the execution of the purposes. As a group, they may arrange to act for the relevant purpose in the situation where they find themselves or indeed repetitively in recurrent instances of that type of situation. But they will not be organized to adjust as the purpose requires over an open range of possible situations or possible variations in that situation: they will not be organized to register the particularities of each scenario and to adapt their behavior appropriately in response.

The lack of such a mode of organization—such a decision-making procedure (French 1979)—will show up in the shortage of grounds for predicting how the partners would respond to various imagined problems. Suppose that the cost of construction went down and that existing funds enabled them to build fancier, higher-priced apartments. We might predict what the partners would be likely to do from knowing something about their individual alertness to that sort of change, their individual incentives, and the likelihood of their reaching agreement on an adjustment to the original plan. But we could not say, as we might with a corporation proper, that it would certainly register that change of conditions, having a watchdog agency in place for monitoring such possibilities; that it would follow a set of agreed accounting routines to determine the benefits of altering the existing plan; and that in view of its commitment

23. When some theorists speak of teams, crediting them with the sort of flexibility displayed by the lifesaving team in our example, they may be targeting such corporate agents, not just jointly acting sets of individuals. See Sugden (2000) and Bacharach (2004). I am grateful to Bob Sugden for alerting me to this possibility.

to maximizing revenue it would adjust to take advantage of the new opportunity presented.

People act in a joint manner across a variety of cases: for example, when they collaborate to carry a piano up a stairway or when they arrange to have a game of tennis or to play chess with one another. In every such case, there is presumably a plan, manifestly in evidence, whereby they can achieve the desired effect together. And in every case, it is presumably manifest to all that they each want to achieve that result, that they can do so—and only do so—by following the plan and, as the action evolves, that the required parties do follow the plan as a matter of fact.

That plan will be designed only for the sort of situation on hand—this may be a one-off or a recurrent scenario—and will not enable the group to adjust for a range of situational changes to realize their purpose or purposes. In that respect it will be unlike the constitution or organization of a corporate agent. The plan may involve pure cooperation, as in the beach and piano cases, but equally it may involve cooperation at one level, competition at another, as when people seek the pleasure of a game of tennis or chess, where that requires them each to compete for victory.[24]

As the plan may be purely cooperative or involve a competitive dimension, so it may evolve explicit or implicit planning by the agents involved or may appear as the unplanned result of the mutual adjustment of those parties. Most obvious examples involve something like planning, as when agents reflect in advance on what they need to do together to achieve a desired end or when they adjust in response to one another's efforts in the process of pursuing a common end. In these cases, the parties light on a pattern of behavior that will ensure the realization of the end and they each play the part that it requires.

A pattern of behavior may emerge without planning, however, as when acting according to a certain convention, say in greeting friends with a handshake rather than a hug, emerges as a pattern under the sort of genealogy presented by David Lewis (1969). In this sort of case, the pattern that evolves is likely to be embraced by those who follow it, now in this encounter, now in that, in the manner of a collective plan; the convention will provide a schema that generates the plan in each case. The participants in that case will not say "Yea," explicitly or implicitly, to the plan of action in which they play

---

24. In some otherwise similar cases, of course, the relevant plan may not itself be salient. But in those cases, it should at least be evident, and evident as a matter of common awareness, that there is a plan whereby they can get together to discuss and form the plan they need.

appropriate parts. They will embrace the plan in a virtual or standby manner by being positioned to say "Nay" and opting not to do so: in effect, by spontaneously employing the available schema.

Accounts differ on what exactly happens at the psychological level when there is joint action. By a first approach, it is sufficient for joint action that the participants should each intend, as a matter of common awareness, that they together act on the plan and realize the result. By a second, it is necessary that they should explicitly or implicitly pledge or commit, as a matter of common awareness, not to let others down in an act of unilateral defection from the plan. And by a third, joint action may involve quite varied packages of individual attitudes. While we follow broadly an approach of the first kind, our argument can be adapted to work with any of these, so that we need not concern ourselves with the detailed considerations on which they divide.[25]

It is enough for our purposes to recognize that joint action materializes insofar as agents, as a matter of shared awareness, follow a plan for achieving a certain result together. The plan may be explicitly or implicitly recognized by the agents, it may or may not involve the spontaneous use of an independently available schema, and it may or may not nest a level at which the parties compete with one another.

One final complexity is worth noting. The groups of which we predicate joint action are sometimes amorphous, and that raises an issue about how many members must play their parts in a plan of joint action to make it reasonable to ascribe the action to the group and not just to a subset of members. The only parts some are required to play may be negative, not positive; they may merely require those members not to object or oppose. But what if there are several members who object to the action undertaken or are wholly indifferent about it? It makes most sense to take a pragmatic line here. If the group is a salient presence, and the members who dissent from the action undertaken do not have a distinct identity, then the fact that enough members play their required parts, positive or negative, should allow us to ascribe the action to the group. Thus, the people in a state may be considered as a jointly acting group,

---

25. To cite just their recent work, the first approach is adopted by Michael Bratman (2014), the second by Margaret Gilbert (2015), the third by Raimo Tuomela (2007). John Searle (2010) holds that no package of individual actions suffices for joint action: that it requires each participant to form a distinctively joint intention, where someone may form such an intention even under an illusion about the presence of other potential partners. For an overview and discussion of the main issues, see Ludwig (2016).

even if that group does something to which a number of random members object. We return to the point later.

The Incorporating People

Joint action is not sufficient for incorporation, as we noted, but it is likely to feature in the process whereby a group attains or sustains a corporate character (Pettit and Schweikard 2006). If several people get together to establish a corporate body for the first time, then they will presumably act jointly, in accordance with a suitable plan, to set up a mode of organization under which they can act as a corporate body. Even Hobbes is committed to this in the political case, as we saw. For when people come together to form his social contract, they must act jointly without yet forming a corporate body. They will act to select a sovereign, each conforming to a manifestly shared plan—presumably that of taking any unanimously supported option—for achieving that result together.

Whether a corporate body appears on such a basis or not, it will presumably continue in existence only when the members manifestly accept and sustain it. They will act individually in delivering such support to the body, whether they played a part in its founding or not. They will each support it on the shared assumption that the continued existence of the group is welcome to all, being generally accepted in at least a minimal sense; that it requires each to play a suitable role in sustaining it; and that they are all willing to discharge their roles. Thus, by our account, members will play their parts in a plan for jointly sustaining the group, albeit a plan that need not presuppose prior planning.

Insofar as they act in this way, the members of any agential body will play an incorporating role and will constitute an incorporating group: this, as distinct from the unincorporated group that exists independently of the organization or the incorporated group that exists in virtue of the organization. And as that is true in general, so it is true specifically of the people in a polity, even a polity that emerges without planning in the manner tracked in our genealogy. Insofar as they act jointly to sustain the state, the people will exist as an incorporating group, not as a group incorporated or unincorporated. The observation directs us to a possibility ignored in the dichotomy that underpins both the absolutist dilemma and the constitutional paradox.[26]

---

26. Despite defending an otherwise persuasive account, even David Ciepley (2017) misses this possibility. He argues that since the people of the United States should be taken to have endorsed or chartered the federal polity in the way in which the English monarch had previously

The unincorporated people are the multiple citizens considered independently of the polity they form, and the incorporated people are the single corporate body that the members of the polity unite to form. Like the unincorporated people, and unlike the incorporated, the incorporating people are a multiplicity of individual agents, not a unified agent or agency that they form. This is a multiplicity of a distinctive kind, however: a multiplicity of agents who jointly sustain the polity, each playing the part or parts required of them in a plan that achieves that effect.

What are the actions that citizens may play as part of a plan to sustain the polity? In any regime, they will include the actions of obeying the law and not objecting to others obeying the law. But why will those actions count as part of a plan to sustain the polity? Because each citizen will take them only because of assuming that others will do so too, where the manifest effect of their all acting in that manner will be to keep the regime going.

If the polity operates on a democratic, decentralized basis, however, there are two further, salient ways in which the incorporating people can be held to sustain the state they accept, one associated with the collective election of certain officials to office, the other with challenging what those officials propose or do while in office.

Taking up the first possibility, people will sustain the state insofar as enough of them stand for office and participate in electoral processes, whether those processes make voting voluntary or compulsory. And they will also sustain the state in this electoral manner insofar as enough of them join in electoral campaigns on one or another side, form political parties, establish public-interest pressure groups, and of course acquiesce peaceably in the results of electoral competition. They will take actions of these kinds, presumably, only because of assuming that others do so too, where it is manifest to all that that shared pattern of action will help to sustain the regime.

The second democratic way in which people can act jointly to sustain an accepted state materializes insofar as enough of them contest or indeed defend certain initiatives of government; again, individuals may take different sides. They will do this in office, when they act faithfully in opposing government

---

chartered individual colonies, they must be assumed to have adopted an incorporated form, albeit one that did not depend on the existence of the polity. "To put this in corporate terms, the People was a Roman corporation for a day—just long enough to promulgate the Constitution, its '*lex regia*'—and thereafter withdrew from the scene (like any other chartering sovereign)."

within parliament: when they act to form a loyal opposition. And they will do it out of office when they take officials to court, or challenge them in the media or on the streets. They will do it also, as they can do it under any constitution, when they resort to civil disobedience for, as we saw, this is not designed to overthrow the regime, only to improve it.

At this point we can see that if a polycentric constitution allows people to have electoral and contestatory power in relation to the polity, then when they exercise such power, they will count in current terms as the people incorporating: the people acting jointly as a group in an exercise associated with determining how an accepted sovereign is to act. It is not the unincorporated people who elect or contest government since electoral and contestatory initiatives assume a capacity for action. And it is not the incorporated people who do so either: the polity does not elect its own officials or contest its own actions. Rather it is the people incorporating: the people or citizenry in a properly political guise.

Someone may balk at the idea that people act jointly to support a democratic state, arguing that joint activity is always cooperative and cannot involve the sort of competition displayed by people at election time and in conflicting contestation. But we know from earlier examples that this assumption is false, since playing tennis with someone or bargaining with them are both instances of joint action. The members of a polity, certainly the citizens of a democratic polity, will sustain that body in existence—will maintain their incorporation as a polity—just insofar as they act for the selection of officials or policies on the competitive basis associated with election and contestation.

The democratic examples of how the incorporating people may sustain the polity are all examples of active, positive involvement. But in what is by now a familiar idea, the incorporating people may also sustain the state—and do so in a manner that engages almost all members—in a negative, virtual mode. As already noted, they will sustain any kind of state, not just by actively obeying the laws, but also by not objecting to the obedience of others: equivalently, by not challenging the state's right to require obedience. In a parallel fashion they will sustain a democratic state, not just by standing for office or voting, but also by not raising any question about the appropriateness of another's doing so or about the rights of a party or person elected to office. And equally they will sustain it, not just by using the courts, the media, or the streets to challenge what government does or proposes to do, but also by not questioning the right of anyone to challenge the government in that manner.

Those who actively support the regime say "Yea" to the sustaining pattern they instantiate, while those who support it virtually fail to say "Nay," in a situation where they can say it if they wish. Citizens will say "Yea" or fail to say "Nay" as individuals but they will do so only on the presumptively shared assumption that others also follow that pattern or plan. Thus, their actions will fit the template for joint action, with the usual sorts of conditions being fulfilled as a matter of common awareness.

Returning to a familiar theme, the people who act in these ways to sustain a given regime might each prefer to be subject to a different sort of constitution and polity. But faced with the regime in which they live, and with the general benefit it confers—say in providing a scheme of coordination that enables them to know where they stand with one another—they will have a common motive to cooperate in supporting it. Some may be radically disaffected, of course, but if enough individuals go along with how things are done, then it is fair to say that the people as a group will act to sustain the polity.

If the benefit the polity provides plays a part in motivating people to sustain it then by our earlier account, they will accept the regime in at least a minimal sense; they will not conform to its requirements, as under a reign of terror, just out of fear of retaliation or punishment for a breach of the law. If that benefit is enough on its own to motivate people to sustain the polity, indeed, then their compliance with its demands will even count as willing or voluntary.

Were those in power to govern by fear alone, as under a repressive regime, then while the polity might well survive, and survive over a considerable period, it would not be supported by the joint action of its subjects. Those subjects would each submit to the laws out of fear for their individual safety and not conditionally on others doing so too; their fear of punishment might keep them in line even if they thought others would be heroically brave and resist their rulers.[27] Under a reign of brute power, the citizens would each act for themselves in obeying the law, not act jointly with one another in doing so. Thus, even if a political regime fails to answer to how its citizens would generally prefer to be ruled, and even if it does not attract fully voluntary compliance, still it will contrast sharply with a dispensation of brute power.

27. As more and more others are expected to be brave of course—as they promise to be numerous enough to overthrow the government—the prospect of suffering retaliation from those in power may become improbable and joining the rebellion may become a more feasible option.

A Political Conception of the People

The unincorporated people are the people in a prepolitical sense of the term; they are the people prior to the formation of the polity, or the people considered in abstraction from the polity. The incorporated people by contrast are the people in a postpolitical sense: the people in a sense that presupposes the formation of the polity; the people politically organized under a sovereign to constitute a state. The incorporating people are situated between those extremes, being the people considered in the role of acting jointly to establish the polity or, more relevantly for most purposes, acting jointly to sustain the polity.

Why has the political conception of the people as the incorporating citizenry not assumed its natural place, side by side with the prepolitical conception of them as the unincorporated populace and the postpolitical conception of them as the incorporated polity? The canonical dichotomy may have been a natural model for absolutists in view of the work to which they put it; and it may have been generally more attractive in an age when it was unusual for those outside a very small elite to have any part in government. But why didn't it make an appearance in the late eighteenth century, when the American and French revolutions proclaimed a more democratic image?

One reason may be that at this very time the Abbé Sieyès (2003) introduced a new version of the old dichotomy and this came to dominate a good deal of later democratic thinking. The people, he said, may assume two forms: one as the constituting people, *le peuple constituant*, the other as the constituted people, *le peuple constitué*. But while the description of the people as constituting may seem to direct us to the incorporating citizenry, Sieyès identified it with the unincorporated people. He suggested that they may have acted in the past to introduce a constitution under which the incorporated people materialized. But he nowhere suggests that they can act in the present, and certainly not to undo the constitution established.[28]

This move on the part of Sieyès directed attention toward what individuals supposedly did, as a matter of joint or collaborative action, in founding the polity; and by the same token, it turned attention away from what individuals continue to do as a matter of joint action in sustaining the polity. He made it difficult to see the incorporating citizenry as the people under an aspect that

---

28. Sieyès's move was all the more confusing because, as we saw, he was one of those who tended to reify the notion of the people, equating it with the nation.

is distinct from the two aspects—or at least from his variation on those aspects—that they were allowed to assume in the older dichotomy.[29]

A Resolution of the Dilemma and the Paradox

It may be true, to return to the absolutist dilemma, that neither the unincorporated nor the incorporated people can act to resist or rebel against the polity: the first, because it lacks a capacity for agency, the second because it lacks the requisite independence from the polity. But that is quite consistent, as we can now see, with holding that the incorporating people can practice such resistance.

The prepolitical, unincorporated people are too inactive and the postpolitical, incorporated too complicit to be able to play a role in opposing the state. But neither difficulty arises with the incorporating, properly political people. The people in this form have the capacity to act together, albeit not as a corporate agent: they are capable of joint action, as they reveal in the joint action of sustaining the polity. And there is no reason in principle why they should not also have the capacity to act jointly in the extra-constitutional attempt to change or replace the constitution. As they can join in sustaining a regime so, presumably, they might join in rejecting it.

The absolutist dilemma ceases to be a problem insofar as the incorporating people can pursue joint actions, unlike the unincorporated multitude, and can do this, unlike the incorporated people, without being organized under a sovereign. They may act to challenge the existing state or sovereign extra-constitutionally, then, and may replace that sovereign without committing suicide at the same time. The postpolitical people might change identity with such change of regime but the political, incorporating people can remain unchanged across the transition. Putting the point in metalinguistic terms, the referent of "the people" in the incorporating sense can act unlike the unincorporated people and can act against the constitution and state—and so against the sovereign—unlike the incorporated people.

As the role of the incorporating people explains away the absolutist dilemma, so it dissolves the paradox of constitutional regress. That regress comes

29. In Pettit (2012, 285–88), I try to reconstrue Sieyès's idea of the constituting people in the image of what I am describing here as the incorporating citizenry. For a view of the people that is broadly congenial to mine, see Espejo (2011). And for an account and defense of approaches that broadly follow the lead provided by Sieyès, see Kalyvas (2005).

of the same dual assumption, first, that the unincorporated people in a polity are incapable of doing anything; and second, that the incorporated people are incapable of changing the constitution on which they depend for agency. The recognition of the role played by the incorporating people resolves the problem this raises. It makes sense of how the people can set up a constitution without reliance on a prior constitution, and without the unanimous contract assumed by Hobbes.

It also explains how the American people, in a continuing sense of the term, could have ratified a novel constitution extra-constitutionally in 1787 and how the English people could have introduced a replacement sovereign in 1688. In neither case, would every member of the people have been on the side of the change. But most of them either took part in the proceedings leading up to the change or acquiesced in others taking part, and those on the losing side as well as those who barely knew of the proceedings generally went along with the upshot. The jointly acting people brought about the change albeit only in a process that embedded competition.

We noted earlier that the incorporated people have virtual control over a constitution insofar as it allows them under certain constraints to amend that constitution itself. But where this power is limited by the nature of the amendment measures allowed by the constitution, the power of the jointly acting citizenry is not restricted in the same manner. While the incorporating citizenry must act under a generally recognized plan of action, there is no limitation on how the plan may be adjusted and amended if it proves unsatisfactory in practice. Those on a beach who try to save a swimmer in the water may vary the plan they adopt as this proves necessary, and the same is going to be true of the incorporating people in a polity who seek to change their constitution. Neither group is locked into a plan in the way in which a corporate body is locked into the constitution, however amendable that may be, on which it depends for its continued existence.

The Power of the Incorporating People

The existence of an incorporating people, side by side with the people incorporated and unincorporated, is enough on its own to undermine the challenges raised by the absolutist dilemma and the prospect of constitutional regress. But for all we have said, and for all that the resolution of those conceptual problems requires, the power of the incorporating people is bound to be limited in one respect and may also be limited in another.

The power of the incorporating people is bound to be limited, to take up the first limitation, insofar as they are not an agent—not a corporate body—but rather a collection of individuals who combine, with whatever degree of individual reluctance, to sustain the polity in existence. Whatever power they may have over the survival of the state, then, it is not the power of an agent or agency that has standing procedures under which it can seek to further that or any other purpose across varying situations. It is not like the power of even a limited corporate body like the lifesaving team that adjusts appropriately, under established procedures, to rescue swimmers in different kinds of difficulty.

It is for this reason that extending the acceptance condition in our revised conception of sovereignty, as we did in the last chapter, does not mean allowing some other agent within the state to control the sovereign. The line we took there in arguing this point is borne out by the recognition that requiring the sovereign, on pain of rejection, to gain acceptance for how it performs does not put it under another agent's control; it means nothing more than recognizing the power of a body, the incorporating people, that is not strictly agential in character but, as we might say, pre-agential.

Turning to a second limitation, however, the power of the incorporating people is not only pre-agential and limited in that sense, it is also likely to be limited insofar as it is a merely potential power: a power that the people may possibly develop rather than one they enjoy as things actually stand. The people or citizens certainly determine as a jointly acting group that a constitution and state is to be sustained. But the possibility that they might withdraw their support does not mean that they are able to do so in actual practice. And so it does not mean that they have actual control—any actual, even pre-agential control—over whether or not the constitution and state are to survive. It does not mean that they have control over that issue of a kind that those in our beach example have over whether or not to rescue the child who is in difficulty in the water.

If the incorporating people are to enjoy the actual, pre-agential power to reject a constitution as distinct from sustaining it, they must satisfy a cognitive and a motivational condition. On the cognitive side, there must be a plan, more or less salient to all, under which they might be able to coordinate with one another in acting for that end. And on the motivational, the cost to them as individuals of coordinating in that way must not be so high that they cannot generally be expected to pay it; the cost must not be such that they could hardly be blamed for refusing to play their part.

The incorporating people may individually accept and sustain a regime, say for the benefit it provides in enabling them to know how they and others may act with impunity and protection; and they may jointly keep it in existence, therefore, despite their each having a preference, and knowing that they each have a preference, for moving to an alternative. But they may still be blocked from acting jointly to achieve that alternative because there is no salient plan under which they might make the move or because participating in any such plan would be excessively costly for them as individuals.

The reason that participation is likely to be costly, especially compared to the option of going along with the regime, is that any act of dissent is liable to attract retaliation by those in power, as in punishment for breaking the law. And that will motivate caution on the part of each, given that they are likely be punished for taking part in an unsuccessful act of joint resistance and that their participation may not be needed for the success of the resistance (Olson 1965). Short of heroic virtue, then, each may be averse to risking retaliation, and they will be able rationalize not taking part in resistance on familiar, free-riding lines. "If others fail to resist in numbers sufficient to change the status quo," each may think, "I will have to endure retaliation without the reward of reform; and if others do resist in sufficient numbers, the reward of reform can come about without my having had to run the risk of retaliation."[30]

When cognitive or motivational problems are present, the citizens may jointly sustain a constitution or regime without having the capacity to reject it in an act of extra-constitutional resistance. They may in principle be able jointly to sustain the regime or to reject it, as we have argued, and in that sense they may have potential, pre-agential control over whether to keep the existing constitution or not. But in actual practice they may not be able to reject the regime or to exercise such joint control. They may actually be powerless.

As this may be true of a regime that people jointly sustain, so it will certainly be true of a despotism or tyranny that people do not accept, even in our minimal sense of acceptance. That explains the absurdity of an infamous claim made by sixteenth-century thinker Étienne de La Boétie (2015), who was immortalized in Michel de Montaigne's essay on friendship. La Boétie maintained that those who live in subjection to any tyrant are guilty of voluntarily sustaining the tyranny. The kernel of truth in the claim is that if all the citizens rose at once, they could almost certainly overthrow any tyrant. But that truth

---

30. Even if individuals do not think in that way, the problem can arise from the fact that each thinks that others think in that way; or that others think that they think that others think in that way; and so on.

scarcely makes it reasonable to argue that they could jointly reject it if they wished.[31]

The incorporating citizenry under any form of constitution will be effectively able to resort to resistance, seeking to change the constitution with some chance of success, only if our two conditions, cognitive and motivational, are fulfilled.[32] First, there must be a relatively salient plan under which an individual citizen or set of citizens can call on others to resist, trying to mobilize enough of them to act. And second, enough of the others must be willing to answer the call and join in the resistance.

Are those conditions sufficient as well as necessary to make it possible for the people to change the constitution? In all likelihood, yes. Assume that there are enough dissatisfied citizens for resistance to be initiated and that the spirit of resistance spreads widely in the group, with some actively resisting and others not opposing them. If there is a salient plan of resistance, and the free-riding problem for resistors is not intimidating, it is very likely that the people will act jointly to change or replace the constitution and state.

How widely must the resistance spread for it to be fair to ascribe the rejection of the status quo to the people as a group, not to a smaller subset? There is no hard line here, as there is no hard line in any comparable case of jointly acting groups. Probably the best answer is that if the resistance spreads widely enough to be successful, then it is fair to ascribe success to the people as a group. The one exception might be where those who support and those who oppose the resistance have distinct identities—the Reds and the Whites, for example—so that it is natural to say that civil strife led to the change of constitution and that it was the Reds who succeeded, not the people as a whole.

Releasing the Power of the Incorporating People

The cognitive and motivational conditions that are necessary and sufficient for the people to be in joint, pre-agential control of the constitution under which they live are not as demanding as they might seem. For they are likely

---

31. In David Estlund's (2020) terminology, they might be subject to a plural requirement—a requirement that each in the set of individuals act in a certain way, provided the others do so—where there is no individual or corporate agent, nor a set of jointly acting agents, who can be held responsible for failing to act.

32. Do they have to be manifestly fulfilled? Not strictly. The fulfilment of the two conditions would lead to the required behavior all on its own, although that behavior would probably then make it manifest that the conditions are fulfilled: it would be clear that their fulfilment explained the behavior.

to be routinely satisfied within a democratic regime. Democracy gives a role to the citizenry, not just in electing certain officials, but also in contesting official actions, whether within the courts, on the media, or in the streets. No democratic constitution makes explicit room for extra-constitutional challenge, of course. But by setting up contestatory procedures of this kind, such a constitution cannot help but make a pattern of potential resistance salient and identify it as a pattern that need not carry heavy costs for those who follow it.

Those procedures will make it possible for individual citizens, without undue fear of redress, to call for and orchestrate a change in the system itself, even a change that cannot effectively be brought about under the procedures for amendment allowed by the existing constitution. No one would be likely to be jailed, for example, for calling in the United States today for a radical upheaval of just the kind that the constitutional founders sought and effected in 1787; this might be a call for a shift, for example, from a presidential to a parliamentary democracy. And if such a call were successful in mobilizing widespread popular support, it is quite possible that one of the political parties might espouse it and, if it won office, might put it up for a popular vote in a way that is not countenanced in the existing constitution.

This observation shows that while democracy is designed for other purposes—for example, to enable the citizenry to enjoy security against the discretionary will of those in office (Pettit 2012)—it is likely to have the unplanned effect of enabling citizens, as if by a spandrel right, to call for change on an extra-constitutional basis. Democratic organization will enable them to overcome the cognitive and motivational obstacles to joint action and to advocate with some chance of success for a constitutionally unratified way of effecting a change in the constitution itself.

This is not the place to explore how far justice argues for allowing the people or citizenry access to extra-constitutional power over the state and constitution. But there is at least one functional consideration that would favor their enjoyment of that power. This is that if ordinary citizens had that power, then that would put pressure on officials to be faithful to the constitution in place and to avoid breaches of its requirements (Pettit 2012, chap. 3).

To argue that the people in a democracy are effectively going to be able to exercise extra-constitutional control over the decision-making rules and indeed that this may be desirable in a just or functional state is not to maintain that the people in the joint, incorporating sense envisaged have power of an unconstrained degree: power of something close to an agential kind. They may be equipped to resist the constitutional status quo, and the decision makers that have power under that constitution, without having much power on other fronts.

Thus, they won't have the power to pick on an individual or set of individuals at random and act to restrict or undermine their choices. There won't be a salient plan whereby they might organize to do this: democratic practices won't offer a template, for example, that might cue them appropriately. And of course, even if there were a salient plan, there might be a free-riding problem to inhibit action; certainly, there will be a problem in any system that is designed to protect individuals against such abuse.[33]

The Polity and the People

The picture emerging in this chapter supports three equations that bear on the relationship between state and people. The prepolitical, unincorporated people are the unorganized material out of which a polity is composed. The postpolitical, incorporated people just are the polity: the people qua properly organized. And the political, incorporating people are those who maintain the polity: the people qua actively organizing.[34]

Our discussion of the constitutional and extra-constitutional power of the people highlights the importance of the political, incorporating people, which has been grossly neglected in political theory. It is people in the sense of active citizens who may exercise constitutional power in civil disobedience or who may interact under a polycentric dispensation with other elements in the polity. And it is the people in this sense who may withdraw support from the state,

33. Pettit (2012; 2014) argues that democratic justice does require that the people have extra-constitutional power over the constitution and state: that otherwise the officials in the state may dominate its citizens, breaching the constitutional constraints on their action. Does this mean that having such power, the people themselves dominate individual citizens, as alleged in Simpson (2017)? Not necessarily, because the people in that sense may lack a salient plan for acting against individuals in that way, and may be inhibited by free-riding considerations. See Lovett and Pettit (2019) and also Ingham and Lovett (2019). Simpson (2019) offers a rejoinder, but one that depends on a view of social norms that is inadequate, by the account of norms defended in chapter 1.

34. These equations should not be surprising to contemporary ears. Adopting a line that is at least consistent with them, John Rawls (1999, 26) describes the state as "the political organization of the people." In two recent studies, Shmuel Nili (2019; 2020) makes imaginative use of the people in broadly this sense: a sense in which, as he himself indicates, "the people" co-refers with "the polity" and designates a group agent.

acting extra-constitutionally to change or replace the constitution. The functional state must give this incorporating people some constitutional and extra-constitutional power and may give them such power in a higher measure than functionality strictly requires: for example, in a measure that justice is likely to support.

Although the metaphor is sometimes misused, we might think of the polity on the analogy of an organism. As the organism is composed of separable cells, so the polity is composed of separate, unincorporated people. As the organism is nothing more than the cells qua organized under a certain biological structure, so the polity—or at least the democratized polity that gives its citizens a share in power—is nothing more than the people qua organized or incorporated under certain constitutional and related arrangements. And as the organism is sustained by the continual action of interconnecting, relentlessly active cells, so the polity is sustained by the continual action of its interconnecting, incorporating people.

The equation of the incorporated people with the state or polity itself—or at least, modifying Hobbes, with the democratized state or polity—may not be as plausible as the other two elements in this picture. If it holds, then presumably we ought to be able to say that whatever a state does, its incorporated people do. Following Bartolus, to return to a point noted earlier in the chapter, we ought to be able to equate the *civitas* in the sense of the state with the *civitas* in the sense of the citizenry (Pettit 2022). And that may not be something we find it natural to say, even assuming its proper democratization, with a complex decentralized polity like the United States of America or the Commonwealth of Australia. The awkwardness about saying this, however, is readily explained and does not mean that the equation is unsound.

It may not be awkward to say that whatever the state does is done by its incorporated people when its full members—its citizens—act together cooperatively, as in the sort of plenary assembly envisaged by Rousseau. But it does become awkward to say this when citizens act competitively rather than cooperatively in maintaining their polity. And in decentralized, democratic regimes, as we have seen, this is precisely how they act, taking different sides on electoral and contestatory issues, and struggling against one another as often as they struggle on the same side. They act together in joint acquiescence to a polity-sustaining plan but they do not act cooperatively. They compete with another under that plan, as players compete with one another in enacting a plan to play tennis, and lack the purely cooperative profile of the citizens in a Rousseauvian assembly.

In the decentralized case, by contrast with Rousseau's assembly, different actions by the state tend to be determined as an upshot of different inputs and different procedures: the inputs of citizens in a referendum, the inputs of different legislators in a parliamentary vote, the inputs of judges in resolving a conflict between the laws and the constitution, the input of administrators in the interpretation and implementation of various policies, the inputs of rival parties in arbitration procedures, and so on. There is no single sort of action, such as assembly voting by all citizens, in which such initiatives are grounded.

But while this helps to explain the awkwardness of saying that whatever is done by a decentralized, democratized state is done by the incorporated people, it gives us no reason to reject that claim. There is no reason why the incorporated people can constitute the polity only if their incorporation is grounded in exclusively cooperative efforts and it has no competitive dimension. We may happily say in the decentralized as well as the other case that what the democratic state does is done by the incorporated people, so long as we silence the suggestion that the incorporating people must act cooperatively in perpetrating such an action. The decentralized constitution does not drive a wedge between the incorporated people and the state; it merely diversifies the roles that different members play under that incorporation.[35]

35. The awkwardness of identifying the state with the incorporated people is exacerbated by the fact that states get cast as legal entities in international law that may even exist for a time without a people: this, in the way Poland existed from the time of its annexation by Russia and Prussia in 1795 to the Treaty of Versailles in 1919.

5

The Individual Rights of Citizens

IN THE FIRST CHAPTER, we looked at the function and nature of the state, and in the second and third we investigated two desiderata on a functional state: that it should be a corporate agent but be organized under a decentralized structure. The last chapter moved on from looking at the desiderata on a functional state to the place and power of the collective citizenry within such a polity. We argued against an alleged constraint on the functional state—or indeed on any state—according to which the people individually or in groups cannot have a constitutional power of contesting the regime, or a power as an encompassing group of forcing it extra-constitutionally to change. We maintained that the functional state must give its citizens both forms of power in some degree and that it may give them such powers in a very substantive measure.

We move on in this chapter to consider a further alleged constraint on the functional state. This is a constraint alleged by libertarians: specifically, by libertarians of a right-wing stripe. The claim is that consistently with being a coercive, territorial power, no state, regardless of how functional it is, can acknowledge significant rights on the part of individual citizens against it or against one another; and this, once again, whether the citizenry be inclusive or not.

The constraint discussed in the last chapter is upheld by absolutists or statists on analytical grounds related to the concepts of sovereignty and of the people. The idea is, on the one side, that the notion of sovereignty implies that no other power within the state, and so no power accruing to its people, can be constitutionally countenanced; and on the other, that the notion of the people does not allow us to think of them as capable of acting together against their sovereign and state. Libertarians argue that the state is constrained by the rights of individual citizens, not on such conceptual grounds, but on metaphysical grounds related to the nature of individual rights.

The idea is that such rights exist by nature, independently of the practices or rules established among the members of a population, and that those rights impose a constraint—perhaps even a disabling constraint—on the territorial coercion that any functional state may exercise over its people. We argue in this chapter that there are no natural rights, only institutional rights; that the functional state must recognize significant, institutional rights on the part of its citizens; and that it may recognize a greater or lesser range of such rights.

The discussion in the chapter divides into three sections. In the first, we look in historical and general terms at the notion of rights, we discuss the variety of rights, and we explain why rights should be valued by any conversable creatures like human beings. The value of having rights explains why it is desirable that the functional state should be able to countenance certain rights on the part of its citizens. But desirability is one thing, possibility another. In the second section we explore and critique the libertarian idea, associated in particular with Robert Nozick (1974), that there are natural, institutionally independent, rights; that these are more significant than any institutional rights; and that they cannot be honored by any territorial, coercive state. In the third section, we argue in favor of the view that there are only institutional rights, and maintain that on this theory it is possible for the functional state to countenance significant rights on the part of its citizens: it must acknowledge some rights on their part if it is to be functional, and it may acknowledge rights on a more or a less inclusive basis and give them a more or a less significant content.

5.1 The Idea of Rights and Their Value

Subjective Rights and Their History

Before introducing the idea of natural or fundamental rights, it will be useful to look at the notion of rights in general. What I have in mind is the notion, in a phrase from intellectual historians rather than moral or political philosophers, of subjective rights. These, intuitively, are rights that give their bearers the power to make demands on others. The power is normative in character and is grounded in the fact that the demands are justified according to relevant authorities and, if appropriate, will be upheld or enforced by them. Who the relevant authorities are will depend on the character of the rights at issue. With legal rights, they will be the legal authorities, for example, and with customary rights the authorities that you and I and others constitute as members of the community.

A right understood in this subjective manner is often contrasted with objective right, where that means what is right according to some law. The contrast amounted in Latin to a contrast between two senses of *jus* and of what it means to be *de jure*. That something is de jure would have meant in classical Latin that it was in accordance with right or law: that it was objectively right. But, building on the work of Michel Villey in the 1970s, historians now argue that it came to mean something different in medieval usage and, even more saliently, in the usage of many seventeenth-century theorists. That something was de jure came to mean, not just that it was in accordance with right or law, but that it was also something whose realization the subject could demand: it was something they could claim in their own name as a subjective right.

Why did the notion of subjective rights emerge in the medieval period? And why did it become such a prominent idea in the seventeenth century that, from then on, there was no need to highlight their subjective status? Rights, period, came to refer, as they still refer, to what historians describe as subjective rights.

The question of exactly when and why the notion of subjective rights emerged in the medieval period has been much debated.[1] One idea that has attracted a good deal of support, however, is that whether they were introduced earlier or not, subjective rights figured prominently in the early fourteenth-century debate on Franciscan poverty and gained articulation in that discussion. In arguing that the Franciscans could use the various resources under their control while remaining true to their vows of poverty, William of Ockham and others maintained that owning a resource meant more than just using it. They held that to own something is to be the master or *dominus* on questions of how it should be used, and by whom, not just to enjoy its use. And this was a power, so he said, that the Franciscans did not claim or enjoy; it belonged ultimately to the Pope.

On this account, owning something, enjoying the power of *dominium* over it, amounts to having a subjective right in that thing: *jus ad rem*. And it did not require any great stretch in the notion of a subjective right to recognize that, even in areas beyond ownership, there could equally be a *jus ad personam*: a right against another person; a right, for example, not to suffer interference at

---

1. For crucial texts, see Michel Villey and Stéphan Rials (2013), Richard Tuck (1979), Brian Tierney (1997), and Annabel Brett (1998). A recent overview of the literature can be found in Van Duffel (2010). For a dissenting voice, see Wolterstorff (2008), who traces the origin of rights to Judeo-Christian scripture.

their hands, a right to gain compensation for some harm, or a right to have them live up to a promise.

With the notion of subjective rights in play, it was natural for seventeenth-century European thinkers to invoke it in a range of contexts that became important in that period. As we saw, it was a period in which the idea of a state of nature became prominent in debate, being apparently illustrated among many native peoples in North America. And equally it was a period in which the rulers of various countries were often at loggerheads with their subjects, as in the case of the French King and the Huguenots. In that context, the concept would have naturally served different sides in debates about the domestic relationship between sovereign and subjects, as well indeed as in debates about the international relationships between sovereigns or states.

The pressing, domestic questions were: what rights each side had against the other, and why people would ever have given up the rights they presumably enjoyed in an imagined state of nature. And among those questions, a particularly crucial question was whether the rights that people enjoyed in the state of nature included rights of ownership or *dominium* over the things they made use of there. We saw that whereas Hobbes argues that there is no mine and thine, and so no ownership, in the absence of a sovereign, Locke holds that property rights already exist in the state of nature; more on this later.

Let us take rights in the subjective sense that emerged in medieval times, that was consolidated in the modern period, and that is now standard. Rights in that sense amount to relatively unconditional claims. And, as we shall see later, they display three distinctive roles, serving as constraints on how others may treat someone, as trumps or powers that that person enjoys, and as the grounds for why others are required to treat them that way.

Rights as Relatively Unconditional Claims

Rights are claims or demands that someone can make on how others ought to treat them, or that third parties can make in the name of that person. The claims must be made against the background of assumptions supporting judgments about what people ought to do. These might be the judgments that are generated by norms accepted generally in the society, for example, such as the norms of nonviolence and truth-telling discussed earlier.

The claims that a person puts forward as rights, to cite some general examples, may require that others should not interfere with saying what they think, with forming relationships of their choice, with choosing location or occupation, with acquiring things by recognized means, or with using the property thereby acquired as they wish. Or they may be demands of a special, relational character that a would-be informant should tell them the truth, that a purported partner should not let them down, or that someone who made them a promise should keep it.

What is it about such claims that makes them into rights? Primarily, the fact that while they may not be unconditional claims—that is, demands that should not be breached under any circumstances—they are at least demands of a relatively unconditional sort. They are claims such that by a common sense of what they involve, others are not entitled to breach someone's claims just because there is a cost associated with conformity. Thus, others will not necessarily be entitled to breach them because they impose some personal cost or indeed a cost to the world at large. And this will be so even when, on at least a first assessment, that cost represents a loss that is not compensated for by the benefit that the satisfaction of their claim means for the claimant. Placed on an impartial scale, so it appears, the good achieved by satisfying the claim may be outweighed by the bad that it causes.

Just to illustrate this point, letting someone say what they think on a given occasion may, on the face of it, do more harm than good, say because of causing upset and even disruption among an audience. And yet it may be that the claim to free speech requires us to let the person speak their mind. Again, keeping a promise that we have made to someone may do more harm than good in virtue of effects on third parties or even, as may be foreseeable, on that person in later life. And yet their claim against us may require satisfaction despite such collateral effects on others or on their later self.

Robert Nozick (1974) focuses on one striking aspect of the relative unconditionality associated with rights. This is that if someone has a claim that counts as a right, then the validity of the claim cannot depend on the fact, if it is a fact, that our granting them the claim maximizes the satisfaction of that sort of claim on the part of others or in the later life of the same person. Thus, we are required to satisfy a person's claim to our nonviolence or our truth-telling, even if it means for whatever reason that doing so will jeopardize the achievement of nonviolence or truth-telling overall, even jeopardize the achievement of those benefits in the life of that person, whether by our agency or that of others. The claim may not be unconditional in the sense that we must refrain from violence or tell the truth, come what may. But it must not be conditional on our satisfaction of the claim serving to maximize the satisfaction of that claim overall, whether by our own hands or those of others, and whether to the benefit of the person involved or that of people more generally.[2]

This shows that a relatively unconditional right will retain its validity even when granting it jeopardizes the overall enjoyment of that very right. But such a right may also retain its validity when acting as it requires jeopardizes other goods as well. And of course, a right may retain its validity even when its satisfaction jeopardizes the satisfaction of certain other rights: those that we deem less weighty. Plausibly, for example, someone's right to life will require us to satisfy it even when this means frustrating their right, or the right of any other, to free speech or free movement. By common reckoning, the right to life outweighs those other rights so that, as it is sometimes put, frustrating or infringing them for that reason does not mean violating them in an objectionable manner (Jarvis Thomson 1990).

Some philosophers hold that there are absolutely unconditional rights that have infinite weight, making demands that remain valid, come what may. The belief in such absolute rights is well-expressed in the Latin tag, *Fiat justitia, ruat coelum*: let justice be done—let the relevant rights be satisfied—even should the sky fall. Historically, the belief in absolute rights went hand in hand with a view of the universe in which God is in charge and people are required, trusting in divine providence, to grant those claims even when the costs seem prohibitive (Schneewind 1998).

Absent such a worldview, however, it is hard to imagine someone giving an absolutely unconditional status to any right. We would surely override your right to life, to take an extreme example, if we had to override it in order to preserve life on earth, say by blowing up a meteor that is going to crash into the planet. Robert Nozick appears to countenance some near-absolute rights, as we shall see, but even he restricts the range in which those rights retain their validity, admitting that they may be overridden in circumstances of what he obscurely describes as "catastrophic moral horror" (Nozick 1974, 30).[3]

2. Nozick's stricture might be softened somewhat. Someone's claim to X-treatment may count as a right even when there is a limit to the level of X-enjoyment it is allowed to jeopardize. It might cease to hold as a claim, in other words, if it jeopardized X-treatment beyond a certain threshold. Someone's claim to enjoying nonviolence at our hands, for example, might cease to hold if it jeopardized the enjoyment of nonviolence beyond a certain threshold in time or in the number of people affected.

3. Nozick is particularly insistent on the importance and status of property rights, and it is worth remarking that even medieval, scholastic theory, despite a commitment to divine providence, denied that anyone's property rights, as we would describe them, were sacrosanct in the

Constraining, Trumping, and Grounding Rights

These comments enable us to shed light on why rights serve three distinct roles. They constrain the choices of other agents in dealing with a rights bearer rather than giving them a goal to pursue; they enable the rights bearer to trump many goals that others might want to pursue; and they provide the ground for why others have duties toward the rights bearer. We shall later defend an institutional theory of rights that explains why rights play these roles, but even in the absence of such a theory, we can see why they are roles that relatively unconditional claims may be expected to play.

To say that someone's right constrains another's behavior is to say that it does not give them a goal to target, not even the goal that might have seemed to be a compelling candidate: that of maximizing satisfaction of the right in some domain. The right restricts how the agent may choose rather than orientating their choices in a certain direction. This constraining role represents one important dimension in which it is relatively unconditional. The right binds the agent in a way that is not conditional on its satisfaction serving to maximize satisfaction of the right.

But a person's right in some area will serve a trumping as well as constraining role, as Ronald Dworkin (1997) emphasizes. It will enable the person to veto any projects by another that would violate it, even a collectively beneficial project undertaken by the government. The status of a right as a trump or power appears especially in the fact that the person involved may choose to waive the claim involved rather than asserting it; they may choose not to avail themselves of the benefit that the satisfaction of the right would bring. Having the right makes them powerful in the sense that they may choose to use it or not; it gives them a degree of control over the projects of others.

But someone's rights will generally play a third role in addition to these constraining and trumping roles. They will ground the correlated duties that others have toward them. When a person asserts a right against others, they will generally do so for the sake of self-protection. Thus, if the right is a claim to the noninterference of others in some choices, the rationale of invoking it will be to protect against interference. That being so, however, it will be natural to say that others have the duty of noninterference because the person has a

---

presence of destitution on the part of others. Aquinas in particular emphasized this possibility; see Aquinas (1958, II.II.7) and, for a useful discussion, Weithman (1993).

right to that treatment. Others will have the duty because the person involved has the right, and not the other way around.

Rights that play the three roles described give people claims against others, and they will be our main focus here (Hohfeld 1919; Wenar 2013). The standard examples are claims involving symmetrically related agents, but there are other claims that also play the three roles, as with the rights of those in political office over other citizens or the rights of other citizens in relation to such authorities.[4] Some rights have a constraining and trumping aspect, however, without a role in grounding the obligations of others. These rights give their bearers privileges that they may assert or waive but do not give them strict claims.

Just to illustrate the category, people each have a shared privilege-right to compete with one another in seeking a good over which no one has an existing claim-right: for example, to race one another in pursuit of a banknote that is blowing in the wind (Hart 1955). In such a case, of course, they each have a duty not to interfere with the other's efforts. But that duty is grounded in the other's general right against interference, not in a specific right they have to lay hold of the money. Spandrel or by-product rights to jury nullification and civil disobedience are also examples of privilege-rights. The ground on which judges are required to accept a nullifying verdict, or those in office required to live with the civil disobedience of citizens, is not a recognized claim on the part of jurors or citizens but simply the fact that the system under which they operate gives the judges or officials no basis for objecting.

The only sorts of rights that transcend the categories of claims and privileges, as they are understood here, are those rights that we loosely ascribe as correlates of independent duties. Examples might be one person's right to expect that others will do their duty by the environment or act according to the duties of etiquette. In what follows, however, we neglect rights in this very loose sense, focusing mainly on claim-rights and, to a lesser extent, on privilege-rights.[5]

---

4. Hohfeld (1919) describes these as authority and immunity rights rather than claim-rights; our category of claim-rights is therefore broader than his. There are some features of authority and immunity rights that distinguish them from other claim-rights in his sense, but they are not of relevance in the current discussion.

5. In an even looser sense, any good for human beings that is deemed to be of great importance is often said to be a human right; we neglect rights in that sense too.

The Value of Rights

There is a distinctive value that attaches to a regime of rights, however narrow or extensive they may be, and to the practice under which they are generally satisfied. Or at least this will be so to the extent that the rights, as we shall assume here, are relatively determinate in content and belong equally to everyone in the relevant constituency. The point is particularly salient with claim-rights, and we shall concentrate on them here. It is the value of having determinate and equal rights that explains why it would be unfortunate, to say the least, if the functional state could not grant significant rights to its citizens.

In order to see why rights are valuable, the first thing to notice is that people do not satisfy one another's rights just in virtue of not violating them (Feinberg 1970). I will not violate your rights to free speech or association just so long as I do not interfere in your choice of what to say or who to associate with. I will not violate your right against me to tell you the truth about something or to keep a promise I made, just insofar as I do not lie to you and I do not act contrary to the promise. But the fact that I do not violate those rights does not mean that I treat the claims involved as relatively unconditional demands: that, in the proper sense, I satisfy those claims.[6]

This becomes clear once we see that I may fail to violate the rights that you have against me, simply because that happens to be in my self-interest or happens to fit with a project of maximizing happiness all round. It may be that my not violating your rights just happens to be what those partial or impartial goals require: that I treat you as your rights require for that goal-related reason only, not on the ground that your rights, being relatively unconditional, require the treatment. You will benefit, to be sure, from how I treat you in such a case. But you will benefit as a matter of luck, not as a matter of right.

When people satisfy one another's claims within a regime of rights, they do not just happen to conform to the requirements involved; they conform to them because of the grounding rights. Not only do they conform to the requirements under the actual circumstances, then, where doing so fits with their own projects; they would conform to those requirements even if circumstances made conformity less convenient or appealing. In other words, they do not conform in the actual circumstances contingently on that fitting with their projects but conform robustly over any variations in the circumstances

6. On the importance of this feature for our conception of freedom of speech, see Pettit (2018c).

where the claims continue to apply and are not outweighed. They may conform more robustly or less robustly, of course, depending on how weighty the
claims are, but they will certainly not conform just because conformity happens to be supported by independent considerations.

Suppose then that the members of a community recognize relatively determinate and equal rights on the part of each and satisfy those rights in how they
treat one another. This regime will manifestly ensure that they enjoy a secure
zone of personal discretion in the exercise of each of the rights. Every individual can be confident that within this zone they will not suffer the interference of others in their choices. The zone will be a domain in which they can
make up their own minds, in the manner proper to conversable agents, without living in fear of how others may react and without having to court their
favor. They can enjoy a degree of self-government or autonomy.

The security that rights would give people constitutes a robustly demanding good, requiring others not just to act in a certain way, but to act robustly
in that manner (Pettit 2015c; 2018b). People will grant a secure zone of discretion to others, not just by how they happen to act—not just, for example, by
happening not to violate the sorts of rights envisaged—but by acting in that
manner because the rights of others require it. This observation explains why
a regime of reciprocal, determinate rights is going to have great value. It will
give those who live under the regime a distinctive security, enabling them to
know how they can exercise their personal discretion without let or hindrance
from others.[7]

Given the value attached to having a regime of determinate and equal
rights, it would clearly be a very serious restriction on the state, in particular
the functional state, if it was unable to countenance significant rights on the
part of its citizens. But that is exactly what libertarians in the mold of Robert
Nozick claim. They argue that certain natural rights are of supreme significance and that any territorial, coercive state, in real-world conditions, is bound
to violate them. We turn to a consideration of that claim in the next section.

7. Apart from the robustly demanding goods of security that rights would give their bearers,
there are robustly demanding goods of intimacy that people would enjoy insofar as they enter
relationships like those of love or friendship or solidarity. In such relationships, people develop
dispositions to favor one another robustly over circumstances where it is inconvenient or unappealing or costly to do so. The goods of intimacy are distinct from those of security insofar as they
are conditional on people retaining the benevolent dispositions associated with the relationship
in question; they need not be secured by norm or law. On the range of robustly demanding
goods, see Pettit (2015c).

5.2 Natural Rights and the State

The Notion of Natural Rights

Whenever people relate to one another under a set of rules of the kind that a practice or institution would put in place, then they enjoy corresponding rule-based rights and duties. Thus, as we saw earlier, individuals who live under shared norms or laws will enjoy the right to act within the limits they put in place, and do so in a suitably unconditional manner. Others will be required by the norms or laws to allow any individual to exercise their discretion within those limits, regardless of a variety of goals, personal or communal, that might be served by not doing so. When the rights established remain relevant and are not outweighed, the bearer of the rights will enjoy their autonomy robustly over the desires of others to advance any such goals.

In the case of institutional rights like these, the rules supporting them do three things. They identify the rights insofar as anyone who knows the rules will know what rights they and others enjoy under the rules. They validate the rights insofar as there is a benefit that the practice or institution serves: say, the collective benefit delivered by general conformity to the social norms like those of nonviolence or truth-telling. And finally, of course, they enforce the rights—they ensure that people act as the rights require—by holding out the prospect of sanctions for offenders.

Natural rights are conceived, at least in general, as rights that do not depend on institutions or on anything of that kind for their identification, validation, or even enforcement. They need not be identified by institutions insofar as they are self-evident, as it is sometimes put: salient to the eye of human reason. They need not be validated by any independent benefit such as that which a general practice might deliver insofar as they are normatively fundamental claims: that is, claims that are not grounded in how much good their satisfaction would generate. And they need not be enforced by institutions insofar as they each entail a right on the part of a bearer to enforce them against others; they are self-enforceable, as we might say.

By this account, natural rights do not depend for their existence on any formal laws or on any informal norms or customs; they are both prelegal and precustomary in character. This being so, they could have existed in the absence of all laws or norms: that is, in a state of nature. Indeed, they would necessarily have existed in such a noninstitutional condition, given that their existence is not contingent on any specific practices or developments. And, existing on such a secure basis, they must continue to exist in the presence of any system of norm or law.

Since natural rights may coexist with customary and legal rights, on this theory, they may obviously come into conflict with such rights. The potential for conflict means that institutional rights may be criticized from the perspective of natural, or natural rights from the perspective of institutional. But, of course, the theory of natural rights treats those rights as normatively more fundamental and significant. It takes them to provide a basis for assessing the rights recognized in law or custom, and the actions adopted by individuals, whether in accord with law and custom or not.[8]

Libertarians maintain the reality of natural rights, subscribing to the view that they are self-evident, self-validating and self-enforceable and, existing of necessity, that they provide a basis for the assessment of human arrangements and actions. But libertarianism in that sense comes in two distinct forms.

Libertarianism, Left and Right

One problem with natural rights as distinct from legal or even customary rights is that, however self-evident they are supposed to be, there is no empirical basis on which to identify them. Traditional theorists of natural rights drew on the classical and medieval idea of natural law, where this came to be conceived as a divinely ordained law governing human beings, that was accessible to reason; it did not have to be derived from any religious revelation (Locke 1990). But what is purportedly accessible to one person's reason does not always prove to be accessible to the reason of others; what is self-evident to some may not be self-evident to others. And so, it is unsurprising that natural rights have been taken to have a very different complexion in different schools of thought.

The main divide among contemporary natural-rights theorists is between those who think of them, particularly in the domain of ownership, in a standard, right-wing libertarian way and those who conceive of them in a left-libertarian manner. Right-wing or standard libertarians take the rights of

---

8. Antipositivist adherents of natural rights will hold that laws that breach those rights do not count as laws in the proper sense of that term, positivist adherents that they do count as laws but do not pass the bar for being good laws. In what follows, I ignore the antipositivist perspective; I do so, not because it is inconsistent with the points made, but for reasons of convenience.

ownership that we purportedly have independently of the institutions under which we live to entitle us, depending on our respective histories of residence and labor, to unequal parts of the external world, including unequal amounts of land and other natural resources. Left-wing libertarians hold that the world's natural resources belong equally to all, so that no one can claim private ownership of resources that would impose a cost on others. Private ownership will accord with our fundamental rights, only if everyone can appropriate an equal amount, or the private owners are taxed to compensate those who are thereby deprived (Vallentyne and Steiner 2000a; 2000b).

Our concern in this chapter is with the commitment to natural rights that would impose a restriction on the functional state. Left-wing libertarianism would impose few limitations; it would argue for one or another pattern of state intervention in economic life on the ground that it is required by people's equal rights to shared resources. Hence, we concentrate here on the right-wing, or standard, libertarian version of natural rights and the restriction it would impose on the polity.

Despite that focus, however, the critique that we run later tells as much against left-wing as it does against right-wing libertarianism. It turns, in the end, on a critique of the very notion of rights that are supposed to be natural in the sense explained. And that critique applies, whether supposedly natural rights are as those on the libertarian right say they are or conform to the profile presented by those on the libertarian left.

Robert Nozick (1974, 1) is the outstanding recent defender of the right-wing libertarian belief in natural rights, beginning his classic defense of that doctrine with the words: "Individuals have rights, and there are things no person or group may do to them (without violating their rights)." The presumptively self-evident rights he ascribes to all individuals include general rights against the interference of others in their actions, at least when those actions are not directly harmful to anyone; general rights to ownership of those goods that they acquire by their own labor or by voluntary transfer (151); and special rights that parties to contracts have against one another to honor contractual terms. As he sees them, the rights in these various categories are "strong and far-reaching" and "raise the question of what, if anything, the state and its officials may do" (1).[9]

9. Nozick will remain the focus of the discussion in view of his centrality to libertarian debates, the systematic way in which he develops his views, and his influence on other thinkers within and without philosophy. But there are important strands of libertarian thinking that follow other routes. See, for example, Kukathas (2003) and Gaus (2011).

According to Nozick's libertarianism, these self-evident rights are appealing or compelling by their very nature and not because of any independent good that their satisfaction would promote; in that sense, they are self-validating. And they are goods moreover that do not strictly need enforcement by an independent agency. This is because natural rights include a right of self-protection against potential offenders and of reasonable retaliation against those who nevertheless manage to offend, where he assumes that it will be rational for people to defend themselves in those ways (Nozick 1974, 10–11). In our sense, they are not only self-evident and self-validating, but also self-enforceable.

The rights on which Nozick focuses are defensive rights of the kind illustrated: rights not to be treated in certain hostile ways by others. They are meant to be relatively few in number and so capable of having absolute status without generating a host of problematic conflicts. They are often represented, in one way or another, as instances of a right against interference, especially interference by the state.[10]

We shall argue later that we should have no truck with natural rights, whether understood in a right-libertarian or left-libertarian way. But before we come to that argument, it will be useful to see how Nozick invokes them to critique the state, however functional it may be, and to soften that critique by trying to show that they would support an appealing set of market arrangements.

Libertarian Rights and the State

The question before us in this chapter is whether the functional state can recognize significant rights on the part of its citizens. On a natural rights theory, the significant rights that a functional state might be expected to countenance are of course natural rights. And if natural rights are conceived of in Nozick's right-wing way—henceforth this is the way we will take them—then it appears that the answer must be negative. The state is required by its very

---

10. Libertarianism in this sense should be distinguished from a teleological or consequentialist libertarianism that has little truck with rights, or at least with fundamental rights, treating noninterference as a goal for the state to promote. This version suggests that the business of the state is to organize its institutions, and to develop its policies, to maximize the enjoyment of noninterference overall, at least among its citizens. Thus, it would countenance measures of interference by the state so long as the interference perpetrated is less than the interference prevented—say, the interference of citizens against citizens—and is justified on that basis.

function to be territorial and coercive, as we have seen, and that means that it is almost certain to breach people's natural right against interference. It would fail to do so only in the vanishingly unlikely event that its citizens all voluntarily agreed, generation by generation, to its interference in their lives.

The notion of interference in a choice is a broad one, of course, usually encompassing the removal of an option from the choice, the replacement of an option by a penalized alternative—either of these may be carried out overtly or covertly—and the misrepresentation of an option in deceptive commentary, fraudulent promise making, or manipulation. Coercion of the kind that the state practices involves two elements: first, replacing the relevant option by a penalized alternative and, second, communicating to people, as in a threat, that they are subject to that penalty if they choose the option. Coercion must be overt insofar as it involves communication and, if it is to be properly coercive, that communication must be sincere; the bluff threat may interfere with victims but only by way of misrepresenting their options: deceiving them about what the options are.

The state exercises coercion in imposing the law, as well as in imposing measures legitimated by law such as taxes, tariffs, and tolls. And so, it interferes with citizens in a manner that is inconsistent with their presumptive, libertarian rights. That is why Nozick holds that those rights raise a question about what the state may do if it is not to violate them. Almost uniquely among libertarians, Nozick acknowledges that every actual state, no matter how functional or impressive, must be deemed inconsistent with the natural rights of those who live under it. The state is essentially hostile toward its citizens, being unable to acknowledge that they have such fundamental rights.

This problem might seem to support the anarchist view that if we care about people's rights then we ought to look at the possibility of doing without states altogether. Rather than embracing that position, however, Nozick (1974, 26) offers an indirect defense of a very minimal kind of state: "the nightwatchman state of classical liberal theory, limited to the functions of protecting all its citizens against violence, theft, and fraud, and to the enforcement of contracts, and so on."

His defense is not that any state of that kind is bound to have been generated with the consent of all its people, or to enjoy their consent in its continuing operations; that would clearly be false. Rather what he argues is this: that starting from a prepolitical world in which people satisfy one another's natural rights—an idealized version, as he sees it, of Locke's state of nature—they would have been led by rational self-interest, combined with a commitment to honoring one another's natural rights, to establish a minimal state and nothing more than a minimal state (293–93).

Nozick tells a story of spontaneous emergence, rather than a story of contractual agreement, in making this claim; he provides us, in effect, with a counterfactual genealogy of the minimal state. The idea is that provided they were committed to honoring one another's rights, those living in Locke's state of nature would have been led, in a cascade of individual, rational adjustments to the problems facing them, to generate institutions of the kind associated with the minimal state.

The genealogy is unusual and cannot serve the purpose of the genealogy of the state in chapter 1, because of the highly unrealistic assumption that the protagonists would be committed only to taking steps that did not violate anyone's rights. Nozick (1974, 119) himself sees this as a weakness: "one would feel more confidence if an explanation of how a state *would* arise from a state of nature . . . specified incentives . . . in addition to people's desire to do what they ought." But however weak the genealogy is in this respect, he thinks that it gives us some reason to prefer the night watchman state to any other sort of regime. Even that state, by his account, would not recognize the natural rights of its citizens, but at least its violation of those rights, unlike the violation by any more interventionist state, might have been acceptable under the development charted in his genealogy.

That genealogy is developed in a series of steps. First, Nozick shows that it would be rational for people in the Lockean state of nature generally to form and join protection agencies that, for a fee, would arbitrate all complaints made by its members and, where appropriate, act in retaliation against offenders: those who have joined the agency themselves as well as those who choose to remain independent and outside (Nozick 1974, 12–15). And then, second, he argues that in any area, a single dominant protection agency would tend to become dominant. This could happen in any of three possible developments: one protection agency might attain dominance straightforwardly in the relevant territory; different agencies might divide up the territory between them, with each then having its own; or the agencies might form a federal agency under which differences between them would be resolved (15–17).

The dominant protection agency in any territory would emerge under the pressure of rational self-interest but without any of those members offending against the rights of others. Would it constitute something akin to the minimal state? Not quite, Nozick concedes, for two reasons. First, even the minimal state would claim a monopoly on the use of force within its territory; and, second, it would extend its protection to all residents. But presumably the independents who do not sign up to the local protection agency would retain their right to use force in retaliating for offenses against them, contrary to the first claim. And presumably the protection agency would not offer them protection, contrary to the second.

Nozick argues, however, that without violating anyone's rights, the dominant protection agency would rationally offer services that at least approximate enforcing a claim to a monopoly on the use of force and extending protection to independents. It would enforce the monopoly claim by defending its own members against the actions of independents in alleged retaliation for offenses by its members; the agency would have no assurance, after all, that those actions were warranted (Nozick 1974, 101–8). And it would extend its services by compensating independents for this usurpation of their right of retaliation, offering them protection against its members (110–11).

If the resulting agency falls short of the minimal state, by Nozick's lights, this is so only in minor respects. It would not protect independents from one another and would allow them to retaliate against one another. Or at any rate it would take that line insofar as the interactions of independents on those fronts did not create danger for its own members.

Nozick does not think that the justifiability of a minimal state that came about by such means would imply that any existing state, however minimal, is itself justifiable. The reason is that the distribution of holdings among its members might be the result of past violations of rights: for example, the sorts of violations committed by Europeans against the indigenous peoples of America. He argues for a principle of rectification under which redistribution would seek to approximate "what would have occurred . . . if the injustice had not taken place" (Nozick 1974, 152–53). It is to Nozick's credit that he thinks libertarians should embrace this principle of rectification. But it is hard to see how, realistically, the principle could be applied, and it is hardly surprising that it has generally been ignored in libertarian or indeed other circles.

Libertarian Rights and the Market

Libertarians can be reconciled only with a very minimal state, then, and can be reconciled only very reluctantly. But the situation is very different, according to Nozick, with the unregulated market—the maximal market—that it would permit and support. He may take this feature to give his libertarianism a certain appeal; it certainly makes it more attractive, for example, than out-right anarchism. The appeal is spurious, however, and it is worth seeing why.

Libertarians hold that the market involves only voluntary exchanges—"capitalist acts among consenting adults," as Nozick (1974, 163) describes them—in which there is no violation of people's natural rights. A mantra that he invokes, albeit with interpretative caveats, sums up the libertarian principle on which it is organized: "From each as they choose, to each as they are chosen" (160). This is designed in conscious contrast, of course, to the Marxist slogan: "From each according to their ability, to each according to their need."

Where the Marxist principle would license relatively unconstrained re-distribution by the state, Nozick's principle would license the unconstrained operation of markets. It would allow only a world in which the state is consti-tutionally restricted from making any attempt to impose a corrective pattern—say an egalitarian pattern—on the aggregate results of economic and social interactions. Of course, those results would likely lead to enormous affluence at one end of the economic spectrum and to great penury at the other. But that, in the libertarian view, is the cost of forcing the state, as far as possible, to recognize the natural rights that all human beings bring to the political world. And the results may not be bad, so libertarians often claim, since voluntary philanthropy may be just as effective as coercive politics in compensating for the market and in bringing about redistribution from the affluent to the penu-rious (Nozick 1974, 265–67).

It is likely in any market transactions that some of the contracts that people enter will give others a power of interference in their activities: say, the power of an employer, at least when losing employment would trigger serious costs, to dictate the conditions in which employees work and the level of their remu-neration. Thus, it is crucial for a libertarian like Nozick to be able to argue that people enter any contracts that limit them in these ways on a voluntary basis. If they have voluntarily consented to the interference they endure, then plausibly there is no wrong done, and no violation of their rights: whatever transpires, transpires by their own choice.

But this claim raises the question as to whether people consent voluntarily to an arrangement that they enter, say an employment contract, when their situation is desperate, and they have little or no choice but to accept the con-tract. Suppose that you are in dire need of food or shelter or clothing, whether for yourself or your family, and that the only way you can get them is by enter-ing employment with me. Does your acceptance of the job constitute a voluntary act, so that the terms I impose on you as my employee are imposed in accordance with your own choice?

In such a situation I may make a generous offer of a decent job and decent remuneration. Or, taking advantage of your lesser bargaining power, I may make an exploitative offer of a job at a subsistence rate of pay, in barely tolerable conditions, and perhaps with a danger to your long-term health (Zwolinski and Wertheimer 2017).[11] In the case of the generous offer you are likely to accept the job very willingly or voluntarily; in the case of the exploitative offer you are likely to accept it only unwillingly or involuntarily: that is, in whole or in part, for want of a comparatively acceptable alternative.

An act will count as voluntary, plausibly, in either of two contexts. One, when the agent chooses it in the presence of at least one apparent alternative that is comparatively acceptable by ordinary criteria.[12] And two, when the agent chooses in the absence of such an alternative but not because of that absence: when the option chosen has sufficient appeal in itself to motivate the choice. Thus, when you philanthropically gift me some money rather than keeping it for yourself, you give it to me voluntarily, since keeping it is comparatively acceptable to you. Or when you give me the money happily, despite being under a constraint to do so, because it appeals to you independently, so that you would have done so even if there had been no constraint in place.[13]

11. There may be other potential employers around, of course, but they will have evidence of your position, as I do. Thus, assuming that you are not the only one in such a dire position—assuming that they can always find someone else to take their job at a subsistence rate—they will not have an incentive to improve on my offer.

12. By such criteria, plausibly, an alternative X to doing something admitted to be objectionable, say Y, would be acceptable to the extent that the fact that it was apparently the only alternative would not credibly excuse that agent for having done Y; the fact that X was the only alternative might excuse the agent's choosing Y if, for example, X was a very costly or difficult—and in that way, unacceptable—option.

13. The account of voluntariness adopted here, and assumed in previous discussions, converges in many but not in all respects with that of Olsaretti (2004). First, unlike hers, it requires that the choice not be made for want of a *comparatively* acceptable alternative rather than for want of an alternative that is intrinsically acceptable; thus, someone faced with a hard choice involving equally unacceptable alternatives may choose willingly. Second, it allows the alternative to be merely *apparent*; thus, the mere appearance that there is no acceptable alternative may make an act involuntary, the mere appearance that there is may make the act voluntary (see Frankfurt (1969). The account differs from that outlined in Pettit (2018a) because it requires of a voluntary act, not that it be chosen in the presence of an apparently acceptable alternative, but

By this criterion, you are very unlikely to consent voluntarily to accepting the exploitative offer of employment; you will likely accept it, at least in part, out of the desire to avoid the harsh, penurious circumstances under which you must otherwise live. No one is to blame for those conditions, we may assume: they may be the unintended consequences of the myriad of actions taken over time by the independent parties in the market. But the hardship they impose is no less effective than the action of another—say, my threat in holding a gun to your head—in making it the case that you do not consent voluntarily to take the job; you take it under force of circumstance, albeit not under a coercive threat.[14]

It is vital for libertarians such as Nozick to be able to argue that the choice you make in response to my offer, even if the offer is exploitative, counts as voluntary. For otherwise, it will be clear that market exchanges need not be as respectful of natural rights as he makes them out to be. The market will begin to seem like a mixed bag, not an unalloyed good.

Nozick and other libertarians respond to this challenge by supporting a different account of voluntariness from that which we have assumed here. They agree that whether an action is voluntary depends in part on how far the agent's alternatives are limited. And they admit that the alternatives for someone in your position will be very limited. But they insist that whether a choice is voluntary depends, not on how far the alternatives are limited, and not on how far that limitation is what moves you, but on the source of any limitation present. "Whether a person's actions are voluntary," Nozick (1974, 262) says, "depends on what it is that limits his alternatives." And he holds that a choice can count as voluntary—say, your choice to work for me, even work for me on exploitative terms—if the alternatives are limited only by "facts of nature," or by the actions of others when they "had the right to act as they did."[15]

---

that it not be chosen because of the absence of any such alternative; this condition can be met, of course, even if there is no apparently acceptable alternative.

14. For a discussion of the difference between taking advantage of someone who is independently in a bad bargaining position—exploitation, intuitively—and taking advantage of them when you have put them in that position—this, as in coercion—see Feinberg (1986). For a chastening analysis of the conditions that workers can be induced to accept, even in an advanced economy, under the force of circumstance, see Anderson (2017).

15. Another line that libertarians might run would be to hold that any intentional or volitional act is voluntary since it reflects the agent's beliefs and desires: it is not a brutely extracted response. But this would imply, absurdly, that even the act of handing over your money when I

When I threaten you with a gun, by this account, that likely means that your transfer of money to me is involuntary; I have no right to threaten you with violence, thereby interfering in the exercise of your natural rights. But when I make you an exploitative offer of employment, recognizing that your desperate circumstances give you little choice but to accept, I act with perfect propriety. It is not the actions, let alone the wrongful actions, of any agent that limit your alternatives. Rather it is the circumstances under which you live, which are presumably the result of the brute facts of nature or the unintentional precipitate of how others behaved when, within their rights, they made a variety of market transactions.

This move makes the libertarian position proof against the objection that entering employment within the market, or accepting any market exchange, will not be voluntary if adopted only under duress. But the move is hardly persuasive, since it remains likely the case by ordinary criteria that you acted as you did, only—or only in part—because you had little or no choice but to accept my offer. You had little or no choice but to accept my offer as you had little or no choice in the mugging case but to submit to my demand. Your response to the exploitative offer was involuntary in a perfectly ordinary sense; it was forced upon you by circumstance, if not by coercion.

Against Natural Rights

If this line of thought is correct, then the libertarian embrace of the market may not seem right or reasonable. And that is so, even if we go along with the libertarian idea that there are natural rights, in particular the sorts of rights postulated by Nozick. But we turn now to a more radical critique of the approach, arguing that the very idea of natural rights is metaphysically suspect. If this critique is sound, then it undermines the claim that the functional state cannot acknowledge significant rights on the part of its citizens. For all libertarians show, the functional state may be able to do this, and we argue later that it will indeed have this capacity.

The idea of natural rights raises a range of problems. One, it is not clear where we are supposed to get the concept of natural rights from and why we are justified in postulating such entities; they are theoretically extravagant posits. Two, even if there are rights of this kind, they are practically indeterminate

---

threaten you is voluntary. Hobbes (1994b, 6.54) holds by this view, as we noted in an earlier footnote; see Pettit (2008a, 67–69).

and would leave people without effective guidance across different cultures and contexts.[16] We review those problems now, and then, in the final section we argue that rights are all institutional in character, contrary to the natural-rights representation of them, and that the functional state can, indeed must, acknowledge such rights among its citizens.

The Problem of Theoretical Extravagance

Natural rights are highly questionable posits. They are supposed to be self-evident, self-validating, and self-enforceable rights that exist as a matter of metaphysical necessity and provide a base for assessing the rules and rights associated with contingent institutions. But why should we give any credence to such alleged entities?

With most of the ideas in which we invest confidence, we expect to be able to offer a plausible account of how creatures like us can gain access to them. In the case of natural rights, this might consist most plausibly in showing how naturalistically intelligible experience presents us with exemplars. It would allow us to construct a counterfactual genealogy explaining how creatures like us might have come to think in terms of rights. The idea of natural rights resists any such vindication, however, so that they must be regarded as highly extravagant posits.

Given our disposition to recognize middle-sized objects, as they feature in our experience, there is no problem about how we come to have concepts for them, applying those concepts as appropriate. Given our color sensations, there is no problem about explaining how we come to predicate properties like red or yellow of objects in our experience, using our sensations to detect them. Given the commitments we make to certain desires, there is little problem in seeing why we think about the things we commit ourselves to desiring as values, contrasting them with things that we treat as attractive in a merely contingent, passing way.[17] And so on through a range of cases. But where in our experience might we come to detect an entity like a natural right?

The most plausible account of where we get the concept of a right from is that, living under one or another set of rules—say, the conventions or norms or laws whose possible emergence we tracked in chapter 1—we see room for

16. They amount to cluster-rights, in a phrase from Jarvis Thompson (1990): that is, rights that demand specification, context by context, in rights of a more determinate kind.

17. For more on the relation between commitment and value, see Pettit (2015c).

the way they may be said to give us robust claims or rights against others and we find a basis on which to introduce such concepts or terms. We return to that account in presenting a rival to the theory of natural rights. But for now, we note only that that plausible account of how we get the concept of right makes sense only against the background of practices or rules under which we do, or at least might, live. And so, it does not hold out a story that would explain how we can gain access in experience to natural rights.

But even if we do not gain access to the concept in experience, perhaps there is reason still to postulate the existence of natural rights. One possibility might be to argue that they figure as part of the best explanatory theory of the world. And that is certainly how they might have been treated among scholastic thinkers in the Middle Ages. Those figures would readily have argued that we need to postulate a law-giving god to make sense of the universe and our place in it, and that in recognizing a divinely ordained natural law we must recognize the natural rights that we enjoy under that law. This line of thought will scarcely serve someone like Nozick, however, nor would it have served the seventeenth-century thinkers who gave natural rights a central place in political theory.

Hobbes (1994b, 15.41) sees the tie between natural laws and a divine lawgiver, when he acknowledges that considered in abstraction from god, natural laws do not strictly deserve the name of laws. "These dictates of reason men used to call by the name of laws, but improperly: for they are but conclusions or theorems concerning what conduceth to the conservation and defense of themselves; whereas law, properly, is the word of him that by right hath command over others." But Hobbes (1994b, 15.41) then adds, as if by way of softening the view, that "if we consider the same theorems as delivered in the word of God that by right commandeth all things, then are they properly called laws." That is in the English edition of *Leviathan*, however, which was published in 1651, and he drops the addition in the Latin edition of the work, which he published in 1668.

Hobbes's own view debunks natural laws, treating them as mere requirements of prudence. Most adherents of the idea in the seventeenth century, however, would have taken natural laws and rights to be more demanding than that, while having some sympathy with Hobbes's wish to loosen the tie with god: this, because of having a desire, at a time of religious strife, to give them a theologically independent status. Even scholastic thinkers had argued that natural laws were knowable by reason alone, without reliance on revelation. And their seventeenth-century successors reiterated that thought, while adding, in a famous phrase from Hugo Grotius (2012, 4), that we would have to recognize their reality "even if we should concede . . . that there is no God": *etiamsi daremus . . . non esse Deum.*

This claim amounts to a brute assertion, however, rather than serious argument. And it is mirrored in the assumption of Nozick and contemporary libertarians that, whether we admit the existence of a god or not, natural rights impose themselves upon us willy-nilly. They are identified and validated by nature itself, so we are assured, as they might have been identified and validated by a law-giving god. And while there is no divine lawgiver to enforce them, they can be enforced by the bearers themselves, so it is assumed, insofar as they include a right of self-protection and retaliation against offenders. This right of retaliation is the right that people outsource to their protection agency, in Nozick's story about how a very minimal state might have emerged from the state of nature.

These observations should underline the theoretical extravagance of postulating natural rights of any kind, including the rather spare, broadly defensive rights that right-wing libertarians privilege. Nothing is said to explain how we might gain access in experience to the complex concept of natural, rule-independent rights. And, given that religious justifications are set aside, nothing is said to explain why we should think that still they are metaphysically compelling. All we are offered, in their defense, is the bland assurance that they are matters of rational intuition: that, in some sense, they are staring us in the face.

The Problem of Practical Indeterminacy

But suppose that despite this problem, reason did give us access to natural rights. The second problem is that even in that case, the natural rights that it delivers would sell us short: they would turn out to be inherently indeterminate. If they are inherently indeterminate, of course, they will be incapable of fulfilling the purpose of identifying how people may or may not behave toward one another, giving each a secure zone of personal discretion.

Rights against the interference of others look like good candidates for rights that might have a universal, culturally independent content. But even rights in that category depend for their specification, not just on a definition of what is to count as interference—this is a point addressed briefly before—but also on an account of the choices that are meant to be protected against interference. Do they include choices, for example, that do not impose deliberate harm on selected victims but generate negative externalities and impose costs on third parties: this, in the way that your dumping waste in a river may harm those who live downstream? It is hard to see how nature on its own could determine whether third parties are harmed enough, or harmed with sufficient probability, to give them rights against such side effects. And even when there are victims, and there is no issue of probability involved, it is not clear how nature could establish when the choice of another does serious enough harm to give a victim a right against such treatment.

The points made about rights against interference apply with even greater force in the case of rights of ownership, contractual rights, and rights of retaliation; like the right against interference these belong with the defensive rights recognized by libertarians. What counts as the reasonable retaliation that I may exercise as a matter of right in seeking recompense from you, or seeking to restrain you? What sort of promise counts as important enough for me to have a right to demand performance or extract compensation from someone who fails to keep it? What titles are sufficient to give me ownership in something? And what does ownership allow me to do: what prerogatives does it confer?

In each of these cases, there are deep differences across cultures and societies in the rights with which people are credited in law or in custom. Almost all take the right of retaliation out of the hands of victims but vary enormously in the penalties they impose. Almost all recognize the significance of contracts but vary greatly on two fronts: first, in the range of promises, verbal and recorded, formal and informal, that they dignify as contracts; and second, in the sorts of compensation they take to be appropriate in the absence of performance. Finally, while almost all societies have some institution of property in place, the conventions of ownership are extremely diverse.

Property regimes differ in several ways. First, they vary in how far they put some things in the category of public or common rather than private ownership: in public ownership, the community or state is the owner; in common ownership, say of shared grazing land, there are many owners. Second, property regimes vary in the sorts of title that they recognize for private ownership: say, in how far authorship gives you copyright in a book, ownership of land extends to natural resources beneath the surface, or being the first-born allows you to inherit from your parents. And third, property regimes vary in what prerogatives the ownership of something confers: say, in how far you may extend or redecorate your house, in how you may treat your pet animals, or in whether you can give an online book that you have purchased to a friend. We return to these matters in the next chapter.

The variation between property regimes underlines the indeterminacy problem for libertarian defenders of natural rights. They can hardly say that at most one of the varying regimes is correct about any right ascribed; that would be downright implausible. They must concede, it appears, that natural rights are inherently indeterminate and that they offer no sure guidance on how individuals should behave or on what social and political arrangements should be established in any society.

Defenders of natural rights might respond to this problem by granting that those rights are indeterminate—that they are schematic rather than substantive rights—but by claiming that nevertheless they serve an important function. Schematic natural rights may not be determinate enough to give detailed guidance at the level of action but can be sufficient, so the idea goes, to put clear limits on the form that customary or legal rights could assume. They could serve as constraints on constraints: higher-level constraints on the sorts of constraints that custom and law might impose as rights at a lower level.

Among natural rights theorists, Immanuel Kant (1996, 416) comes close to adopting the schematic view, arguing that in the state of nature our natural rights to bodily integrity, property, and contractual fidelity are "provisional" as distinct from "conclusive." They are provisional both in the sense of not being determinate and in the sense of not being subject to the proper, impartial form of enforcement that a state would provide. He argues the point with a focus on property rights, maintaining that "conclusive acquisition takes place only in the civil condition": that is, in a condition that the state is needed to establish.[18]

In holding that natural rights are indeterminate in the absence of the state, Kant takes a different view from Locke, and from Nozick and others who follow the Lockean line. On that view, for example, people may come to own private property, most conspicuously land, by mixing their labor with it, where, as the *Second Treatise of Government* says, "there is enough, and as good, left in common for others" (Locke 1960, s27). Kant gives no indication that he endorses that sort of view, merely observing that the state is needed to make natural rights determinate.

Kant also emphasizes the need for the state to make rights enforceable, where any rights enforced will have to be relatively determinate. By saying that natural rights are not properly enforceable in the state of nature, he means that they are not established in a way that would make them consistent with everyone's enjoying the same "external freedom" as others living in the

18. I have been helped in my construal of Kant by Bradley (2022).

same territory (Ripstein 2009). Unusually among natural rights theorists, he rejects the idea that people might each have a right to defend themselves against others, enforcing their rights "unilaterally," and holds that only an egalitarian system of enforcement, expressive of an "omnilateral" will, could give them equal freedom.

Having the same external freedom as others means enjoying, as a matter of common assurance, the same rights with the same security (Hodgson 2010). And such security, say of ownership, is available only when it is supported by law in the civil condition, under the state. As Kant (1996, 409) himself expresses the point, it is only "a general (collective) and powerful will that can provide everyone this assurance. But the condition of being under a general external (i.e. public) lawgiving accompanied with power is the civil condition. So only in a civil condition can something external be mine or yours."[19]

Putting aside the argument about enforceability, does Kant provide a satisfactory response to the indeterminacy problem raised? He does exemplify the claim that natural rights might be taken by defenders to be wholly schematic, requiring a state to fill them in. But he provides little or no indication of the constraints that natural rights would impose on state-enforced rights, apart from the stipulation that ideally there should be a basis for mutual assurance that they are the same for everyone, and available to everyone with the same security. Thus, for all he says, a regime might aim mainly to establish public or communal property rights, not rights of private property, and might specify the titles to private ownership or the prerogatives of private ownership in any of a range of different ways.[20]

Kant's position on the need for law parallels that of Herbert Hart in an interesting way. As we saw in chapter 1, Hart thinks that in a prepolitical society, people would establish primary rules and corresponding rights in an unplanned

---

19. The Kantian position is supported by our claim that enjoying a right means being secured against its violation by others, not just happening not to suffer violation: that it means robustly avoiding violation. If enjoying any right requires such security or robustness, and if people in a society are to enjoy it equally, then it must be protected by a law that treats citizens as equals.

20. Louis-Philippe Hodgson (2010, 62) puts the point as follows: "Kant's argument only requires some system of rights allowing one to exclude others from using a certain object for a certain amount of time, regardless of whether one is holding it or not. That could be achieved by a system under which the means of production are communally owned, so long as it appropriately determines who has the right to use a given object at a given time. The considerations presented here thus do not amount to an endorsement of capitalism, or of the sort of absolute private property rights advocated by libertarians." See too Korsgaard (1997, 325–26).

fashion, using them to guide them in their interactions. Like the rights that Kant thinks nature itself provides, these rights would rule out certain offenses like deception and infidelity, violence, and theft. But then Hart argues, like Kant, that the norms and rights in question would be indeterminate and ineffective and would need the support of laws in order to achieve determinacy and to be effectively enforced on an impartial basis. Where his custom-based norms and rights would seem to put some constraints on law, however, it is not clear that Kant's natural rights would impose any.

5.3 Institutional Rights and the State

The Institutional Theory

The question raised in this chapter is whether the functional state can recognize significant rights on the part of its individual citizens. If significant rights are natural rights of the kind that Nozick postulates, then the answer is that in virtue of being territorial and coercive, it cannot plausibly give them recognition. Our critique of natural rights directs us to a distinct theory, however, under which rights are not natural but institutional in character. And we shall see that if rights have this character, then it is possible to identify ones that might count as significant and to argue that the functional state can indeed recognize such rights on the part of citizens.

The problems of extravagance and indeterminacy may seem to support Bentham's (1843) famous thought about natural rights, in particular the imprescriptible rights that no law could supposedly ignore. "Natural rights is simple nonsense: natural and imprescriptible rights, rhetorical nonsense, nonsense upon stilts." They may even lend support to Alasdair MacIntyre's (1987, 69) claim that belief in natural rights "is one with belief in witches and in unicorns." But to reject natural rights is not to be driven to embrace Bentham's utilitarianism, or indeed MacIntyre's Aristotelianism. It is simply to acknowledge that if we are to make room for the notion of rights—as we should in view of the value, documented above, of a regime of rights—then we need to introduce a different way of thinking about what is required for rights to exist.

We observed already in chapter 1 that regularities such as conventions and norms and laws can introduce rights and correlative duties for those who live under them. The obvious alternative to a theory of natural rights, then, is a rule-dependent or institutional theory. This would be a theory to the effect that rights come into existence only in virtue of being established by a system of rules, be those rules conventions, norms, laws, or whatever. Rights, so the line would go, are identified by the rules that support them; they are validated, if they have value, by the good that those rules ensure; and they are enforced, where enforcement is necessary, by the sanctions that the rules would trigger for offenders.

The institutional theory has a metaphysical and a normative side. As against natural rights theory, it maintains, first, that it is always rules that account for the reality of rights and, second, that the rights sustained by the rules are valuable just insofar as the sustaining rules are valuable. In serving these two goals, the theory mimics the dual role played by natural rights in the view of defenders. Nicholas Wolterstorff (2008, 386–87) emphasizes that dual role when he says that while natural rights constitute metaphysical constraints of a kind with "legally and socially conferred rights," they also serve a normative purpose since "to dishonor a natural right is to wrong someone."[21]

We shall consider institutional theory in its normative aspect later, when we argue that the functional state is bound to support significant institutional rights for its citizens. But first we look at three advantages of the institutional theory as an account of the metaphysical status of rights. The first is that it fits well with some general assumptions that we make about rights. The second is that it enables us to get over the problems of theoretical extravagance and practical indeterminacy that we raised for natural rights. And the third, which we spend more time elaborating, is that it explains the constraining, trumping, and grounding character of rights.

The First Advantage

Taking up the first of the advantages, the idea that rights depend on institutions and practices—in effect, on one or another system of rules—is borne out by the common assumption that when someone can be said to have a certain

---

21. There is a well-known debate in legal and political philosophy between the will theory and the interest theory of rights. Because of distinguishing between the metaphysical and normative aspects of rights, we can avoid that issue. The metaphysical view of rights embedded in institutional theory emphasizes their role in enabling the bearers of rights to exercise their will within a secure zone of discretion, and thereby reflects the main theme of will theory. The normative view that fits with an institutional theory would argue that rules ought to be established, and rights put in place, only if they benefit the individual persons who live under them, thereby aligning itself broadly with the interest theory.

right, there are almost always rules in the background that support the right. This applies to the right of a player in a game of chess to move a bishop on the diagonal, the right of any citizen to say their bit in a political debate, or the right of the people to oust the government in an electoral democracy. When such rights hold, we generally assume that they do so in virtue of the background rules: the conventions of chess in the first case, norms of free speech in the second, and democratic procedures in the third.

This assumption suggests, in support of the institutional theory, that where there are rights, there are supportive rules. But there is one sort of case where we ascribe rights to an agent in the absence of supportive rules, and we need to be able to make sense of why we do that, if we are to give weight to this first consideration. In this type of case we ascribe a right to someone that they would have under a system of rules that we favor but don't have under the rules that actually obtain. For example, we say of someone living under a system of laws that limits freedom of political speech that still they have the right to speak their mind on political matters. If it is manifest that they do not have that right in the system under which they live, then this may seem to clash with the assumption that rights presuppose background rules.

The institutional theory of rights can easily account for this sort of case, however. If it is manifest to all, and a background presupposition of our remark, that the deprived person we are talking about does not have a legal right of free speech, then saying nonetheless that they have such a right can mean only one thing: that the local system of laws is unsatisfactory in that regard. That regime of laws may be unsatisfactory, however, not in failing to encode presumptively natural rights, but in failing to meet any of a variety of presumptively normative criteria: for example, in reducing trust between people, in weakening democratic institutions, or in undermining free inquiry and the discovery of truth. What the remark conveys, in strict paraphrase, is that the person would enjoy the right of free speech under the system of law that ought to be in place, by whatever normative criterion, in their society.

This explanation of what we say in ascribing to someone a right that they do not have in their own system of law is not ad hoc. By all accounts there are rights established under legal systems; even natural-rights theorists admit this, taking natural rights to dictate the rights that ought to be established in law. By the institutional account, it is the rights established by laws, or by any suitable rules, that serve canonically as referents for the concept; the idea is that if there were no such rights given in experience, then people would not gain access to the concept of a right. But if the notion of a right is fixed by its utility on such canonical occasions of use, then it is entirely intelligible why it should be invoked in the sort of context illustrated to criticize a system of law.

The relationship between the canonical content of the notion of a right and its content in such a context of use is rather like the relationship between a word in its literal usage and that same word used metaphorically. It is only because of the literal content of "lion" that we can communicate something true by saying that Richard is a lion, and it is only because of the literal content of "island" that we can communicate something significant as well as true by saying that no man is an island. Similarly, it is only because of what it means to say that someone has a right to free speech within a given legal system that we can communicate something by saying of a person living under a restrictive system—perhaps with appropriate emphasis or intonation—that they too have a right to be able to speak their mind.[22]

The Second Advantage

The second thing to be said in favor of an institutional theory is that not only does it square with our ordinary assumption that rights presuppose rules; it also avoids the problems of extravagance and indeterminacy that plague the natural rights approach. If rights exist only in virtue of a system of rules under which their bearers live, then rights are going to be no more mysterious than rules. But by the account offered earlier of conventions, norms, and laws, there is absolutely nothing mysterious about how systems of rule—practices, in our sense—might come into existence. And so, there is equally nothing mysterious about the existence of the rights that they support.

Let the reality of rules be granted, then, as we have argued that it should be granted, and the reality of corresponding rights must be granted as well; they come along for free. Let the concept of rules gain currency among those who live under rules, as we have argued that it would appear in the presence of conventions, norms, and laws, and the concept of rights is likely to gain

---

22. Another way of expressing this point might be to posit the existence of moral norms or laws, treating these as ideal counterparts of the social norms and laws under which people live, and to say of the person imagined that they have a right to free speech relative to those ideal rules, if not relative to the actual rules under which they live. This is an acceptable way of making the point, but it is important to notice that it too relies on something like metaphor. The ideal rules envisaged are only rules in a secondary, derivative sense; they are not rules of a kind that are embedded in actual human practice. I am grateful to Eliot Litalien for a discussion of this issue.

currency at the same time. And if the concept of rights gains currency, then there will be a natural opening for employing it in noncanonical as well as canonical usage, as in ascribing a right of free speech to the subjects of a repressive regime.

But not only does the institutional theory avoid the problem of theoretical extravagance that confronts the idea that there are natural rights; it also clearly avoids the problem of practical indeterminacy. The rules on which rights depend for their existence, according to this theory, will give the rights they support a content that is as determinate as they are determinate. The rules will be determinate insofar as they specify the conditions where they apply or, such a specification being impossible at some margins—say, in their weighting against other rules—establish a procedure for determining how they apply in such cases. Whatever determinacy they come to enjoy as a result, they will bequeath it to the rights they establish.

Let the rules be precise in the demands they make on how people are to be treated and the rights of those individuals will also be precise. Let them remain indeterminate in some cases, and the rights they support will inherit that marginal indeterminacy. But no such indeterminacy of rights need constitute a problem. If we wish to make the rights more determinate, we can do so by introducing a greater determinacy into the rules: this, in the way that formal laws, by Hart's account, would introduce a degree of determinacy lacking in social norms.

The Third Advantage

The third thing to say in favor of the institutional view of rights is that it does extremely well in explaining why rights have three features we listed earlier: why they constrain people's actions rather than providing a target to pursue; why they provide trumps that an individual can assert or waive against the potentially hostile ventures of others, even collective ventures for the common good; and why they serve as grounds for the duties that others may owe to a bearer.

Suppose there are rules in place that are designed, like norms and laws, to govern how people should treat one another in certain interactions. The point of such a system of rules will be to form a basis on which the parties can each tell the range of options available to them and the range of responses others are likely to make. The rules will rule out certain choices and responses and, perhaps only by ruling out alternatives, rule in others: that is, present them as available under the rules.

If I break such a rule in dealing with you I may be able to make any of a number of acceptable excuses. In other words, I may be able to provide a plausible explanation of my behavior that purports to show that I am not an opportunistic or pathological rule-breaker, and that you can generally rely on me to abide by those rules. One sort of explanation may be an appeal to an epistemic failure: "I forgot for a moment what I was doing," "I didn't realize we were operating under those rules." Another may invoke a practical obstacle: "I was distracted by hearing some very bad news," "I couldn't show up because I fell and broke a leg."

One sort of excuse I cannot offer for a failure to conform to such rules, however, is that by breaking the rule in dealing with you I managed, for whatever reason, to reduce such rule-breaking overall: I inhibited others from breaking the rule. Indeed, I will not even be in a position to offer the excuse that by breaking the rule in dealing with you now I managed, due to whatever perversity of circumstance, to reduce the extent to which others—or perhaps even I myself—will break the rule in dealing with you later. To offer any such excuse will betray a misunderstanding of the role of the rules in coordinating our mutual relations and expectations (Pettit and Smith 2004).

These observations explain why rights of the sort that systems of rules establish are bound to figure as constraints on the behavior of parties to the rules. But the connection with rules also explains the capacity of rights, or at least of protective rights, to trump the otherwise beneficial actions of others, giving the agent a power of asserting or waiving the rights.

Since the rights established in law are primarily designed to establish a secure zone of discretion for the individuals who live under them, the rules supporting such rights will generally be protective in character. The person such rights protect will be positioned to assert a right against any behavior on the part of others, even the state, that would breach them. But any protected person may voluntarily opt out of the protection provided, since it is only their own welfare that is at risk: in the old tag, *injuria non fit volenti*; no harm or wrong is done to the person who consents to what is done. And that means that as they may choose to assert a right against other agents, so on occasion they may choose to waive it. Thus, the right will give them a degree of trumping control over others, enabling them to block or allow certain actions by those others.[23]

---

23. It is consistent with recognizing that that is so, of course, that the norms or laws that give you a certain right may impose a duty on you not to waive that right, at least in certain

Consistently with rules enabling people to enjoy such control, the power that they give others may be wide or narrow. Different rules may offer a more robust or a less robust form of protection and control, depending on the seriousness of the harms against which they guard. The customary or legal rules against violence will tend to offer more robust protection and control, for example, than any rules against insult or infidelity. Thus, the connection with rules explains, not just why rights serve a trumping part, but also why they differ in the degree to which they serve as trumps (Sumner 1987, 124). Indeed, the connection also explains why no rights are ever likely to serve as absolute trumps. The status of a right depends on how significantly protective the associated rules are, and it is unlikely that any rules are going to be required to protect you under every conceivable circumstance: say, under the circumstance imagined earlier in which saving the lives of most people on earth requires us to take an action that will lead to your death.

The third feature of rights, or at least of protective rights, is that they ground the correlated duties of others. The connection with rules also makes this intelligible. Suppose that the rules supporting certain rights are protective in character, as are customary or legal rules that protect you against general interference or contractual infidelity. On that assumption, it will be natural to cite the right as the ground of the duty imposed on others in dealing with you. The point of the general rule will be to enable you to enjoy noninterference in a certain range of behavior, the point of the contractual right to enable you to enter contracts without fear of being vulnerable to others. And that means that the primary goal is to give you a right that protects you against interference and infidelity, so that it is the right thereby conferred that grounds the duty that others owe you.

This argument about the grounding role of rights is relevant, as we know, only to claim-rights, not to privilege-rights. But not only does the connection with rules explain why claim-rights ground duties; it also explains why privilege-rights do not serve such a grounding function.

There are two ways in which rules may permit you to act in a certain manner. One is the standard case where rules protect you in a range of action, giving you by design the right to act as you wish within that domain and, at the same stroke, imposing correlative duties on others. The second is where the rules say nothing for or against a certain type of action and allow you by default to

---

conditions. And some rules, like the rules of chess, do not support rights that lend themselves to waivers; to waive your rights against an opponent would be to change the nature of the game.

act in that way or not. In this case, the rules will give you a privilege-right to act as you please and will do so without imposing a corresponding duty on others. Rights in the design category will enable you to act appropriately with impunity and, by imposing duties on others, with protection; rights in the default category will enable you only to act in that manner with impunity.

Privilege-rights of the kind illustrated earlier are rights that a system of rules allow people to exercise, not by design, but by default. Thus, the right of each of us to compete for the banknote blowing in the wind arises from the fact that property rules say nothing about the ownership of such an unclaimed good. And the right of juries to nullify the law or the right of people to practice civil disobedience arises from the same source. The rules of common-law criminal justice do not explicitly allow jury nullification, but they say nothing against it. And similarly, the rules in a constitutional system say nothing for or against civil disobedience and license it in the same default manner.

The Cheshire Cat Fallacy

So much for the main advantages of the institutional theory of rights over the theory of natural rights. But there is a further, less salient advantage that the institutional theory also enjoys. A good question to raise about two rival theories in any area is whether either can plausibly debunk or explain away the intuitions supporting the other. It turns out that on this front too, the institutional theory scores better than its competitor.

If rights are the precipitates of practices and rules, as we have argued, then the libertarian intuition that human beings have rights against one another independently of conventions, norms, or laws, must be mere appearance: if you like, an illusion. Is there any explanation of why libertarians might be misled by such an illusion? Plausibly, there is. It may well be that they are subject to what I have elsewhere described as the Cheshire cat fallacy (Pettit 2018a).

Alice, in Lewis Carroll's story, seemed to see the grin of the Cheshire cat remain after the disappearance of the cat itself; it stayed with her in the manner of an afterimage. And it may be that those who think they see rights in the absence of rules are subject to a similar illusion. They focus on rights that certain systems of rules do or might ground and then, overlooking the rules themselves, treat the rights as autonomous existences; they mistake the after-image of the rights for the real thing.

This explanation of how people might come to have postulated natural, rule-independent rights is plausible to the extent that when rules give rise to rights, they may recede into the background while the rights assume a fore-ground salience. Arguably, the implied rules of conversive exchange, which is a practice deeply embedded in our nature, support rights like the right to be told the truth, have promises fulfilled, and enjoy an absence of the aggression or coercion that would undermine such exchange (Pettit 2021). But such rules often fade into the background when attention is given to the associated rights: demands associated with the second-person viewpoint, as Stephen Darwall (2006) calls it. And it would hardly be surprising if those rights might then seem to exist independently of the rules generating them.

The idea that those who believe in natural rights are guilty of this mistake is reminiscent of a suggestion made by Elizabeth Anscombe (1958, 5–6).[24] One strand in her famous lecture on modern moral philosophy is the idea that the discipline has been betrayed by two simultaneous moves: first, dropping "the conception of God as a law- giver"; and, second, continuing to give moral terms like "should" and "ought" and "needs"—and, we might add, the concept of moral or natural rights—the sort of sense they would have had in the pres-ence of divine law. This, as she casts it with some irony, is "a special so-called 'moral' sense." "It is as if the notion 'criminal' were to remain," she says, "when criminal law and criminal courts had been abolished and forgotten."

Anscombe suggests that only a natural law, grounded in a conception of God as lawgiver, would provide the basis required for legitimating talk of natu-ral rights and cognate ideas; she implies that they will have a place only under what we earlier cast as the divine incorporation theory (Schneewind 1998). She supposes that her opponents forget about the divine law presupposed to the existence of duties and rights, suggesting that they try to make use of "a concept outside the framework of thought that made it a really intelligible one." They imagine, in our analogy, that they can keep the grin and lose the cat.

The Functional State and Institutional Rights

We can return now to the question of whether the functional state can counte-nance significant rights on the part of its citizens. According to libertarian theory, it cannot do this because the best candidates for significant rights are the natural rights favored in the tradition and no territorial, coercive state is going to satisfy these. But what if rights are institutional in character, as we have ar-gued? Does that make it more likely that the functional state can acknowledge significant rights among its citizenry?

24. I am indebted to James Doyle (2017) for illumination on this theme.

The question breaks down into two distinct issues. The first is whether there is a ground for determining whether certain institutional rights count as significant in a relevant sense. And the second is whether and how far the functional state can acknowledge such rights on the part of its citizens while remaining territorial and coercive.

What Makes Rights Significant?

Our earlier discussion of the value that attaches to rights, however they are constituted, gives us a way of determining whether rights are going to count as significant. Rights will be significant to the extent that they provide people with a secure zone in which they can exercise their personal discretion, without worrying about whether others are going to object to that exercise or obstruct it. And rights will achieve this result, as we saw, insofar as they are determined and enforced under constraints that apply equally to members of the relevant constituency.

The value of having a zone of personal discretion is a perfect criterion for determining whether rights are significant or not. By the account sketched in chapter 2, we human beings are inherently conversive creatures who can intentionally make up our minds about what to believe and desire, can help one another to make up our minds in a parallel way, and can form our decisions, including commissive decisions, on that basis. A social precondition of enjoying the exercise of such a capacity—a precondition of our operating properly as human beings—is that we know what we can and cannot do with impunity and protection. Let any arrangement compromise that good, and it is liable to be unstable and ineffective, attracting the resentment and resistance of those to whom it denies that benefit. Let it support that good among any group of people, and it is bound to be cherished by each of them.[25]

Can the State Acknowledge Such Rights?

Can the functional state recognize significant rights on the part of its citizens? On this reading, the question is whether it can deliver rights that support a secure zone of discretion for each of its citizens. The assumption is not that the rights that count as significant in delivering a secure zone of discretion will preexist the state, as in a natural rights approach. Rather it is that whatever

25. For more on the demands supported by our conversive character as a species, see Pettit (2021).

rights the state countenances, including rights that turn out to be significant, they must be established or reinforced institutionally under the laws. And the question, then, is whether indeed the laws of the functional state can establish such rights of civic security: whether they can enforce suitably equal and determinate rights among its citizens.

By coercively establishing laws under which its citizens live, perhaps framing those laws to regiment and reinforce preexisting social conventions or norms, the state is bound to establish a range of such rights. It will identify those rights in the way in which any set of rules will identify corresponding rights. It will validate those rights insofar as the rules provide citizens with a secure zone of personal discretion. And it will enforce the rights on the basis, not just of the sanctions it puts in place, but of the ratified status that by our earlier argument its laws will assume among the citizenry.

The functional state will do this all the better, of course, insofar as it satisfies the functional desiderata of being incorporated and decentralized. The characteristics of that ideally functional regime will guard against the danger that the laws will not be uniformly interpreted across different agencies or that individual officials or groups of officials will abuse their power, acting without check to take the law into their own hands. Thus, we may expect the functional state, in establishing such laws, to enforce determinate rights among its citizens.

In order for rights to be significant, giving security to every citizen, they will have to apply equally among those individuals. That ought not to be a problem for the functional state, however, for by the account given earlier it must give equality before the law to all its citizens. It may give special rights of authority to various officials, but these will be required by the offices occupied by such citizens and need not reflect any special status they enjoy as individuals. And they will be balanced in any case by the rights of ordinary citizens against those in office: rights, for example, that require the authorities to stick to their briefs in office and not to act *ultra vires*.

The ideally functional state will be incorporated and decentralized and, among other consequences, that would ensure that it satisfies standard rule-of-law constraints. Those constraints require that the decision-maker laws that it incorporates should reduce the discretionary power of the authorities and reduce the vulnerability of citizens to that power. Decision-maker laws would reduce the power of authorities by requiring generality in the framing of decision-taker laws, stability in their alteration, and uniformity in their interpretation across different agencies. And they would reduce the vulnerability of citizens by requiring that decision-taker laws should be promulgated and

THE INDIVIDUAL RIGHTS OF CITIZENS 263

knowable, clear and intelligible, and capable of serving citizens as guidelines: this, in virtue of not being incoherent, retrospective, or overdemanding.

The state that meets such conditions in its laws is bound to further the security of its citizens in making their own choices and to establish significant rights among them. Citizens will know where in general they stand in relation to others, especially in relation to officials, if the laws are required to apply to all, if they cannot change without warning, and if they cannot be interpreted differently by different agencies. And that general sense of where they stand will be further assured if the laws are well known to citizens, are intelligible to all, and are capable of guiding them in their behavior and expectations.

These observations show that the answer to the question raised in this chapter is certainly affirmative. There is nothing about the functional state, not even its territorial and coercive character, that blocks it from recognizing significant rights of civic security among its citizens. On the contrary, indeed, a state would not count as functional, by our earlier account, and certainly not ideally functional, if it did not recognize some such rights in the citizenry. Not only can it countenance those rights, then, it has no choice but to do so.

But the rights of civic security that the functional state must recognize may fall well short of the rights we might expect to be honored in a fully just regime. The citizens for whom it establishes those rights need not include all intuitively eligible members of the society, contrary to what justice on almost any account would require. And the rights that it accords to its citizens may fall well short of what many theories of justice would support. For all that functionality demands, the state might operate with decision-maker laws that give authorities intuitively unjustifiable power, for example, and it might establish decision-taker laws that allow some citizens to have an intuitively unjustifiable degree of private power over other citizens: the wealthy over the poor, for example, men over women, or the mainstream over minorities.

This is to say that while the functional state must countenance significant rights on the part of its citizens, specifically rights of civic security, it may recognize those rights on a narrower or wider front and may give them a poorer or richer content. Still, this is not bad news from the point of view of a theory of justice, for it shows that the state may be required to satisfy the requirements of justice, according to one or another theory, without ceasing to be functional. The functional state need not be just, but it need not be unjust either. The ideal of statehood that it encodes coheres with the ideal of justice but it does not entail it.

6

The Demands of
a Market Economy

WE HAVE been concerned in the last two chapters with how far the functional state characterized in part I can transcend some alleged limitations. In chapter 4, we argued that in such a state, contrary to absolutist or statist views, the people as subjects of the law must collectively enjoy a certain degree of countervailing power, constitutional and extra-constitutional, in relation to the sovereign, and that they may enjoy quite a high degree. And then in chapter 5, we saw that while people do not individually have the natural rights that libertarians take to corral or even disable the state, there are good grounds for holding that the functional state must acknowledge some significant institutional rights on the part of its citizens, specifically rights of civic security; that it may acknowledge such rights quite widely, making the citizenry inclusive; and that it may give rights that are richer in their demands than statehood strictly requires.

These discussions all bear on the question as to how far the potential of the state is limited by the fact of being functional. The question is important for several reasons, not least because justice by most accounts would require the state to be able to empower its citizenry collectively and to be able to grant them significant individual rights; thus, it is only if the functional state has the sort of potential ascribed that justice constitutes a feasible ideal. In this final chapter, we address that same sort of issue in another context. We ask how far the demands of a market economy require the functional state to restrain its exercise of power, letting economic arrangements evolve autonomously, and how far therefore those demands limit its potential.

Absolutists rely on conceptual grounds, related to the analysis of the notions of sovereignty and the people, when they argue that the functional state

is deeply limited in the collective powers it can grant its citizens. And libertarians rely on metaphysical considerations—the alleged reality of natural
rights—in arguing that the functional state is limited, even blocked, when it
comes to acknowledging significant rights on the part of those citizens. In a
parallel fashion, laissez-faire theorists, as we may call them, maintain on empirical grounds that the functional state is limited in how far it can intervene
productively in the market economy. They argue that it would be hazardous
at best, self-defeating at worst, for the state, including the functional state, to try
to regulate and shape that economy.

Those who maintain a laissez-faire point of view may embrace any of several
pictures. In one, the economically interventionist state is criticized on the
pragmatic ground that it cannot hope to access information about people's
often changing preferences, and that it could not intervene to a reliably beneficial effect in the workings of the economy and civil society more generally
(Hayek 1944; 1960).

In another the interventionist state is derided on the ground that the freedom of the market from government regulation should be maximized for a
mix of pragmatic and principled reasons. The pragmatic consideration is that
market freedom is needed if the economy is to perform well; the principled,
that the maximal enjoyment of such freedom is a good in itself (Friedman
1962).

In yet another picture, the interventionist state is criticized on the purely
principled ground, first, that a naturally evolving civil society and economy is
an essentially respectful form of association, in which people each pursue their
own ends; and, second, that the benefits it provides for its members are jeopardized if a rationalistic state redirects it to a centrally dictated end, treating it
like a corporate organization (Oakeshott 1975; 1991).

Those who defend pictures like these may often wish to criticize, not strictly
the intervention of the state in the economy, but only that species of strategic,
policy-based intervention that is made by the government of the day or its
agencies. Such thinkers might be willing to countenance the more stable intervention embedded, perhaps on the basis of constitutional or common law,
in long-established practice. Both sorts of interventions are perpetrated by the
state, however, and what we take as laissez-faire theory is a position opposed
to interventions of either kind.[1]

---

1. Conservative economists of the public choice school typically recognize the role of the
state in the economy but hold that it ought to be limited in good part to interventions that are

Is this fair? Yes, for two reasons. First, there is no sharp divide between strategic and stable intervention, as our discussion should reveal, although there is a good issue in institutional design—an issue connected with the ideal of a rule of law—about how far the state should stabilize its economic interventions. Second, the critique of the role of the state in the market economy is usually presented in abstract theory, and certainly in public rhetoric, as one that applies to any form of state intervention. Laissez-faire theory projects an ideal of the market economy as an allegedly autonomous, self-regulating sphere independent of the state. And that image is simply false. Far from being autonomous and self-regulating, the modern market economy depends for its very existence on the law and the state.

Where we relied on relatively a priori arguments in dealing with statism and libertarianism, we must invoke more empirical considerations in arguing against laissez-faire theory. We shall look at three aspects of the market economy and trace the interventions that the state has been forced to make in response to distinctively modern pressures. This history suggests that as the modern state was forced to respond in that interventionist way, so any functional state would be forced to adopt similar measures in response to such pressures: not necessarily the same measures, of course, but measures of an equally interventionist character.

The lesson of the history, as Karl Polanyi (2002) puts it in a classic work from 1944, is that under modern pressures the economy has had to become "politically embedded." The claim, in Katharina Pistor's (2019, 4) words, is that "legal coding" has been essential in the modern world: that "the economic success" of "modern economies . . . tracks the rise of nation-states that rely on law as their primary means of social ordering."[2]

The three aspects of the economy on which we focus are the property regime, the monetary system, and corporate arrangements. When it provides for property rights, the state determines the commodities and services that can be exchanged in the market; when it provides for money, it establishes the means of exchange that are essential to any market; and when it provides for

---

constitutional or quasi-constitutional in character. See Buchanan and Tullock (1962), Buchanan (1975), and Brennan (1987).

2. There is much in both the studies cited that supports the lines argued in this book, especially the argument that the self-regulating, state-independent economy is a myth. But their concern is mainly empirical and historical, so that they do not focus on the normative issue of what the state might be allowed or required to do if it is to be functional or even just.

the appearance of corporations, it introduces novel but important players into the to-and-fro of market exchange. We argue that as modern pressures have forced the actual state to be highly interventionist, so they would force any state, in particular any functional state, to be interventionist too.

The chapter is in four sections. We look in the first at the role of the state in defining and defending people's property rights; in the second at its role in establishing a monetary system; and in the third at its role in making possible the formation of corporations: in older terminology, joint stock companies. Then in the fourth section we defend the sort of moderate realism about corporate bodies presupposed in our account of corporations, and indeed in our earlier account of the state; this can be seen as an appendix to the chapter and even the book.[3]

6.1 Property

Constraining and Enabling Market Exchange

There are two broadly distinct ways in which the state connects with the market economy. On the one side, it introduces laws that constrain market activities, as it might constrain any activities whatsoever; on the other it establishes laws that enable the market to assume distinctive forms. Almost everyone acknowledges the constraining role of the state in relation to the market, and we shall focus here on its enabling role. But before adopting that focus, it may be useful to mention the main ways in which the laws of a functional state may be expected to constrain market activity.

Market exchanges are contracts that people make with one another and inevitably take place under social norms that are accepted, as a matter of common awareness, on all sides. It is such norms that enable people to form reliable expectations about one another's performance, about what factors may excuse a failure of performance, and about what is due to them in the event of another's unexcused failure.

As the functional state will play a role in regimenting and reinforcing social norms that are generally beneficial, by our genealogical argument, so it will play this role in relation to the norms governing contracts. Specifically, it will do this in developing various bodies of criminal and contract law, tort law, and the law of commerce.

---

3. In developing the chapter, I called on the advice of several colleagues and friends, and I should acknowledge especial debts to Will Bateman, Geoffrey Brennan, and Paddy Ireland.

The state plays a part in shaping contracts insofar as it determines within criminal law that certain sorts of contract are illegal. And with those that it allows, especially in formal, enduring relationships, it introduces laws of contract to which the parties are subject or can choose to be subject. Contracts made under these laws will clarify the terms of the exchange—these may or may not be negotiable by the parties—and will usually lay down the sort of redress that an aggrieved party may seek from the courts when the other breaches those terms. Laws of that kind typically apply to relatively formal contracts like those of marriage, partnership, employment, rental arrangements, and the like.

Apart from directly shaping contracts in this way, the state typically shapes market exchanges indirectly by introducing rules under which parties may complain in the courts about how they fare informally at the hands of others. Prominent among these are tort laws that determine when someone who suffers harm at the hands of another, even perhaps the unwitting hands of another, can sue for damages. Laws of economic tort will be particularly relevant to market exchanges, and can be regarded also as market rules, insofar as they bear on effects like the negative externalities—say, effects in the pollution of a local water supply—that industrial and related enterprises can generate.

Contract law and tort law provide the most general constraints on legal market exchanges, regimenting norms that would be likely to materialize in any case. But exchanges of a distinctively commercial kind will also be governed by emerging norms and will engage the law of commerce, in a broad sense of that term, in supporting and improving such norms. This law too may reach quite far into the operations of the market, establishing rules to guard against the formation of monopolies, for example, to protect consumer rights, and to regulate relations between employers and employees.

Contract law, tort law, and the law of commerce illustrate nicely the role we might expect the state to play in setting up rules to constrain legal market exchanges. But the state also plays a role in defining the rules that make market exchanges possible in the first place, and it is these that we shall focus on here. Such enabling rules are especially important and are more likely than constraining laws to escape notice within the laissez-faire perspective.

The three outstanding examples of market-enabling rules are the laws that define property rights in the goods exchanged, the laws that establish the financial system under which exchange takes place, and the laws that enable corporations to be players in the exchange system. We look at the rules governing property in this section, in particular private property; at the rules governing money in the next; and at the rules governing corporations in the third.

Laissez-faire theorists have much to say about the constraining laws of contract, tort, and commerce, arguing that the state should give them this or that shape. But they tend to ignore or downplay the role of laws in enabling property, money, and corporations, when they adopt a stance that is hostile to what is cast as unnecessary regulation or intervention by the state. The aim of the chapter is to highlight the extent to which in today's world property, money, and corporations depend on law and the state for their very existence, and to argue that the functional state would be required to play an equally constructive role, albeit not necessarily a role with the same constructed effects.

The Nature of Ownership

Before looking at the role of the state in relation to property, and the form it took under modern pressures, we need to think about what ownership involves. The first thing to notice is that owning something—holding it as private property—amounts to more than acquiring it, keeping it, and monopolizing its use. Someone might gain possession of certain resources and commodities—a particular patch of land or some items they had made or inherited—but still not enjoy ownership in those assets.[4] Suppose that no one other that the person in possession was likely to resist someone who tried to take from their holdings; suppose it was a dog-eat-dog society in which everyone, or perhaps every family, had to defend the things they had acquired in order to maintain possession. There would then be no sense, intuitively, in anyone's claiming to own what they possessed; there would be no such thing as property.

The reason for this is that ownership, to return to a theme from the last chapter, is a robustly demanding good. I do not own something just because other people happen not to want to dispossess me or are too weak or timid to take it from me. I must have possession of what I own, and the ability to use it as I wish, in a relatively robust degree. I must retain possession robustly over variations in the desires or attitudes or capacities of others. Or at least I must robustly retain possession so long as I use what I have only in certain ways:

---

4. Thus, in a classic article on ownership, A. M. Honore (1961, 107) writes, "A people . . . who meant by *meum* and *tuum* no more than 'what I (or you) presently hold' would live in a world that is not our world."

ownership may not allow me to use what I own, for example, in a way that imposes certain costs on others.

As a robustly demanding good of this kind, ownership requires, not or not just that others should be firmly disposed to leave me in possession of what I own, but also that they should be constrained to do so. If ownership is generally available across a society, as we may assume it is, then the constraints that establish it must identify the conditions under which someone will count as owning something as well as the conditions under which they can maintain possession and monopolize the use of that property.

The constraints that can do this job must have the form of general rules, whether social norms or formal laws: laws, if we go with the lesson of our genealogies in chapter 1, that will often regiment and reinforce norms that preexisted them. Such rules will establish rights of acquisition and rights of usage. Rights of acquisition determine when you or I have a title to own something, say as first possessor, maker, purchaser, inheritor, or whatever. Rights of usage determine the prerogatives that you or I will enjoy in what we do with the things to which we have a title; they will determine how far, for example, and under what conditions we may trade, gift, bequeath, or indeed retain such items. Needless to say both the rights or titles to ownership as well as the rights or prerogatives of ownership vary across societies and have varied across time within almost every society (Honore 1961).

The norms or laws supporting property would protect the owner against those who might try to dispossess them of what they own or interfere with how they use it. More specifically, they would impose a sanction on anyone who interfered in that way with the property holder: in the case of a norm a sanction of disesteem or ostracism; in the case of a law, a sanction of a more directly punitive kind. Such rules would enable each to claim a right to own that which they hold, and it is just such a form of rightful possession that the concept of ownership is used to ascribe. No ownership without rights and, by the argument of the last chapter, no rights of ownership without rules.

Like any rights, property rights will enable their bearers to assert or waive certain demands that are justified under the relevant rules and, where appropriate, the claims they assert will be upheld by the authorities who implement those rules. The relevant authorities in the case of social norms will be members of the community like you and me—it is we who will impose sanctions of disesteem on offenders—and in the case of legal rights, the officials of the state.

Property may be private, public, or common. The owner in the first case is a particular agent, individual or corporate in character; in the second, it is the state; and in the third, it is people considered as individuals: they share in ownership insofar as they enjoy shared rights of usage, as in the way the people may own and use common land. In what follows, we may restrict attention to private property only, since the lessons supported carry over to the other categories.

Three Theories of Ownership

These remarks argue that whenever property began, it began with the advent of constraints like norms or laws to establish ownership, and with the robust demands that such constraints would have put in place. But how did such constraints come into existence among our forebears? Here it may be useful to review the sorts of stories associated with three classical theories of property within the common-law tradition: those, respectively, of Hobbes, Locke, and Hume.[5]

Hobbes denies, as we know, that any rules, and so any rights—that is, any claim rights—can be effectively implemented in the absence of the state. The practice that establishes the relevant rules and rights cannot emerge and stabilize just on the basis of spontaneously emerging conventions and norms, by his account; it must involve coercive law and a coercive state. In a prelegal world, by his lights, there would be only dissension. And consequently, there would be no established customs and of course no property rights. When it comes to matters of property and the like, Hobbes (1994b, 5.3) suggests, there is "want of a right reason constituted by nature." And in the absence of a polity, therefore, there could have been "no mine and thine distinct; but only that to be every man's, that he can get; and for so long, as he can keep it" (1994b, 13.13).[6]

---

5. For useful overviews of theories of property, normative and empirical, see Ryan (1984) and Waldron (1988; 2016a). For a collection of articles on the history of theories of property, see Parel and Flanagan (1979); and for a recent introduction to theories of property in law and philosophy, see Alexander and Penalver (2012).

6. For a fuller discussion of Hobbes on this theme, see Pettit (2008a, 130–32). It is worth noting that Kant supports something like a Hobbesian point of view when, as we saw, he argues a twin thesis about property rights. First, that in order for a system of property rights—or indeed any system of rights—to provide external freedom equally for all, which is a requirement of justice on his account, it has to provide them each with the assurance that they are given the same rights as others and given them with the same security. And second, that this condition can be properly fulfilled—that is, as we saw, fulfilled in an egalitarian manner expressive of an

It is true, of course, that Hobbes (1994b, 14.1) posits a "right of nature" that people have before the state is established; this consists, he says, in "the liberty each man hath to use his own power as he will himself for the preservation of his own nature; that is to say, of his own life." But, as he goes on to explain, this right or liberty consists just in "the absence of external impediments . . . to do what he would," not a right that gives the bearer a claim against others. In our terminology, his right of self-defense is the limit case of a privilege-right, not a claim-right; it is a right that people have by default, in the absence of any rules dictating how they should behave.[7]

Our genealogical account of norms gives us reason to reject the story about the origin of property constraints that Hobbesian theory suggests. By that account it was at least possible that property rights got to be established by legally unenforced norms; Hobbes is wrong to think that the state had to be involved. In taking this view, we agree with Locke, who argues that there is a particular set of property rights that would have been likely to gain recognition as a matter of custom or norm in the condition of nature.

Locke begins from the assumption that people have and are aware of having natural rights and argues that this would have prompted them in the state of nature to seek to enforce their rights against others. He puts the argument in a passage from the *Second Treatise of Government* that we already cited. Everyone "hath by nature a power," Locke (1960, s87) says, "not only to preserve his property, that is, his life, liberty and estate, against the injuries and attempts of other men; but to judge of, and punish the breaches of that law in others, as he is persuaded the offence deserves." If people in the state of nature each exercise the power of preserving their naturally rightful property, and of punishing those who trespass against them, they will presumably give rise to corresponding norms. And at that point those norms will presumably serve as rules to specify rights of property and, if they are generally recognized, as rules that others will uphold in supporting anyone against a trespasser.

"omnilateral" will—only insofar as there are coercive, state-supported laws in place, and so a supportive system of coercive taxation.

7. Famously, Hobbes argues later that by the laws of nature—in effect, self-interest—no one can fail to defend themselves against aggression, especially when their life is at stake, and that no one can consent to a system of law that would take this right away. Thus, under any system of law, subjects will have the right to resist individually, however futile resistance may be, if the sovereign seeks to punish them.

While Hobbes is mistaken that property could have emerged only in the wake of the state, it may be that as a matter of historical fact, at least in some countries, it was the state that prompted its development. And while Locke is mistaken that property emerged only with the recognition of natural rights, he may be right to think that it would have first appeared before the advent of laws.

David Hume offers a story about how property appeared that differs from both Hobbes's and Locke's. He maintains that it could have appeared by custom and norm alone, so that its appearance need not involve the state. But he argues that it could have appeared in a way that does not require people to be aware of supposedly natural rights of property. On his account of ownership, as in the genealogies we presented in the first chapter, the very concept of property—and so of property rights—is likely to have appeared only simultaneously with a corresponding practice.

Hume assumes that in the world without property, it would still have been the case that people gained hold, where they could, of goods they desired, acquiring and maintaining possession so far as that was within their power. And, assuming that there was such a distribution of possessions already in place, he argues that each would have recognized the tit-for-tat attraction of accepting it, as they might accept a social norm.

He defends that argument by reference to how any one of us would think in such a scenario. "I observe," Hume (1978, 3.2.2) says, "that it will be for my interest to leave another in the possession of his goods, provided he will act in the same manner with regard to me." And, he goes on, this recognition by each of what it is in their interest to do in relating to any other—and, of course, what it is in the interest of the other to do also—will give rise to an appropriate regularity and, assuming this is widely if reluctantly accepted, a corresponding norm. "When this common sense of interest is mutually express'd, and is known to both, it produces a suitable resolution and behaviour."

The Premodern History of Property

Where does this review of classical theories leave us on the question of how property first emerged? Rejecting Hobbes, we may assume that it did not necessarily require the prior introduction of laws of ownership by the state. Rejecting Locke, we may assume that it emerged without any recognition of supposedly natural rights on the part of people. We may endorse the Humean lesson, instead, that even if the state had not previously introduced laws of ownership, and even if there are no natural rights, still property rights would have been likely—indeed, robustly likely—to be established by social norms.

This lesson leaves open the possibility that such norms and rights appeared in many countries only after the state had imposed laws. The message is that property rights were established in premodern history either by spontaneously emerging norms or, perhaps less likely, by laws that the state introduced. It may even be that they appeared in some places in the first way, in others in the second.

While this is a very schematic conclusion, we may add a little more substance and detail if we grant two assumptions, already defended in chapter 1. First, that any social norms that spontaneously emerged were likely to have attracted the support of laws; and second, that any laws that the state introduced de novo would have won enough acceptance, however reluctant in some quarters, to have enjoyed the status of social norms, as we put it earlier. The conclusion is that property rights must first have appeared with the combined support of norms and laws.

We may embrace that conclusion while leaving open the question as to whether norms preceded laws or laws preceded norms. This conclusion is congenial insofar as it is certainly the case that the property system that modern pressures began to transform in the modern period—in Europe, to concentrate on that example, from about the seventeenth century—was precisely a system supported by a combination of traditional norm and established law.

But the property system transformed by modern pressures would have already involved another element that we can also ascribe to premodern developments. This is the taxation, levied at whatever point, that the state would have depended on for its support. The functional state would not have appeared or survived, unless it could modify existing property rights to legitimate taxation—to distinguish it, in effect, from outright theft—with general acceptance on the part of the citizenry.

Taxation remains controversial even today, and it is worth emphasizing that it is an essential part of any legislatively regimented system of property rights. Such rights would amount to little in the absence of the tax-derived resources that the state uses to establish the institutional infrastructure they presuppose. While taxation may look and feel like an intrusion on those who are required to pay it, this is because it usually comes after possession and is naturally seen as a sort of dispossession. Far from being an assault on ownership, however, taxation is required, and would have been required in the premodern period, to make ownership legally effective.[8]

Modern Developments

With this sketch of how property would have been organized previously, we may turn to the impact on patterns of ownership that came about in the modern period, initially in Europe and then worldwide. Institutional and technological developments as well as associated changes like increases in population and urbanization forced the state to make some quite dramatic changes in the organization of property. They led regimes to expand the range of ownership and property, to recognize novel property titles—novel rights *to* ownership—and to introduce novel property prerogatives: novel rights *of* ownership.

Consider the economic shift whereby joint stock companies got to be recognized from about the sixteenth century in Europe; more on this when we consider corporations in the final section. This shift forced the law to treat those entities as novel types of owners. And it also pushed the law into recognizing that individuals—and indeed corporate agents—may invest in a joint stock company and own a sort of property that did not preexist that development: namely, company shares. Another sort of property that did not preexist the joint stock company, of course, is the corporate bond: an IOU on which the company pays a regular return. Corporate bonds were modeled on government bonds that were also introduced in the modern period: IOUs on which the government paid a regular return to its creditors.

Thus, the appearance of the joint stock company generated a new type of owner, the corporation, and new types of property for owners to hold: shares and bonds. And as that sort of institutional change led to deep alterations in the property regime, so new technologies had a similar effect. As a result of new technologies, the law had to allow ownership, not just in familiar tangible assets, but in intellectual property such as that which is recognized in copyright or patent law. And under similar pressures, it had to allow ownership in

---

8. This is not to defend any specific pattern of taxation, of course, only to maintain that taxation as such is essential under any state, functional or not, and that the property rights we may expect to be present in any functional state cannot preclude it. For a defense of a congenial view of taxation, see Murphy and Nagel (2004).

other intangible assets like software, established brand names, professional licenses, customer lists, online books, and so on.

As novel types of owners and novel forms of property emerged under institutional or technological developments, so inevitably the rights of ownership also altered. Thus, with the introduction of patent and copyright law, the titles to ownership in such assets turned on claims to originality and the like. And prerogatives of ownership came to be defined in a manner suited to the novel items owned, disappearing with the lapse of time and in some cases—say, that of online books—not allowing for transfer in a trade or as a gift.

Other developments led to changes in the prerogatives associated with traditional ownership. Thus, under environmental and other pressures, the law in many countries came to deny landowners control over whether a canal or railway or road could pass through their property, control over areas of their land on the sea, or control over the natural resources that lie beneath the surface. Almost everywhere population pressures prompted the law to impose zoning restrictions on what could be built and owned in residential areas and to deny householders prerogatives like those of extending their dwelling at will or of painting it any color they liked. And humanitarian commitments put limits on how people could treat their domestic or farm animals.

The Implications of These Developments

As property titles and prerogatives have historically evolved under the pressures of modern society, they have become creatures of law that are dependent on the state for their very existence and maintenance. They exist in virtue of the laws that have been introduced to cope with various changing and novel circumstances, and they could hardly have come into existence otherwise. This historical lesson teaches us that insofar as such adjustments proved necessary in fact, so adjustments of that general kind, if not necessarily those that actually occurred, would have to be introduced by any functional state.

Thus, the laissez-faire, empirical argument against the state's making the sorts of economic interventions required under modern circumstances is scarcely compelling. The contemporary economy in most countries is now an economy of intangible assets, corporate owners, and qualified ownership. It is so complex, and so dependent on the innovations of the state in establishing appropriate laws, that it seems downright silly to suggest that the state does more harm than good in its interventions in this area. We may not approve of some of the interventions that have occurred, either on grounds of function or justice, but we can hardly deny that a functional state would be required to make some such interventions under modern conditions.

The laissez-faire point of view might have had some credibility prior to the emergence of the novel institutional and technological developments of recent centuries, and prior to the impact of environmental and population pressures. In that period the principal owners were individuals, the paradigm goods that they owned under norm and law were the land they individually inherited or purchased, the dwellings and other goods they made or purchased, and the money they gained from parting with those items or selling their services. And the taxes imposed by government did not involve income taxes, or even indeed many wealth taxes; they were mainly tariffs that could be seen as tolls paid to government for the use of seaports, bridges, roads, and the like.

In the context of such a simple, predominantly agrarian economy, it might have made sense to think that the titles to ownership were always determined by established patterns of inheritance and transfer, discovery and creation. In that context, it might equally have made sense to think that the prerogatives of ownership were unqualified and unchanging. And in that context, finally, it might have seemed sensible to think that property rights in general were fixed in stone and, if not metaphysically natural in the sense discussed in the last chapter, were salient enough to be rights that we might expect to find established under any functional state.

In that predominantly agrarian economy, then, people might have been excused for thinking that the state is liable to do more harm than good in intervening to adjust property titles and rights. But in the modern economy that prevails almost everywhere today, that laissez-faire view must look little short of absurd. Urbanization, population growth, and the appearance of the joint stock company, together with industrialization, financialization, and the digital transformation of society have introduced a radically different economy. Most property is owned by nonindividual owners in this world, ownership is subject to substantial constraints derived from the pressures of population or the requirements of technology, and the property owned and exchanged is mainly of a sort that cannot be seen by eye or touched by hand. In this sort of society, property and property rights depend inherently on the state and the law, and it makes no sense to think that the state should stay out of the picture.

To argue that the modern regime of property is dependent on the state, and that it is futile to argue that the functional state cannot productively intervene in the domain of ownership, is not to say that such a regime is what justice requires. The argument is consistent with the claim that the state should consider whether the property regime it establishes is just and, if not, how it should be amended. Contrary to the laissez-faire claim, the state does not stand outside the property regime like an alien force and its initiatives on this front do not have the character of foreign interventions. The property regime exists in virtue of political support, and there can be no functionally based objection to the state's considering whether justice requires that it should alter that regime and, if so, in what specific ways.[9]

6.2 Money

The lesson of the last section is clear. As property rights have been historically regimented and extended by the state under modern pressures, so any functional state would have to make some such adjustments in response to those pressures. And so, consistently with its function, the state might be able to make deeper changes of the kind that justice presumptively requires: say, for example, changes in the unqualified title to acquisition associated with inheritance (Halliday 2018); changes in the rates of taxation attached to different income streams of a kind that many have supported; or, to anticipate discussion in the next section, changes in the range of things that corporations may own. But if the market rules of property are dependent in this way on the state, contrary to laissez-faire doctrine, the dependence is even more marked in the case of the market rules of money.

The Premodern History of Money

As the property system is likely to have emerged historically on a customary basis, and as a system of law is likely to have emerged to regiment and transform property rights in response to modern pressures, so the same is true of money. There is good reason to think that a rudimentary kind of monetary system appeared independently of the law or the state. This is because the

9. It may be said against this that in some countries the constitution dictates a relatively unchangeable basis for the sorts of property rights that ought to obtain under the polity. Richard Epstein (1985; 1990) argues in this spirit that the U.S. Constitution dictates that the property rights recognized in statutory law should meet certain strict constitutional limits. But what the constitution dictates in any country, if indeed it dictates anything, may not be what justice dictates. And the demands of justice on what the state should do in establishing property include demands on what the constitution should do—if it should do anything—as well as demands on what the constitutionally established government should do.

counterfactual genealogy of money shows that this is a live possibility, and because that tends to happen even currently when, in times of crisis, the state-sponsored currency breaks down. By all accounts, for example, cigarettes emerged among the local population in postwar Berlin as the most common currency, serving the standard role of money as a medium of exchange and consequently a metric of price and a means of accumulating wealth (Petrov 1967).

The cigarette example suggests that things may have been historically similar, with some widely sought commodity such as gold or silver assuming a role in exchange, as in our genealogy. Under such a development, a regularity would have emerged whereby the commodity was employed and expected in exchange between people. And being recognized as such, the regularity would have assumed the role of an accepted, collectively beneficial norm among the populace. Many might have preferred that a different regularity should take its place, involving a commodity more accessible to them. But while conformity might have been relatively burdensome for those individuals, still the arrangement would have had sufficient appeal as a way of coordinating mutual expectations to be accepted and internalized by all.

Even if such a currency was supported only by custom or norm, and did not depend on the support of law, its appearance would have introduced a properly financial market; gold or silver or whatever would have come to be sought, not for its own sake, or not just for its own sake, but for the sake of its exchange value. The point is nicely underlined by the joke reportedly common in Berlin immediately after World War II: that while everyone wanted cigarettes, the common medium of exchange, no one wanted any longer to smoke.

The currency norms in different societies may have emerged on this pattern without reliance on the law. But whether that pattern obtained or not, it is likely that in every society the state would have taken initiatives to support the currency. It would have had reasons to make the identity of the preferred currency clear, akin to the reasons for making any norm determinate and effective. And it would have had a ready means of achieving this, nominating it as the currency in which taxes should be paid. As people saw that tax bills had to be paid in gold or silver or whatever, they would have recognized the commodity chosen as a uniquely reliable means of exchange, a good metric of price and a safe way of accumulating wealth.

Exchange in any society would have been greatly facilitated, presumably to people's benefit overall, if it became possible, not just for the relevant commodity like gold or silver to be used in exchange, but also for IOUs in that commodity to play the same role. And as the state could have made the commodity into a reliable currency by accepting it in taxation, so it could have enabled the IOUs issued by certain agents or agencies to be equally reliable by accepting them in payment of taxation as well. This may have been possible only in some societies, of course, depending on the commodity recruited as currency. But it may well have happened in the case of gold-based economies, for example, with various private bodies—in effect, banks—being recognized by the state as providers of acceptable IOUs: in effect, banknotes.

Those banks would presumably have been motivated to lend some of their reserves to others, presumably in the form of IOUs: say, banknotes or checks; they would have ensured that the loans were secured and would have charged interest for the reserves or IOUs they lent. Moreover, they could have charged others for depositing surplus gold in their vaults or if those others were willing to have IOUs issued against that gold, they could profitably have paid them some interest against the deposits, provided that the rate was lower than the rate demanded from borrowers.

This sketch of the possible prehistory of money is wholly conjectural and may not be faithful to what historically occurred. For all we need to assume, for example, it may be that norms did not always precede laws, as in the story just sketched, but that the state's laws came first, and the norms second. But whatever occurred in times lost to us, it bequeathed to many societies at the beginning of the modern period, a commodity-based financial system supported, like the property system, by a mix of norm and law. This was a system in which the supply of money was fixed by the level of relevant reserves—gold in our example—and in which IOUs, being easier to handle, played the role of facilitating exchange. We can now take things up at that point and document what happened to the system under the pressures that began to emerge, especially in Europe, in the sixteenth century.[10]

We shall see that from then on, the historical state responded to evolving pressures by intervening more deeply in the financial system, thereby making money, like property, essentially state dependent. In that period state intervention came to be necessary for the success of money, and it has continued to play an essential part. Money had to become international insofar as trade developed between countries. And with this development various organizations were established to facilitate international trade and some currencies

---

10. Thus, the approach taken here, like the counterfactual genealogy of money explored in chapter 1, is consistent with the claims in Graeber (2011) about the actual prehistory of money.

gained special favor for their perceived reliability. We ignore the international aspect of the financial system for our purposes, however, focusing on the role of the individual state—a role, inevitably, with both domestic and international aspects—in providing an infrastructure for the money recognized within its borders.[11]

From our viewpoint the lesson of the history outlined in what follows is that any functional state that operates under modern pressures would likely have to play an interventionist role—even the sort that justice might require it to play—of a kind with the role that the state has historically played. There is nothing to the laissez-faire claim on the side of finance, as there is nothing to that claim on the side of property, according to which the state cannot interfere with benefit in the economy.[12]

Modern Developments

The developments of the financial system over the past three or four centuries are complex, and they varied from country to country. In view of the limited purpose of our review of that history, it will be enough to document the developments that took place in a rather sketchy and stylized form, ascribing them to the state, as if they materialized in the same way and at the same pace in all countries. The developments charted began in trading countries like Holland, Sweden, and England in the sixteenth and seventeenth centuries and have now spread to most countries on earth (Ferguson 2008). We may chart the developments of particular importance in ten stages.

1. When the state accepted the IOUs in gold that were issued by certain banks in payment of taxation, it effectively credentialled those bodies, recruiting them in the service of providing a reliable and indeed portable currency. The IOUs issued by such banks took the form, in the most straightforward version, of banknotes—or indeed coins in other metals—that could be cashed in for the reserve commodity: gold, as we have been assuming. This recruitment of the banks served the community well in establishing those IOUs as an accepted currency, thereby facilitating trade and indeed taxation.

---

11. For a useful study of the performance of the state on this front, specifically in some parliamentary regimes, see Bateman (2020).

12. For an accessible and appealing critique of more recent developments in financial systems, see Kay (2015). And for an overview of where change is needed and not needed, see Rouch (2020).

2. The state had a motive to bolster its own operation, however, by establishing in law a central bank to fund various ventures that it undertook and to serve as its own banker; the bank could organize loans to the executive, say by auctioning government bonds that attracted domestic or overseas lenders. The state sometimes established that bank coercively, sometimes by giving lenders interest-based and other incentives to provide government with the required reserves of gold or of recognized IOUs. Thus, the Bank of England was established in 1694—as a privately held joint stock company—in order to provide the government with a war chest.

3. But even if it was not moved by the wish to fund its own operations, every modern state had independent reasons to want a publicly owned central bank: typically, one that seemed relatively impartial, operating at arm's length from domain-general authorities in the legislature and executive. For, as became apparent over the centuries, such a bank could regiment and reinforce the financial system—the norms likely to emerge in the development of that system—in a variety of ways. It could provide a single clearing house where commercial banks were able to exchange one another's IOUs, it could give short-term loans to private banks to facilitate their day-to-day operations, and it could issue IOUs of its own to serve as currency. But even more important, a central bank could play a safeguarding as well as a simplifying role, protecting the economy against the risks associated with private banking.

4. One of those risks became salient in the mid-seventeenth century when banks began, in effect, to create money. They did this via fractional reserve banking, which began in Sweden and gradually spread elsewhere. In nonfractional reserve banking, the bank holds gold reserves in its vaults sufficient to cover all its IOUs in circulation. In fractional reserve banking, it holds reserves sufficient to cover only a fraction of those IOUs; the remainder are covered by the liabilities—presumably, adequately secured—of those who borrow those IOUs. The system promises to work because the depositors in a bank are hardly likely to want to withdraw all their deposits at once and hardly likely to create a run on the bank. While fractional reserve banking may first have emerged without legal recognition, it would have appealed in any state insofar as it increased the money supply, the quantity of trade, and the taxable base on which a state can draw.

5. The central bank in many countries was called upon, often only in the last century or so, to guard against the danger of a run on a bank by serving as a backup lender—a lender of last resort—for any bank whose creditors lost faith in its reliability; and, at least in some countries, by having the power to require

commercial banks to hold reserves against a higher fraction of its liabilities, and so to lend less money to borrowers. Furthermore, the government often supplemented those measures by guaranteeing those with savings and deposits in designated commercial banks that their funds, or their funds up to a certain level, would be safe, if a run on such a bank did lead to its collapse.

6. With the emergence of financial systems in each country, people depended on the IOUs in circulation, and related forms of credit—in short, on the supply of money—for being paid for the commodities they made, or the services they provided, at a level that enabled them to stay in business. At an ideal level, the supply of money would be large enough to meet this requirement, enabling full employment, yet not so large as to cause prices to rise in an inflationary spiral. But there is a constant danger of movement away from this level, as an economy responds slowly to changes in local productivity or to challenges from more productive trading partners elsewhere. Every state had an incentive, therefore, to guard against the problems to which unregulated conformity to existing norms and laws might have led: an incentive, in effect, to steer a passage between the dangers of high unemployment and uncontrolled inflation.

7. The state generally helped to guard against the dangers of unemployment and inflation by taking steps to decrease or increase the money supply at any moment. It could do this, for example, insofar as the central bank had the power to set the interest rates at which it gave credit to commercial banks, or to vary the fractional reserve requirement mentioned above. If commercial banks had to pay lower interest rates for money borrowed from the central bank, or if they had to cover a smaller fraction of their liabilities to depositors with reserves, then they would be able to lend more money at lower rates to borrowers. If they had to pay higher interest rates, or hold more reserves, then they would have less money to lend and would be able to lend it only at higher rates.[13]

8. The state generally supplemented monetary control with fiscal policy—the administration's policy in taxation and spending—in the search for attractive levels of employment and inflation. Since the viability of the currency depends on how effectively those goals are achieved, that meant that the actions of a state via its central bank and executive government became crucial to determining how far the country's money commanded confidence as a

---

13. I do not discuss other measures such as the quantitative easing that central banks have also taken to deal with financial crises.

means of national and international exchange: in effect, how far people were willing to accept it in payment of debts.

9. Thus, the credibility of the money in every country came to be tied to the success of the economy in such a close manner that the size of the gold reserves that the central or commercial banks retained ceased to be of much relevance. And that being so, it became possible for the state not to rely on any fraction of such metallic reserves at the central bank to back its money and to impose fractional reserve constraints of a nonmetallic kind on private banks. It could decide to let the viability of the currency—the confidence it commands in national and international markets—depend instead on the performance of the economy and on its perceived prospects.

10. This, of course, is what happened with the currency of existing countries when the gold standard, which had required at least fractional backing in national gold reserves, was generally rejected in the mid- to late twentieth century; it had become a mainstay of international finance from about a century earlier when the supply of gold became sufficient to enable gold to play that role. Thus, the utility of the money on which markets depend came to be fixed in each country—and its exchange rate with other currencies—only by the success of the local economy in achieving a balance between inflation and employment, and by the corresponding level of popular confidence in the capacity of the currency to retain its purchasing power over time.[14]

With these developments, money became fiat money, as it is often called: that is, money created and supported by the *fiat* or dictate of the state, not by confidence in the availability of material reserves to back the currency. The success of the financial system in any country may not be determined by just the state's say-so, but it came to be determined everywhere by the actions of the state in shaping monetary and fiscal policy. The utility of a country's money is grounded in the confidence that the markets have in the performance of that state on those fronts, not in any putative reserves that the money reflects.

14. The gold standard ruled industrial countries for fifty to sixty years after the 1870s, when gold became sufficiently available due to the gold rushes in California and Australia. While it lost some of it importance in the 1930s, it remained in effect while currencies were tied to the U.S. dollar and the United States relied on the gold standard domestically; this ceased only in the early 1970s. The use of the gold standard tended to support protectionism, to the detriment of the world economy, as each country sought to guard its gold reserves against international trade; and it may even have sponsored colonialism, as major countries sought to expand their protectionist regimes to encompass colonies abroad. See Polanyi (2002).

The Implications of These Developments

It should be clear from this short, stylized history that in modern times money has come to be essentially dependent, like property, on the performance of the state as an economic manager. That being so, it is a little short of unthinkable that the functional state might be prohibited, on pain of being counterproductive, from interfering in the financial sector of the modern economy. Like property, money has become a state-dependent reality, and the laissez-faire idea of keeping the state out of the economy on these fronts is deeply misconceived. As the modern state has become interventionist, so any functional state operating under modern pressures must be interventionist too, and may be required, for example in the service of justice, to develop novel modes of intervention.

The dependence of the financial system on people's confidence in the state can give rise to a sense of vertigo, and this has driven many to yearn conservatively for a system in which gold reserves would continue to play some role. The gold standard may seem to promise a solid base for the credibility that a currency commands. But returning to the gold standard would not insulate the value and viability of a currency from the overall performance of the state in achieving a balance between employment and inflation. There is no escape from the fact that in the maintenance of a financial system, as in the maintenance of a property regime, we depend in every country on the crucial, foundational role of the state.

Revulsion against the dependence of the economy on the performance of the state, and on the general level of national and international confidence in government may have prompted the rise of Bitcoin and similar would-be currencies. These are designed to operate independently of states and to serve as an international medium of exchange. It is too early to say how far the initiatives will succeed in transforming the international financial system. And it is certainly too early to say whether on balance they ought to be appealing, and ought to command attention in on grounds of efficiency or justice. But it is very unlikely that any of them will succeed without the active support of different states. If they develop to maturity, that development may call for a revision of the points argued in this section, but it is hardly likely to make money wholly independent of the state.

The fear of vertigo that our account of money can prompt may be heightened or lessened, depending on how exactly that account is presented. Thus, the fear is unnecessarily heightened under the otherwise appealing way of thinking about institutional realities, money included, that John Searle (1995; 2010) defends. He argues broadly that an institutional reality such as money depends for its existence on the attitudes displayed by people in their jointly assigning a suitable status and function to things that count as money. The idea is that a certain piece of paper has the status and function of a dollar bill—it constitutes money—in virtue of people's jointly subscribing to a formula according to which such a piece of paper counts in perfectly ordinary circumstances, and not for example in a game, as a dollar bill.

There is nothing strictly mistaken in this sort of claim, since it can be taken to support a point we made earlier, that the people of any state sustain its institutions by jointly acting in accord with corresponding demands. People sustain the electoral institution insofar as they together vote in sufficient numbers and go along with the results of their voting. And in the same way people sustain an institution of money insofar as they together treat tokens of a certain currency in an appropriate manner.

But, as we saw earlier, people may jointly sustain an institution without having any collective, let alone individual, control over it. This is because, there may be no accessible route whereby they might upend that institution and put another in its place. They may be blocked from acting in such a revisionary manner by the lack of a salient plan for doing so or by the fact that free-riding problems might inhibit anyone from taking the risk that seeking to mobilize the group would require. Étienne de La Boétie (2015) failed to recognize this when he argued that because the people together are required to sustain even a state where a dictator rules, there is no such thing as involuntary servitude to such a ruler.

The problem with Searle's formulation of the way in which an institution like money depends on people's collective attitudes and actions is that it can be read as supporting a control-centered or decisionist view of the kind that La Boétie presupposes. It may be true that when people collectively establish money, they endorse a formula to the effect that such and such items count as money. But that claim can be easily taken to suggest that what the people give in endorsing an appropriate formula they can take away—and take away at will—by withdrawing their support. And that would be quite misleading.

As citizens may jointly sustain the state without having control over whether to keep it or not, so people may jointly sustain a financial system without having control over whether to maintain it. In each case this is because control requires the ability jointly to cease to sustain the institution and they are unlikely to have this, because of lacking a plan or because of free-riding problems. Searle's formula obscures that inability and may well elicit a sort of vertigo, suggesting that money is a totally flimsy, fictional thing: an entity that has an effect, like the Wizard of Oz, only so long as people are willing to give it credence.

This is not to say, of course, that the money of a country—the value it has as a medium of domestic and international exchange—is insulated from the effects of a government's policy and of the behavior of its citizens. As we have stressed, the monetary and fiscal policy of the government is quite likely to impact on the value of its currency, as of course may the relative productivity of other players in the market. But to acknowledge that vulnerability is not to identify a danger that is peculiar to fiat money. That danger would be likely to remain present, and even worse dangers might come into prospect, if fiat money were replaced by a gold-based currency.

If these considerations move us to resist the idea of requiring the state to introduce a gold standard at the base of the financial system, they should not lead us to think that that system is likely to remain unchanged under future developments. It may become clear as things continue to change that there is room for beneficial improvements to the system, whether from the perspective of justice or statehood. It may be, as some now say, that the role of commercial banks could be profitably reassigned, at least in part, to the central bank in any country: that people might be able to lodge their savings with, and draw loans from, the central bank itself. The consideration of such possibilities, however, lies beyond our brief in this book. It is enough for us just to register that the functional state is bound to play an interventionist part in entrenching the financial system and that it may play a smaller or a larger part, depending on the ideals it embraces.

6.3 Corporations

From Regulation to Construction

In the areas of property and money that we have just reviewed, the functional state is going to be pushed, as the state has been pushed in modern times, from a detached into a more interventionist role. The state that emerged with the appearance of a legal system—a system of secondary rules and authorities— may initially have had a relatively passive, regulative role in these areas, the job of its officials being to regiment and reinforce the primary rules of ownership and finance—the conventions and norms—that obtained independently. But discharging that task under changing cultural and technological developments moved the modern state to adopt a more and more actively interventionist profile. Novel opportunities elicited the recognition of new domains of ownership. And the needs of an economy that exploits those opportunities pushed legal systems to expand or restrict property titles and to adjust the prerogatives of ownership. In the same way, the needs and opportunities associated with an expanding commercial society pushed countries toward the sort of financial system that prevails almost everywhere today.

The state's move from a passive to an active role in the property and financial areas is replicated in the case of corporate law. Here too we can see why commercial corporations spontaneously appeared at a certain stage in the development of society. And here too we can see why modern developments created needs and openings that led to the corporatization that is now a feature of almost every economy in the world. Insofar as that corporatization depends on the law and the state for its emergence and maintenance, the history suggests that it is bogus to argue that there is a strict limit of the kind imagined by laissez-faire thinkers on how far the state can productively intervene in the economy.

In charting the developments in systems of property and finance, we stressed that the functional or just state might well depart in some ways from the actual developments we have identified, avoiding functionally or morally unappealing effects. This observation is even more important in relation to the changes mapped in this final section. As we shall see, readily intelligible and generally welcome initiatives in the legal regimentation of commercial norms led in a manner that few could have predicted to results of a highly questionable kind. The rights that corporations have managed to achieve in our world, and the extent to which they have been able to escape corresponding responsibilities, call out for reconsideration within political theory. But we shall not pursue such reconsideration here. The point of mapping the historical developments is only to undermine the laissez-faire charge that the functional state must keep out of the market economy.

The Premodern History of Commercial Bodies

As property and money could have existed independently of legal or state involvement—and as they probably did exist prior to such involvement—so the same is true of the corporate commercial body. The universities, monastic orders, and professional guilds of the medieval world existed as corporate bodies, plausibly, before they became recognized as such in law. And trading organizations or companies of merchants enjoyed a similar status.

All such bodies were taken to be groups of individuals who operated, in virtue of representation, as singular agents. They were systems that pursued certain purposes, fixed or variable, in an executively reliable manner and on the basis of evidentially reliable judgments. In Thomas Hobbes's (1994b, chap. 16) articulation of the idea, they were groups that satisfied two connected conditions. First, they could speak for themselves coherently in the manner of natural persons: this, by virtue of an authorized spokesperson or of a voice emerging from authorized procedures. And second, they could generally be relied upon to live up to the attitudinal avowals and pledges thereby issued in their name. This was true of the trading companies of the high Middle Ages in Europe, as it was true of the universities, monastic orders, and guilds.

Existing by virtue of an enduring connection between words uttered and words acted on, such corporate entities could continue to exist over changes in their membership and procedures; all that continuation required was that regardless of other changes, the connection between utterance and action remained reliably in place. And existing by virtue of that connection, those bodies could credibly subscribe to standing rules or norms, with members being ready to satisfy associated expectations and to hold others to similar expectations. Their credibility was grounded in their advertised readiness to accept sanctions—reputational and sometimes material sanctions—for failing to abide by commitments.

While corporate bodies of this kind may have initially appeared in the Middle Ages without explicit legal recognition, the conventions and norms involved in their appearance would have been ripe for legal articulation and regimentation. But even if laws preceded norms rather than norms preceding laws, the upshot was that at the beginning of the modern period there were various corporate organizations that existed and operated under the combined support of norm and law. In this respect the prehistory of incorporation resembles the prehistory of property and money.

The status of these bodies is nicely captured in William Blackstone's magisterial *Commentaries on the Laws of England*, which offer a characterization that already applied in the late Middle Ages, although they were first published in the 1760s. Blackstone ascribes five rights to any corporate body, noncommercial as well as commercial, that reflect features with which we are familiar. The rights ascribed are: first, to continue indefinitely in existence, enjoying "perpetual succession"; second, "to sue or be sued . . . by its corporate name"; third, "to purchase lands, and hold them"; fourth, to "manifest its intentions," which it can do when it "acts and speaks only by its common seal": that is, by an authorized procedure that can "bind the corporation"; and fifth, to "make by-laws or private statutes for the better government of the corporation, which are binding upon themselves, unless contrary to the laws of the land" (Blackstone 2016, bk. 1, chap. 18, 308–10).

Incorporation for Blackstone may assume a municipal, ecclesiastical, educational, commercial, or other form; he uses the generic term "corporations" to cover all. In each case the body formed has one single duty: "that of acting up to the end or design, whatever it be, for which they were created by their founder" (bk. 1, chap. 18, 311). And in each case, it involves the empowerment of individuals, by explicit or implicit permission of the king, to unite in pursuit of such a corporate end. A corporate body exists when, with such permission, "a number of private persons are united and knit together, and enjoy many liberties, powers, and immunities in their politic capacity, which they were utterly incapable of in their natural" (bk. 1, chap. 7, 311).

The Modern Emergence of Joint Stock Companies

For all that Blackstone's characterization implies, and for all that our notion of the incorporated group requires, the bodies he describes constitute what in the commercial area might count as partnerships: aggregates of individuals organized for the pursuit of common commercial ends on the basis of common judgments. But while commercial partnerships were immensely important from the Middle Ages on, and right down through the eighteenth century in which Blackstone was writing, a new sort of incorporated body—the joint stock company, as it came to be known—had emerged in the service of commercial goals in the sixteenth and seventeenth centuries, although it achieved wide popularity and effectiveness only in the nineteenth. There were Italian precedents for the joint stock company, particularly in Genoa (Schmitthoff 1939). But it was in the newly prominent trading countries of Holland and England that it first came into its own.[15]

15. For an overview of the history and character of the joint stock company, see Ireland (1996), Hansmann, Kraakman, and Squire (2006), O'Neill (2007), and Ireland (2018). For a useful history of joint stock companies in the United States, see Horowitz (1992) and Winkler (2018). For an accessible discussion of the overall properties of the joint stock company, see Ciepley (2013). And for a good introduction to the standing of the company in current law, see Orts (2013).

In order to understand the distinctive features of the joint stock company, it may be useful to contrast it with the partnership, as it would have existed in the period when it appeared and indeed for centuries afterward.[16] The partnership is a commercial venture that operates in broadly the same manner as the other corporate bodies we have been considering. The partners join together to further their commercial fortunes, organizing themselves under a procedure that generates an authorized voice to follow on relevant matters: say, on matters to do with the subgoals to aim at and the means to be adopted in their pursuit. Partners in such an enterprise are distinguished from the members of other corporate bodies, municipal, ecclesiastical, or whatever, only by the commercial character of the end they pursue. And like those other bodies, the partnerships constitute agents and persons in law.

The partnership, so conceived, is an abstract type that can and has been realized in different concrete forms. Taken under the abstract model, however, it offers an illuminating foil for the joint stock company: for short, the company or, in equivalent terms, the firm or corporation. The partnership is subject to three distinct, if interconnected vulnerabilities, and the genius of the design behind a company or corporation is that it guards in part or in full against these dangers.

First, the partnership is vulnerable to one or more of the partners withdrawing their funds from the common enterprise, thereby leaving others in the lurch. Second, it is vulnerable as an entity to being pursued for the debts of a partner who goes bankrupt as an individual. And third, the partners or owners are vulnerable to being pursued as individuals for the debts of the entity—the partnership as a group—should it go bankrupt.

The most basic feature of a joint stock company is that it guards against the first danger, that partners may withdraw their funds at any time from the enterprise. As a safeguard against that danger, the joint company requires its contributing members to commit their assets to the common enterprise and to forego their right ever to withdraw those funds (Blair 2003). Such asset commitment means that once members provide the funds, they are locked into the arrangement; they cannot choose to pull out their money. Asset commitment probably grew out of the tendency of partnerships to require their members to commit for at least a certain period—not, say, for just one venture—to the common fund (Walker 1931).

16. Today the partnership is often allowed in law to have many of the features of the company or corporation. See Orts (2013).

Why would members be willing to commit their assets in this way? They would have a right to share in the profits of the company, regularly paid as dividends, in the proportion in which they hold shares of the common stock, and asset commitment would make those profits more dependable, guarding against the danger of a withdrawal of funds. But asset commitment still makes it impossible for members to recover their investment if they need liquid funds. So why commit? It was probably in response to the perception of this issue that Dutch practice and law introduced an important innovation early in the seventeenth century. The innovation was to allow investors to sell their shares in a company—their rights to dividend payments—and to establish stock exchanges in which shares could be traded. That innovation spread rapidly to England and eventually to the rest of the commercial world.

Asset commitment guards a company against the first vulnerability of the simple partnership. But how to guard the entity against the creditors of an individual shareholder who goes bankrupt? And how to guard the owners of shares against the creditors of the company if the enterprise itself goes bankrupt? How to provide entity shielding on the one side, owner shielding on the other?[17]

Entity shielding is closely tied up with asset commitment, since contributing to an entity in a way that does not allow you to withdraw the assets committed is close to alienating those resources, so that henceforth they belong to the company, not to you. All that you own after you make your contribution are your shares, and while these tradable rights to profits will be vulnerable to your personal creditors, that will not be so with anything that belongs to the company as such; the company need not be affected, then, by your personal bankruptcy.

Owner shielding is not so tightly tied up with asset commitment, since that device still leaves in place the possibility that should the company fail, your personal assets—the resources you hold independently of the company—may still be exposed to the claims of the company's creditors. But from early in the history of the joint stock company, the general practice was to presume that as the company's assets were protected against the bankruptcy of individuals, so individual assets were protected against the bankruptcy of the corporate entity. This practice became fully and formally ratified only in the nineteenth century, however, with recognition of the limited liability of owners.

17. This terminology is employed by Hansmann, Kraakman, and Squire (2006), whom this account broadly follows.

These developments all began in the great seventeenth-century trading powers, Holland and England. On each of the three fronts, laws were introduced—sometimes de novo, sometimes in regimenting novel norms—to establish something like the required arrangements, thereby benefitting the trading companies and, as it was widely assumed, benefitting the society at large. Firmer legal protection against the dangers listed enabled trading companies to improve their performance, to attract investors, and to bring greater prosperity to the society overall.

The Temporary Decline of Joint Stock Companies

When the joint stock company emerged in the seventeenth century, it could take a legally incorporated or unincorporated form; it could be chartered or unchartered, as we will put the distinction here. The chartered companies in England, and to a good extent in Holland, were created by act of parliament or by royal assent and were generally designed to foster foreign trade that promised to be of public utility, bringing a benefit to the country as a whole. Often provided with monopoly rights, and in some cases military protection, they were exemplified in the English case by corporations like the East India Company, founded in 1600, and the Hudson Bay Company, founded in 1670.

Side by side with chartered companies of these sorts, however, various unchartered commercial groupings, many of them with the features of joint stock companies, also came into existence in the late seventeenth and early eighteenth centuries. These mainly operated in local manufacture, in short-haul trade, and in various forms of banking, and were often established as family enterprises.

By the early eighteenth century, chartered and unchartered companies were proliferating in England, with the Bank of England figuring prominently among them; it was established as a joint stock company in 1694. In 1711 Parliament established the South Sea Company at a time of large government debt and an active economy. It was to provide shares that government creditors could be offered in payment of its debts; to enjoy the support of government by means of an annual grant that would ensure the payment of dividends on those shares; and to have monopoly rights in trading in South America: this, implausibly, since Spain controlled the relevant territory. The company thrived in a very buoyant share market, but that led to one of the most famous of stock market bubbles: this eventually burst in 1720, and the shares of the company plummeted in value.[18]

That collapse caused a serious setback to the English economy and had an inhibiting effect on the growth of joint stock companies for over a hundred years. And in that hundred years England was the main center of international trade, as the influence of Holland went into decline. The inhibiting effect was bolstered by the Bubble Act, so called, that had been passed earlier in 1720—ironically, under pressure from the South Sea Company itself. While the act was not applied regularly or rigorously, it signaled a retreat from belief in the joint stock company. It stipulated that chartered companies had to stick rigidly to the purpose, associated with a form of public utility, for which the company was established by Parliament or the king. And it also denied shareholders in unchartered companies the right to trade their shares on the stock market.

While the activity of joint stock companies may have been inhibited in the eighteenth century, however, they were still a prominent enough feature of economic life to attract the criticism of Adam Smith (1976, 5.1.3) in *The Wealth of Nations*, published in 1776. He argued that the directors of a company do not put their own fortunes at risk and that being "managers rather of other people's money," they will not "watch over it with the same anxious vigilance with which the partners in a private copartnery frequently watch over their own."

The Rapid Resurgence of Joint Stock Companies

But notwithstanding the reservations of commentators like Adam Smith, the joint stock company grew rapidly and powerfully in nineteenth-century Britain and the United States, and this development was paralleled in other European countries and eventually throughout the world. The main pressure that nurtured the return and gradual empowerment of corporations was the need to capitalize the development of canals and railways in the service of an ever more networked economy and society.

The legal initiatives that marked the new age were the reversal of the Bubble Act in England in 1825 and then, more significantly, the introduction of statutory acts that enabled joint stock companies to form as chartered entities just

18. For an account of the political and constitutional turmoil associated with the bubble, see Lebowitz (2018).

by registering appropriately with a notary; the assent of the king or parliament was no longer required. With this change, joint stock companies ceased to depend on the king or parliament and began to seem like free-standing, independent entities.

Blackstone (2016, bk. 1, chap. 18, 306) had emphasized in the 1760s that all corporate bodies depend on law for their existence but held that this dependence meant little for traditional municipal, ecclesiastical, and educational bodies, since they would exist "by force of the common law" and so only by "the King's implied consent." But, presumably in deference to the Bubble Act, he had stressed that things were different at that time in the commercial area, holding that "no trading company is with us allowed to make by-laws which may affect the king's prerogative, or the common profit of the people, under penalty of law unless they be approved" (bk. 1, chap. 18, 307–08).

It was this difference that disappeared with the reversal of the Bubble Act. Trading companies began to enjoy greater independence from government, as it became possible for a company to register as a chartered entity without appeal to anyone in office and power. They were still dependent on law, of course, since the law was required to help them form; to establish the rules governing relations between directors and managers, workers and shareholders; and to implement asset commitment and related measures. But they were freed from the requirement for statutory or royal recognition. With this liberation, the possibility of forming a joint stock company ceased to look like a privilege conferred by the grace of government and came to be seen more and more as a right that any individuals could exercise.

Like England, various jurisdictions of the United States in the nineteenth century also allowed joint stock companies to form on just the basis of registering appropriately. But other developments in that country underlined a second aspect of corporate independence.

The evolving jurisprudence of the Supreme Court emphasized early in that century, for example, that whatever the basis on which it was formed, any company was protected in common law, if not against the introduction of general statutes that might affect corporate rights, at least against the interference of government in its particular affairs. In 1819 the Supreme Court found for the appellant in *Dartmouth College v. Woodward*, a famous case in which the college, which had been chartered in 1769, challenged the right of the state of New Hampshire to take it over as a public enterprise, establishing a new set of trustees; Woodward represented those trustees. That finding established that corporate bodies, including joint stock companies, did not exist at the mercy of the policies adopted by the executive government. It reinforced the image of corporate bodies as private associations that people had the right to form and maintain under common law, with the protection of the courts.

Building on this development, the Supreme Court went further in 1886, maintaining that corporate bodies like joint stock companies were even protected against laws that a particular state might introduce to favor its own companies over those from other states. They were protected, not just in common law, but under the constitution.

In *Santa Clara County v. Southern Pacific Railroad*, the Supreme Court had to decide whether the railroad was required to pay taxes on the wooden fences that bordered the track it used in Santa Clara County. In its defense, the railroad made several points: at the more mundane end, that it did not actually own the fence; at the more elevated, that it was protected against allegedly unfair treatment on the part of the county by the Equal Protection Clause of the Fourteenth Amendment: this was a clause introduced to protect emancipated slaves. The Court found for the railroad on the grounds of its not actually owning the fence on which the county wished to tax it. But the court report cited the Chief Justice at the time—he died before the report appeared—as offering this important remark or *obiter dictum*, on the constitutional defense. "The court does not wish to hear argument on the question whether the provision in the Fourteenth Amendment to the Constitution, which forbids a State to deny to any person within its jurisdiction the equal protection of the laws, applies to these corporations. We are all of opinion that it does" (Horowitz 1992, chap. 3).

The Eventual Dominance of Joint Stock Companies

As the nineteenth century wore on, further legislative and jurisprudential developments in England, the United States, and other economically advanced countries enabled the joint stock company to operate ever more independently and effectively. One measure was an explicit recognition of the limited liability of shareholders: a formal stipulation that shielded them in the event of the enterprise's collapse. A second measure enabled such bodies to move at ease between different jurisdictions: for example, between different states of the United States of America in the nineteenth century—this was underlined in the Santa Clara decision—and between different countries across the globe in the twentieth century. And a third, reversing a provision of the Bubble Act, enabled companies to alter their sphere of activity, moving from banking into industry or from industry into agriculture, or maintaining a presence in a range of fields at once.

While these measures were important in the development of the corporation, however, it remained the case that most commercial enterprises in England and the United States operated within the partnership form—sometimes amended from its earlier shape—until late in the nineteenth century (Hansmann, Kraakman, and Squire 2006). About that time, however, a change occurred in both countries that led to a massive migration toward the form of the joint stock company.

The change was marked in England by the finding in 1897 of the House of Lords, the ultimate court of appeal, in *Salomon v. Salomon & Co.* Salomon had transferred his personal enterprise of boot making to a company constituted by himself and other family members, enticing various creditors to lend the company funds. He was paid for the transfer by shares in the new company and by a privileged status that made him the first claimant in the event of bankruptcy, on the company's assets. The company did indeed go bankrupt, and his claim on its assets meant that unsecured creditors were left with nothing.

Those creditors brought a case against him, arguing that the company was merely a device of obfuscation, since it was so small that it could be identified with Salomon and his family. While lower courts supported that argument, the House of Lords found in his favor. The company, it said, had a legal personality distinct from that of Salomon and his family, and the claim he made on its assets were therefore comparable with and, by the arrangement he had made, weightier than the claims of those creditors.[19]

That finding was echoed in a wave of legislation within the United States, with the result that in both countries many unchartered companies and partnerships sought a legally chartered status (Hansmann, Kraakman, and Squire 2006). These developments put a veil in place between a corporation and

---

19. While solidly supported in the law of joint stock companies, it is worth emphasizing how far the finding offends against common sense. It would suggest that one and the same individual can act under one hat—that of a company—in order to benefit themselves under another: that of the individual. It calls up the figure of Pooh-Bah, the Lord High Everything Else, in Gilbert and Sullivan's operetta *The Mikado*. He too operates under many hats but takes seriously the separateness he enjoys in each persona. Thus, he advises another official, Ko-Ko, who asks him to be deceptive, that "as Paymaster-General, I could so cook the accounts that, as Lord High Auditor, I should never discover the fraud. But then, as Archbishop of Titipu, it would be my duty to denounce my dishonesty."

those who established or controlled it, and, while the courts have sometimes allowed that veil to be pierced, its existence led those in many unchartered entities to avail themselves of the strengthened rights associated with formal incorporation under the law.

One effect of the corporate veil was to ensure that if a corporation is a majority or sole shareholder in another company—this too had been allowed in the nineteenth century (Horowitz 1992, chap. 3)—then it can control that other company without incurring responsibility for much that the company does. As Salamon and Co. is a distinct person from Salamon himself, separated from him under the corporate veil, so a controlled company is going to be a distinct and separate entity from the company that controls it. That makes it possible for a company to establish a distinct company as a subsidiary, to enjoy total control over that company—this, as the majority or only shareholder—and nonetheless, as a shareholder, to be shielded from the liabilities that the subsidiary may incur, if it goes bankrupt or attracts legal sanctions.

There is nothing unusual about giving the shareholders some control over a company, however standby and indirect in character. Together with directors, managers, and other employees—at least if such employees are allowed a formal or informal input to company policy—they are the individuals who constitute the company: the members of the corporate body involved. And who should have arm's-length control over a corporate body, even a joint stock company, if not its membership?

But things do not look so natural, given that a company may be a majority shareholder, perhaps the only shareholder, in another company. For at that point the control of the principal company over its subsidiary amounts to a form of control exercised by the management of one body in determining what another body—a distinct legal person—should do. This is not the control of a membership over a corporate agent that they constitute so much as the control of one agent over another.

Worse than that, it is control with little or no responsibility. Once a company is allowed to be the majority or sole shareholder in a subsidiary, then the limited liability of shareholders helps to ensure that the controlling company in such a case is not liable for the debts or penalties, even the legal penalties, of its subsidiary. Thus, the controlling company can outsource its possible liability for a specific, perhaps risky project—the risk may be economic or legal—by assigning it to a distinct company that it creates, capitalizes, and controls. If the project should fail, then it will not generally have to bear the costs of the failure, since they will accrue entirely to the subsidiary body.

Ensuing legislation and jurisprudence has enabled companies to form themselves into networks or groups, perhaps operating under the control of a single holding company, that can command connected ranges of commercial activity and establish dominance in one or another market. And it has enabled them to avoid paying taxes in higher-taxing jurisdictions by creating shell companies in lower-taxing countries and assigning the bulk of their profits to those companies (Braithwaite and Drahos 2000).[20]

Controlling the Controllers

We have seen how corporations have benefitted from the infrastructure provided by law to become independent and dominant organizations in economically advanced societies. That has raised a factual question about who is in control of such a corporation, which is related in turn to a normative issue as to how they ought to be controlled. The normative issue has not generally focused on how they ought to be controlled in justice, but rather on how they ought to be controlled if they are to flourish economically. This is unsurprising, since, like the factual question, the issue has mainly been discussed by economists and business theorists.

As joint stock companies evolved, it became less and less appropriate to describe individual shareholders as owners, a term we would happily use to describe the members of a commercial partnership. They did not own the company, only shares in the company, and they did not even own its assets; the company itself was the proprietor. Their relationship to the company became ever weaker from the nineteenth century on, as shareholding was extended to ever more people and shareholders tended to hold a small number of shares in many companies rather than a large number in few (Ireland 2018).

The demotion of shareholders from the status of owners was registered from early days in restrictions on how they could exercise influence over the company in which they held shares. As company law emerged, regimenting predominant norms, it gave active control of a company to an appointed board of directors and to a management team that operated under their supervision.

---

20. Another more recent development is the shrinking of certain companies and the outsourcing of functions, including manufacturing and wholesaling functions, that would traditionally have been kept in-house. This has enabled companies to avoid traditional, sometimes legally enforced, obligations to their employees: those who do the work they commission have the status of independent contractors. See Davis (2016).

And it restricted the control of shareholders to their role, for example at annual general meetings, in appointing directors and perhaps laying down some general guidelines for the directors to follow; in effect, it gave them an indirect form of standby control: they could veto proposals, not initiate them, and veto them only within certain limits.

A famous study by Adolf Berle and Gardiner Means (1967), first published in 1932, argued that with the rise of the modern company or corporation control had passed effectively from shareholders to managers; only a majority shareholder could exercise a decisive influence over company policy. For many years after that work, this managerialist theory of company control was accepted on all sides, both as a view of how corporations ought to be controlled, and as a view of how they generally are controlled. The idea was that the managers of a successful company should, and do mostly, pursue the interests of those who have a stake in its success, including shareholders and creditors, employees and suppliers, as well perhaps as members of the local community and citizens of the country at large.

Many economists in the 1970s began to question this approach on the ground, among other considerations, that it seemed to justify giving a dangerous level of power to managers or inviting government to dictate how they should use that power (Jensen and Meckling 1976; Jensen 1983). What emerged from this critique, spearheaded by economist Milton Friedman (1962), was the replacement of stakeholder theory by shareholder theory. This was greatly boosted by two developments: first, the practice of remunerating chief executive officers with shares in their own firm; and second, the rise of pension funds and mutual funds that sought only to maximize financial returns when purchasing shares on behalf of their members (Winkler 2018, Conclusion).

The normative idea in this approach is that managers should be allowed to take account only of the interest of shareholders and that they should seek, within the limits of the law, to make the firm so profitable that returns to shareholders are maximized, whether in dividends or in the value of the shares. The theory has remained dominant for a long period, to the point that it has helped to make it the case that corporations are generally run with a view to the interests of shareholders, and shareholders only.

In this way, shareholder theory, which was originally a normative theory of how corporations ought to be run, has become the best empirical theory of how corporations actually are run. Whether it remains the best empirical theory of corporate control will depend, of course, on whether the normative theory comes to be rejected, as many of those who argue for corporate social responsibility—ultimately, a view of how in justice the corporation should behave—believe it ought to be rejected.

It is worth mentioning, finally, that fidelity to the theory does not put control in the hands of shareholders, since they do not act as a corporate agent. Shareholders seek to invest, or to belong to funds that invest, where the returns are best or where others are likely to invest, driving up the value of shares. The markets they create in this competitive, often speculative pursuit of profit can be highly volatile. When managers seek to maximize the appeal of their companies for shareholders, then, they may end up slavishly tracking a target that is unstable in itself and may be further destabilized by their very efforts.

The Implications of These Developments

The upshot of these considerations is a lesson akin to that which we drew in the case of property and money. Like those institutions, the corporation has come to depend for its existence on the law and the state. As there are no natural property rights, only rights recognized in norm and law, and as there is no natural money, only the money supported by the state, so the observations made here show that there is no natural corporation, only the sort of corporation recognized in custom and in law.

As rudimentary property rights may have come into existence merely in virtue of social norms, and a basic form of money may have emerged merely on the basis of interpersonal confidence, so corporate bodies, including commercial bodies, may have first formed in virtue of prelegal conventions and norms. But under the influence of modern pressures, the state has used its laws to give a novel, powerful shape to these organizations; it has assumed an active rather than a passive role in their development (Ciepley 2013).[21]

It may be thought that corporations did not have to assume their modern form and that the history reviewed here charts a series of wholly fortuitous changes. But that is not right. The pressures of trade in the seventeenth century, and the emergence of norms within trading associations, made it natural for

21. Does the view adopted amount to an acceptance of the grant or concession theory of the corporation, as it is often described, according to which corporate bodies other than the state depend necessarily on it for their existence (Bratton 1989, 433–36)? Not really, since the dependence alleged is contingent rather than necessary and applies only to the corporation in its contemporary form.

the state to legally regiment asset commitment, entity shielding, and owner shielding; doing so would have seemed to regiment emerging norms, or elicit novel norms, in the general interest of the citizenry. And the call for canals and railways in the nineteenth century made a strong case for an amendment of the law to facilitate the formation and operation of the companies needed to capitalize such works.

But was it necessary for a state to take precisely the measures that were generally adopted, including measures that have had some extraordinary, unforeseen consequences? Absolutely not. The claim defended here is merely that a functional state that operates under modern pressures is bound to maintain laws that keep corporations in existence, not necessarily in the exact form that corporations have taken, but in some form of the same general kind. This is sufficient to support the main thesis defended: that the dependence of the corporate form on the law and the state, like the dependence of the property regime and the financial system, makes nonsense of the laissez-faire claim that the functional state cannot intervene with benefit in the economy.

The fact that most states have taken the initiatives described, and the fact that a functional state is bound to take some such initiatives under modern conditions, does not imply that the initiatives actually taken pass muster in the theory of justice. One of the tasks of the theory of justice, as distinct from the functional theory of the state, is to determine how far established initiatives in these areas should be preserved, amended, or regulated. Thus, one question raised by our history is whether companies should have the right to control other companies, making possible the emergence of powerful multinational groups of companies. And another, assuming that it is not possible to reverse this development, is how a theory of justice should pronounce on the claims of individuals, be they workers, consumers, or neighbors, against these titans. But those questions take us beyond our current brief.

6.4 Three Corporate Ontologies

The main business of this final chapter is now complete, but it may be useful, in view of the attention we have given to corporations, to provide an appendix on the moderately realist view of corporations, and of corporate bodies more generally, that it supports. There has been much discussion in recent years of the ontological and legal status of such entities, and it would be remiss not to address some of the issues that it has raised.

The Ontology of the Corporate Body

We have made use throughout the book of a distinctive idea of incorporation, distinguishing it from more episodic collaboration between individuals— their pursuit of joint goals—and of course the looser linkages they maintain in other groups and in networks like the market. Thus, we argued in the second and third chapters that the state or polity should be fully incorporated if it is to discharge its function well and that such incorporation is quite consistent with decentralizing the body into independent modules. In the fourth chapter we made much use of the idea of incorporation again in distinguishing be- tween the incorporated, the unincorporated, and the incorporating citizenry. And in this final chapter we looked at the developments that have sponsored commercial incorporation, scouting out the ways in which joint stock compa- nies have developed over recent centuries.

In pursuing this discussion, we presented a view of the corporate agent that builds on the medieval materials used in Hobbes's influential theory. Accord- ing to that approach, individuals will incorporate as a single agent insofar they rally effectively behind a single authorized voice, following its instructions and upholding its commitments. But in light of the discursive dilemma and associ- ated impossibility theorems, we amended the Hobbesian approach in one important respect. The lesson we took from these results is that when it is not controlled by a single individual, the voice behind which corporate members rally must be authorized under procedures that avoid problems of incoherence that arise with bottom-up arrangements like majority voting.

According to the position defended, then, a collection or aggregate of people may organize themselves via the authorization of a group voice—and this in an egalitarian or hierarchical, centralized or networked fashion—so as to simulate an individual agent. Organized around a voice that speaks for them coherently, they can pursue common purposes reliably on the basis of reliably formed common judgments and even make and live up to avowals and pledges. They can conform to the requirements of agency and personhood.

This is a moderately realist theory of the corporate agent. Such an agent involves a collection of individuals who will operate severally under their personal names, speaking for themselves as individuals, but operate collec- tively under a group name, following a corporate voice that their procedures establish. The organized group is distinct from the collection of members in- sofar as it is an agent and a person, while the collection is not, so that realism is vindicated. But the organized group is constituted by that collection of individuals—it does not require any extra component in its makeup—so that the realism vindicated is moderate in character.

The corporate body may be a distinct entity qua agent or person—this, because its attitudes cannot be a bottom-up function of the individual attitudes of members—but it is identical with the collection qua set of individuals. The relation between the group agent and the individual members who make it up is like that of the statue to the material out of which it is constructed. It is formally distinct but materially identical.[22]

This moderately realist theory contrasts with two alternative views that are present in the literature, especially the literature on corporations, and it may be useful, in this discussion, to distance it from those rival views and show how well it compares with them. One of these alternatives is hyperrealist or inflationist in character, the other antirealist or deflationist. The first is mainly defended in law and jurisprudence, the second in economic and business circles.

According to the inflationist theory, a corporate body like a firm or corporation is a natural or real entity, in the favored phrase, that exists in some obscure sense over and beyond its members. Thus, it enjoys something more than the formal distinctness accorded it under our moderately realist view. According to the deflationist alternative, the corporation doesn't enjoy even that distinctness. It is nothing more than a nexus of contracts, to use a phrase applied particularly to corporations, between individual agents. On this view, corporations or firms are "simply legal fictions which serve as a nexus for a set of contracting relationships among individuals" (Jensen and Meckling 1976, 310).

The Inflationist, Natural-Entity Ideology

The inflationist ideology may be supported in part by considerations that often apply to the state, as we noted earlier. Like the state, the company or corporation—as well as some other corporate bodies—may cast its would-be members in diverse, often competitive roles, so that it is awkward, if not impossible, to think of what it does as something done by the membership. Like the state, it is reified by its association with a natural resource: in this case not territory or language or religion, but the funds and assets that survive changes of directors, managers, and employees, even changes in its sphere of activity (Stoljar 1973). And like the state, it is juridified by its recognition in law; it begins

---

22. There are different ways in which this relationship may be philosophically articulated, but they are not relevant to our concerns here.

to look like an entity that might even continue to exist on the legal books without having any existence in the social interactions and life of individuals.[23]

These considerations may make it tempting to think in an inflationist way that the corporation is something over and beyond its membership, as they may introduce a similar temptation with the state. But historically the inflationist ideology about the corporation was probably more directly sourced by the appearance of an extravagant enthusiasm for corporate modes of organization in the early twentieth century. This enthusiasm is often, if not invariably, expressed in terms that suggested that the corporation is a living and breathing organism: a body that gets cast as a natural entity—almost a natural agent or person—rather than being described as the sort of artificial agent or person defended in our moderate realism.

This view of the corporation, and of some other corporate bodies, was sourced, rightly or wrongly, in the scholarship on medieval and later notions of incorporation developed in the late nineteenth and early twentieth centuries by figures like the German legal historian Otto Gierke and his English translator and counterpart Frederic Maitland (Runciman 1997; Runciman and Ryan 2003). Gierke's work—and, with lesser justification, Maitland's—inspired a view of corporate bodies that is certainly realist but that often veers toward the inflationist extreme. In introducing a translation of one of Gierke's works, Sir Ernest Barker (1950, 61) displays the inflationist tendency of the approach when he associates incorporation with "the pulsation of a common purpose which surges, as it were, from above, into the mind and behavior of members."

The natural-entity approach to corporate bodies in general, and corporations in particular, is metaphysically so obscure that it ought not to appeal to anyone. If it attracted those writing in the wake of Gierke and Maitland, that may be because it appeared to represent the only way of being realist about such bodies. It may have seemed to be the only way of acknowledging, in a passage that Maitland (2003, 63) quotes from the constitutional theorist A. V. Dicey, to the effect that when "men bind themselves together to act in a particular way for some common purpose, they create a body, which by no fiction of law, but by the very nature of things, differs from the individuals of whom it is constituted."[24]

23. For a radical possibility of a company continuing to operate in the absence of people, see Dan-Cohen (1986).

24. It is not clear that Maitland himself, who was elusive on all matters philosophical, would actually have agreed.

The approach prospered in all likelihood, however, not because of its meta-physical attractions, but because of its political appeal, both on the left and on the right (Dewey 1926; Hager 1989; Runciman 1997). It probably appealed on both sides for the way in which it displaces the absolutist picture in which people confront the corporate state as individuals, not in independent associations, and owe allegiance only to that Leviathan. It may have appealed on the left as a way of supporting a view of society in which individuals can find fulfilment and a capacity for action in collective association—the trade union is more likely to be the exemplar than the corporation—not just as atomistic market players. And it may have appealed on the right—more pertinently to our concerns—for how it justifies the ascription of various rights to the corporations that play such a crucial role in the modern economy.

The invocation of the natural entity theory in support of corporations is surely implicit in the Chief Justice's remark in *Santa Clara County v. Southern Pacific Railroad* that corporations are protected as persons under the Fourteenth Amendment. It may be, as some have argued, that the Court need not have been thinking of the railroad corporation as itself a natural entity: that they may have thought of its rights under that amendment as just the rights of the incorporating members.[25] Still, the remark rapidly came to be interpreted as a vindication of the corporation's claims as an entity in its own right: a person, now depicted in inflationary terms, that can claim a certain equivalence with a natural person (Horowitz 1992, chap. 3).

That interpretation certainly fits with the judgment of the Court in 1909 in *Southern Railway Co. v. Greene*: "That the corporation is a person, within the meaning of the Fourteenth Amendment, is no longer open to discussion" (Schane 1987). And arguably, this assumption played a role in many later judg-ments by the Court. These included the right to protection against search and seizure under the Fourth Amendment (1906); the right to jury trial in criminal cases under the Sixth Amendment; the right to jury trial in civil cases under the Seventh Amendment; and, on the grounds that money is speech, the same right as individuals to independent political expenditures under the First Amendment (2010): this latter, in the much-discussed judgment on *Citizens United v. Federal Election Commission*.[26]

25. Thus, Adam Winkler (2018) argues that in the 1886 remark and in other judgments the Court may have meant to ascribe rights to corporations as rights they enjoyed as associations of natural persons.

26. In this judgment, the Court emphasized the benefits for listeners of the increased quan-tity of political speech that corporations might generate. But speech hardly offers any benefits

It should be clear that there is nothing in our argument for the reality of corporate bodies, and nothing in the case we made for thinking of them as artificial persons, to suggest that they ought morally to enjoy something like the rights of natural persons, let alone have those rights constitutionally protected. It may be useful to say a little on this issue, although strictly it belongs to the theory of justice.

Assume, as argued in chapter 5, that people's rights are law-dependent and that the rights that any person, natural or corporate, ought to enjoy are those that they would enjoy under the right or best law, however that is determined. Assume, second, that the right or best law is to be determined by how it serves relevant interests overall, however interests are understood. And assume, finally, that the interests that ought to be served in the human world are those of individuals and that if corporate bodies are taken to have interests, they will deserve attention only insofar as they reflect the interests of members or of others whom the bodies affect.[27]

What rights should we grant to corporate agents, including corporations, under these assumptions? Clearly, those rights that are supported by the interests of the members they benefit, as well as the interests of other individuals affected. Thus, it might be appropriate to grant the right of asset commitment to commercial corporations, given the capitalization of socially important enterprises that it makes possible. But it might not be appropriate to give them the right to set up shell companies that they control.

What is or is not appropriate will be determined in the theory of justice by what serves the interests of individuals overall. And it will hardly serve the interests of individuals overall—interests worthy of equal consideration in any plausible theory of justice—to have a law that gives corporate bodies, including commercial corporations, the same rights as individuals themselves. Corporate bodies may be agents unto themselves, corporate bodies may even count as persons in the sense elaborated earlier, and yet not deserve in justice

---

to listeners unless there are speakers—presumably, corporate speakers—that can be interrogated and checked for the accuracy and consistency of what is said; the speech of automated bots, tuned to the presumed biases of the listener, is surely of no benefit whatsoever.

27. To take a difficult example, the corporate interest of an Indigenous tribe within an advanced, colonially introduced economy might argue for the preservation of its language and culture. But would that interest deserve to be satisfied if doing so required current members to remain part of the tribe, regardless of their own preferences? Those who argue that the corporate interest might support such a restriction on current members could plausibly do so only because of taking it to reflect the interests of other individuals: say, the interests of future members of the tribe.

to be given the same status in law as individual persons themselves. Indeed, depending on the end for which they form, different corporate bodies will hardly deserve to be given the same rights and status as one another. The interests of individuals may dictate, for example, that the rights of a political association to participate in elections may be quite different from any such rights on the part of a commercial corporation.

The Deflationist, Nexus-of-Contracts Ideology

But if this legal tradition ascribes a status to corporations and other corporate bodies that goes well beyond the moderate realism supported by our discussion, a rival economic tradition falls far short of that realism. It maintains that not only are corporations not natural entities, they are not agents or persons of any kind, however artificial in character. They are pretend or fictitious entities of the kind that, as we saw, medieval philosophers took the expression *persona ficta* to describe: this, by contrast with medieval lawyers, who took it to characterize corporate bodies as artificial, not fictitious, persons.

The nexus-of-contracts view was introduced in the later twentieth century by economists as an improvement on the managerialist view of things that had become orthodox earlier in the century. Under that managerialist view, the corporation is not a natural entity of the inflationist kind but an agent or agency that is organized to pursue common purposes—so far this is just moderate realism—and organized in particular by its managers: they have the say-so on what purposes to pursue in any scenario and what means to employ in that pursuit (Bratton 1989, 425–27).

Many economists became unhappy with this approach, on two counts. First, as mentioned earlier in this chapter, on the moral ground that it seems to justify giving a dangerous level of power to managers or inviting government to dictate how they should use that power. And second on the methodological ground that it presents the corporation as a black box that economists are not allowed to explore with the tools developed in the analysis of market contract (Jensen and Meckling 1976; Jensen 1983).

In response to these problems, economists have argued that the corporation involves nothing more than the network or nexus of members interacting under distinctive contractual terms. What makes the contractual terms distinctive, so it is often said, is that they involve fewer transaction costs than would arise if the different sorts of interactions each had to be negotiated separately in the open market (Coase 1937; Williamson 1989).

We need have no issue with the argument that corporations form or survive because of reducing the transaction costs faced by members. And we need have no objection to the idea of looking within the corporation at how the contractual terms reduce those costs or achieve other effects. The only element in the picture that clashes with our moderate realism about corporate agency is the implied assumption that the interactions between members cannot make the group an agent in its own right.[28]

That assumption routinely appears in the deflationist claim, as one commentator casts it, that a corporation or group agent is just "a collective noun for the web of contracts that link the various participants" (Grantham 1998, 579). This amounts to an eliminativism about group agents akin to the medieval philosophical view that they are pretend entities. Such eliminativism is characteristic of the utilitarian tradition associated with economics and is well expressed in the claim by the utilitarian jurist John Austin (1869, 364) that we speak of corporate bodies as subjects or agents "only by figment, and for the sake of brevity of discussion." The philosopher Anthony Quinton (1975, 17) sums up this way of thinking quite nicely: "We do, of course, speak freely of the mental properties and acts of a group in the way we do of individual people. Groups are said to have beliefs, emotions, and attitudes and to take decisions and make promises. But these ways of speaking are plainly metaphorical. To ascribe mental predicates to a group is always an indirect way of ascribing such predicates to its members."

Consistently with thinking that corporations emerge on the basis of contract and interaction among members, however, we may hold that nevertheless any corporation, indeed any corporate body, will meet the conditions for counting as an agent, even a personal agent, in its own right. It will count as an agent insofar as it is organized to pursue certain purposes reliably according to reliably formed representations. It will count as a personal agent insofar as it uses an authorized voice to invite others to rely on its having a suitable range of purposes and representations and generally lives up to the attitudes thereby self-ascribed.

Why might economists be led to think otherwise just because they look within the corporation, seeking for example to identify the cost-reducing

---

28. The assumption, as we shall argue, is not needed by economic analysts of the corporation. And some defenders of the assumption come close to acknowledging this, as when they allow that it may occasionally be useful to treat the corporation as an elementary component: an entity as basic as the individual agent. "When it is appropriate for a scientist to treat a complex subsystem as an elementary component is a subtle and difficult issue" (Jensen 1983, 326).

contracts that typically bind members to one another? One line of thought that may operate is the following. "Markets and corporations are both built out of contracts; but markets are not agents; and so, neither can corporations be agents." That line of thought, however, is manifestly fallacious. It involves the same line of reasoning as the following: "Trees and human beings are both built out of cells; but trees are not agents; and so, neither can human beings be agents."

As the cellular structure of human beings enables them to be agents, unlike the cellular structure of trees, so the contractual structure of corporate bodies enables them to be agents, unlike the contractual structure of markets. That structure makes it possible for corporations, and corporate bodies in general, to authorize a voice that speaks for them as a unified agent in a conversable, and indeed commissive manner. Contractual or quasi-contractual arrangements will give rise to such an agent insofar as they ensure that members recognize a voice that speaks for them as a group and dispose them to rally behind that voice in their role as members.

But the objection to group agency may not be that corporate bodies do not meet the functional specifications for counting as agents. It may rather be that there is no explanatory purpose served by treating them as agents. The thought behind this construal goes as follows. We would not have to rely on an agential characterization of an animal to understand how it behaves, if we had a full account of how it functions at a neuronal level. And, in the same way, we would not have to rely on an agential characterization of a corporate body, if we had a full account of how it functions at the individual level: at the level of member contracts and interactions. But economics can deliver just such an individualistic account of member behavior, so the thought goes. And the search for such an account naturally supports sidelining or rejecting an agential perspective on the corporate body.

This way of thinking is also mistaken (List and Pettit 2011). A comprehensive theory at the neuronal level would not give us a full understanding of an animal's behavior if we did not see why the neuronal organization helps it to meet the conditions for agency, and if we did not recognize that natural selection explains why such an agential profile is present. Equally a comprehensive theory at the level of individual contract and interaction would not give us a proper understanding of a corporate body's behavior if we did not see that its organization at that individual level is designed to enable it to perform as an agent that pursues corporate purposes.

If a corporate body is to perform as an agent, as we know, then it must reliably pursue common purposes according to common judgments that it has a reliable method for generating. But, unless they were designed to have that effect, it would be miraculous if the contracts that members made with one another, and the interactions that they instantiated under those contracts, just happened to support such a reliable pattern of performance. And not only would the contracts have to be designed to generate such a pattern; this would have to be more or less manifest to the contractors themselves. Why would individuals be motivated to enter the contracts, and to assume corresponding roles, unless they could see that this would enable them to benefit from the agency of the body as a whole?

Think in this context of the standard structure of the joint stock company, with rules governing the role and appointment of a board, the part that shareholders may play in controlling the board, the place that is given to managerial and other employees in running the company, the shielding of the company against the bankruptcy of shareholders, the limited liability of shareholders in the event of company failure, and the relative claims of shareholders and creditors in the event of such failure. It should be clear that while any corporation is going to operate on the basis of contracts among its members—shareholders, directors, managers, and other employees—it will do so successfully only insofar as the contracts are designed to allow the body as a group to operate reliably as an agent. And it will attract members to enter such contracts only insofar as it is manifest to all that by doing so they can secure a personal benefit that derives, directly or indirectly, from the agential performance of the group as a whole.

The issue that arises here can be put as follows. Does the corporate body perform as a group agent because of the independent character of the contracts that members make with one another? Or do the contracts between members have their specific character because they are designed to enable the corporate agent to perform as a group agent? The answer, so we have suggested, is that the direction of priority is of the latter rather than the former kind. And that is why no social scientists can hope to give us a proper understanding of corporations and other corporate bodies without taking account of how such entities are designed to perform as agents in their own right (List and Pettit 2011).

The nexus-of-contracts approach, as already mentioned, may do well to identify the role of contracts within corporations in reducing transaction costs for relevant players. More generally, it may serve a useful purpose in opening up the black box of the corporation to economic analysis. And it may do a welcome service in questioning the traditional, managerial form of the corporation. But none of its initiatives on those fronts undermines the sort of moderate realism about corporations and similar bodies that has been defended here. None offers reason to be eliminativist about corporate agents.

The deflationary view of corporate bodies that is built into the nexus-of-contracts view may be motivated by a reaction to the inflationism of the natural-entity way of thinking. But neither extreme is appealing. We may be realist about corporate agents without thinking that they come into existence by virtue of the appearance of a pulsation of common purpose from above, to recall Ernest Barker's words. And we may be realist about such agents without denying that the attitudes they form, and the actions they display, are wholly grounded in the interactions of their members.

CONCLUSION

Outlining the Argument

WE HAVE COVERED A great deal of ground, including some swampy and some rocky terrain. It may be useful in conclusion to offer an account of the main points made in each chapter, including the introduction. This may not make ready sense on its own, but it should at least serve as a map of the territory covered and as a memo of the points made in developing the argument.

Introduction. Motivating the Argument

1. The global state system is likely to be inescapable, since any state that dissolved itself would be replaced by another, no state has the power to govern the world unilaterally, and distrust between peoples makes the prospect of an agreed world government elusive.
2. This means that, realistically, justice is achievable only in the presence of states, more or less as we know them, and in view of the power of the state needs to be brought about, domestically and internationally, by states themselves.
3. But does the state or polity have the capacity to serve as an instrument of justice? That depends on its role or function. Specifically, its role or function, on the minimal normative assumption that there is an approximate balance of power between rulers and those—or at least many of those—over whom they rule. The theory defended here is that the state does have such a function and, as it happens, a justice-compatible function.
4. That theory is historically realist insofar as it assumes that the state is inescapable and normatively realist insofar as it seeks to identify requirements on the state that derive from its function rather than focusing on requirements of a moral kind. Those requirements reflect

313

an ideal of statehood that is more basic than, and presupposed to, any ideal of justice.

5. What might count as the function of the state? An effect that would materialize in any settled society like ours where there is an approximate equality of power among most of the membership; an effect that need materialize only when those who run the state act as it requires them to act; and an effect that would explain why the state exists: at least why it exists resiliently over many, if not all, possible changes of circumstance, retaining a shape fitted to producing that effect.

6. Our theory relies on a genealogical thought experiment to identify a possible function. Would a recognizable state be robustly likely to emerge among agents like us, living in settled conditions like ours without widespread imbalances of power? And if so, what effect would explain the emergence of a state in that counterfactual scenario? Such an effect, if there is one, is a candidate for the function of the state.

7. Our argument is that something like a state would likely emerge in that scenario and that there is an effect that would explain its emergence. This effect consists in its establishing and entrenching a regime of law among a class of relatively powerful members—the proper citizens— that may or may not be inclusive of all. That regime would give citizens security against one another and allow them to know what they may do with legal impunity and protection.

8. This theory of the function of the state is consistent with recognizing that many regimes may be oppressive or ineffective and not serve this function properly. As hearts that no longer pump blood are still hearts, these regimes will still count as states, albeit of an outlier or improper kind. They will be states but not functional or proper states.

9. Chapter 1 develops this theory of the function of the state and then the other two chapters of part I argue that the function will be better served if the state meets a further pair of conditions. First, it is incorporated as a group agent that serves its function reliably among a perhaps restricted citizenry. Second, it is decentralized in such a manner that the component agencies and groups that shape its behavior check and balance one another.

10. The three chapters of part II go on to look at the potential of the state, arguing against a supposedly conceptual constraint on how far it can give collective power to its citizens; an allegedly metaphysical constraint—the existence and austerity of natural rights—on how far

it can acknowledge suitable rights among citizens; and an imagined empirical constraint according to which it cannot satisfy the needs of an autonomous market economy.

11. The functionally ideal state may fall well short of promoting domestic or global justice. Domestically, it may limit the citizenry unjustifiably, or give them rights that are not rich enough to secure them appropriately against those in office—citizens themselves, we assume—and against other ordinary citizens. But it will at least be capable of improving its performance on those fronts, satisfying a plausible ideal of justice as well as that of statehood.

12. A neo-republican form of justice is foreshadowed in this account of the state. It would endorse the idea of a citizenry but require citizens to be an inclusive class. It would require the law to give each citizen an effective degree of security against others, including those in office. And it would require the state to work for a global order in which different peoples enjoy effective security in relation to other international actors. But statehood, not justice, is the topic here.

Part I. The Role of the State and Its Demands

Chapter 1. The Function of the Polity

1. We know from the introduction that the state must be able to promote justice if justice is to be a realistic ideal. And we know that that depends on whether the state has a function and on how far the function is consistent with justice. We need a theory of the state to determine those matters.

2. How might we develop such a theory? We propose a counterfactual genealogy of the kind given in economics for money. That narrative shows how something like money would be robustly likely—likely regardless of various contingencies—to emerge without planning in an unmoneyed society, generating an effect that explains its appearance and survival in that world and, presumptively, in ours.

3. We explore whether a similar genealogy might argue for the robust likelihood that something like a state would appear and survive in a prepolitical society because of unplanned adjustments by individuals to the pressures of their world. The chapter outlines a genealogy that supports an affirmative answer.

4. The genealogy of money directs us to the function of money in serving as a medium of exchange: this is an effect in virtue of which it would

remain resiliently present; it identifies money as having a functional nature that might be realized via gold or whatever; and it suggests that in origin, money need not have had to be planned.

5. Our genealogy of the state aims to illuminate the function and nature of the state, with lessons about its possible origin, on a similar basis. Arguing that the state would be robustly likely to emerge without planning within a suitable prepolitical society, it implies that it would not have had to be agreed upon, for example, in a social contract.

6. The genealogy starts from a prepolitical society of moderately self-regarding, moderately rational, and mutually dependent agents, operating under conditions of relative scarcity and an approximately equal balance of power: this, among the members of a privileged class, if not more widely. The members of that class figure as the participants in the genealogy and as the citizens of the emerging state.

7. The first stage in the genealogy is to argue, with Lewis and against Hobbes, that conventions will emerge spontaneously in a prepolitical world, being generated by unplanned adjustments to coordination predicaments, where each party just wants to do what others do: for example, to drive on the right or on the left side of the road.

8. In such a case the adjustments will give rise to a regularity that is recognized as a matter of common awareness and invoked in instructing others about what is in their best interest. But the regularity will also be internalized as collectively beneficial, so that each will prefer that everyone conform. And it will be recognized as such, so that anyone can speak for all in supporting it categorically: in effect, it will be treated as a socially ratified requirement.

9. As conventions will arise spontaneously, so will collectively beneficial regularities that may be individually burdensome, like telling the truth. Each individual will adjust to the need to get others to be reliable by proving reliable themselves, seeking a reputation for reliability. This will generate a regularity—a norm—that is recognized in common awareness and can be invoked in regulating others, advising them on what is in their prudential interest.

10. As in the convention case, the regularity will be internalized as something each wishes that all would follow. And this being recognized as a matter of public awareness, the regularity will be socially ratified. It will be manifest that anyone may speak for all in presenting conformity as a categorical demand of the society; in Hobbes's language as a

command made in the name of the society, not just as a counsel of prudence.

11. A society where social norms rule will generate problems of a sort that Herbert Hart identifies. The norms—primary rules, he calls them— will be vague at some limits and incapable of being adjusted to new circumstances. And the application of the rules will be confounded in many cases by rival claims about whether an offense occurred or not.

12. People may be expected to adjust to such problems, he says, introducing on an ad hoc basis, secondary rules or routines for clarifying and changing the social norms, and for determining if an offense was committed in a particular case, what compensation is due, and, should reputational effects not suffice, what further sanctions should be imposed.

13. Those adjustments will generate a system for running and amending social norms that should count as a legal system. There will be decision-taker rules imposed on all—old primary rules and novel amendments— and decision-maker rules governing how those rules—and, if relevant, the decision-maker rules themselves—should be decided. Such regularities will be manifest to all and available to be invoked in prudential counsel.

14. The emerging rules, however imperfect, are likely to be accepted by all in this sense: that conformity is not just motivated by fear of sanction, but also by the benefit of enabling citizens to coordinate expectations. Thus, they are likely to be internalized as rules that each wishes all should follow and, this being manifest across the society, they will be ratified as categorical demands on citizens. Some laws will regiment existing norms but even novel laws will elicit norms: regularities supported in the manner of norms, not just by legal sanction.

15. While this genealogy suggests that a state is not necessary to produce a legal system, it shows that a rudimentary state will materialize simultaneously with any such system. There will be legislative routines for clarifying and changing law, judicial routines for judging offenses, and executive routines for promulgating and implementing decisions made.

16. Such a state may be very different from the modern state. But under conditions typical of the modern era it will be subject to pressures that lead it, again in an unplanned, spontaneous fashion, to take on a familiar profile. Those pressures will involve four sorts of problems related to

getting people to comply, suppressing competing forces, making the system impermeable to fleeing or intruding offenders, and protecting the system against other states.

17. The compliance problem will lead the authorities in the system to attach coercive sanctions to laws; the competition problem to suppress other forces or accommodate to them; the permeability problem to establish and police borders; and the protection problem to set up a defensive military force and international representation.

18. The function of the modern state, so this suggests, is to establish a coercive, territorial regime of law that orders the lives of the citizenry vis-à-vis one another and that entrenches that system against internal and external dangers. This is the role the state will assume under the plausible circumstances invoked in our genealogy, and the role that will help to make it resilient—to keep it in a suitable shape—in similar, actual circumstances.

19. The genealogy suggests that the state has a functional nature that requires it, no matter how it is institutionalized, to secure an inclusive or noninclusive citizenry against one another and to stabilize that system internally and externally. And it suggests that the state need not originate in planning or contract; it may emerge behind people's backs, so to speak.

20. That the state has this function does not entail, of course, that there are no states that fail their function. Under special circumstances, as for example when those in authority wield an irresistible power over those outside their family or clique, it is likely that the state will be denatured and cease to function properly, according to our account here.

21. The function of the state proper is nomothetic, by this account: it consists in laying down law. As it happens this account fits with a long Western tradition, well expressed by Immanuel Kant when he says that living under a proper state—in a civil condition, as he puts it—is a great boon. Even if it does not mean living under a just or rightful order, it excludes subjection to a ruler who relies on fear alone, as in a reign of terror.

Chapter 2. The Polity Incorporated

1. The questions addressed in this chapter are whether the state can incorporate as an agent and, if it can, whether it should do so to

promote its function as well as possible. Much of the chapter provides background, relevant also in other chapters, on what basic agency, human agency, and corporate or group agency involve.

2. The basic agent, robotic or biological, is a system that is organized to reliably pursue a purpose or set of purposes across varying situations, registering and adjusting to the specificities of each situation and of the behavior needed there. When things are intuitively normal, it will reliably act for its purposes according to reliably formed representations.

3. While robotic and especially animal agents vary enormously in the range of purposes pursued, in the perceptual inputs sourcing their representations, and in the flexibility of their adjustments, the big divide is between agents who interpret themselves to one another, as we conversable humans do, and nonhuman agents who give us no such help.

4. A human agent's self-interpretation can help others to know what they pursue or desire and how they represent or believe things to be, although only if they can speak with authority on their mind. The agent will enjoy that authority by grace of a capacity that language gives them to make up their mind about what to say and what to think.

5. To be reliable speakers with whom others happily cooperate, human agents must be able to make assertions truthfully and carefully—on the basis of data with belief, desiderata with desires—in response to the questions of others. If they do this, then what they say ought to match attitudes newly formed or confirmed; otherwise, language would be dysfunctional: even sincere speech would fail to correspond with attitude or to predict action.

6. This being manifest, individuals will also be able, where data and desiderata are available and adequate, to form their own attitudes by making the intentional effort to ask themselves questions about what to believe or desire and the intentional effort to answer them carefully, on the basis of data or desiderata. They will be able to make up their own minds.

7. That being so, they will have a basis on which to know what they believe or desire, where desire may involve a qualified preference or an unqualified intention. As speakers, they must be able to recognize the attitudes they should and presumptively do hold, insofar as they recognize that they are led by data and desiderata to make this or that sincere assertion: this or that judgment. The attitudes recognized may be novel or may just be reconfirmed in such judgment.

8. Speaking a common language, people will be able to communicate such attitudes to one another. And insofar as they can choose to do so in utterances that are relatively expensive, betting on themselves to have the attitudes communicated—insofar as they can commit in that sense to the attitudes—they will be able make the utterances more credible.

9. They will be able to do this if they use words that indicate a mind made up rather than a mind on which they report, as they might report on another's mind. They will thereby foreclose the later excuse of having misread the evidence on their minds and will make their communication more credible than an evidence-based report. They will avow the belief that p by asserting that p, as we may say, and avow the desire to X by citing the desiderata that argue for X-ing.

10. Apart from avowing attitudes, humans may choose to pledge intentions, if not any other attitudes. Pledging involves manifestly foreclosing the changed-mind as well as the misleading-mind excuse and will be possible with an intention insofar as declaring an intention to do something may provide a reputational reason for doing so: a reason that they may expect to keep the intention unchanged, even if circumstances alter.

11. Conversable, commissive agents will count as persons insofar they can make up their minds about what to think; present to one another as intelligible and addressable; and bet on themselves to display the attitudes they communicate, thereby inviting the reliance of others. With that perspective available, they will also be able to see themselves as addressable and make commitments to themselves.

12. How can human groups become agents? How can they reliably act for group purposes according to reliably formed group representations across varying situations? Drawing on earlier thinking, Hobbes gives us a clear answer. Individuals can form such a group agent insofar as they each authorize a certain voice to speak for the group, as they might each speak for themselves, and commit to acting according to that voice when acting in the group's name.

13. When members rally behind a voice in this way, they agree to be committed to the attitudes that it avows and pledges when it speaks for the group. Thus, they ensure that the group will enact the mind enunciated by that voice and that they will constitute an agent by virtue of their organization. The voice authorized may be that of an individual,

according to Hobbes, or the voice of a majoritarian committee, but we put aside those details until chapter 3.

14. If that is how a group agent forms, as Hobbes himself insists, then the group will count as a person. It will make up its own mind in the process whereby the directive voice is settled, it will be intelligible to other agents and addressable by them, it will be able to make commitments that it can invite others to rely on, and of course it can prove reliable in practice.

15. Clearly there is no problem about whether the polity can incorporate as a group agent. It can do so insofar as each member pledges to rally behind the guiding voice of the law that establishes how decisions are to be made and what decisions to implement. This theory is found in Hobbes but has medieval origins in the work of Bartolus and others.

16. Does the polity have to incorporate as an agent with a single voice and mind or can it exist without full incorporation? Yes, it can. It can operate without eliciting universal compliance from its officials or citizens: without their fully rallying around it. And it can even operate without the law establishing a univocal voice for citizens to rally around. In classical Athens, for example, the voice of the law was equivocal insofar as the *dikasteria* or courts were liable to pass different judgments in interpreting the law across similar cases.

17. There are reasons related to its nomothetic function why the polity should fully incorporate. It will not properly secure citizens under a stable regime of law unless it meets two conditions: it speaks with a univocal voice across different agencies, and it elicits universal conformity among the citizenry, particularly among members of the police and the military and among officials who are called upon to enact the domestic and international commitments of the state.

18. The need for a univocal voice argues on functional grounds for rule-of-law constraints that restrict the discretionary power of decision makers by requiring that laws be general, relatively unchanging, and uniformly interpreted; and that restrict the vulnerability of decision takers to that power by requiring that the laws imposed be promulgated, be intelligible, and—not being inconsistent, retrospective, or overdemanding—be capable of providing guidance.

19. The need to elicit universal conformity to the voice of law bears particularly on the police who are commissioned to guard against internal problems and the military whose job is to protect against external

dangers. If these agencies are not brought firmly under the control of a single decision-making voice, they can go rogue and be inimical to the functional polity.

20. The need for the state to constitute a responsible or accountable agency that can be held to its commitments requires those who enact state commitments to follow the voice enunciated by those who made them. This need is especially salient in the international domain, where a polity must assure other states that it will not defect from individual treaties, or breach a code of international law; otherwise, it will be vulnerable to hostile treatment by those states.

21. If the nomothetic state is fully incorporated—if it is guided by a univocal voice eliciting universal compliance—then it will satisfy each of these requirements. Incorporation entails their satisfaction although it does not constitute a more readily accessible means of satisfying them; the question about the best means is one in institutional design that we ignore here.

Chapter 3. The Polity Decentralized

1. If the state is incorporated, then it will represent a particularly powerful agency. And since that raises the danger that some authorities may use it for their own purposes, there is a functional case for decentralizing the state by establishing distinct centers of power that can check and balance one another, making the state polycentric.

2. A constitution will be polycentric insofar as it separates the legislature, administration, and judiciary; requires each branch to share out its power among different centers; and in a more recent development, introduces an outsourcing of responsibility designed to guard against incompetence or corruption on the part of any bodies or officials.

3. The dispersion of power under such a constitution—a mixed constitution, as it is traditionally known—was celebrated in the long republican tradition from ancient Rome, through the medieval Italian cities, to eighteenth-century Britain and the United States, being defended by Polybius, Cicero, Machiavelli, Harrington, Montesquieu, Blackstone, and the authors of the *Federalist Papers*.

4. The mixed constitution was utterly rejected, however, by the absolutist tradition represented canonically in the work of Jean Bodin in the sixteenth century, Thomas Hobbes in the seventeenth, and Jean-Jacques

Rousseau in the eighteenth. They insisted that an effective polity needs a single sovereign and that the mixed constitution rules this out.

5. Notwithstanding their opposition, however, decentralization has an obvious appeal as a way of countering the possibility of political abuse by officials. Separating out the judiciary would force legislators to satisfy rule-of-law constraints, for example, sharing power would guard against takeover by a particular faction, and outsourcing power would create reliable informational, invigilating, and, where needed, detached, impartial agencies.

6. Such checks and balances would protect people against political abuse, giving them defenses against potential abusers and imposing deterrent sanctions on the abusive. The measures contrast in that way with the introduction of incentives, as envisaged for example by Hobbes, that would make political abuse less appealing for authorities but leave it still within their reach.

7. There is a problem about embracing decentralization, however, since the absolutists make a good case for the indispensability of a single sovereign. This argument is persuasive, at least in a somewhat revised form, and raises the question as to whether it rules out the polycentric or mixed constitution.

8. The argument begins from the claims that the function of the state is to establish a regime of law, that laws are commands imposed on members of the society, and that they presuppose an accepted, sovereign commander. That the sovereign is accepted means for absolutists that the sovereign was duly appointed, but a plausible revision would require that citizens should continue in some sense to accept their sovereign.

9. But in what sense should they give acceptance? They should accept the sovereign in the sense explained earlier, of accepting the sovereign's laws. The regime established by the sovereign's laws should have such an appeal in enabling the coordination of expectations that citizens will not obey the laws, and submit to their sovereign, out of fear alone.

10. The sovereign, so the absolutist argument continues, must be an effective agent, natural or corporate, and while operating beyond legal and other enforced forms of domestic control, may be subject to normative, unenforced ideals, may be constrained by voluntarily contracted constraints, and may have to satisfy certain constitutive constraints that help define sovereignty: say, the constraint, ideally

understood in the revised form, that the sovereign should enjoy acceptance.

11. Bodin and Hobbes allow the sovereign to be a majoritarian committee of an elite or of the whole citizenry, and Rousseau requires that the sovereign be a majoritarian committee of the whole. But the members of a majoritarian committee may vote up inconsistent policies, even when consistent themselves—a lesson of the discursive dilemma—so that no such polity could work.

12. The absolutists compound this oversight with the error of holding that officials could not operate under the mixed constitution they reject. For there is no reason in principle why, for example, one subagency in the state might not propose and another dispose: why one might propose laws, and another decide to accept, reject or revise them, whether on grounds of consistency or some other value.

13. If there must be a single sovereign, and if a polycentric system might enable officials to operate perfectly well, unlike the majoritarian, then a question arises as to where the sovereign is to be found in such a system. The people under a decentralized state do not rally behind the personal voice of an individual sovereign nor behind the algorithmic voice of a majoritarian sovereign. So, what is the voice that they treat as a sovereign authority?

14. The answer is the voice that the authorities create when they operate under procedures for reaching decisions about the framing and imposition of law: for example, the voice that emerges in our simple example from the interaction between a committee that proposes law and another that decides on whether to accept it. This procedurally generated voice can guide citizens, provided the procedures ensure consistency.

15. If we go along with this, then clearly the polycentric sovereign is the polity itself: in our example, the agency constituted by the two committees that constrain one another in determining what laws are implemented overall. The sovereign is the corporate body that operates in this way to pursue lawmaking purposes according to judgments about what that purpose requires in this or that scenario.

16. This polity, operating within constitutive constraints, will be the sovereign source of all its laws, transcending legal or domestic control of any kind; it will involve checks and balances but only on officials and citizens acting within the system, not on the polity itself. There may be limitations on how far it can revise decision-maker laws but

only if they reflect constitutive constraints. Such limitations would resemble the limitation on the absolutist majoritarian committee, that it must operate by majority vote.

17. Why do the absolutists overlook this possibility? Perhaps because of a category mistake like that made by the Oxford visitor who sees the colleges and asks then to see the university. The mistake appears in the idea that the sovereign under any constitution must be a concrete entity within the constituted state, not the state itself: not the corporate agency that is constituted by interacting agencies, as the university is constituted by its colleges.

18. But if the polycentric sovereign can be a corporate agent of this kind, it may assume any of a variety of shapes, depending on the centers the constitution countenances and on the procedures it establishes to govern their interaction. One division is between presidential, radically polycentric systems like the United States and parliamentary systems like Australia that require a separate judiciary but bind legislation and administration tightly together.

19. In Australia the prime minister is chosen by the elected legislature so that the legislative group or party that supported the leader must maintain that support, if the government is not to fall. In the United States the president and legislators are both elected so that no legislators are required to support the leader. In Australia there is a fixed majority to support government proposals, then; in the United States each proposal must find its own majority.

20. Legislative negligence and gridlock are a threat for the presidential system, where representatives vote to please their districts and lobbies, but not a threat for the parliamentary, where the governing party will control all legislation. That being recognized in the parliamentary system, a further advantage is that each party can promise specific policies at election time and cannot easily excuse a failure to enact them in government; this is unlikely to happen in the presidential counterpart.

21. The parliamentary system that allows a highly proportional representation, unlike Australia's, is exposed to problems like that in the United States since differing parties can act like mutually independent legislators. But since parties are fewer in number, they may commit to policies before forming government, if not before the election, and proportionality may appeal insofar as it enables voters to reflect their policy preferences more finely.

Part II. The Potential of the State and Its Dimensions

Chapter 4. The Collective Powers of Citizens

1. Absolutists or statists claim that the sovereign state cannot allow its citizens or people to enjoy a countervailing power of making complaints and imposing demands. It cannot give them the power to challenge it in groups, even in a singleton group, under the constitution; and it cannot admit a power on their part—as the people—to act together outside the constitution to challenge or replace it.

2. The constraints alleged are conceptual in character. The claim is that the sovereign state cannot give the people—that is, its citizens—the constitutional power envisaged consistently with the conceptual demands of sovereignty and that it cannot recognize the envisaged form of extra-constitutional power consistently with the demands associated with the concept of the people.

3. The people envisaged in these debates are not to be taken in the restricted sense of the poor or plebs or commons but to encompass all citizens; and this, whether the citizenry is inclusive or not. And they are not to be taken in a reified sense in which they, like the nation or the public or the folk, could be cast as a purely passive entity.

4. The claim that the people cannot enjoy constitutional power against the sovereign, and so against the sovereign state, turns on the assumption that the constitution that establishes a sovereign must grant that individual or body domestically uncontrolled power and cannot therefore give the people any degree of countervailing power.

5. A common argument in support of this restriction is that if the constitution gave ordinary people the right or power to challenge the sovereign, then it would have to identify an agent, individual or corporate, to adjudicate the challenge. Could the judge be challenged in turn? If no, the judge is the real sovereign. If yes, there is a regress. It is therefore best, so the argument goes, to stick with the claim that the sovereign is beyond popular challenge.

6. One reason why this argument must fail, no matter what the form of the sovereign, is that people will always be able to break the law by acknowledging the authority of the courts to try them—thereby accepting the constitution—and then advertising their offense as an act of civil disobedience or contestation. The constitution may not design for the existence of such a right, but it must admit it by default: the right exists as an inescapable by-product of any constitution.

7. Another reason why the argument fails, or at least why it loses practical import, is that if the state is itself the sovereign, as under a mixed or polycentric constitution, ordinary people may be allowed to voice complaints and make demands that can reshape what that sovereign does; their inputs in interaction with other bodies, legislative, executive, or judicial, may be recognized as appropriate under the decision-making procedures that the constitution legitimates.

8. The second, absolutist claim, that the people, acting as a group, cannot challenge or oust their sovereign in an extra-constitutional way, turns on the general assumption that "the people" or "the citizens" has only two possible meanings. It can refer to the residents of the state considered as a multitude of separate individuals or to the corporate body of citizens that constitutes the state; it can refer to the unincorporated or to the incorporated people.

9. The unincorporated people cannot perform an action together, on the absolutist picture, at least in the absence of an unlikely unanimity. They will lack a single voice, personally or procedurally generated, behind which they could rally—to which they could pledge allegiance— pursuing the purposes it ascribes to the group according to the judgments it makes about the means to pursue them: specifically, about who is to do what in pursuing those purposes.

10. The incorporated people in a state can act together, of course, but they will do so only in virtue of the existence of the sovereign—and ultimately, therefore, the state—and the sovereign's directive role in setting out the purposes of the group and the means to be adopted in furthering those purposes.

11. There is a dilemma, therefore, for those who think the people of a state might act together extra-constitutionally to challenge or oust the sovereign. If the people are taken to be unincorporated, then absent unanimity they will lack the ability to act on any front; and if they are taken to be incorporated, they will not be sufficiently independent of the state to be able to act against it. Thus, the people cannot act as complainants to oust a sovereign or even to change the sovereign's will.

12. Constitutional and democratic theorists revive this line of thought when they argue that the people in a democracy can only change their constitution under rules the constitution itself provides. The people may be able to amend their constitution if it has an amendment clause, but they cannot change it otherwise. If taken as unincorporated, they

will be unable to act at all; if taken as incorporated they will be unable to act against the constitution.

13. Unlike the absolutists, these thinkers focus on a regress that arises when we ask if a people could have acted to adopt their constitution. If the people did do this, then that must have been under a prior constitution$_1$, and if they actively adopted constitution$_1$, that must have been under a distinct constitution$_2$. The looming regress is avoidable only if at some point, paradoxically, the people acted on a constitution they did not choose.

14. As it happens, Hobbes avoids this regress version of the problem. While he takes unanimity to be so unlikely that the unincorporated people cannot generally act, he holds that there is one striking exception: the situation where, recoiling from the war of all against all—the state of nature—they agree to seize contractually on the possibility of peace, selecting one or another agent, individual or corporate, as their sovereign.

15. Both the absolutist position, and the position of those upholding the paradox of constitutional regress, are built on the mistaken assumption that the people as a group must constitute either an unincorporated multitude or an incorporated body indistinguishable from the state. The idea is that there is nothing else that the concept—or an equivalent concept like that of the citizenry—could pick out: there is no other referent it could have.

16. This dichotomy is misleading, since a group of individuals may act together in this or that situation, episodic or recurring, without being organized, on our account, as an agent. They may be able to pursue one sort of purpose in one type of situation, without having procedures that would enable them, as agency proper requires, to pursue that or any other purpose across different situations, registering what the pursuit requires in each case.

17. In the role envisaged, the participants will act jointly as a group. They may do so in a purely cooperative spirit, as when those on a beach act on a plan to rescue a swimmer together; or they may do so in a way that nests competition, as when two or more individuals play a game: they act on the game plan for the sake of common enjoyment, but this shared goal requires them each to pursue victory for themselves.

18. The people as a group will act jointly to sustain their polity when at least most of them generally conform to the law and do so on the assumption that others will conform too; take any part that the polity

assigns or accept the part played by others selected for the job; compete in elections, if the polity is democratic, and opt to contest government decisions within the constitution; or just accept that it is appropriate for the state to demand such responses.

19. But if the people act jointly to sustain a polity, then they must be able in principle to act jointly in refusing to sustain it by no longer going along with the established constitution and state. Thus, the issue of whether it makes conceptual sense to say that the people can change their constitution and state is resoluble; the people in this sense—the incorporating people—can in principle change or replace the state they would normally sustain.

20. It also follows that the paradox of constitutional regress is no longer compelling. For it should be clear, to take an historical case, that the American people who changed the constitution in 1787 did not act under the 1776 Articles of Confederation, or under any other constitution. It was the American people understood in the incorporating, jointly acting, sense that made that change, not the American people incorporated or unincorporated.

21. That the people jointly sustain a polity does not mean that they actually control it. They may be unable to reject or replace it in practice, for lack of a salient plan about how to do that, or because the free-riding temptation means that few would be likely to play their required parts. But there needn't be a problem if democratic contestation is constitutional and common since it will offer a template for resistance; arguably, this is why the American change of constitution in 1787 was unproblematic.

22. Can the functional state assign collective power to its citizens, then? Well, it must grant them some constitutional power, as in civil disobedience, and some extra-constitutional power, in principle if not in practice. And as it must grant them some such power, it may grant them much more. Thus, if justice requires the people to have considerable constitutional power and extra-constitutional power in practice, it can make that available.

23. The upshot of the chapter is that there are three distinct notions of the people: the prepolitical, unincorporated populace; the postpolitical, incorporated people; and the political, incorporating citizenry. It is to the people in this third sense that the functional state must give some constitutional and extra-constitutional power, and it is to the people in this sense that it may give it in quite a high degree.

Chapter 5. The Individual Rights of Citizens

1. Libertarians like Robert Nozick argue that in virtue of being territorial and coercive, the functional state cannot acknowledge significant rights on the part of its individual citizens. Every state must offend against such rights, he argues, although an ultra-minimal state will be less objectionable on this count than any other polity.
2. This constraint is presented as metaphysical in character, deriving from the claim that independently of norm and law, and of all institutions, there are certain natural rights—intuitively the most significant rights conceivable—that belong to every human being and that rule out coercion of the kind that is characteristic of the state.
3. Whether they are taken to be natural or to be established under the rules of a practice, rights are demands that individuals may make on how others should treat them. They may not be absolutely unconditional, but they are bound to be unconditional in some degree. Thus, no right will demand to be satisfied only if its satisfaction maximizes satisfaction of the right overall or even over the lifetime of the bearer.
4. Rights may vary in how far they are unconditional. One type of right may make a demand that weighs over only moderately important goods, another over goods of intuitively even high importance, although hardly anyone, Nozick included, thinks that any rights are absolutely unconditional. Depending on how they score, of course, rights will weigh also against one another, with one type of right making demands that outweigh another's.
5. Every right constitutes a constraint on how others may treat someone rather than a claim whose satisfaction might be a goal. But it will serve at the same time as a trump that the person may play against the agent, asserting or waiving the right, as they choose. Finally, a claim-right of the kind in focus here will ground the correlated duty of others to honor it, although a privilege-right such as the right to civil disobedience mentioned earlier would not.
6. Whether rights exist naturally or institutionally, living under a regime of equal rights will have tangible value for people. The regime will ensure not just that others do not violate a person's rights but that they robustly avoid violation. Thus, the person living under a regime of rights will enjoy a secure zone of discretion where they may choose

as they wish, knowing that they are acting with impunity and even protection.

7. When rights are established by a practice or institution, the rules will identify the rights, validate them by virtue of the good that the rules generate, and enforce them with sanctions. Natural rights, by contrast, are meant to be self-evident and self-validating and fit to be enforced by the bearers of the rights: as we might say, self-enforceable.

8. Libertarians like Nozick take natural rights to be few and unquestionable. They require others not to interfere in a person's unharmful actions, for example, not to steal what they have non-harmfully acquired, and not to breach any promises made. They also allow the person to protect themselves against others and to retaliate against the offender; the exercise of that right may be the only mode of enforcement possible in the state of nature.

9. While Nozick holds that all real-world states breach the natural, significant rights of citizens, not having the consent of those individuals, he argues that a minimal, night watchman state might have emerged in an unplanned fashion among rational agents without any rights being breached along the way. Although that does not properly vindicate such a state, he thinks it shows it to be superior to alternatives.

10. Nozick also argues that the unregulated market that the minimal state ensures is ideal in natural rights terms. It enables people to order their relations and affairs on a wholly voluntary basis, so that everything happens by the consent of those involved. While the relatively deprived may accept an offer for want of an acceptable alternative, he argues counterintuitively that the act is voluntary if the deprivation is not wrongly imposed.

11. Whether in the libertarian form or not, natural rights are hard to take seriously as metaphysical posits. In general, we only countenance entities that are empirically compelling or explanatorily indispensable. But natural rights are neither. On the face of it, they belong with the notion of a god and a god-given law and have little to be said for them when they are taken as independent posits.

12. But not only are natural rights theoretically extravagant posits, they are also practically indeterminate and incapable of playing the role assigned to them by libertarians or others. Rights are carved out in detail within systems of law, and lacking such detail, it is hard to see how natural, noninstitutional rights could provide any normative guidance, say in

the domain of property, on how laws should be framed and how people should behave.

13. Some, like Kant, have argued that natural rights in themselves are provisional and that they require positive laws to fill in the detail and indeed to provide impartial enforcement. But for all that he says, such provisional rights might be articulated in any of an open variety of ways by the law, so that they do not usefully constrain the form that laws should take.

14. The institutional theory of rights argues that the only rights people have depend for their existence on the rules of some practice, customary, legal, or whatever. This makes those rights metaphysically unproblematic by contrast with natural rights since, by the argument of chapter 1, such rules are unproblematic. And since those rules can be determinate, it also avoids the problem of indeterminacy raised by natural rights.

15. The institutional theory makes sense of the fact that in general we associate rights with rules of some kind. We may say that someone has a right to something like free speech when the norms or laws of their country do not give them that right. But this can be seen as a claim that the norms or laws ought to give that person, and others like them, such a right.

16. The institutional or rules-based theory of rights explains why rights are constraints: rules would be redundant if they did not constrain. It explains why rights are trumps insofar as the rules are protective: an individual may assert or waive a right, depending on how they prize that protection. Finally, it explains why the rights given under protective rules serve as grounds for the duties of others: this is implied by the protective rationale.

17. The institutional theory not only does better than natural rights theory in this regard; it can also explain why people might have been attracted to its rival. If rights are dependent for their existence on rules and enjoy a salience of their own that eclipses the rules, then it is intelligible why someone might neglect the rules and take the rights to exist independently. As its grin survives the Cheshire cat, so the rights might be taken to survive the rules.

18. These observations bear on the metaphysical claims of the institutional theory. But does the theory enable us to argue, as against a libertarian like Nozick, that the functional state can recognize a significant range of individual rights on the part of its citizens? Yes, it does.

19. The discussion of the value of rights directs us to what might make a range of rights significant. Individual rights will be significant to the extent that they provide those who have such rights with a secure zone of personal discretion, protecting them against others.

20. The functional state must acknowledge some significant rights on the part of citizens. It is required by its function to establish or enforce a regime of law under which citizens enjoy the same range of rights against other citizens, including others in office. When it does this, it provides a zone of civic security, in which the citizens each know how they can act with legal impunity and under legal protection.

21. While the functional state must acknowledge some significant rights on the part of its citizens, of course, it may do so in a richer measure, and for a more inclusive class of citizens, than its function strictly requires. If justice demands the enrichment and extension of rights, therefore, the state can serve justice without compromising its function on this front.

Chapter 6. The Demands of a Market Economy

1. Laissez-faire theorists argue that the functional state cannot intervene beneficially in the workings of the market: that the market will perform best if it is left to evolve on its own, assuming a relatively unregulated form. The reasons cited may be that the state lacks the knowledge needed to interfere, that interference reduces the appeal of the free market, or that interference undermines the naturally evolving character of the market.

2. Those reasons for why the potential of the state is supposedly limited are empirical in nature. But they are brought into question by a history in which the state, under modern pressures, has played a central role in establishing property rights, a financial system, and a network of corporations. The lesson of this chapter is that any functional state must play some such role and that it may play an even bigger role, especially if it pursues justice.

3. Many conservative economists who cite considerations like those mentioned may be opposed, not so much to the intervention of the state in the economy, as to the intervention by government on a day-to-day basis. Laissez-faire theory is taken here to oppose the intervention of the state, even in the stable form it assumes under common or

constitutional law. It takes the economy to be a relatively autonomous, self-regulating system that the state should leave alone.

4. The state invariably plays an economically constraining role as the source of criminal law limits on market exchanges; contract law determinations of contractor obligations; tort law remedies for various grievances; and commercial law requirements on a range of matters. But in legislating on property, money, and incorporation it plays a primarily enabling role, and it is this role that gives the lie to laissez-faire theory.

5. Taking up property, the first thing to mark is that ownership is a robustly demanding good that requires not just that others respect the holdings of owners, but that they be constrained to do so. Owners must be secure in their possessions, having rights that are established by constraints of norm or law. Those rights will include titles to property—rights of acquisition—as well as prerogatives of ownership: rights of usage.

6. Which constraints are likely to have operated in the initial development of property? Hobbes is wrong that they must have been laws since conventions and norms can emerge independently. And Locke is wrong that a sense of their natural rights would have led people to protect their property themselves, establishing a prelegal regularity and norm, since there are no natural rights. Hume strikes the right note in offering a genealogy of norms of ownership akin to our genealogies.

7. It is possible for norms of ownership to have evolved independently of laws, on the pattern identified by Hume, and to have been regimented later in laws. But even if this is possible, indeed robustly probable, it also remains possible that the state first introduced the laws, and elicited norms of property as those laws gained acceptance in the society.

8. The safest take on the premodern history of property is that it may have emerged either under the influence of customary norms or under that of innovative law. Since customary norms would have had to be reinforced by laws, however, and since innovative laws would have elicited norms in their support, we may say that property was supported by a combination of norm and law before it began to be transformed in the modern period.

9. The development of corporations in that period, reviewed later in the chapter, introduced new owners and new sorts of property that agents could own: shares in those corporations and associated financial

instruments like bonds. And the development of technology also introduced new intellectual property like patents and copyrights and other intangible assets such as licenses, brand names, trademarks, and software.

10. These and other developments meant that the property regime shifted in other ways too. Intangible assets necessarily introduced new titles to ownership and new prerogatives of ownership. And various social changes affected the prerogatives of even traditional ownership. Thus, there were novel developments in the rights of landowners to mine their land, in the rights of householders to extend or paint their houses, and in the rights of farmers or pet owners over their animals.

11. As modern pressures led the state to change property rights in such ways, so they would lead any functional state to adopt a similarly interventionist role, perhaps with a view to different results. A belief in natural titles to property and natural prerogatives of property might have made sense in the premodern period, but the state-dependent nature of property in the world today gives the lie to the laissez-faire claim that the state cannot productively intervene in the economy.

12. The history of money supports a similar lesson. It is likely that some commodity, say gold, would have been given that role on a customary basis. This is supported by the way in which such a form of money spontaneously develops when the state fails: for example, in the turn to the use of cigarettes in exchange in Berlin immediately after World War II.

13. But even if money did first emerge in this way, the state would have had little choice but to support the emerging currency, given the need to specify an acceptable means of paying taxes. By requiring people to use a certain commodity like gold in payment of taxes—or by allowing the use of IOUs that it judged reliable—it would have given credibility to that commodity, and to those IOUs, and reinforced the currency.

14. This development would have enabled the rise of banks, as we may call them. These would have held reserves in the commodity, as gold-smiths might have held gold, and would have had an incentive to lend IOUs to borrowers against those reserves, demanding some security on each loan and charging interest for it. Such banks would also have been able to hold deposits of gold for others and even to pay them for using them to back IOUs.

15. Moving into the modern era, the state had a motive to establish a central bank, side by side with private banks, and many regimes did. It

would have served as the state's own banker as well as furthering other purposes too. It could operate as a clearing house for the IOUs from other banks, offer short-term loans to private banks to facilitate day-to-day trading, and issue IOUs or banknotes of its own. And it could help in various ways to safeguard the emerging financial system.

16. Thus, it could guard against the danger of a run on a bank, introduced by fractional reserve banking, which began in the seventeenth century. Under that system banks issued IOUs against which they held only a fraction of metallic reserves; unbacked IOUs would be supported only by the assets offered by borrowers to secure their loans. The system would have increased the supply of money and the level of economic demand, facilitating trade and taxation.

17. The central bank in many countries guarded against this danger of a run on a bank by serving as the lender of last resort when depositors panicked and wanted to retrieve their money, and by imposing constraints on the fraction of reserves that private banks were required to hold. In taking these measures, it reinforced guarantees that many governments provided to protect the funds of depositors in the case of a bank run.

18. The central bank also began to play a role in ensuring that inflation and unemployment were avoided, so far as that was possible. By varying the interest charged to private banks for loans, it could vary the interest that those banks charged borrowers, thereby controlling the supply of money. That monetary policy was combined with the fiscal policy of government in an attempt to balance demand and supply within the economy.

19. With these developments, the credibility of a currency, domestically and internationally, began to depend on how well the economy was doing and its perceived long-term prospects. At that point metallic reserves mattered less and less. Central banks ceased to rely on gold reserves to support the national currency and recast fractional reserve requirements in currency terms only. Money then became fiat money, dependent for its utility on the performance of the state.

20. As in the case of property, this history shows how modern pressures have led to a situation where money is essentially state dependent. Those pressures would force any functional state to take similar initiatives in constructing its financial system, including initiatives of the kind that justice might be taken to require. Once again, the laissez-faire claim that the state cannot intervene productively in the economy is undercut.

21. That same lesson is borne out even more clearly in the case of corporations. While corporate bodies operated before then for commercial purposes, the modern era saw the emergence of the joint stock company that more reliably attracts investors. Unlike the partnership, it locks in company assets, shields the company against the personal bankruptcy of any shareholder, and shields shareholders against the bankruptcy of the company.

22. Despite a decline in the eighteenth century, the joint stock company gained in dominance in the nineteenth, with the need to capitalize canals and railroads. It was enabled to form without a legislative act, to move territory, to change its business, and was given a status independent of government. Being recognized as an entity in its own right, it was even allowed to have shares in other companies, including majority shares that gave it control over those companies.

23. These developments ensured that by the twentieth century, the joint stock company, registered in law, became the most powerful private actor in the economy. It could gather around itself a set of companies that it controlled as the majority or only shareholder without being held responsible for their failures or misdemeanors: the shielding of shareholders enabled the controlling company to be shielded too.

24. But who is to control such corporate controllers? Not shareholders, since many dissipate the limited power that they enjoy by spreading their investments thinly over several corporations and by investing indirectly via pension funds and the like. The dominant approach holds that managers control corporations for the maximization of returns to shareholders, but that can generate a volatile market in which managers try to track a target that changes in response to their own efforts.

25. As with property and finance, the lesson of this history is that corporations exist in virtue of the will of states, and operate under state given terms, so that the laissez-faire claim against state intervention in the economy is bogus. The functional state must support commercial incorporation, essential as it is to the modern economy, but it may—and in justice probably should—break in many ways with how incorporation currently operates.

26. Implicit in this account of corporations, and in previous discussion of corporate bodies, is a moderately realist ontology of such entities. This contrasts with the inflationist theories that legal theories have sometimes defended, which make corporate bodies into natural

entities, and with deflationist theories, often held by economists about corporations, which deny them any reality as agents, treating each as just a nexus of market contracts.

27. The corporate body, commercial or not, is certainly a real agent by our account, and while it is composed of nothing more than a collection of individuals, it has a distinctive agential form lacking in a mere collection. It achieves this form by virtue of explicit and implicit contracts between those individuals. But, unlike contracts in a regular market, these are essentially designed to enable the body as a whole to operate as an agent.

REFERENCES

Ackerman, B. 1991. *We the People*, vol 1: *Foundations*. Cambridge, Mass.: Harvard University Press.

Alexander, G. S., and E. M. Penalver. 2012. *An Introduction to Property Theory*. Cambridge: Cambridge University Press.

Allen, D. 2000. *The World of Prometheus: The Policy of Punishing in Ancient Athens*. Princeton, N.J.: Princeton University Press.

Amar, A. R. 1988. "Philadelphia Revisited: Amending the Constitution outside Article V." *University of Chicago Law Review* 55:1043–1104.

Anderson, E. 2017. *Private Government: How Employers Rule Our Lives (and Why We Don't Talk about It)*. Princeton, N.J.: Princeton University Press.

Ando, C. 2015. *Roman Social Imaginaries: Language and Thought in Context of Empire*. Toronto: University of Toronto Press.

Anscombe, G. E. M. 1958. "Modern Moral Philosophy." *Philosophy* 33(124).

Appiah, K. A. 2010. *The Honor Code: How Moral Revolutions Happen*. New York: Norton.

Aquinas, T. 1958. *Summa Theologica*. Madrid: Biblioteca de Autores Cristianos.

Aristotle. 1996. *The Politics*. Edited by S. Everson. Cambridge: Cambridge University Press.

Aubrey, J. 1994. "The Brief Life." In *Thomas Hobbes: The Elements of Law, Natural and Politic*, edited by J. C. A. Gaskin. Oxford: Oxford University Press.

Austin, J. 1832/1954. *The Province of Jurisprudence Determined*. London: Weidenfeld.

———. 1869. *Lectures on Jurisprudence, or the Philosophy of Positive Law*. London.

Axelrod, R. 1984. *The Evolution of Cooperation*. New York: Basic Books.

Bacharach, M. 2004. *Beyond Individual Choice: Teams and Frames in Game Theory*. Edited by N. Gold and R. Sugden. Princeton, N.J.: Princeton University Press.

Badiou, A., P. Bourdieu, J. Butler, G. Didi-Huberman, S. Khiari, and J. Rancière. 2016. *What Is a People?* New York: Columbia University Press.

Barker, E. 1950. "Introduction." In *Gierke, Natural Law and the Theory of Society*, edited by E. Barker. Cambridge: Cambridge University Press.

Bar-on, D. 2004. *Speaking My Mind: Expression and Self-Knowledge*. Oxford: Oxford University Press.

Bartolus. 2012. *On the Government of a City*. Translated by J. Robinson. Toronto: University of Toronto.

Bateman, W. 2020. *Public Finance and Parliamentary Constitutionalism*. Cambridge: Cambridge University Press.

Bentham, J. 1843. "Anarchical Fallacies." In *The Works of Jeremy Bentham*, vol. 2, edited by J. Bowring. Edinburgh: W. Tait.

Beran, K. 2020. *The Concept of Juristic Person*. Prague: Wolters Kluwer.

Berle, A., and G. Means. 1967. *The Modern Corporation and Private Property*. 2nd ed. New York: Harcourt, Brace and World.

Berman, H. J. 1983. *Law and Revolution*. Cambridge, Mass.: Harvard University Press.

Bicchieri, C. 2006. *The Grammar of Society: The Nature and Dynamics of Social Norms*. Cambridge: Cambridge University Press.

———. 2017. *Norms in the Wild: How to Diagnose, Measure, and Change Social Norms*. Oxford: Oxford University Press.

Blackstone, W. 2016. *Commentaries on the Laws of England. Book 1*. Oxford: Oxford University Press.

Blair, M. 2003. "Locking in Capital: What Corporate Law Achieved for Business Organizers in the Nineteenth Century." *UCLA Law Review* 51:387–456.

Block, N. 1981. "Psychologism and Behaviorism." *Philosophical Review* 90:5–43.

Bodin, J. 1967. *Six Books of the Commonwealth*. Edited by M. J. Tooley. Oxford: Blackwell.

———. 1992. *On Sovereignty: Four Chapters from the Six Books of the Commonwealth*. Cambridge: Cambridge University Press.

Boyle, M. 2009. "Two Kinds of Self-Knowledge." *Philosophy and Phenomenological Research* 78:133–64.

Bradley, J. C. 2022. "Means, Context, and Property Rights." Princeton University.

Braithwaite, J. 1997. "On Speaking Softly and Carrying Big Sticks: Neglected Dimensions of a Republican Separation of Powers." *University of Toronto Law Journal* 47:305–61.

Braithwaite, J., and P. Drahos. 2000. *Global Business Regulation*. Cambridge: Cambridge University Press.

Brandom, R. 1994. *Making It Explicit*. Cambridge, Mass.: Harvard University Press.

Bratman, M. 1987. *Intention, Plans, and Practical Reason*. Cambridge, Mass.: Harvard University Press.

———. 2014. *Shared Agency: A Planning Theory of Acting Together*. Oxford: Oxford University Press.

Bratton, W. W. 1989. "Nexus of Contracts Corporation: A Critical Appraisal." *Cornell Law Review* 74:407–65.

Brennan, G. 1987. "The Buchanan Contribution." *Finanzarchiv* (Band 45): 1–24.

Brennan, G., L. Eriksson, R. E. Goodin, and N. Southwood. 2013. *Explaining Norms*. Oxford: Oxford University Press.

Brennan, G., and L. Lomasky. 1993. *Democracy and Decision: The Pure Theory of Electoral Preference*. Oxford: Oxford University Press.

Brennan, G., and P. Pettit. 2004. *The Economy of Esteem: An Essay on Civil and Political Society*. Oxford: Oxford University Press.

Brett, A. 1998. *Liberty, Right and Nature*. Cambridge: Cambridge University Press.

———. 2011. *Changes of State: Nature and the Limits of the City in Early Modern Natural Law*. Princeton, N.J.: Princeton University Press.

Buchanan, J. 1975. *The Limits of Liberty*. Chicago: University of Chicago Press.

Buchanan, J., and G. Tullock. 1962. *The Calculus of Consent*. Ann Arbor: University of Michigan Press.

Burke, E. 1999. "Speech to the Electors of Bristol." In *Select Works of Edmund Burke*, edited by E. J. Payne. Indianapolis: Liberty Fund.

Cammack, D. 2019. "The Demos in Demokratia." *Classical Quarterly* 69:42–61.

Canevaro, M. 2013. "Nomothesia in Classical Athens: What Sources Should We Believe?" *Classical Quarterly* 63:1–22.

———. 2017. "The Rule of Law as the Measure of Political Legitimacy in the Greek City States." *Hague Journal of the Rule of Law* 9:2011–36.

Canning, J. P. 1980. "The Corporation in the Political Thought of the Italians Jurists of the Thirteenth and Fourteenth Century." *History of Political Thought* 1:9–32.

———. 1983. "Ideas of the State in Thirteenth and Fourteenth Century Commentators on the Roman Law." *Transactions of the Royal Historical Society* 33:1–27.

———. 1987. *The Political Thought of Baldus de Ubaldis*. Cambridge: Cambridge University Press.

Canovan, M. 2005. *The People*. Cambridge: Polity.

Carey, C. 2017. *Democracy in Classical Athens*. London: Bloomsbury Academic.

Cicero, M. T. 1998. *The Republic and the Laws*. Oxford: Oxford University Press.

Ciepley, D. 2013. "Beyond Public and Private: Toward a Political Theory of the Corporation." *American Political Science Review* 107.

———. 2017. "Is the US Government a Corporation?" *American Political Science Review* 121.

Clark, A. 1997. *Being There: Putting Brain, Body and World Together Again*. Cambridge, Mass.: MIT Press.

Clastres, P. 1987. *Society against the State: Essays in Political Anthropology*. New York: Zone Books.

Coase, R. 1937. "The Nature of the Firm." *Economica* 4:386–405.

Coleman, J. 1990. *Foundations of Social Theory*. Cambridge, Mass.: Harvard University Press.

Collins, S. 2019. *Group Duties: Their Existence and Their Implications for Individuals*. Oxford: Oxford University Press.

Collins, S., and H. Lawford-Smith. 2021. "We the People: Is the Polity the State?" *Journal of the American Philosophical Association* 7:78–97.

Couzin, I. D., and S. A. Levin. 2015. "Special Issue: Collective Behavior." *Journal of Statistical Physics* 158(3).

Craig, E. 1990. *Knowledge and the State of Nature*. Oxford: Oxford University Press.

Crawford, J. 2006. *The Creation of States in International Law*. Oxford: Oxford University Press.

Crispo, E. 2007. "The Baldwin Effect and Genetic Assimilation: Revisiting Two Mechanisms of Evolutionary Change Mediated by Phenotypic Plasticity." *Evolution* 61:2469–79.

Curley, E, ed. 1994. *Hobbes Leviathan*. Indianapolis: Hackett.

Dan-Cohen, M. 1986. *Rights, Persons and Organizations: A Legal Theory for Bureaucratic Society*. Berkeley: University of California Press.

Darwall, S. 2006. *The Second-Person Standpoint: Morality, Respect, and Accountability*. Cambridge, Mass.: Harvard University Press.

Davis, G. F. 2016. *The Vanishing American Corporation: Navigating the Hazards of a New Economy*. Oakland, Calif.: Berrett-Koehler.

De la Boetie, E. 2015. *The Politics of Obedience: The Discourse of Voluntary Servitude*. Auburn, Ala.: Mises Institute.

Dennett, D. 1987. *The Intentional Stance*. Cambridge, Mass.: MIT Press.

———. 1992. *Consciousness Explained*. New York: Penguin.

Dewey, J. 1926. "The Historic Background of Corporate Legal Personality." *Yale Law Journal* 35:655–73.

Diamond, M. 1978. "The Separation of Powers and the Mixed Regime." *Publius* 8:33–44.

Dicey, A. V. 1982. *An Introduction to the Law of the Constitution*. Indianapolis: Liberty Fund.

Dietrich, F., and C. List. 2007. "Arrow's Theorem in Judgment Aggregation." *Social Choice and Welfare* 29:19–33.

Doyle, J. 2017. *No Morality, No Self: Themes from Anscombe*. Cambridge, Mass.: Harvard University Press.

Duff, P. W. 1938. *Personality in Roman Private Law*. Cambridge: Cambridge University Press.

Dworkin, R. 1986. *Law's Empire*. Cambridge, Mass.: Harvard University Press.

———. 1997. *Taking Rights Seriously*. London: Duckworth.

Dyzenhaus, D. 2015. "Kelsen, Heller and Schmitt: Paradigms of Sovereignty Thought." *Theoretical Inquiries in Law* 16:337–66.

Elman, B. 2002. *A Cultural History of Civil Examinations in Late Imperial China*. Berkeley: University of California Press.

Elster, J. 1979. *Ulysses and the Sirens*. Cambridge: Cambridge University Press.

———. 1999. *Alchemies of the Mind: Rationality and the Emotions*. Cambridge: Cambridge University Press.

Epstein, R. 1985. *Takings: Private Property and the Power of Eminent Domain*. Cambridge, Mass.: Harvard University Press.

———. 1990. "Property and Necessity." *Harvard Journal of Law and Public Policy* 13:2–9.

Erskine, T. 2003. *Can Institutions Have Responsibility? Collective Moral Agency and International Relations*. London: Palgrave.

Eschmann, T. 1946. "Studies on the Notion of Society in St Thomas Aquinas, 1. St Thomas and the Decretal of Innocent IV Romana Ecclesia: Ceterum." *Medieval Studies* 8:1–42.

Espejo, P. O. 2011. *The Time of Popular Sovereignty: Process and the Democratic State*. University Park: Pennsylvania State University Press.

Estlund, D. 2020. *Utopophobia: On the Limits (if Any) of Political Philosophy*. Princeton, N.J.: Princeton University Press.

Fehr, E., and S. Gächter. 2002. "Altruistic Punishment in Humans." *Nature* 415:137–40.

Feinberg, J. 1970. "The Nature and Value of Rights." *Journal of Value Inquiry* 4:243–57.

———. 1986. *Harm to Self: The Moral Limits of the Criminal Law*. Vol. 3. Oxford: Oxford University Press.

Ferguson, N. 2008. *The Ascent of Money: A Financial History of the World*. New York: Penguin.

Flower, H. I., ed. 2014. *The Cambridge Companion to the Roman Republic*. Cambridge: Cambridge University Press.

Fodor, J. 1983. *The Modularity of Mind*. Cambridge, Mass.: MIT Press.

Forsdyke, S. 2018. "Ancient and Modern Conceptions of the Rule of Law." In *Ancient Greek History and Contemporary Social Science*, edited by M. Canevaro, A. Erskine, B. Gray, and J. Ober, 184–212. Edinburgh: Edinburgh University Press.

Frankfurt, H. 1969. "Alternate Possibilities and Moral Responsibility." *Journal of Philosophy* 66:829–39.

Franklin, J. 1973. *Jean Bodin and the Rise of Absolutist Theory*. Cambridge: Cambridge University Press.

———. 1991. "Sovereignty and the Mixed Constitution: Bodin and His Critics." In *The Cambridge History of Political Thought 1450–1700*, edited by J. H. Burns and M. Goldie. Cambridge: Cambridge University Press.

French, P. A. 1979. "The Corporation as a Moral Person." *American Philosophical Quarterly* 16:207–15.

Friedman, M. 1962. *Capitalism and Freedom*. Chicago: University of Chicago Press.

Fukuyama, F. 2011. *The Origins of Political Order: From Prehuman Times to the French Revolution*. New York: Farrar, Straus and Giroux.

Fuller, L. L. 1971. *The Morality of Law*. New Haven, Conn.: Yale University Press.

Gardner, J. 2013. "Why Law Might Emerge: Hart's Problematic Fable." In *Reading HLA Hart's The Concept of Law*, edited by D. d'Almeida, J. Edwards, and A. Dolcettit, 1–23. Oxford: Oxford University Press.

Gaus, G. 2011. *The Order of Public Reason: A Theory of Freedom and Morality in a Diverse and Bounded World*. Cambridge: Cambridge University Press.

Gilbert, M. 2015. *Joint Commitment: How We Make the Social World*. Oxford: Oxford University Press.

Gilovich, T., D. Griffin, and D. Kahneman, eds. 2002. *Heuristics and Biases: The Psychology of Intuitive Judgment*. Cambridge: Cambridge University Press.

Gould, S. J., and R. Lewontin. 1979. "The Spandrels of San Marco and the Panglossian Paradigm: A Critique of the Adaptationist Programme." *Proceedings of the Royal Society of London* 205:581–98.

Graeber, D. 2011. *Debt: The First 5000 Years*. London: Melville House.

Graeber, D., and D. Wengrow. 2021. *The Dawn of Everything: A New History of Humanity*. New York: Farrar, Straus and Giroux.

Grantham, R. 1998. "The Doctrinal Basis of the Rights of Company Shareholders." *Cambridge Law Journal* 57:554–88.

Grimm, D. 2015. *Sovereignty: The Origin and Future of a Political and Legal Concept*. New York: Columbia University Press.

Grotius, H. 2012. *The Law of War and Peace*. Student ed. Cambridge: Cambridge University Press.

Gwyn, W. B. 1965. *The Meaning of the Separation of Powers*. The Hague: Nijhoff.

Habermas, J. 1995. *Between Facts and Norms: Contributions to a Discourse Theory of Law and Democracy*. Cambridge, Mass.: MIT Press.

———. 2001. "Constitutional Democracy: A Paradoxical Union of Contradictory Principles." *Political Theory* 29:766–81.

Hager, M. M. 1989. "Bodies Politic: The Progressive History of Organizational 'Real Entity' Theory." *University of Pittsburgh Law Review* 50:575–654.

Halliday, D. 2018. *The Inheritance of Wealth: Justice, Equality and the Right to Bequeath*. Oxford: Oxford University Press.

Hankins, J. 2010. "Exclusivist Republicanism and the Non-monarchical Republic." *Political Theory* 38:452–82.

Hansen, M. H. 1999. *The Athenian Democracy in the Age of Demosthenes*. London: Duckworth.

Hansmann, H., R. Kraakman, and R. Squire. 2006. "Law and the Rise of the Firm." *Harvard Law Review* 119:1333–1403.

Harrington, J. 1992. *The Commonwealth of Oceana and A System of Politics*. Cambridge: Cambridge University Press.

Harris, E. M. 2006. "The Rule of Law in Athenian Democracy: Reflections on the Judicial Oath." *Dike* 9:157–81.

Hart, H. L. A. 1955. "Are There Any Natural Rights?" *Philosophical Review* 64:175–91.

———. 1961. *The Concept of Law*. Oxford: Oxford University Press.

———. 1965. "Review: Lon Fuller 'The Morality of Law.'" *Harvard Law Review* 78:1281–96.

———. 2012. *The Concept of Law*. 3rd ed. Oxford: Oxford University Press.

Hayek, F. A. 1944. *The Road to Serfdom*. Chicago: University of Chicago Press.

———. 1960. *The Constitution of Liberty*. Chicago: University of Chicago Press.

Heider, F., and M. Simmel. 1944. "An Experimental Study of Apparent Behavior." *American Journal of Psychology* 13:243–59.

Hickey, T. 2019. "The Republican Core of the Case for Judicial Review." *International Journal of Constitutional Law* 17:288–316.

———. 2023. "Legitimacy—Not Justice—and the Case for Judicial Review." *Oxford Journal of Legal Studies* 43.

Hinsley, F. H. 1967. "The Concept of Sovereignty." *Journal of International Affairs* 21:242–52.

———. 1986. *Sovereignty*. Cambridge: Cambridge University Press.

Hobbes, T. 1990. *Behemoth; or, The Long Parliament*. Edited by F. Tönnies. Chicago: University of Chicago Press.

———. 1994a. *Human Nature and De Corpore Politico: The Elements of Law, Natural and Politic*. Oxford: Oxford University Press.

———. 1994b. *Leviathan*. Edited by E. Curley. Indianapolis: Hackett.

———. 1998. *On the Citizen*. Edited and translated by R. Tuck and R. Silverthorne. Cambridge: Cambridge University Press.

Hodgson, L.-P. 2010. "Kant on Property Rights and the State." *Kantian Review* 15:57–87.

Hohfeld, W. 1919. *Fundamental Legal Conceptions*. Edited by W. Cook. New Haven, Conn.: Yale University Press.

Holton, R. 2009. *Willing, Wanting, Waiting*. Oxford: Oxford University Press.

Honore, A. M. 1961. "Ownership." In *Oxford Essays in Jurisprudence*, edited by A. Guest, 107–47. Oxford: Oxford University Press.

Horowitz, M. J. 1992. *The Transformation of American Law 1870–1960: The Crisis of Legal Orthodoxy*. Cambridge, Mass.: Harvard University Press.

Hume, D. 1978. *A Treatise of Human Nature*. Oxford: Oxford University Press.

———. 1994. *Political Essays*. Cambridge: Cambridge University Press.

Ingham, S., and F. N. Lovett. 2019. "Republican Freedom, Popular Control, and Collective Action." *American Journal of Political Science* 63:774–87.

Ireland, P. 1996. "Capitalism without the Capitalist: The Joint Stock Company Share." *Journal of Legal History* 17:41–73.

———. 2018. "Corporate Schizophrenia: The Institutional Origins of Corporate Social Irresponsibility." In *Shaping the Corporate Landscape: Towards Corporate Reform and Enterprise Diversity*, edited by N. Boeger and C. Villiers, 13–35. London: Bloomsbury.

Ivison, D. 2020. *Can Liberal States Accommodate Indigenous Peoples?* Cambridge: Polity.

Jackson, F. 1992. "Block's Challenge." In *Ontology, Causality, and Mind: Essays on the Philosophy of David Armstrong*, edited by K. Campbell, J. Bacon, and L. Rhinehart. Cambridge: Cambridge University Press.

James, A. 2005. "Constructing Justice for Existing Practice: Rawls and the Status Quo." *Philosophy and Public Affairs* 33:281–316.

Jarvis Thompson, J. 1990. *The Realm of Rights.* Cambridge, Mass.: Harvard University Press.

Jensen, M. C. 1983. "Organization Theory and Methodology." *Accounting Review* 58:319–39.

Jensen, M. C., and W. H. Meckling. 1976. "Theory of the Firm: Managerial Behavior, Agency Costs and Ownership Structure." *Journal of Financial Economics* 3:305–60.

Jones, E. E. 1990. *Interpersonal Perception.* New York: Freeman.

Kalyvas, A. 2005. "Popular Sovereignty, Democracy and the Constituent Power." *Constellations* 12:223–44.

Kant, I. 1996. *Practical Philosophy.* Translated by M. J. Gregor. Cambridge: Cambridge University Press.

Kantorowicz, E. H. 1997. *The King's Two Bodies: A Study in Mediaeval Political Theology.* Princeton, N.J.: Princeton University Press.

Kay, J. 2015. *Other People's Money: The Real Business of Finance.* New York: Public Affairs.

Kelsen, H. 1992. *Introduction to the Problems of Legal Theory.* Oxford: Oxford University Press.

Kharkhordin, O. 2010. "Why Res Publica Is Not a State: The Stoic Grammar and Discursive Practices in Cicero's Conception." *Political Theory* 31:221–45.

Kornhauser, L. A., and L. G. Sager. 1993. "The One and the Many: Adjudication in Collegial Courts." *California Law Review* 81: 1–59.

———. 2004. "The Many as One: Integrity and Group Choice in Paradoxical Cases." *Philosophy and Public Affairs* 32:249–76.

Korsgaard, C. 1997. "Taking the Law into Our Own Hands: Kant on the Right to Revolution." In *Reclaiming the History of Ethics: Essays for John Rawls*, edited by A. Reath, B. Herman, and C. Korsgaard, 297–328. Cambridge: Cambridge University Press.

Kropotkin, P. 1902. *Mutual Aid: A Factor in Evolution.* New York: McClure, Phillips.

Krygier, M. 2016. "The Rule of Law: Pasts, Presents, and Two Possible Futures." *Annual Review of Law and Social Science* 12.

Krygier, M., A. Czarnota, and W. Sadurksi, eds. 2022. *Anti-constitutional Populism.* Cambridge: Cambridge University Press.

Kukathas, C. 2003. *The Liberal Archipelago: A Theory of Diversity and Freedom.* Oxford: Oxford University Press.

La Boétie, E., de. 2015. *The Politics of Obedience: The Discourse of Voluntary Servitude.* Auburn, Ala.: Mises Institute.

Laborde, C., and M. Ronzoni. 2016. "What Is a Free State? Republican Internationalism and Globalization." *Political Studies* 64:279–96.

Lai, T.-H. 2019. "Justifying Uncivil Disobedience." *Oxford Studies in Political Philosophy* 5:90–114.

Languet, H. 1994. *Vindiciae, Contra Tyrannos.* Cambridge: Cambridge University Press.

Lanni, A. 2006. *Law and Justice in the Courts of Classical Athens.* Cambridge: Cambridge University Press.

Lawford-Smith, H. 2019. *Not in Their Name: Are Citizens Culpable for Their States' Actions*. Oxford: Oxford University Press.

Leat, M. 2010. "Bernard Williams and the Possibility of a Realist Political Theory." *European Journal of Political Theory* 9:485–503.

Lebowitz, A. 2018. "An Economy of Violence: Financial Crisis and Whig Constitutional Thought, 1720–1721." *Yale Journal of Law and the Humanities* 29:165–238.

Lederman, H. 2018. "Common Knowledge." In *Handbook of Social Intentionality*, edited by M. Jankovic and K. Ludwig. London: Routledge.

Lee, D. 2016. *Popular Sovereignty in Early Modern Constitutional Thought*. Cambridge: Cambridge University Press.

———. 2021. *The Right of Sovereignty*. Oxford: Oxford University Press.

Lewis, D. 1969. *Convention*. Cambridge, Mass.: Harvard University Press.

Lieberman, D. 2006. "The Mixed Constitution and the Common Law." In *The Cambridge History of Eighteenth-Century Political Thought*, edited by M. Goldie and R. Wokler, 317–46. Cambridge: Cambridge University Press.

Liebert, H. 2016. *Plutarch's Politics: Between City and Empire*. Cambridge: Cambridge University Press.

Linz, J. J., and A. Valenzuela, eds. 1994. *The Failure of Presidential Democracy*. Baltimore: Johns Hopkins University Press.

List, C. 2006. "The Discursive Dilemma and Public Reason." *Ethics* 116:362–402.

List, C., and P. Pettit. 2002. "Aggregating Sets of Judgments: An Impossibility Result." *Economics and Philosophy* 18:89–110.

———. 2004. "Aggregating Sets of Judgments: Two Impossibility Results Compared." *Synthese* 140:207–35.

———. 2011. *Group Agency: The Possibility, Design and Status of Corporate Agents*. Oxford: Oxford University Press.

List, C., and B. Polak. 2010. "Symposium on Judgment Aggregation." *Journal of Economic Theory* 145(2).

Locke, J. 1960. *Two Treatises of Government*. Cambridge: Cambridge University Press.

———. 1975. *An Essay Concerning Human Understanding*. Oxford: Oxford University Press.

———. 1990. *Questions Concerning the Law of Nature*. Ithaca, N.Y.: Cornell University Press.

Loughlin, M. 2010. *Foundations of Public Law*. Oxford: Oxford University Press.

Loughlin, M., and N. Walker, eds. 2007. *The Paradox of Constitutionalism: Constituent Power and Constitutional Form*. Oxford: Oxford University Press.

Lovejoy, A. O. 1961. *Reflections on Human Nature*. Baltimore: Johns Hopkins University Press.

Lovett, F. 2009. "In Defense of the Practice Theory." *Ratio Juris* 32:320–38.

———. 2012. "Harrington's Empire of Law." *Political Studies* 60:59–75.

Lovett, F. N., and P. Pettit. 2019. "Preserving Republican Freedom: A Reply to Simpson." *Philosophy and Public Affairs* 46:363–83.

Lovett, F. N., and M. Sellers, eds. Forthcoming. *Handbook of Republicanism*. Oxford: Oxford University Press.

Ludwig, K. 2016. *From Individual to Plural Agency: Collective Action*. Vol. 1. Oxford: Oxford University Press.

Macedo, S. 1990. *Liberal Virtues: Citizenship, Virtues and Community in Liberal Constitutionalism*. Oxford: Oxford University Press.

Machiavelli, N. 1997. *Discourses on Livy*. Oxford: Oxford University Press.

MacIntyre, A. 1987. *After Virtue*. London: Duckworth.

Madison, J., A. Hamilton, and J. Jay. 1987. *The Federalist Papers*. Harmondsworth: Penguin.

Maitland, F. H. 2003. *State, Trust and Corporation*. Cambridge: Cambridge University Press.

Malcolm, N. 1991. *Sense on Sovereignty*. London: Centre for Policy Studies.

Malmendier, U. 2005. "Roman Shares." In *The Origins of Value: The Financial Innovations That Created Modern Capital Markets*, edited by W. Goetzman and G. Rouwenhorst, 31–42. Oxford: Oxford University Press.

McAdams, R. H. 1997. "The Origin, Development and Regulation of Norms." *Michigan Law Review* 96:338–433.

McCormick, J. P. 2007. "People and Elites in Republican Constitutions, Traditional and Modern." In *The Paradox of Constitutionalism: Constituent Power and Constitutional Form*, edited by M. Loughlin and N. Walker. Oxford: Oxford University Press.

———. 2011. *Machiavellian Democracy*. Cambridge: Cambridge University Press.

McGeer, V. 1996. "Is 'Self-Knowledge' an Empirical Problem? Renegotiating the Space of Philosophical Explanation." *Journal of Philosophy* 93:483–515.

———. 2008. "The Moral Development of First-Person Authority." *European Journal of Philosophy* 16:81–108.

McLean, J. 1999. "Personality and Public Law Doctrine." *University of Toronto Law Journal* 49:123–49.

———. 2004. "Government to State: Globalization, Regulation, and Governments as Legal Persons." *Indiana Journal of Global Legal Studies* 10:173–97.

———. 2012. *Searching for the State in British Legal Thought: Competing Conceptions of the Public Sphere*. Cambridge: Cambridge University Press.

Menger, C. 1892. "On the Origin of Money." *Economic Journal* 2:239–55.

Michelman, F. I. 1999. *Brennan on Democracy*. Princeton, N.J.: Princeton University Press.

Mill, J. 1978. "An Essay on Government." In *Utilitarian Logic and Politics: James Mill's "Essay on Government," Macaulay's Critique, and the Ensuing Debate*, edited by J. Lively and J. Rees. Oxford: Oxford University Press.

Miller, D. T., and D. A. Prentice. 1994. "Collective Errors and Errors about the Collective." *Personality and Social Psychology Bulletin* 20:541–50.

———. 1996. "The Construction of Social Norms and Standards." In *Social Psychology: Handbook of Basic Principles*, edited by E. T. Higgins and A. W. Kruglanski, 799–829. New York: Guilford.

Montesquieu, C. d. S. 1989. *The Spirit of the Laws*. Cambridge: Cambridge University Press.

Moran, R. 2001. *Authority and Estrangement: An Essay on Self-Knowledge*. Princeton, N.J.: Princeton University Press.

Morgan, E. S. 1988. *Inventing the People: The Rise of Popular Sovereignty in England and America*. New York: Norton.

Morris, C. 1998. *An Essay on the Modern State*. Cambridge: Cambridge University Press.

Morris, I., and W. Scheidel. 2009. *The Dynamics of Ancient Empires: State Power from Assyria to Byzantium*. Oxford: Oxford: University Press.

Mueller, J. W. 2003. *A Dangerous Mind: Carl Schmitt in Post-war European Thought*. New Haven, Conn.: Yale University Press.

———. 2016. *What Is Populism?* Philadelphia: University of Pennsylvania Press.

Murphy, L., and T. Nagel. 2004. *The Myth of Ownership*. New York: Oxford University Press.

Näsström, S. 2007. "The Legitimacy of the People." *Political Theory* 35:624–58.

Negri, A. 1999. *Insurgencies: Constituent Power and the Modern State*. Minneapolis: University of Minnesota Press.

Nelson, E. 2010. *The Hebrew Republic: Jewish Sources and the Transformation of European Political Thought*. Cambridge, Mass.: Harvard University Press.

Nietzsche, F. 1997. *On the Genealogy of Morals*. Cambridge: Cambridge University Press.

Nili, S. 2019. *The People's Duty: Collective Agency and the Morality of Public Policy*. Cambridge: Cambridge University Press.

———. 2020. *Integrity, Personal and Political*. Oxford: Oxford University Press.

Nozick, R. 1974. *Anarchy, State, and Utopia*. Oxford: Blackwell.

Oakeshott, M. 1975. *On Human Conduct*. Oxford: Oxford University Press.

———. 1991. *Rationalism in Politics and Other Essays*. Indianapolis: Liberty Press.

Ober, J. 1999. *Mass and Elite in Democratic Athens*. Princeton, N.J.: Princeton University Press.

———. 2004. "Aristotle's Natural Democracy." In *Aristotle's Politics: Critical Essays*, edited by R. Kraut and S. Skultety, 223–43. Lanham, Md.: Rowman and Littlefield.

———. 2008a. *Democracy and Knowledge: Innovation and Learning in Classical Athens*. Princeton, N.J.: Princeton University Press.

———. 2008b. "The Original Meaning of 'Democracy.'" *Constellations* 15:3–9.

O'Connor, C. 2019. *The Origins of Unfairness: Social Categories and Cultural Evolution*. Oxford: Oxford University Press.

Olsaretti, S. 2004. *Liberty, Desert and the Market*. Cambridge: Cambridge University Press.

Olson, M. 1965. *The Logic of Collective Action*. Cambridge, Mass.: Harvard University Press.

O'Neill, A. 2007. *The Constitutional Rights of Companies*. Dublin: Thomson Round Hall.

Origgi, G. 2018. *Reputation: What It Is and Why It Matters*. Princeton, N.J.: Princeton University Press.

Orts, E. 2013. *Business Persons: A Legal Theory of the Firm*. Oxford: Oxford University Press.

Parel, A., and T. Flanagan. 1979. *Theories of Property: Aristotle to the Present*. Waterloo, Ont.: Wilfred Laurier University Press.

Pasquino, P. 1998. *Sieyès et l'invention de la constitution en France*. Paris: Edition Odile Jacob.

Pasternak, A. 2021. *Responsible Citizens, Irresponsible States: Should Citizens Pay for Their State's Wrongdoings?* Oxford: Oxford University Press.

Peacocke, C. 1983. *Sense and Content*. Oxford: Oxford University Press.

Petrov, V. 1967. *Money and Conquest: Allied Occupation Currencies in World War II*. Baltimore: Johns Hopkins University Press.

Pettit, P. 1986. "Free Riding and Foul Dealing." *Journal of Philosophy* 83:361–79.

———. 1990. "*Virtus Normativa*: Rational Choice Perspectives." *Ethics* 100:725–55. Reprinted in Pettit 2002.

———. 1996. "Functional Explanation and Virtual Selection." *British Journal for the Philosophy of Science* 47:291–302. Reprinted in Pettit 2002.

———. 1997. *Republicanism: A Theory of Freedom and Government*. Oxford: Oxford University Press.

———. 2001a. "Deliberative Democracy and the Discursive Dilemma." *Philosophical Issues (suppl. to Nous)* 11:268–99.

———. 2001b. *A Theory of Freedom: From the Psychology to the Politics of Agency*. Cambridge: Polity.

———. 2002. *Rules, Reasons, and Norms: Selected Essays*. Oxford: Oxford University Press.

———. 2008a. *Made with Words: Hobbes on Language, Mind and Politics*. Princeton, N.J.: Princeton University Press.

———. 2008b. "Value-Mistaken and Virtue-Mistaken Norms." In *Political Legitimization without Morality?*, edited by J. Kuehnelt, 139–56. New York: Springer.

———. 2010. "Varieties of Public Representation." In *Representation and Popular Rule*, edited by Ian Shapiro, Susan Stokes, E. J. Wood, and A. S. Kirshner. Cambridge: Cambridge University Press.

———. 2012. *On the People's Terms: A Republican Theory and Model of Democracy*. Cambridge: Cambridge University Press.

———. 2014. *Just Freedom: A Moral Compass for a Complex World*. New York: Norton.

———. 2015a. "Justice, Social and Political." In *Oxford Studies in Political Philosophy*, vol. 1, edited by D. Sobel, P. Vallentyne, and S. Wall, 9–35. Oxford: Oxford University Press.

———. 2015b. "The Republican Law of Peoples: A Restatement." In *Domination and Global Political Justice: Conceptual, Historical, and Institutional Perspectives*, edited by B. Buckinx, J. Trejo-Mathys, and T. Waligore, 37–70: London: Routledge.

———. 2015c. *The Robust Demands of the Good: Ethics with Attachment, Virtue and Respect*. Oxford: Oxford University Press.

———. 2016a. "Making Up Your Mind." *European Journal of Philosophy* 24:3–26.

———. 2016b. "Rousseau's Dilemma." In *Engaging with Rousseau: Reception and Interpretation from the Eighteenth Century to the Present*, edited by A. Lifschitz, 168–88. Cambridge: Cambridge University Press.

———. 2017. "Political Realism Meets Civic Republicanism." *Critical Review of International Social and Political Philosophy* 20:320–33.

———. 2018a. *The Birth of Ethics: Reconstructing the Role and Nature of Morality*. Oxford: Oxford University Press.

———. 2018b. "Three Mistakes about Doing Good (and Bad)." *Journal of Applied Philosophy* 35:1–25.

———. 2018c. "Two Concepts of Free Speech." In *Academic Freedom*, edited by J. Lackey, 61–81. Oxford: Oxford University Press.

———. 2019a. "Analyzing Concepts and Allocating Referents." In *Conceptual Engineering and Conceptual Ethics*, edited by A. Burgess, H. Cappelen, and D. Plunkett, 333–57. Oxford: Oxford University Press.

———. 2019b. "Social Norms and the Internal Point of View." *Oxford Journal of Legal Studies* 39.

———. 2020. "My Three Selves." *Philosophy* 95:363–89.

———. 2021. "A Conversive Theory of Respect." In *Respect: Philosophical Essays*, edited by R. Dean and O. Sensen, 29–54. Oxford: Oxford University Press.

———. 2022. "Popular Sovereignty and Constitutional Democracy." *University of Toronto Law Journal* 72.

———. 2024. *When Minds Speak: The Social Nature of Our Mental Life.* Oxford: Oxford University Press.

Pettit, P., and D. Schweikard. 2006. "Joint Action and Group Agency." *Philosophy of the Social Sciences* 36:18–39.

Pettit, P., and M. Smith. 2004. "The Truth in Deontology." In *Reason and Value: Themes from the Moral Philosophy of Joseph Raz*, edited by R. J. Wallace, P. Pettit, S. Scheffler, and M. Smith, 153–75. Oxford: Oxford University Press.

Pettit, P., and R. Sugden. 1989. "The Backward Induction Paradox." *Journal of Philosophy* 86:169–82.

Pistor, K. 2019. *The Code of Capital: How the Law Creates Wealth and Inequality.* Princeton, N.J.: Princeton University Press.

Plunkett, D. 2013. "Legal Positivism and the Moral Aim Thesis." *Oxford Journal of Legal Studies* 33:563–605.

Poggi, G. 1990. *The State: Its Nature, Development and Prospects.* Cambridge: Polity.

Polanyi, K. 2002. *The Great Transformation.* Boston: Beacon.

Polybius. 2011. *The Histories.* Vol. 3. Cambridge, Mass.: Harvard University Press.

Pufendorf, S. 2005. *Of the Law of Nature and Nations: Eight Books.* Buffalo, N.Y.: Hein.

Queloz, M. 2021. *The Practical Origins of Ideas: Genealogy as Conceptual Reverse-Engineering.* Oxford: Oxford University Press.

Quinton, A. 1975. "Social Objects." *Proceedings of the Aristotelian Society* 75.

Rawls, J. 1999. *The Law of Peoples.* Cambridge, Mass.: Harvard University Press.

Raz, J. 2003. "About Morality and the Nature of Law." *American Journal of Jurisprudence* 48:1–15.

Ripstein, A. 2009. *Force and Freedom: Kant's Legal and Political Philosophy.* Cambridge, Mass.: Harvard University Press.

Rouch, D. 2020. *The Social License for Financial Markets: Reaching for the End and Why It Counts.* London: Palgrave Macmillan.

Rousseau, J.-J. 1997a. *The Discourses and Other Early Political Writings.* Edited by Victor Gourevitch. Cambridge: Cambridge University Press.

———. 1997b. *The Social Contract and Other Later Political Writings.* Edited by Victor Gourevitch. Cambridge: Cambridge University Press.

Rovane, C. 1997. *The Bounds of Agency: An Essay in Revisionary Metaphysics.* Princeton, N.J.: Princeton University Press.

Rubenfeld, J. 2001. *Freedom and Time: A Theory of Constitutional Self-government.* New Haven, Conn.: Yale University Press.

Runciman, D. 1997. *Pluralism and the Personality of the State.* Cambridge: Cambridge University Press.

———. 2000a. "Is the State a Corporation?" *Government and Opposition* 35:90–104.

———. 2000b. "What Kind of Person Is Hobbes's State? A Reply to Skinner." *Journal of Political Philosophy* 8:268–78.

———. 2003. "Moral Responsibility and the Problem of Representing the State." In *Can Institutions Have Responsibilities?*, edited by T. Erskine, 41–50. London: Palgrave.

———. 2006. "Hobbes's Theory of Representation: Anti-democratic or Proto-democratic?" In *Political Representation*, edited by I. Shapiro, S. C. Stokes, E. J. Wood, and A. S. Kirshner, 15–34. Cambridge: Cambridge University Press.

Runciman, D., and M. Ryan. 2003. "Introduction." In *F. H. Maitland: State, Trust and Corporation*, edited by D. Runciman and M. Ryan. Cambridge: Cambridge University Press.

Ryan, A. 1984. *Property and Political Theory*. Oxford: Blackwell.

Ryan, M. 1999. "Bartolus of Sassoferrato and Free Cities." *Transactions of the Royal Historical Society* 6:65–89.

Ryle, G. 1949. *The Concept of Mind*. Chicago: University of Chicago Press.

Sangiovanni, A. 2008. "Justice and the Priority of Politics to Morality." *Journal of Political Philosophy* 16:137–64.

Scafuro, A. C. 1997. *The Forensic Stage: Settling Disputes in Graeco-Roman New Comedy*. Cambridge: Cambridge University Press.

Schane, S. A. 1987. "The Corporation Is a Person: The Language of a Legal Fiction." *Tulane Law Review* 61:563–609.

Schmitt, C. 2005. *Political Theology: Four Chapters on the Concept of Sovereignty*. Chicago: University of Chicago Press.

Schmitthoff, M. 1939. "The Origin of the Joint-Stock Company." *University of Toronto Law Journal* 3:74–96.

Schneewind, J. B. 1998. *The Invention of Autonomy*. Cambridge: Cambridge University Press.

Schwenkenbecher, A. 2021. *Getting Our Act Together: A Theory of Collective Moral Obligations*. London: Routledge.

Scott, J. C. 2017. *Against the Grain: A Deep History of the Earliest States*. New Haven, Conn.: Yale University Press.

Searle, J. 1995. *The Construction of Social Reality*. New York: Free Press.

———. 2010. *Making the Social World: The Structure of Human Civilization*. Oxford: Oxford University Press.

Selinger, W. 2019. *Parliamentarism: From Burke to Weber*. Cambridge: Cambridge University Press.

Shapiro, S. 2011. *Legality*. Cambridge, Mass.: Harvard University Press.

Shoemaker, S. 1996. *The First-Person Perspective and Other Essays*. Cambridge: Cambridge University Press.

Sieyès, E. J. 2003. *Political Writings*. Indianapolis: Hackett.

Simpson, T. 2017. "The Impossibility of Republican Freedom." *Philosophy and Public Affairs* 45:27–53.

———. 2019. "Freedom and Trust: A Rejoinder to Lovett and Pettit." *Philosophy and Public Affairs* 47:412–24.

Skinner, Q. 1978. *The Foundations of Modern Political Thought*. Cambridge: Cambridge University Press.

———. 1999. "Hobbes and the Artificial Person of the State." *Journal of Political Philosophy* 7:1–29. Reprinted with revisions in Skinner 2002b.

———. 2002a. *Visions of Politics*. Vol. 2: *Renaissance Virtues*. Cambridge: Cambridge University Press.

———. 2002b. *Visions of Politics*. Vol. 3: *Hobbes and Civil Science*. Cambridge: Cambridge University Press.

———. 2005. "Hobbes on Representation." *European Journal of Philosophy* 13:155–84.

———. 2009. "A Genealogy of the Modern State." *Proceedings of the British Academy* 162:325–70.

Smith, A. 1976. *An Inquiry into the Nature and Causes of the Wealth of Nations*. Oxford: Oxford University Press.

———. 1982. *The Theory of the Moral Sentiments*. Indianapolis: Liberty Classics.

———. 2010. *Lectures on Jurisprudence*. Indianapolis: Liberty Fund.

Smith, M. 1994. *The Moral Problem*. Oxford: Blackwell.

Sober, E., and D. S. Wilson. 1998. *Unto Others: The Evolution and Psychology of Unselfish Behavior*. Cambridge, Mass.: Harvard University Press.

Stilz, A. 2019. *Territorial Sovereignty: A Philosophical Exploration*. Oxford: Oxford University Press.

Stoljar, S. J. 1973. *Groups and Entities: An Inquiry into Corporate Theory*. Canberra: Australian National University Press.

Straumann, B. 2020. "Leaving the State of Nature: Polybius on Resentment and the Emergence of Morals and Political Order." *Polis* 37:9–43.

Sugden, R. 2000. "Team Preferences." *Economics and Philosophy* 16:175–204.

Sumner, L. W. 1987. *The Moral Foundation of Rights*. Oxford: Oxford University Press.

Sunstein, C., and A. Vermeule. 2020. *Law and Leviathan: Redeeming the Administrative State*. Cambridge, Mass.: Harvard University Press.

Tamanaha, B. Z. 2004. *On the Rule of Law: History, Politics, Theory*. Cambridge: Cambridge University Press.

Tanguay-Reynaud, F. 2013. "Criminalizing the State." *Criminal Law and Philosophy* 7:255–84.

Tierney, B. 1997. *The Idea of Natural Rights: Studies on Natural Rights, Natural Law and Church Law: 1150–1625*. Atlanta: Scholars Press.

Tilly, C. 1975. "Reflections on the History of European State-Making." In *The Formation of National States in Western Europe*, edited by C. Tilly. Princeton, N.J.: Princeton University Press.

Tomasello, M. 2014. *A Natural History of Human Thinking*. Cambridge, Mass.: Harvard University Press.

Tuck, R. 1979. *Natural Rights Theories. Their Origin and Development*. Cambridge: Cambridge University Press.

———. 1998. "Hobbes and the Body Politic." Cambridge, Mass.: Harvard University, Department of Government.

———. 2006. "Hobbes on Civil Persons and Representation." Cambridge, Mass.: Harvard University, Department of Government.

———. 2016. *The Sleeping Sovereign: The Invention of Modern Democracy*. Cambridge: Cambridge University Press.

Tucker, P. 2018. *Unelected Power: The Quest for Legitimacy in Central Banking and the Regulatory State*. Princeton, N.J.: Princeton University Press.

Tuomela, R. 2007. *The Philosophy of Sociality: The Shared Point of View*. Oxford: Oxford University Press.

Tyler, T. R. 1990. *Why People Obey the Law*. New Haven, Conn.: Yale University Press.

Ullmann-Margalit, E. 1977. *The Emergence of Norms*. Oxford: Oxford University Press.

Urbinati, N. 2019. *Me the People: How Populism Transforms Democracy*. Cambridge, Mass.: Harvard University Press.

Vallentyne, P., and H. Steiner, eds. 2000a. *Left-Libertarianism and Its Critics*. New York: Palgrave.

———, eds. 2000b. *The Origins of Left-Libertarianism*. New York: Palgrave.

Van Duffel, S. 2010. "From Objective Right to Subjective Rights: The Franciscans and the Will and Interest Conceptions of Rights." In *The Nature of Rights: Moral and Political Aspects of Right(s) in Late-Medieval and Early-Modern Philosophy*, edited by V. Mäkinern, 65–93. Helsinki: Philosophical Society of Finland.

Vatter, M. 2014. "Republics Are a Species of State: Machiavelli and the Genealogy of the Modern State." *Social Research* 81:217–41.

Vergara, C. 2020. *Systemic Corruption: Constitutional Ideas for an Anti-oligarchic Republic*. Princeton, N.J.: Princeton University Press.

Vile, M. J. C. 1967. *Constitutionalism and the Separation of Powers*. Oxford: Oxford University Press.

Villey, M., and S. Rials. 2013. *La formation de la pensée juridique moderne*. Paris: Presses Universitaires de France.

Vincent, A. 1987. *Theories of the State*. Oxford: Blackwell.

Waldron, J. 1988. *The Right to Private Property*. Oxford: Oxford University Press.

———. 1989. "The Rule of Law in Contemporary Liberal Theory." *Ratio Juris* 2:79–96.

———. 2006. "Kant's Theory of the State." In *Kant: Towards Perpetual Piece and Other Writings*, edited by P. Kleingeld, 179–200. New Haven, Conn.: Yale University Press.

———. 2016a. "Property and Ownership." In *Stanford Encyclopedia of Philosophy*, edited by E. N. Zalta. https://plato.stanford.edu/entries/property/.

———. 2016b. "The Rule of Law." In *The Stanford Encyclopedia of Philosophy*, edited by E. N. Zalta. https://plato.stanford.edu/entries/rule-of-law/.

Waley, D. 1988. *The Italian City-Republics*. 3rd ed. London: Longman.

Walker, M. U. 1931. "The History of the Joint Stock Company." *Accounting Review* 6:97–105.

Weale, A. 2018. *The Will of the People*. Cambridge: Polity.

Weber, M. 1946. "Politics as a Vocation." In *From Max Weber: Essays in Sociology*, edited by H. H. Gerth and C. W. Mills, 77–128. New York: Oxford University Press.

Weithman, P. J. 1993. "Natural Law, Property and Redistribution." *Journal of Religious Ethics* 21:165–80.

Wenar, L. 2013. "The Nature of Claim-Rights." *Ethics* 123:202–29.

Wendt, A. 2004. "The State as Person in International Theory." *Review of International Studies* 30:289–316.

Whelan, F. G. 1983. "Prologue: Democratic Theory and the Boundary Problem." *Nomos* 25:13–47.

Whitehead, A. N. 1997. *Science and the Modern World*. New York: Simon & Schuster.

Williams, B. 2002. *Truth and Truthfulness*. Princeton, N.J.: Princeton University Press.

———. 2005. *In the Beginning Was the Deed: Realism and Moralism in Political Argument*. Princeton, N.J.: Princeton University Press.

Williamson, O. E. 1989. "Transaction Cost Economics." In *Handbook of Industrial Organisation*, vol. 1, edited by R. Schmalensee and R. Willig, 135–82. Amsterdam: North Holland.

Winch, P. 1963. *The Idea of a Social Science and Its Relation to Philosophy.* London: Routledge.

Winkler, A. 2018. *We the Corporations: How American Businesses Won Their Civil Rights.* New York: Norton.

Wolterstorff, N. 2008. *Justice: Rights and Wrongs.* Princeton, N.J.: Princeton University Press.

Woolf, C. N. S. 1913. *Bartolus of Sassoferrato.* Cambridge: Cambridge University Press.

Zuckert, M. P. 1996. *The Natural Rights Republic: Studies in the Foundation of the American Political Tradition.* Notre Dame, Ind.: Notre Dame University Press.

Zurn, C. F. 2010. "The Logic of Legitimacy: Bootstrapping Paradoxes of Constitutional Democracy." *Legal Theory* 16:191–227.

Zwolinski, M., and A. Wertheimer. 2017. "Exploitation." In *Stanford Encyclopedia of Philosophy,* edited by E. N. Zalta. https://plato.stanford.edu/entries/exploitation/.

INDEX

Acton, Lord, 114

agency, 69–72, 173, 194; basic, 319; characterization of, 289; corporate, 84–91, 173, 289, 307–11, 319–22, 338; human, 73–84, 304, 309–10, 319–20

Albericus de Rosciate, 90

Allen, Danielle, 93n22

amour propre, 191n9

anarchy, 3, 120, 239, 241–42

Anscombe, Elizabeth, 260

Aquinas, Thomas, 90

Aristotle, 64, 94, 177, 178, 252

Articles of Confederation, 199–200, 217, 329

asset commitment, 291–92, 302, 307

Athens, 134; integration failures of, 93–98; uniform laws of, 99–100, 105–6

Austin, John, 132, 146, 309

Australian parliamentary democracy, 164–70, 223, 325

Badiou, Alain, 176n2

Baldus de Ubaldis, 90

Bank of England, 282, 293

bankruptcy, 291–92, 297–98, 311, 337

Barker, Ernest, 305, 312

barter society, 18–19

Bartolus of Sassoferrato, 90, 91, 191–92, 321

Bentham, Jeremy, 252, 309

Berle, Adolf, 300

Bitcoin, 285

Blackstone, William, 116, 161n30, 289–90, 295, 322

Block, Ned, 72n2

Bodin, Jean, 114–15, 176, 322–24; on democracy, 136; on Justinian law code, 129–30; on mixed constitution, 120, 121; on Roman Republic, 120; on social contract, 132, 142–43; on sovereignty, 118–21, 131–32, 138–39, 182

Bratman, Michael, 52n32, 210n25

Bratton, W. W., 301n21, 308

Bubble Act (1720), 294–97

Buchanan, James, 35

Burke, Edmund, 169–70

by-product rights. *See* spandrel rights

Callisthenese of Olynthus, 93

Carroll, Lewis, 259

central banks, 116, 123; establishment of, 280–84, 287, 335–37; market system and, 179, 336

Charles I, English king, 119, 195, 199, 200

chartered companies, 293, 294, 297–98. *See also* joint stock company

Cheshire cat fallacy, 259–60, 332

Chinese civil service, 66

Cicero, 65, 117, 126, 322; on citizenry, 177–78; on public safety, 65, 125

Ciepley, David, 211n26

citizenry, 10, 173; Aristotle on, 177, 178; Cicero on, 177–78; collective powers of, 173–76, 326–29; constitutional power of, 177–87; definition of, 327; extra-constitutional power of, 176, 187–89, 193–99, 204–24; Harrington on, 178; incorporating of, 211–22; individual rights of, 225–26, 330–33;

citizenry (*continued*)
　　Machiavelli on, 178; political conception
　　of, 215–16; polity and, 222–24; reification
　　of, 179–80
Citizens United v. Federal Election Commission
　　(2010), 306
civil disobedience, 213, 326, 329; nonviolent,
　　183n6; right of, 182–84, 187, 232
civitas, 191–92, 223
claim-rights, 232–34
Cleisthenes of Athens, 94
coercion, 239, 241; monopoly claim to, 57–58;
　　need for, 55–57
Collins, Stephanie, 204n21
commercial law, 267–69, 275–76, 334–35
common law, 129, 183–84, 201–2, 232, 295
compliance problem, 55–57, 318
constitution, 197, 278n9; amending of, 156–58,
　　196, 217, 327–29; Blackstone on, 161n30;
　　Kant on, 161; polycentric, 115–21, 174–75,
　　178–87, 322–23. *See also* U.S. Constitution
constitutional regress, 196–200
contract law, 267–69, 304, 308–12, 334
conventions, 29–30, 32, 124, 316. *See also* norms
copyright, 275–76, 335
corporations, 267, 287–302; bankruptcy of,
　　292, 297–98, 311, 337; Blackstone on, 289–90;
　　controlling of, 299–302; deflationist
　　theory of, 304, 308–12, 338; development
　　of, 288–90, 334–38; Hobbes on, 289; infla-
　　tionist theory of, 304–8, 337–38; multina-
　　tional, 107, 302; ontology of, 302–4;
　　outsourcing by, 299n20; transaction costs
　　of, 308–9, 311
Craig, Edward, 18
criminal law, 101, 144, 170, 260, 268, 334
cryptocurrencies, 285

Dartmouth College v. Woodward (1819), 295–96
Darwall, Stephen, 260
decentralization, 124, 163–70, 195–96, 223–24,
　　322–25; of sovereignty, 155–63, 174, 187.
　　See also polycentric organization
deflationist theories, 304, 308–12, 338

democracy, 202, 221–22; majority rule and,
　　136, 149–53; parliamentary, 164–70, 223,
　　325; presidential, 165–70, 223, 325
Dennett, Daniel, 70
Descartes, René, 160–61, 162
Dicey, A. V., 148, 305
dikasteria (courts), 321
discursive dilemma, 150–51
doctrinal paradox, 150n24
Dworkin, Ronald, 67, 93, 231
Dyzenhaus, David, 146n23

East India Company, 293
eliminativism, 309
eminent domain, 276
enforcement dilemma, 34–35
entity shielding, 292, 302
environmental laws, 276
Epstein, Richard, 278n9
esteem economy, 35–37, 41
Estlund, David, 220n31
extra-constitutional power, 176, 187–89,
　　193–99, 204–24

Federalist Papers, 116, 117, 161, 322
Forsdyke, Sara, 95n25
free speech, 229, 230, 233, 306, 332
Friedman, Milton, 265, 300
Fuller, Lon, 103n30
functional state, 4–6, 15–16, 260–64, 314–18;
　　individual rights and, 225–26, 330–33;
　　libertarian rights and, 238–41; natural
　　rights and, 237–39, 245–52; nomothetic
　　role of, 62–67, 173–76, 318, 322; rule of law
　　and, 128–29, 173, 318. *See also* state

genealogy, 16–18; of money, 18–20, 278–81;
　　starting point of, 24–27; of state, 21–24,
　　240, 316
Gierke, Otto, 305
Gilbert, Margaret, 210n25
gold standard, 284, 285, 287, 335–36
goods of intimacy, 234n7
Graeber, D., 280n10

A NOTE ON THE TYPE

This book has been composed in Arno, an Old-style serif typeface in the classic Venetian tradition, designed by Robert Slimbach at Adobe.